CHILTON'S
MECHANICS' HANDBOOK

VOLUME 3 AUTO BODY SHEET METAL REPAIR

Robert L. Sargent

Managing Editor	Kerry A. Freeman, S.A.E.
Senior Editor	Richard J. Rivele, S.A.E.

OFFICERS

President	William A. Barbour
Executive Vice President	James A. Miades
Vice President & General Manager	John P. Kushnerick

CHILTON BOOK COMPANY
Chilton Way, Radnor, Pa. 19089

Manufactured in USA
© 1981 Chilton Book Company
ISBN 0-8019-7033-4 (softcover)
0-8019-7034-2 (hardcover)

Library of Congress Catalog
Card No. 80-67324

1234567890   987654321

ACKNOWLEDGMENTS

Sincere and grateful acknowledgment is made to the following organizations that supplied copyrighted illustrations and information used in this edition of this book or whose material has been re-used from previous editions:

Air Reduction Sales Co.
Albertson & Co., Inc.
Applied Power, Inc., Automotive Division
Controlled Systems (Windsor), Ltd.
Fairmount Tool & Forging, Inc.
General Motors Corporation, Fisher Body Division
Guy Chart
Hougen Manufacturing, Inc.
Hobart Brothers Co.
Lenco, Inc.
Marquette Manufacturing Co.
H. K. Porter, Inc.

This and previous editions could not have been written without the cooperation of many businesses and individuals. I extend sincere thanks to the following firms for their cooperation in furnishing information and material on request: Lenco, Inc.; Guy Chart; Air Reduction Sales Co.; Controlled Systems (Windsor), Ltd.; Fairmount Tool & Forging, Inc.; Applied Power, Automotive Division; General Motors Coproration, Fisher Body Division; Hougen Manufacturing, Inc.; Hobart Brothers Co.; Albertson & Co., Inc.; H. K. Porter, Inc.

Within General Motors Corporation, the help of the following subsidiaries and divisions is acknowledged and appreciated: General Motors Institute, Motors Insurance Corporation, Chevrolet Motor Division, and Fisher Body Division.

I greatly appreciate the contributions of persons who helped in many ways with the previous editions: E. D. Hougen, M. B. Nelson, H. O. Swanson, John C. Pursell, E. E. Smith, C. A. Brown (deceased), Uriel Hoskins, Harry Ferguson (deceased), Keith Willoughby, Morris D. Thomas, Neil Lucey, Willard Duddles, Morley Wiederhold, and R. J. Kakuska. It is a pleasure to add the names of Warren Bok, Douglas Hammond, Guy Chartier, E. R. Maynerick, David Fleming, Wilson Burry, Frank Flynn, Robert Hamlyn, Edward Vatcher, and Dermot Linegar, who have been very helpful in the preparation of this edition.

Morris Thomas deserves special mention for assistance with ideas and specific suggestions that have improved the electric welding section of Chapter 5.

Special mention must be made also of Mrs. Janet Kelly, a typist who brought a sometimes confusing manuscript to beautiful legibility.

Although now far removed from the field, I still remember with gratitude the help and encouragement Glenn Madere gave in the preparation of the first edition.

Robert L. Sargent

CONTENTS

PREFACE

The automobile industry has changed direction in the years since publication of the second edition of this book. At that time the average American-built automobile was still growing larger, with the accent on performance and luxury rather than fuel economy. There were some small models, but the general viewpoint was "bigger is better." As I prepare the material for this third edition, the trend is to "down-sized" big models and smaller small ones. I won't attempt to predict where it will end, but it seems reasonable to assume that some type or size of automobile will continue to be the primary means of personal transportation.

It also seems reasonable to assume that, as long as there is an automobile industry, there will be a continuing need for trained people to repair automobiles. I have revised, improved, and expanded the material in this book to meet the needs of the training programs necessary to recruit new people into the body repair industry.

In past editions I concentrated almost entirely on the techincal aspects of metal working and left teaching methods largely to the individual instructor. For this edition, I have expanded the technical aspect, particularly as it applies to new metals, such as aluminum and thinner, harder steels, and have added a series of Skill Development Exercises to provide the autobody instructor with a prepared program for skill training. Some instructors may prefer their own system, but my contacts convince me that many will welcome a prepared program.

I have added three new chapters: Doors, Body Shop Management and Estimating, and Job Opportunities. The Doors chapter is strictly technical, but Body Shop Management and Estimating delves into the business aspect of the body shop business to acquaint the reader with that side of shop management. Job Opportunities provides a brief glimpse into some of the other occupations related to the auto body repair trade. The student is assured that learning his trade can be a qualification for other, related employment as well as being a desirable end in itself.

The pronouns "he" and "his" are used throughout the text, as are "repairman," and so on. These references should not be viewed as exclusionary; they are simply conventions, used to eliminate an unwieldy and unnecessary struggle with language.

Robert L. Sargent

This chapter will provide information about the material used in making automobile body sheet metal parts. Prior to the world-wide shortage of oil, which arose in the early 1970s, mild steel was the only material used. Legal restrictions and economic pressures resulting from the shortage have forced automobile manufacturers to develop more fuel-efficient automobiles. The manufacturers took the two obvious approaches to the problem: one, to develop more fule-efficient engines; two, to develop lighter automobiles that would require less fuel consumption from any engine. The drive to reduce weight affected all components of the automobile, but was most effective with the parts made of stamped sheet metal, because it outweighs all other materials. Mild steel parts have been reduced in weight and size as much as possible, aluminum has been substituted for steel where practical, and thinner but much harder steels are being substituted for many body structural parts. For the first time since the beginning of the mass production of automobiles, the repairman is forced to widen his skills so that he can work new metals.

It is impossible to predict the ultimate design of the automobile of the distant future, but it is reasonable to assume that the present trends will continue for some time into the immediate future. Mild steel probably will continue to be the basic material for most automobiles for long years to come. The use of aluminum and lighter, harder steels will surely increase, and the time could come when some automobiles are built with one or the other as the primary material. If so, the transition will be gradual rather than abrupt. Revolutionary changes must come slowly in any large industrial operation.

Any discussion of automobile body construction must consider the use of plastics and plastic-reinforced materials. Use of these materials started long before the oil shortage developed and has accelerated rapidly since. The materials manufacturers and the automobile companies have many experimental and development programs working to produce lightweight substitutes for steel. The possibility of a non-metallic automobile body structure cannot be ruled out, but it is still in the future. If and when it comes, it will not cause an overnight change in the entire automobile industry. Plastics and other non-metallic materials, however, are outside the scope of this text and will not be discussed further.

In the following non-technical discussions of steel and aluminum, the intention is to interpret the technical language of the metallurgist and engineer into plain language for the repairman, to provide basic information about the material with which he will work. Sections on the general subject of steel include a discussion of the nature of steel, with emphasis on the properties that determine whether it is *hard* or *soft*, an explanation of grain structure, an explanation of plasticity as it applies to steel, an explanation of the tendency of steel to harden further as it goes through plastic deformation, and an explanation of the plastic limits of various grades of steel.

Sections on the general subject of aluminum follow the pattern used for steel, because it has some degree of

AUTOMOBILE SHEET METAL

the same properties. Pure aluminum is basically a soft metal. Other elements are combined with aluminum to produce an alloy with sufficient rigidity to permit its use in automobile body or chassis parts.

On the specific subject of *sheet metal*, which encompasses both steel and aluminum, included are the essential properties of either metal that make it suitable for automotive use, a brief explanation of the process by which any metal can be made into sheets, and a brief explanation of the stamping process by which metal sheets are made into body panels and parts.

STEEL

An exact definition of steel is difficult, because it is made in many grades for use in almost countless products. The fact that it can be produced with special properties to meet almost any need has made it the world's most important industrial alloy. The different grades of steel are produced by varying the combination of basic materials, or *elements*, used in its manufacture. Some of these elements are common to all grades of steel; others are used only to impart special properties to a particular grade or type of steel.

A broad definition of steel often is used in which it is described as a commerical form of iron containing carbon as an essential alloying element. The amount of carbon in steel is very small in comparison to the amount of iron; it is rarely ever more than 1.7 percent, and most often it is much less. It is the amount of carbon that determines the hardness and strength of a particular grade. Mild or soft steel has the least carbon, less than 0.23 percent; this type is also called low carbon steel. Medium steel has from 0.25 to 0.60 percent carbon. High carbon steel has over 0.80 percent carbon.

Other elements also common to all grades of steel, though found in only very small amounts, are manganese, silicon, phosphorus, and sulfur. Still others are added to produce special properties such as toughness, corrosion resistance, high strength, wear resistance, and so on.

The original steel available to the automobile industry when it entered the mass production era was relatively hard. It was adequate to the needs of the times, but the demands of styling led the automobile manufacturers to demand better materials to make more complicated shapes and make them faster. Essentially, this meant softer but tougher steels made available by lowering the carbon content, use of special alloys, and improving manufacturing methods. Use of softer steels does not imply that the strength of the automobile structure was made weaker, because, as explained more fully in later sections, the metal is stiffened by the stamping process in forming the panels. Further strength can be provided where needed by using welded-on reinforcements or heavier metal.

The state of the art of sheet metal forming limits the use of the thin, hard steels to relatively simple shapes such as frame members, reinforcements, and inner

body parts. This is not a static situation, however; historically, progress of the automobile industry has been as much a matter of improving manufacturing methods as of improving the product. There is good reason to believe that improved methods of sheet metal forming will extend the use of hard steels far beyond today's limits.

GRANULAR STRUCTURE OF STEEL

The properties of any piece of steel—hardness, weldability, strength, and so on—are the result of the particular combination of elements that make it up. These elements are not combined in a smooth, uniform mixture such as found in glass, however. Steel is made up of tiny grains.

The individual grains of steel are large enough to be seen with the aid of a microscope, if the sample has been prepared properly. In preparation, the surface is polished and etched with acid to bring out the shape of the individual grains. The grains will form a pattern called the grain structure. A photograph of a steel sample prepared in this manner and magnified 150 times is shown in Figure 1-1.

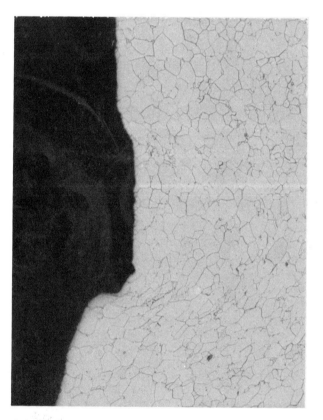

1-1 Grain structure of steel, magnified 150 times after polishing and etching with acid.

The grain structure of a particular grade of steel will vary according to the way it has been heat treated and worked. The changes follow a definite pattern, however, so that a microscopic test of grain structure can be used to determine important information for the metallurgist and engineer. The condition of the grain structure of any piece of steel determines the extent to which it can be bent or formed. To change the shape of the piece, it is necessary to change the shape and position of every grain in the affected area. In mild steel, which bends easily, the individual grains can withstand a considerable amount of deformation and movement. In harder steels and many other common metals, this amount is much less. In all steels, there is a definite limit of such action, and when it is reached the piece breaks.

A simple demonstration of the action of the grains in a piece of sheet metal can be made by bending it back and forth several times rapidly. There will be noticeable increase in temperature because of internal friction among the grains.

SHEET STEEL

The properties of sheet steel that make it suitable for use in body panels are due to the combination of elements in its composition and the way it was processed in the steel mill. It is essential that sheet steel for a particular part be soft, or pliable enough to withstand the necessary deformation required to make it by existing manufacturing methods. Complicated shapes require very soft, low carbon steel. Less complicated shapes can be made of harder, higher-carbon-content steel. In years past spot heating has sometimes been used to soften panel areas, because the design required deformation beyond the limit of the then available low carbon steel. This was usually an interim step between successive stamping operations on the same panel. The purpose was to relieve the grain structure; the heated piece was partly cooled before going to the next stamping operation.

There is often a very definite surface difference in the metal used for inner and outer panels. Many of the inner panels show patterns of wavy lines on the surface, called *stretcher strains* (Figure 1-2). These patterns are duplicated exactly on both sides of the metal. They are the result of yielding under tension when the panel is stamped. These lines may have almost any pattern; some may look like fern or grass leaves, others like the branches of a tree. Sometimes they have the appearance of worms pressed into the surface. Successive parts coming from the same stamping press will have different patterns; some may have no marks at all.

Metal used for outside panels is processed in the steel mill prior to stamping so that it will not form stretcher strains; otherwise, excessive labor would be necessary to file or power-sand the panel smooth. Inner panels that cannot be seen are not harmed by the presence of these marks, so the metal used to make them need not be processed. There is no difference in strength or in the way such metal can be worked when it is being straightened, so stretcher strains are not a problem to the repairman.

1-2 Typical stretcher strain pattern.

WORKING PROPERTIES OF SHEET STEEL

Certain properties or characteristics of sheet steel which vary for different grades of steel, determine and limit the manner in which it may be worked. Automotive sheet metal requires primary properties that will permit it to be formed into the shape of the various panels and be fabricated by welding. It also must have a surface with which paint can form a lasting bond. Strength and surface texture are related to the primary properties discussed in the following paragraphs.

The desired properties of sheet steel are determined by manufacturing requirements. These same properties, however, permit and limit the work that may be done by the repairman, and for that reason they should be studied so hat they become ingrained in his thinking on the job. Those that directly affect his work are (1) plasticity, (2) work hardening, and (3) elasticity.

Although each of these properties will be dealt with separately in the following pages, it must be remembered that they are all closely related in that they are different aspects of the effect of force applied to sheet steel. The key point in this relationship is the *yield point*, which may be defined in terms of the amount of force that any piece of metal can resist without bending or otherwise deforming. The yield point has been reached when enough force has been applied to cause deformation.

Plasticity

Plasticity is the property of any metal or other material that permits it to change shape when sufficient force is applied to it. Plasticity permits the flat sheet to be reshaped into any of the body or other stamped parts with one stroke of the press. Since in this process the sheet metal is subjected to tremendous forces, without sufficient plasticity it would break or split. A high degree of plasticity is required to make some of the complicated shapes found on the surfaces of present-day automobiles.

Changing the shape of a sheet of metal may be called *plastic deformation*. The amount of plastic deformation that a piece of sheet metal can undergo without breaking is related to its hardness. Harder grades of steel cannot withstand as much plastic deformation as can the softer grades. Although closely related, however, softness and plasticity are not necessarily the same. It would be possible to have two pieces of steel of equal softness, but one could have a greater degree of plasticity than the other.

The opposite of plasticity is rigidity. The best example of metal with no plasticity is cast iron, which is used for engine blocks because it will not bend or deform in any way. A cast-iron part designed to withstand the forces that will be applied to it will maintain its shape permanently. Instead of bending, it will break under a severe overload.

Plastic deformation takes place under both tensive and compressive forces. The property that permits deformation under tension is *ductility*. The property that permits deformation under compression is *malleability* (not to be confused with malleable iron, which is cast iron heat-treated to give it some degree of the malleability of steel). The result of deformation under tension is *stretching*. The result of deformation under compression, or pressure, is *upsetting*.

Plasticity is important to the repairman because both stretching and upsetting take place in various areas of most of the damaged panels with which he works. This is explained in much more detail in the section dealing with the effects of force on sheet metal.

Work Hardening

The common term used to describe the plastic deformation of steel without the use of heat is *cold working*, or sometimes the more simple term *working*. These terms are used in all discussions that follow. Any area of *any metal* that has been bent, upset, stretched, or changed in shape in any way below a temperature of approximately 500°F. (260°C.) has been cold worked; above that heat level, the effect gradually lessens until it is lost at red temperature.

The amount of cold working possible for a certain piece of steel has a limit; when worked past this limit, it breaks. As cold working approaches this limit, the metal becomes progressively harder. This causes a corresponding increase in stiffness and strength. This increased hardness is called *work hardening*.

A very simple experiment can be performed to demonstrate the effect of work hardening. A 1¾ in. piece of soft utility wire may be used. It has essentially the same properties as automotive sheet steel and is small enough so that it can be stretched by hand. To perform this experiment, tie one end of the wire to a rigid support and the other end to something that will serve as a handle. Best results will be obtained if the wire used is several feet in length, because the increase in length will be more apparent. Measure the overall length, then

stretch the wire until it breaks. The total increase in length should be close to 25 percent.

A noticeable increase in stiffness can be felt by bending a section of the stretched wire between the fingers and comparing it to the stiffness of another section of the same wire that has not been stretched. This increase in stiffness is due to the strain on the individual grains. For the wire to grow thinner and longer, it is necessary for the individual grains to grow longer and smaller in diameter. It is this distortion of the shape and position of the individual grain that causes the metal to work harden. When comparing the stiffness of the stretched wire to that of the unstretched wire, the full increase is not apparent because stretching reduces the diameter of that piece. If an unstreteched wire of the smaller diameter were available for comparison, the difference would be more evident.

This experiment can be carried out under more scientific conditions by supporting the wire overhead and attaching weight, in increasing amounts, to the lower end. If this is done, it will be found that when enough weight is added to reach the yield point, the wire will stretch a short distance and stop. It will then be necessary to add still more weight to cause further stretching. This can be repeated several times, each time with additional weight, until the limit is reached and the wire breaks. The need for additional weight is proof of additional strength resulting from the stretching. Each time the wire is stretched, the yield point is raised slightly.

This experiment can be carried further by using a strip of automotive sheet metal and the proper equipment. A hydraulic body jack and sheet metal clamps, such as those shown in use in the repair section of this book, are satisfactory for the purpose. If the proper gauges are available to record the force used, it will be found that a strip of mild steel will more than double in strength if it is stretched to the breaking point. This is illustrated in Figures 1-3 to 1-7.

Figure 1-3 shows a strip of metal 1 inch (25.4 mm) wide and 0.037 inch (0.93 mm) thick set up in clamps. A length of salvage steel tape has been clamped to it at one end, and crayon marks, 8 inches (203.20 mm) apart, have been aligned with the 1- and 9-inch marks of the tape. Note that the gauge hand is slightly below the 0 mark of the gauge.

In Figure 1-4, the jack has been extended enough to stretch the strip ⅛ inch (3.17 mm), as indicated by the crayon mark of the right side which is one eighth past the 9-inch mark. Note that the gauge hand now reads slightly over 1,000 pounds.

In Figure 1-5, the jack has been extended enough to stretch the strip inches (44.45 mm), as indicated by the crayon mark now at the 10¾ inch mark. Note that the gauge pressure has built up to about 2,100 pounds, approximately double the force needed to stretch the strip the first eighth. It was expected that the strip would break soon after this picture was taken, but after the jack had been extended another ¾ inch (19.05 mm), the picture in Figure 1-6 was taken. This shows a reading of approximately 2,500 pounds on the gauge, which was the maximum.

1-3 *(Top)* Tensile test of body sheet metal strip. The gauge hand registers 0. Arrows indicate crayon marks on the strip, 8 inches (approx. 200 mm) apart and aligned with numerals 1 and 9 on the tape.

1-4 *(Bottom)* Strip stretched ⅛ inch (approx. 3 mm). The gauge registers slightly over 1,000 pounds on the jack.

1-5 *(Top)* Strip stretched 1¾ inches (approx. 45 mm). The gauge registers 2,100 pounds—more than twice the original yield point.

1-6 *(Bottom)* Strip stretched 2½ inches (approx. 63 mm). The gauge registers 2,500 pounds, the maximum pressure reached.

Figure 1-7 shows the strip stretched another ⅜ inch (9.52 mm), and the gauge reading has dropped back to 2,000 pounds. Note that the strip has begun to fail by narrowing sharply close to the clamp on the left end. The actual breaking point is not shown, but only a little more stretching was needed; the gauge pressure dropped rapidly as the piece was stretched from the point shown in Figure 1-7.

Both the amount of stretching and the increase in yield strength obtained with the strip in these illustrations are more than can be expected normally. Failure at twice the first yield point, in this case about 2,000 pounds, would be more probable. In fact, another strip cut from the same piece of sheet stock did yield at the lower figure. The significance of this test is that unworked sheet steel elongated more than 25 percent and, in doing so, increased in strength more than 100 percent. (Actual figures for the strip shown are 34 percent increase in length and 150 percent increase in strength; however, they are probably higher than can be expected with most available sheet steel.)

The harder, thinner sheet steel coming into use for some body parts can be expected to stretch less and to build up resistance to further stretching more rapidly than milder steel. Its use is a radical departure from previous design practices of the automobile industry, caused by the need to reduce weight. It is reasonable to assume that the weight reduction efforts will continue; it seems equally reasonable to assume that various grades of harder steel will come into use as the industry gains experience with it.

Another example of work hardening is shown in Figure 1-8. This strip of mild steel was bent double by pressing on the ends and then straightened by resting the bent area against a solid surface and pushing the ends apart. When bent double, this piece was in the shape of the piece shown in the left in Figure 1-9. The work hardening caused by the first stiffened the metal in the bent area. The additional stiffness resisted the straightening action, causing two new bends to form on each side of the first one.

The importance of understanding how metal stiffens, making it stronger, in areas that are bent or otherwise worked, cannot be over-emphasized in the study of sheet metal repair. It is the basis of practically all damage. Some work hardness will be found in any undam-

1-7 Strip beginning to break at arrow.

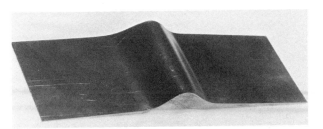

1-8 Typical buckle formed by bending and straightening a piece of sheet metal.

aged automobile body panel; it is the result of the cold working done in the die that originally formed the panel. The bending caused by a collision adds still more work hardening in the areas affected. More, sometimes much more, will be added by the cold working used as the metal worker straightens the damaged area. Excessive work hardening caused by working the metal improperly will make the job more difficult.

Elasticity

Automotive sheet metal has a limited amount of *elasticity*, which may be defined as the ability of an object to regain its original shape after a deflecting force has been removed. Reducing this to a simpler statement as it applies to automotive sheet metal, elasticity may be considered as the tendency of the metal to spring back after a force has been applied to it and released.

Elasticity is not the exact opposite of plasticity, but the two properties are closely related. Very soft steel has very little elasticity but a high degree of plasticity; the opposite is also true to a large extent. However, it would be possible for steel having low elasticity to have varying degrees of plasticity. In the example of stretching shown in Figures 1-3 to 1-7, the shown strip has stretched more than another cut from the same stock, showing differences in plasticity in the same material.

Any metal has an *elastic limit*. Going back to the simple definition of elasticity above, the eleastic limit is the point at which enough force has been applied to overcome some of the tendency to spring back. This is the yield point. However, even though yielding relieves some of the elastic strain, there is always enough of it left to cause a partial spring-back. This may be proved by bending any piece of metal as the piece shown in Figure 1-8 was bent. There will be partial spring-back when it is released.

This partial spring-back tendency makes it highly desirable for the metal worker to learn to recognize the elastic strains in the damaged panels on which he works. The work should be planned to take advantage of any spring-back tendency that is present. Spring-back will be found in almost any area that is still relatively smooth but has been carried out of position by buckles formed in adjoining areas. Some areas will spring back to shape if released by relieving the distortions in the buckled areas that hold them out of place.

ALUMINUM

The use of aluminum in automobile body construction seems to many experienced repairmen to present new and difficult metal repair problems, to the point that some consider aluminum panels not repairable. This reaction is not surprising, because it is human nature to distrust and avoid new routines. But there is no reason for the student to share this distrust as he begins his training, because he has not yet developed routines to cling to. He will find that working aluminum and working steel are in many ways quite similar, but each has its own combination of properties that govern repair procedures. If these properties are understood, skill in working aluminum should develop as fast as it does for steel. The fact that aluminum requires a "finer touch" may make the student more sensitive to the problems of working steel and make him a better performer on both metals.

The adoption of aluminum as one of the automobile body construction materials should be regarded as permanent—at least, until some as yet undiscovered element or process comes along. Ignoring world politics, the world's supply of petroleum is finite. The development of substitutes for petroleum motor fuels is based on an economy that is governed by relatively high-cost petroleum. Whether the world's supply of petroleum runs out in the twentieth century or lasts for centuries to come, the return of relatively low-cost petroleum-based motor fuel seems remote, if not impossible. Use of aluminum provides one of several ways to build lighter automobiles that require fewer quantities of relatively expensive fuel. The student entering the automobile collision field should be aware that his services may not always be limited to working on steel. Both steel and aluminum may eventually be replaced by other substitutes; but, for the foreseeable future, at least some skill should be acquired on aluminum as well as steel.

THE GRADES OF ALUMINUM

The term aluminum, as it is used normally, refers to some alloy of aluminum and several other metals. Pure aluminum is too soft for most industrial uses. But, just as iron can be combined with other elements to produce various grades of steel, aluminum can be combined with many of the same elements—silicon, copper, manganese, magnesium, zinc, chromium, titanium, and even iron—to produce alloys having special properties for special purposes. The aluminum industry produces well more than a hundred different alloys, referred to here as grades. Of these, only a few are suitable for use in automobile body panels. It is reasonable to assume that, as experience is gained with aluminum use on mass production, more suitable grades will be developed.

Sheet aluminum suitable for body panel use must have sufficient strength or rigidity for the specific panel. In addition, it must have properties that permit it to be stamped into shape by mass production methods, withstand 180-degree bends in making hem-flanges, and have a smooth surface to which paint can adhere as well as it does to steel. Some of the weight advantage of pure aluminum, as compared to steel, must be sacrificed to produce an alloy that meets these requirements. Pure aluminum weighs approximately one third as much as steel, but the addition of other elements to produce a metal suitable for body use increases the weight, because most of those added are considerably heavier. Allowing for the extra weight and probable design differences required for aluminum, it is possible to make body panels that weigh approximately one half of what they would if made of steel. This is a distinct advantage, which the body designer will use, when necessary, to meet the demand for reduced weight. The limits of possiblity are established by safety and manufacturing problems.

Safety for the body structure is, primarily, a matter of protection for the passengers if and when the automobile suffers physical damage due to collision, upset, or other causes. Safety requirements are established by law and approved by the automobile industry. No automobile manufacturer would knowingly design an unsafe automobile because the repercussions from both legal sources and the general public would be financially devastating. The first use of aluminum in the current weight-reduction program has been in hood panels and deck lids, areas where the passengers are least exposed in an accident. Aluminum could be used in door assemblies if sufficient reinforcement was provided to meet safety requirements.

Aluminum cannot be joined directly to steel, particularly by welding, because corrosion will develop. This eliminates the use of steel for reinforcing parts, and thus eliminates the use of aluminum for the large area panels. Aluminum could be joined to steel by using mechanical fasteners and providing insulation between the contact surfaces, but that would eliminate the advantage of welding, and the cost would be prohibitive. For these reasons, the current use of aluminum is limited to separate assemblies that attach to the main structure by bolts or other mechanical fasteners. If aluminum is ever adopted for the main body structure, it will probably be an all-welded aluminum structure. The possibility of this should not be ruled out, particularly in the luxury automobile field, because there is little evidence that the demand for such automobiles will diminish in the future. As the aluminum industry and automobile engineers find ways to retain the weight-saving features of aluminum and improve its strength, its competitive position as a substitute for steel will improve proportionally.

WORKING PROPERITES OF SHEET ALUMINUM

For aluminum to be an economically feasible substitute for steel in automobile body manufacture, grades must be available that either can be worked by existing methods for steel or require the minimum development of new methods. Aluminum grades must perform in much the same manner as steel when it is pressed into shape, welded, assembled, and painted. Ideally, the grade selected would have properties identical to those of steel. In practical use, the alloys available have varying degrees of those properties, sometimes more and sometimes less. For that reason, the properties of aluminum are discussed by comparing them to the properties of steel.

Elasticity

Pure aluminum, being quite soft, has much less elasticity than steel. When it is mixed with other elements to produce an alloy that can be used as a substitute for steel, the hardness and corresponding elasticity are increased, but neither reaches a degree equal to that of steel, when compared on the basis of volume. It would be possible to use extra-thick aluminum to acquire equivalent strength, in terms of rigidity, but to do so would defeat the purpose of the substitution. All grades of aluminum suitable for body use have less elasticity and hardness than steel.

Plasticity

Aluminum has more plasticity than steel. It will stretch, upset, bend, and tear more easiy than steel. To the repairman, this means it will suffer more damage in collision and react differently to the force he applies when repairing collision damage. Also, it means that he must use more care in applying force to aluminum than to steel to avoid adding to the existing damage.

Work Hardening

Aluminum tends to work harden differently from the sheet steel used in body construction. Although softer, aluminum of the grades suitable for automobile body panels can withstand less deformation without breaking than the steel it replaces. But this is more a problem for the body engineer than for the repairman. The engineer must select a grade of aluminum that can be pressed into shape without breaking in the draw die. The work hardening that occurs in the stamping operation as the panel is formed affects the entire panel area. Even though some areas are affected more than others, none are worked to the total limit of the aluminum, or the panels would break and become scrap.

The work hardening caused by a damaging impact can be quite severe, but in most cases it is limited to small areas where the metal has not been severely worked in the manufacturing operation. Examination of a typically damaged panel—if there is such a thing—would reveal that most of the severe buckles are in the relatively flat sections that have had very little working when stamped. The most severe cold working of the aluminum in the stamping operation is in the sharp bends, particularly the 180-degree bends in hem-flanges, and the few high crown areas. When these areas are affected by a severe impact, more breakage can be expected than for similar damage to a steel panel.

EFFECT OF HEAT ON SHEET METAL

Heat, from one source or another, is involved in many of the repair operations performed on the sheet metal panels of an automobile. The most common source of heat is the oxyacetylene welding torch. Another source is friction, resulting from power-driven abrasives such as the disc-sander. Because of the different characteristics of the two metals, the effects of heat on aluminum and steel are discussed separately.

EFFECT OF HEAT ON SHEET STEEL

The repairman should understand the effect of heat on steel over the full temperature range from normal ambient temperature to the melting point, which is over 2,600°F. (1,427°C.); but most of his concern is in the temperature range from 400° to 1,600°F. (204° to 871°C.). Heat above this temperature range is not, or at least it should not be, used, except for welding. Except for the effect of welding temperatures on grain structure, the temperature above 1,600°F. (871°C.) will not be considered.

Three separate effects of heat are to be considered: (1) scaling, (2) changes in grain struture, and (3) expansion and contraction. These effects occur at the same time, but for study purposes it is easier to consider them separately.

Scale and Heat Colors

A light film of scale, which is iron oxide, will begin to form on steel when it is heated to 430°F. (221°C.). If the surface is clean and bright, it will be visible as a pale, yellow coloring. As increased further, the color deepens progressively through straw, brown, purple, light blue, and dark blue, which is reached at approximately 600°F. (315°C.).

Further heating will cause the dark blue to fade into a gray or greenish shade until the first reddish glow appears at approximately 900°F. (482°C.). Above this temperature the colors usually are described as blood red, dark cherry, medium cherry, or full red, which is reached at approximately 1,550°F. (825°C.). Above this, the red color increases in brightness through salmon, orange, lemon, light yellow, and white, which is reached at approximately 2,000°F. (1,093°C.). At approximately 2,600°F. (1,427°C.), steel melts.

The colors below the red heat range will not be affected by the light in which they are viewed, because they are simply a film that coats the surface. They can be used as an indication of the approximate temperature of the surface, essential in many of the straightening and shrinking operations the repairman uses.

However, the way we see the colors in the red range is affected to some extent by light conditions, because those colors are a form of light. Metal that appears to be at bright red heat in dim light will not appear to be so bright in sunlight. This can be confusing, because shop lighting conditions can vary widely at different hours of the day. This is not a critical problem, but it is well to learn to make allowance for light conditions when doing work where temperature is important, particularly in shrinking operations.

Metal heated to the higher temperature range will accumulate a heavy scale on the red-hot area unless it is protected from the air. When the metal is heated with the oxyacetylene torch flame, the scale will be much heavier on the underside than on the side to which the flame was applied, because the gases burned in the flame exclude air and prevent oxidation. The scale on the protected side does not begin to form until the flame has been removed, but the underside is subjected to the attack of oxygen in the air as soon as the proper temperature is reached.

Although the formation of scale is an acutal burning of the metal, it is impractical to attempt to prevent its formation in the normal use of heat on sheet steel. Most spots are heated only once, so the effect is not of great importance. Nevertheless, it is desirable to avoid heating the same area of metal to high temperature repeatedly. Each reheating will cause some loss of metal by oxidation, so that after enough reheatings, the piece is weakened because part of it has been burned away. Such reheating and consequent metal loss rarely occurs in normal repair operations, however.

EFFECT OF HEAT ON GRAIN STRUCTURE

A progressive change in grain structure takes place when steel is heated from room temperature up to the melting point. The structures that result have a direct effect on hardness. Hardness and strength are so closely related that they are almost the same thing; therefore, the structure also affects strength.

The effect of heat on mild steel, such as automotive sheet, is more limited than it is on higher carbon steels. The carbon content of mild steel is too low for the metal to harden to any appreciable extent by heat treating; the effect of heat on it is almost completely limited to softening or *annealing*. Higher carbon steels may be annealed or hardened by following the proper procedure.

Work hardening of automotive sheet steel as a result of cold working was explained earlier. It can be completely relieved by heating to slightly above the bright red heat range. When the metal is turning to a salmon color, it has reached 1,600°F. (871°C.). Metallurgists call this point the *critical temperature*, because the grain structure undergoes a complete rearrangement. The new grains have none of the effects of working that hardened the old grain structure, because they have been entirely reformed. Cooling from this temperature to normal by exposure to air will leave automotive sheet steel in a very soft or annealed condition.

The effect of annealing is illustrated in Figure 1-9. These two pieces of metal were cut from the same sheet and were bent in the same manner, by pressing on the ends. The only difference is that the piece on the right had a band of metal annealed across the width before it was bent. This was done by passing the flame of a welding torch across it just fast enough to bring the metal to a salmon red heat, just slightly above bright red, and allowing it to cool to normal temperature before bend-

1-9 Effect of heat on bending. The piece on the right was heated to bright salmon red; the piece on the left was not heated. Both were bent by pushing the ends together.

ing. Note that all of the bending has taken place within the area affected by the heat, and that it has bent in a much shorter radius than the unheated piece on the left. The shorter radius bend is due to the loss of strength caused by the annealing.

The pieces of steel shown in Figure 1-9 were cut side by side from flat stock that had not been worked in any way other than the cold rolling they were given in the steel mill. The same metal would show an even greater effect if it first had been through a stamping operation that would have cold worked it further. Similar pieces cut from a salvage panel would show greater resistance to bending than the unheated one. The heated piece would bend the same whether it had been further worked or not, because the work hardening would be lost.

Figure 1-10 shows the same piece of metal after it had been straightened and further cold worked by hammer-on-dolly blows over the annealed area. The entire area was covered with closely spaced, hard hammer blows to ensure uniform and severe cold working. Bending was done by pressing on the ends, just as the previous ones, shown in Figure 1-9 were bent. Note that the previously soft area has become so stiff that it has bent less than the unheated piece in Figure 1-9. It is now the stiffest area in the strip.

Part of this work hardening was the result of the bending and straightening; the rest of it was the result of the hammer-on-dolly work. More work on this area with the hammer-on-dolly would make it even harder. However, there is a limit to the hardening that can be obtained by cold working mild steel; further working past that point would cause the metal to break when bent.

The discussion so far has been limited to the effect on the metal of heating up to the critical temperature fol-

lowed by slow cooling. Fast cooling, by immersing the heated metal in water, will tend to harden any steel. The hardening effect on automotive sheet steel is very slight, however, too little to have any practical significance. On higher-carbon steels, such as would be used in a punch or chisel, the hardening effect is of great importance; such tools would be useless unless they were properly hardened by heating and quenching.

A simple experiment performed with a strip of mild steel will show another effect of cold working. Bend it back and forth rapidly, and it will get quite hot, due to internal friction. Also, a slight increase in stiffness will be felt at first, but this will drop off and the strip will break if bending continues long enough.

The hardening effect gained by quenching— immersing hot steel in water or oil—results because the rapid loss of heat traps the metal in its finest, hardest grain structure. The hardness that can be obtained is directly related to the amount of carbon in the steel; however, the increase in hardness tends to level off when the carbon content exceeds 0.6 percent. Most ordinary hand tools are made of steel having less carbon than this.

Another characteristic of higher-carbon steel is that it reaches the critical point at lower temperatures than mild steel. Steel used in a chisel will reach the critical point at about 1,450°F. (788°C.), when it will be between cherry and bright red when viewed in bright light. Steel of the quality used in chisels will be too hard and brittle when quenched from bright red to normal temperatures. This is corrected by reheating to a much lower temperature and requenching, in an operation called *drawing* or tempering. The reheating would be up into the color range, usually light or dark blue. The old-time blacksmith's method of tempering tools such as chisels was to heat an inch or more of the end up to bright red; he then quenched part of the red-hot metal by dipping the end into water, keeping the tool moving

1-10 Effect of cold working. This is the same piece shown on the right in Fig. 1-9 after straightening, working the annealed area with hammer-on-dolly, and rebending.

up and down to avoid a sharp break-line between the hot and cold metal. When the end cooled enough to stop boiling off water, he scratched the scale off quickly, so he could see the color change as heat flowed back into the end, and when the shade he wanted reached the tip, he plunged the complete tool into the water. This same procedure can be used in the repair shop to reclaim many dull or soft tools. Heat from the welding torch and either a pail of water or a quantity of oil are all that is needed. To be safe, quench the tool in oil first. If that does not make it hard enough, redo it using the water. If the tool is made too hard, it will break in use and be ruined.

The effect of heating above the critical point, into the orange or white range, is to set up a coarse and weak grain structure. Such a structure always is formed in the metal next to a weld. Most so-called weld failures occur in this area, rather than in the weld proper. Unless this condition is removed by reheating or cold working, the area becomes the weakest in the welded panel. More detailed information on the proper treatment of this area is found in Chapter 5 on Welding.

A very common mistake is to overheat a section of metal that is to be straightened. Many sharp kinks are found that will straighten best if heat is applied, but best results will be obtained if heating stops at or below the critical point. Where overheating has occurred, it can be relieved by allowing the area to cool and then reheating to the critical temperature.

Free Expansion and Contraction

Expansion is the increase in size that occurs in nearly everything when its temperature is raised. Contraction is the decrease in size that occurs when the temperature drops. Some materials expand and contract more than others. Automotive sheet steel expands and contracts more than many other materials, particularly non-metallic substances.

The amount of expansion and contraction of anything is expressed in *linear* measurement; length, width, and thickness are the linear measurements used to measure size or volume. As expansion occurs, each of these dimensions increases at the same rate. The rate at which 1 inch of linear dimension increases when the temperature is increased or decreased 1°F. is called the coefficient of expansion. In the metric system, the coefficient of expansion is expressed in terms of the change of 1 centimeter caused by a change of 1°C. in temperature.

The coefficient of expansion of automotive sheet steel in the temperature range from normal to 1,500°F (816°C.) is approximately six millionths of an inch per degree. Above that range it is less, decreasing to practically nothing at the melting point. This may seem to be an amount so small that it has no significance. However, it is a matter of simple mathematics to determine that 1 inch of steel heated to 1,500°F. (816°C.) will expand 0.009 inch (0.23 mm); 10 inches (254 mm) heated 150°F. (65.5°C.) will expand the same. This becomes a matter

of great importance, particularly when something acts to restrict the movement caused by expansion.

It should be kept in mind that the expansion takes place in all directions. Reference was made to 1 inch of steel. This inch could be measured in length, width, or thickness. Expansion would be equal in all three if the application of heat were uniform. Although 1-inch thickness is never found in sheet metal construction, the expansion in thickness would be proportional for the fractional part of an inch that it measures.

RESTRICTED EXPANSION

When sheet metal expands, it pushes outward in all directions. When a condition exists that tends to restrict this outward push, tremendous forces can be generated. The exact amount of such force will be governed by the amount of restriction offered, the amount of heat, and the strength of the metal expanding. If sufficient heat is applied to a small area, the result will be serious heat distortion, as shown in Figure 1-11.

In the case of a spot heat application to sheet metal—which includes nearly every repair operation in which heat is used—the restriction to expansion is offered by the surrounding metal that is either unheated or at a much lower temperature. The restriction is only to the expansion of surface area. No similar restriction is offered to the expansion of thickness.

The limit of outward push is established by the force required to cause the particular area to bend or buckle. Once buckling has started, further expansion will not increase the outward push, because it will be taken up in the buckle. This condition is further complicated by the fact that as the temperature rises, the resistance to buckling is lowered proportionately; thus, as the metal expands, it begins to push up into a higher and higher bulge.

The same piece of metal shown in Figures 1-11 and 1-12 was scribed with parallel lines before heat was applied, so the heat distortion could be seen better. Note

1-11 *(Top)* Heat distortion due to spot heat application.

1-12 *(Bottom)* The same piece of metal as shown in Fig. 1-11 after cooling.

that, in Figure 1-11, the buckle is lightly higher than in Figure 1-12, which shows the piece of metal after cooling. This buckle remains because the expansion of the heated area has caused a bend strong enough to resist the tension set up by cooling. The tension tends to pull the buckle out, but it is never as effective as the pressure of expansion. This is because of the time lag between the development of highest pressure and tension. Rapid cooling in this very short time restores the strength in the distorted area so that much greater resistance is offered when tension develops.

The heat experiment shown here was performed on a piece of unworked metal. A similar experiment on a flat body panel would create a similar but probably smaller condition, because the outer edges would not be free to flex with the expansion of the hot spot. After cooling, such a spot on a body panel may cause hollow buckles to form on opposite sides of the heated area. If such buckles do form, they will be in the direction of the greatest curvature of the panel.

A distortion much different in appearance would be caused by heating an area of metal reinforced by its shape in such a way that it tends to resist swelling—for example, a section of a panel with a bead pressed into it. The bead is too stiff to swell; instead, most of its expansion would be taken up as an upset into the heated spot. When such an area cools, it will draw sharp buckles into the adjoining metal. The upset in the stiffer area will serve as a drawstring on the adjoining metal surface.

An explanation frequently offered for heat distortion is that it is the result of relieving existing strains in the metal. An experiment similar to the one shown in Figures 1-11 and 1-12 has proved this to be untrue. The experiment involved several pieces of metal of the same size, three of which were annealed by heating and long cooling in a heat treat furnace. An experiment similar to the one shown in Figures 1-11 and 1-12 was then performed. No appreciable difference could be seen in the amount of heat distortion on the annealed pieces and the unannealed pieces. As the result of this experiment, it appears that the primary cause of heat distortion is the restriction offered by the adjoining, cooler metal.

The three photographs in Figure 1-13 indicate the importance of very slight changes in the length of flat, or very nearly flat, panel surfaces. In the upper photograph, a flat strip of sheet metal is shown lying on a flat surface and fitting exactly between square blocks on each end. In the center picture, the strip has been lifted out, a 0.005-inch (0.127 mm) feeler gauge placed against the edge of one block, and the strip fitted back into place. Note that the thickness of the feeler gauge added to the length of the strip has caused it to bulge upward nearly ¼ inch (6.35 mm).

In the lower picture, the strip has been fitted back into place without the feeler gauge, but it has been expanded by passing a torch flame along its length. Note that it has bulged upward about twice as high as it did when the feeler gauge was in place. This amount of bulging has been obtained without heating the strip enough to cause it to discolor.

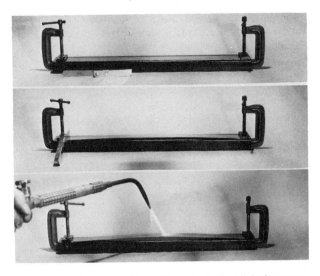

1-13 *(Top)* Demonstration of the effect of a slight increase of length of a section of flat metal. *(Center)* A 0.005-inch (0.127 mm) feeler gauge has been added to the length of the flat strip. *(Bottom)* The strip has been heated but kept below red heat.

The significance of these three photographs is in what they reveal concerning the need for precise length restoration if flat metal is to remain flat after it has been heated. The feeler gauge in the center photograph shows that only a few thousandths of an inch will create a bad wave. The torch application in the lower photograph shows that only slight heating will cause much more difference in length.

The same amount of expansion would be obtained by heating a much smaller area to a much higher temperature. This was done in heating the metal sheet shown in Figures 1-11 and 1-12. Of course, the effect would not be the same on a narrow strip as on a wide piece of metal because the strip, being free to move, does not offer the restriction to expansion that the larger piece does. Thus, the strip would not tend to distort nearly as much when heated as the surface of a panel would under the same conditions.

The repairman must understand the effect of heat distortion. Heat concentrated on a small spot causes the metal to push outward against the adjoining, cooler metal. This resistance will cause the heated spot to bulge and shorten, because it is under a compressive strain. Then, when the surface cools, the heated spot remains shorter, tending to have a gathering effect on the adjoining metal surface. In relatively flat panels, this effect may be enough to cause buckles to extend on each side of the heated spot for several inches.

A very common mistake is to think of metal affected in the manner just described as being stretched. Stretching is dealt with in greater detail in later sections, but we can quickly demonstrate a condition similar to stretching by folding a pleat in the edge of a piece of paper. The shortening effect of the pleat will cause the adjoining paper to bulge. The fact that only a few thousandths of an inch of upset will cause an appreciable bulge in a flat surface indicates how important it is to be able to differentiate between heat distortion and stretching.

EFFECT OF HEAT ON ALUMINUM

The following discussion of the effects of heat on aluminum is separated into these closely related topics: (1) melting points of different alloys, (2) heat conduction, (3) scaling, and (4) expansion and contraction.

Melting Point

The exact melting point of aluminum varies with the composition of the alloy involved, but all alloys melt in the temperature range in which steel is just beginning to show red heat in bright light. The lowest temperature at which any aluminum alloy melts is approximately 1,150°F. (621°C.), and the highest is over 1,200°F. (649°C.). All grades of aluminum retain the distinctive aluminum color when heated from normal temperature almost to the melting point. Unlike steel, which goes through a wide range of colors before melting at white heat, aluminum indicates melting only by the appearance of tiny bubbles and a slight greying, sometimes called an ashen appearance. The molten aluminum retains its distinctive aluminum color unless heated far beyond any practical heat range.

Scaling

Aluminum differs from steel in that it does not form a scale that varies in color and thickness as it is heated from approximately 430°F. (221°C.) to red hot. Instead, a thin scale, aluminum oxide, forms on aluminum; it has properties much different from those of scale on steel.

An important characteristic of aluminum oxide is that it forms a protective layer over the surface of the metal. If it did not, oxygen in the air would continue acting on the metal until it was all consumed, leaving nothing but aluminum oxide. The formation of aluminum oxide can be seen on pure aluminum by watching closely as the surface is scraped with a knife blade. The scraping action breaks the existing surface film, revealing a much lighter-colored metal. The lighter color darkens almost instantly as oxygen attacks it and replaces the scraped-off film. This same action takes place on the various aluminum alloys, but is easier to see on the pure metal.

The film of aluminum oxide, or scale, complicates welding and brazing procedures, because it remains in place at the temperature at which such work is done. Flux is required to break down the oxide before aluminum can be either welded or brazed.

Expansion and Contraction

In comparing the expansion and contraction of aluminum to steel, consideration must be given to three basic differences in the properties of the two metals: (1) aluminum conducts heat approximately twice as fast as steel, (2) aluminum expands approximately twice as far as steel; the contraction by volume will be equal to the expansion, but the linear contraction may be different, and (3) aluminum yields at lower temperature than steel.

The rapid conduction of heat in aluminum, as compared to steel, presents repair problems, because most of the heat applications involved are to a relatively small area; in most cases heat will be applied with welding equipment, although occasionally overheating may occur if a power-driven abrasive tool is held too long in one spot. A much larger area expands more rapidly than would be expected by a person whose experience was limited to steel.

Restricted Expansion is involved in any spot heat application. Experiments such as the ones shown in Figures 1-11, 1-12, and 1-13 would not produce quite the same results if performed on aluminum. The metal surface would rise higher, even though heated to a lower temperature, in Figures 1-11 and 1-13, but the remaining bulged area would be less than shown in Figure 1-12.

Linear expansion and contraction may not always be the same because, as the metal expands, upsets occur at relatively low temperatures. Once an upset has formed, it will not be released by cooling. The overall expansion and contraction will be equal, but the shape and dimensions of area will change.

Heat conduction in aluminum is approximately four times as fast as it is in steel. The effect of this is that heat spreads over a much larger area when it is caused either by welding operations or by friction when power-driven abrasives are used on it. The repairman should consider this as heat absorption. Any spot heat application below the melting point will require more heat, or take longer, to reach a given temperature than a similar application to a similar piece of steel.

The rapid conduction of heat by aluminum is an advantage in some instances and a disadvantage in many others. At least to some degree, it is a limiting factor in using heat to shrink stretched areas, and compared to the same operations performed on steel, it produces different heat distortion, or warpage, patterns caused by welding operations. These differences are partly offset, or minimized, by the fact that all operations involving heat are performed on aluminum at lower temperature levels than similar operations on steel.

Heat conduction should not be considered a major problem or difficulty, but techniques suitable for steel must be refined to be suitable for use on aluminum. A part of the refinement is to recognize that the nature of aluminum places some limits on what can be done with heat, as compared to steel.

Weldability

In the discussion of steel and its properties, weldability was taken for granted and not discussed as a separate topic. Welding of both metals is discussed in detail in Chapter 5, but brief mention of some of the differences in their welding problems is made here.

The primary difference is in the melting point temperatures. The exact melting temperatures of both vary according to their composition, but aluminum melts at or above 1,150°F. (621°C.), which is approximately one half the melting temperature of steel. At this relatively low temperature there is very little color change to indicate that it is close to melting. The surface becomes ashen in appearance and tiny bubbles appear on the surface just before it melts; there is no emission of light. At the higher melting temperature of steel, it glows white hot, giving off considerable light. The welder can judge the melting point of steel much more easily than that of aluminum.

A second difference is in the need for flux. Aluminum is always covered by a thin layer of scale that melts at a higher temperature than the metal does. The flux breaks this scale down by chemical action to bare the metal so that filler metal can be added. Steel does not require flux for fusion welding.

Finally, particles of molten steel seem to have an attraction for each other, which aluminum lacks or has to a much smaller degree. The combined differences make aluminum more difficult to weld than steel, but aluminum welding techniques can be developed by any person who has learned to weld steel.

MAKING SHEET METAL PANELS

The sheet metal panels of the automobile are made by dies that form and trim the metal to shape. The dies are mounted in huge presses that are the operating or power unit. We may consider the methods used for pressing steel and aluminum to be the same. Any real differences are manufacturing problems that do not concern the finished product.

Different types of dies are required to perform all the operations involved in making any of the larger panels of the automobile. The panel has to be formed, or *drawn*, into shape; this is done in the *draw die*, Figure 1-14. After being drawn, it has to be trimmed, flanged, and pierced. These operations may be performed by separate dies, or they may be combined; the complexity of each individual panel is the determining factor.

Knowledge of the action of the draw die is helpful in understanding the effect that force can have on automobile sheet metal, whether steel or aluminum. The plastic properties that permit either metal to be permanently deformed in the draw die also permit them to be permanently deformed by the force of a collision and also by the forces the repairman uses in correcting the collision damage.

Operation of the draw die includes two separate actions: clamping the sheet metal blank around the outer edges, and pushing the male die against the center area of the sheet metal blank to form it. These actions are illustrated in Figures 1-15 and 1-16, which

1-14 Typical draw die mounted in a draw press.

represent a cross-sectional view of a die stamping circular metal pan. The basic principle of stamping such a pan or a hood or roof panel is essentially the same.

Figure 1-15 represents the die in the open position, with a sheet metal blank in place ready to be pressed. The press that operates this type of die has two separate actions: the first raises and lowers the movable clamp ring; the second raises and lowers the male die. These actions are timed so that the clamp ring pressure is maintained throughout the entire downward stroke of the male die. Thus, the male die draws the edge of the blank inward through the clamp ring as it shapes the panel.

The pressure on the clamp ring must be adjusted properly. If it is too tight, the metal will break instead of drawing inward around the die; if it is too loose, the metal will wrinkle as it is drawn inward. However, when this pressure is correct, sufficient metal will be drawn through the clamp ring to permit a smooth, unbroken panel to be formed. It is here that manufacturing techniques are varied to suit the different operating problems of aluminum and steel.

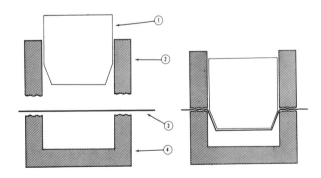

1-15 *(Left)* Cross-sectional sketch of a simple draw die in operation: 1, male die; 2, movable clamp ring; 3, sheet metal blank; 4, stationary clamp ring.

1-16 *(Right)* Cross-sectional sketch of male die at the bottom of a stroke.

In stamping a part with a complicated shape, the draw die exerts a tremendous tension of the sheet metal even though some of it is relieved by the movement through the clamp ring. This tension is enough to cause a slight spring-back after the die pressure is released.

The press action is completed when the clamp ring and male die return to the positions shown in Figure 1-15. The drawn panel is then removed, a new blank put in place, and the operation repeated.

The action of the draw die produces a piece of sheet metal that has the overall dimensions and shape of the finished part, but instead of being properly trimmed and flanged, it is surrounded by the excess metal that has been held between the clamp rings. To remove this excess, the piece then is put into a trim die, which is simply a shear built to the proper shape for the particular part. The excess metal trimmed off in the trim die is useless for other purposes because of the beads pressed into it and the working it has undergone in being pulled through the beaded surfaces of the clamp rings. In any large pressroom operation, this scrap is baled and shipped back to the steel mill.

Up to the point of trimming, the operations in making the round pan and a body panel are approximately the same. The differences lie in the shape of the dies and the fact that the die with the more complicated shape would have more complicated operating problems. For example, the clamp rings for a hood panel would follow its outer edge, and the male die would have the exact shape of the inside of the hood. In some cases, trimming the edge of the automobile panel is all that is needed; in others it is necessary to form special flanges.

The action of a flanging die is to fold the edges of the panel to shape. The widely varied types and shapes of flanges used on the different panels of the automobile make it necessary that such dies be designed to perform a specific operation. These dies are never interchangeable from one operation to another; some are very simple, others quite complicated. Detailed information on this type of die is beyond the scope of this book, however, and will not be considered further.

The important fact to gain from the preceding discussion of die operation is that any die-stamped panel is left in a state of *tension*. As pointed out, there is some spring-back as the die pressure is released, but the tendency to spring back is not relieved completely by this action. Remaining in the panel are locked-up forces, properly called *residual stresses*, that continue to pull against the shape. Being less than the strength of the metal in which they are found, these stresses have no effect unless the panel is weakened in a spot or area. The presence of such stresses may be demonstrated easily by cutting through a flat section of any stamped panel. The edges of the metal adjoining the cut will pull out of shape. A straightedge laid across the cut will show that the edges have dropped below the original contour.

The amount of residual stresses remaining in the panel is governed by the amount of stretching required in drawing it. Panels that have been subjected to minor forces may be expected to have fewer stresses than those subjected to much greater forces. Also, the condition will not be uniform over the entire surface of any particular panel.

Since the natural condition of the residual stresses in a panel is a slight state of tension, it should be remembered that when a damaged panel is repaired properly, it is restored to a state of tension. This matter will be considered in much greater detail in later sections on metal finishing and shrinking with heat.

BASIC SHAPES

The effect of a damaging force on a panel is governed by the shape, size, and reinforcements of that panel. Many different areas on the surface of an automobile have the same or similar shapes, and even though such panels vary in both size and the kind of reinforcements that support their outer edges, they may be expected to form the same damage patterns when subjected to similar damaging forces.

The similarity of shapes is more readily understood when the various areas of the panel are considered separately. The overall shape of the panel is a combination of the various areas representative of the basic shapes. The shape of a particular part, such as a door or hood panel, may vary for different year models of the same automobile, but it still is a combination of the basic shapes.

By classifying panels according to basic shapes, it is possible to establish basic damage patterns and related repair procedures. These can be applied to any sheet metal panel, whether it is on past, current, or future models.

Another factor that makes it desirable to classify panels according to shape is that it is rare for the damage to extend to the entire area of a panel. The repair problem will be confined to a portion of the larger panels, and the repairman need only concern himself with the portion that is damaged. There is always a direct relationship between the basic shape involved and the damage pattern that results.

There are different damage patterns for a basic shape, because damaging forces may be applied in many different ways. However, two different panels of the same basic shape will be damaged in a similar pattern if the damaging forces are the same. Damage patterns are discussed in the following chapter.

An easy way to describe shape is to consider the curvature of the length and width of an area separately. The shape of any particular area may be described accurately by placing two curved lines, at right angles to each other, over the area. In establishing these lines, length would lie along the front-to-rear length of the automobile. Width would be taken either vertically, as on the side of the automobile, or crosswise, as on the top or bottom. Front- and rear-end panels having their length in the crosswise direction to the automobile would be considered whichever way their overall shape would suggest.

The combined effect of the shape of length and width

1-17 Example of high crown panels. Most of the surface is high crown except the flat cowl side and reverse crown at headlight.

will be considered as the *crown* of the area of the panel being discussed. Four basic classifications are used to describe the crown of any panel: (1) low crown, (2) high crown, (3) combined high and low crown, and (4) reverse crown. Examples are shown in Figures 1-17 and 1-18.

High Crown

Surfaces in the high crown classification have enough curvature to give the impression of rounding shape in both directions. The curvature in both directions may not be the same, but in both cases it is enough to be obvious.

True high crowns were very common in the automobiles built in the early years of the automobile industry, but became less common immediately following the end of World War II. The weight reduction program caused by the world oil shortage of the early 1970s started a trend toward plainer, boxier shapes having even fewer high crowns than before. Those that are found are relatively small and usually in such locations as roof panel corners, rear end of quarter panels, and sometimes on the front end of hood panels.

As with the low crown, it is difficult to define exactly the amount of curvature necessary for a surface to be classified as high crown. Defined in terms of stiffness, it cannot be flexed out of shape by hand pressure; when enough force is applied to a high crown to push it out of shape, it will not spring back when the pressure is released. Examples of high crown are shown in Figure 1-17.

Metal in high crown areas has been worked by the draw die more severely than low crown metal, and for that reason it is slightly stronger due to additional work hardening.

Low Crown

Panels in the low crown classification have very little curvature; many of them can be found that are straight in the lengthwise direction. The impression gained from a glance at a small area is that it is a flat surface. For all practical purposes, the repairman must treat such panels as though they were flat. Figure 1-18 shows the shape of typical low-crowned panels.

The best examples of low-crowned panels are door lower panels, quarter lower panels, fender skirts, hood tops, and the center area of roof panels. Of this list, the roof panel has the least appearance of being flat because if has more curvature both lengthwise and crosswise than most other low crown panels. However, it is also the largest panel on the automobile, which causes it to react to a force, either damaging or repairing, as if it were flat. This is because the load-bearing strength of such long, slight curves is very low.

It is difficult to define exactly the amount of curvature that a panel can have and still be considered low-crowned. It is easier to define in terms of springiness or elasticity. The surface of an undamaged low-crowned panel will spring or flex out of shape when hand pressure is applied to it and snap back when the pressure is released.

In some cases, the entire area of a panel will be in the low crown classification; in others, only a portion will be low-crowned; the rest of the area may blend into any combination of the other basic crowns.

Combined High and Low Crown

The rounding edges of many low crown areas are actually low-crowned in one direction and high-crowned in another. Many such panels, like doors and front fenders, are very nearly flat lengthwise but curve away very sharply in the crosswise or width direction

1-18 Examples of low crown panels. The door and quarter panel are relatively flat but blend into sharp reverse crowns at the upper and lower edges.

along the edges. Many such surfaces can be compared to a portion of the outside of a cylinder.

Combined low and high crown surfaces have the strength characteristic of the high crown rather than the low crown surface. Although relatively flat in one direction, the relatively short radius of the curvature in the other provides strong bracing to resist force.

Reverse Crowns

In contrast to the other crowns, one curve of the reverse crown is hollow when viewed from the outside. This may be considered an inside curve, because the center point of the curve is on the side from which it is viewed. Usually, the inside curve has a relatively short radius as compared to the radius of the outside curve. It is quite common to find considerable variation in the radius of the inside curve of a reverse crown that runs the length of a panel. The outside curve will usually have a relatively long radius. Variations of either of these conditions will be found.

The reverse crown presents a particular repair problem because of its strength. A simple bend is not possible, because the two curves are braced against each other. A collapse of the metal surface is necessary for a bend to occur. As a result, damage in a reverse crown is usually severe as compared to damage in either a low or high crown. However, when damage does occur, often it is localized in one or more small areas. Because the reverse crown is stiffer, damage tends to spread less than it will in the other crowns.

Examples of reverse crowns can be seen in Figures 1-17 and 1-18.

REINFORCING METHODS

The strength of crowned panel surfaces on an automobile body is not enough to provide the rigidity necessary to hold alignment of parts and resist the strains of normal operation. The desirability of keeping weight down to the minimum rules out the use of heavy reinforcing members; this has always been important to good body design, but its importance has increased tremendously with the demand for more fuel-efficient automobiles. This demand has placed even greater emphasis on the development of lightweight reinforcements using minimum amounts of material.

Reinforcements are of three basic types: (1) those formed in the surface of an inner or outer panel, (2) those welded to the panel, and (3) those made by bonding inner and outer panels together with thermosetting or catalyst-activated adhesives; this is relatively new, as compared to the first two, and is discussed in more detail later in this section.

The reinforcements formed in a panel are the flanges, beads, and offsets used primarily for stiffness. Examples are such sections as the flange on the lower edge of a fender skirt and the ribs or beads on door inner panels and floor pans; reinforcements of this type

are essentially stiffeners intended to prevent vibration or flexing. Welded-on reinforcements are usually channel or box section pieces that serve as structural members. Examples include roof rails, windshield headers, and the crossbars used under the floor pan, among many others.

Body engineers design light structural members of thin sheet metal by taking advantage of the stiffening effect of an angular bend. A strip of sheet metal has relatively little strength to resist bending when force is applied to it at right angles to the surface. The same strip can support far greater loads when it is turned so that the load is applied to the edge instead of to the flat surface. A flange turned on the edge of flat sheet is, in effect, an attached strip. The far greater resistance to bending of the edgewise strip is added to the relatively low strength of the flat sheet.

The reinforcing effect is greatest when the flange is turned away from the load and least when turned toward it. These two conditions are illustrated in Figures 1-19 and 1-20. In Figure 1-19 the outer edge of the flange is under tension and cannot yield except by breaking or stretching. The inner edge of this flange is under a compressive force that would tend to buckle it if it were free; attachment to the flat sheet prevents buckling. In Figure 1-20, the opposite is true. The attached edge of the flange is under tension, and the outer edge is under compression; unsupported, the outer edge is free to buckle as the flat sheet bends. A second flange has been added in Figure 1-21, making a channel.

Maximum strength can be obtained by adding the fourth side to the three-sided channel, making what is

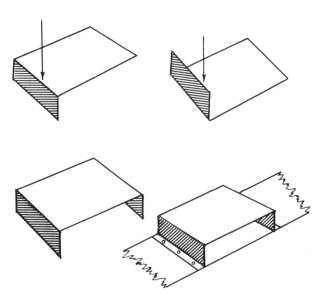

1-19 *(Top, left)* Flange turned away from the load, indicated by the arrow

1-20 *(Top, right)* Flange turned toward the load, indicated by the arrow.

1-21 *(Bottom, left)* Channel formed by adding a second flange.

1-22 *(Bottom, right)* Box construction.

1-23 Cutaway section of roof and box construction roof rail. Roof rail construction varies widely.

1-24 Cutaway section of typical rocker panel; showing box construction.

commonly termed a box construction. Figure 1-22 is representative of a very commonly used form of box construction. It is essentially a channel with narrow flanges turned on the outer edges of the wide flanges. These narrow flanges serve as a means of welding to the broad section of sheet metal. The crossbars on the underside of floor pans are excellent examples of this type of box construction.

Box construction is not limited to the square shape shown in Figure 1-22. The possible variations of the shape of such parts, usually called members, are almost limitless. Regardless of shape, however, box construction offers more strength than can be obtained by any other method used to provide reinforcement in automobile bodies.

An actual cutaway section of a typical roof and roof rail is shown in Figure 1-23. This is true box construction, as is the cutaway rocker panel shown in Figure 1-24.

Adhesive bonding of inner to outer panels started in the years following World War II as a means of prevent-

ing flutter in large, nearly flat areas of sheet metal. It has been used primarily on hoods and deck lids, but one manufacturer has used it on roof panels. Wherever it is used, an inner panel is required to serve as the support for the outer; the inner panel may have pressed-in reinforcements and cut-out sections, but will be designed so that the bonding points will be close to the outer.

The adhesive is a viscous material that forms artificial rubber when subjected to heat or when a catalyst is added to it. In factory assembly, blobs of the material are put on one panel, in a predetermined pattern, and the other panel is put in place. The panel will later go through a heated paint drying oven, which will provide the heat required to cure the adhesive. When a catalyst is used, the material cures immediately.

Adhesive material used to install windshield glasses, either the caulking or the tape type, can be used to re-attach a broken bond whenever necessary.

2

COLLISION DAMAGE

When a collision occurs and damage results, it is because the sheet metal was subjected to more force than it could resist. The study of collision damage is complicated by the fact that it is the result of an impact instead of normal wear. Each case of damage is an individual problem to be solved by the repairman. This is in sharp contrast to the repair of the operating units of the automobile, because similar units develop similar problems, so that exact procedures can be prepared and published in a shop manual or service bulletin for the mechanic to follow. In solving his problems, the repairman must be guided by what he knows about the effect of impact force on the particular metal involved and the repair methods that may be used to restore it to original shape.

This chapter explains the basic damage conditions that result when impact force is applied to the basic shapes. By understanding these basic conditions, it is possible to reduce a highly variable situation to a combination of basic patterns. Training and experience allow us to see the damage on any panel as a combination of these conditions instead of as just a tangled mess of sheet metal.

To grasp these basic factors, it is necessary to understand the relationship of shape to the effect of force on it. This relationship is a variable factor, because it involves different speeds, impact angles, size and rigidity of the impact object, and the construction of the area affected. The use of different metals, mild steel, hard steel, and aluminum, may seem to complicate the problem. This should not be a matter of great concern; the repairman's problems are with panels that are repairable. Panels of different metals may suffer more or less damage under the same conditions, but shape and force will react in much the same manner regardless of the type of sheet metal involved.

This chapter has been arranged so that the relationship of shape to the effect of force on it is discussed first. This is followed by a list of the basic conditions and a discussion of the physical effects of each. The chapter concludes with an explanation of the variable factors of speed, angle, rigidity, and so on, and how they are related to the severity of the damage conditions.

EFFECT OF FORCE ON SHAPE

The term *impact*, as used here, means the force involved when an automobile strikes, or is struck by, another object. The other object may be another automobile, but could be anything. To cause damage, the *impact object* must strike the *impact area* hard enough to overcome its elasticity, meaning that it will not spring back. The deeper the impact area is driven in, the wider its effect spreads. As it spreads, force from the impact either pushes or pulls on the adjoining surface, depending on the shape of the areas affected. This spreading action is referred to in later sections as the *flow of force*.

Figure 2-1 shows the outward flow of force from a direct impact on a combination high and low crown. The solid lines AA and BB represent vertical and lengthwise cross sections of a typical panel. The arrow C represents a direct impact on the intersection of the cross section lines. The dotted lines show the effect of the impact on the original shape, and the arrows indicate the flow of force. Note that the arrows under the high crown point outward, indicating that the force following this path has pushed outward against the adjoining metal; the arrows under the low crown point inward, indicating an exactly opposite effect.

An impact on a high crown always can be expected to push outward against the adjoining metal; the same impact on a low crown always can be expected to pull inward on the adjoining metal. When these crowns are combined, as they are on most body panels, the effect of pushing and pulling will act along lines as shown. The panel's material will not change the flow of force; steel, aluminum, or a non-metallic substitute will react in the same manner. The strength of the material involved, however, will determine the extent of damage; softer material will be driven in farther and damaged more than a hard material.

The reaction of any sheet metal when subjected to a force that pulls will be different from that to a force that pushes on it. Pressure on the opposite edges of a sheet toward the center will cause it to crumple because of its low resistance to bending. An outward pull on the same edges will draw it tight, and no further effect will occur unless enough force is applied to exceed the metal's yield strength. For this reason, the damage conditions found in a high crown area will be different from those found in the adjoining low crown area, even though both are the result of the same impact.

THE BASIC DAMAGE CONDITIONS

Force spreading from the impact point into other areas of the panel or into other panels causes damage by changing the shape of the areas affected. The nature of such damage varies too widely to attempt to establish what could be called a typical condition. However, when a detailed examination is made of the damage area, it will be found to be a combination of the following basic damage conditions: (1) displaced areas, (2) simple bends, (3) rolled buckles, (4) upsets, and (5) stretches. The combination is called the *fold pattern* in this book.

Displaced Areas

In almost every case, examination of a damaged panel will reveal that parts of the area are not affected by bending or other distortion. Such areas are part of the overall damage only because they have been pushed out of position. Quite often they are under an elastic strain that, when relieved, will allow the area to snap

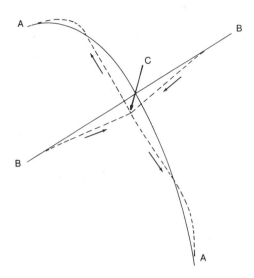

2-1 Showing the flow of force from a direct impact on a combination high and low crown surface.

back into shape. Such areas may be considered displaced. Much of the center area of the door panel shown in Figure 2-2 is displaced. Such an area is sometimes called *elastic metal*, because it will tend to snap back to place if the buckles holding it are relieved properly. The word "elastic" in this sense is technically wrong, because all metal is elastic. The area should be considered under an elastic strain, or springy.

It is important to recognize all displaced areas and plan the repair procedure so that the buckles holding them out of place will be relieved properly. Large displaced areas often can be released so that there is little or no repair work except on the buckled areas that hold them.

One measure of the severity of any damage is in the amount of displaced metal that makes up the damaged area. It is obvious that an area that can be made to snap back into shape will not require as much straightening work as a similar-sized area that is badly bent and distorted.

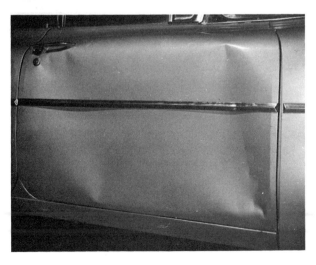

2-2 Displaced metal. Much of the center area will snap back into shape when the sharp buckles are relieved.

Simple Bends

As the surface of a panel collapses under impact, it folds. Some of the folding is the result of simple bends, particularly in relatively flat areas. A simple bend is essentially a long, usually narrow, area of metal that has served as a pivot for the movement of the adjoining metal and in doing so has changed shape.

The deformation in a simple bend is due to the opposing action of tension and pressure forces. As force, which tends to cause bending, is applied to a piece of sheet metal, it causes tension on the outer surface and pressure on the inner. Bending occurs when the force is enough to overcome the metal's resistance to this tension and pressure. Under normal conditions, the outer surface of the bend is *stretched* and the inner is *upset.* Upset means shortened, and stretched, obviously, means lengthened. The bending action is illustrated in Figure 2-3.

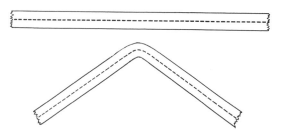

2-3 Enlarged cross section of a piece of sheet metal before and after bending. The outer surface is stretched, and the inner surface is compressed. The center line remains unchanged.

If stretching occurs on the outer surface and upsetting occurs on the inner, it is quite apparent that somewhere in between the metal would not be affected by either. The dotted center line in Figure 2-3 represents this unaffected part, which is actually a plane, located approximately in the center of the thickness. The metal on each side of this plane is solid, so that both tension and pressure are resisted equally at the start of the bending. When breaking occurs in a sharp bend, however, it appears on the outside, because the action tends to pull it apart. The inner surface will be at the breaking point but will not separate until the bend is straightened.

In studying the effect of bending, it is essential to direct attention to the very small unit of metal instead of being concerned with the entire panel. Figure 2-4 represents an enlargement of a piece of sheet metal slightly less than ½ inch (13 mm) long and ⅓ inch (18 mm) wide. The lines on its surface are spaced apart the thickness of the metal. Thus, if flat, each square formed by these lines represents one face of a cube joined on four sides to similar cubes.

In Figure 2-5, A and B represent a much greater enlargement of one of these cubes before and after bending. In A, the upper and lower halves are exactly the same size and shape; in B, bending has distorted the

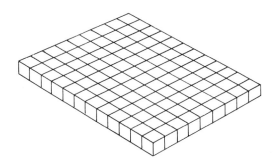

2-4 Enlarged piece of metal with lines scribed on the surface, representing interconnected cubes.

square into the shape of a wedge. The upper and lower halves are still the same in bulk, because nothing has been taken away or added, but they are different in shape, the upper being stretched and thinned and the lower being pressed together and thickened.

The total amount of metal involved in a simple bend is determined by its length and how sharply it is formed. Quite often an area several inches long and a fraction of an inch wide, made up of many sections of metal the size of the cube illustrated, is affected. The effect of bending on various sections throughout such an area would vary considerably. It follows logically that to straighten such an area, force must be applied so that these effects are relieved, regardless of the extent of individual section distortion.

Hinge Buckles

A hinge buckle is one form of a simpe bend. There is no major difference, but the term hinge suggests a straight, simple bend that has served as a pivot point for one section of a panel to swing around another. Many simple bends are curved, particularly when they have been formed into a curve by pressure flowing out from an impact area.

Rolled Buckles

The rolled buckle is so named because of the rolling action that occurs in much of the area of a panel as it collapses under an impact. This action is similar to the pivot action of a hinge buckle, except that the pivot

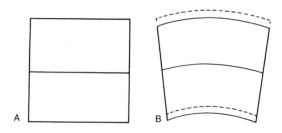

2-5 The shape of a single cubical section (A) before and (B) after bending.

point travels across an area instead of remaining in one place. An example of a severe rolled buckle is indicated by arrow 1 in Figure 2-6. Less severe rolled buckles are indicated by the arrows 2 and 3. The sharp dent between 1 and 3 is a direct impact area from which spread the force causing the rolling. This example is from an older car, because rolled buckles as severe as this one are becoming quite rare, due to the design trend to squarer bodies. They still occur, however, and represent one of the repairman's major problems in straightening panels.

The distinctive feature of a rolled buckle is two ridges running together at an angle. These ridges are generally sharply formed at the meeting point, which is usually in the area where a low crown blends into a combination low and high crown. On each side of the meeting point, the sharpness of these ridges will be reduced gradually, until in many instances they will blend into the shape of the adjoining surfaces. This is not true of the rolled buckle shown here, however, because the ridges are in an area of metal that is quite high crowned in both directions, and the dent is quite deep.

As the buckle rolls into the high crown area, flattening of the crown forces the meeting point of the two ridges above the proper level of the panel. Referring to Figure 2-1, this is the raised effect shown by the dotted line AA. The rolling action always causes a valley section to form between the two ridges; this valley forms a stiff prop under the raised area.

The damage caused by a rolled buckle can vary from a condition no more severe than a simple bend to one of the worst conditions with which the repairman will work. The severity of the distortion of the individual rolled buckle is governed by the amount of force that caused it. The rolling action starts as a curved ridge around the impact point and moves, or rolls, outward. The shape of this ridge is relatively smooth until it reaches the point where the low crown blends into a combination crown. At this point, the inner surface of the ridge collapses, forming the valley buckle. If the roll-

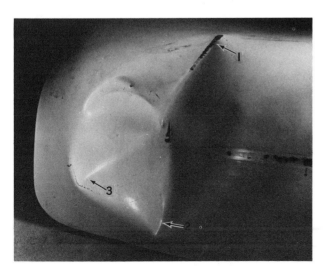

2-6 A typical example of rolled buckles. Arrow 1 points to the break-over path of the most severe buckle. Arrows 2 and 3 indicate less severe buckles.

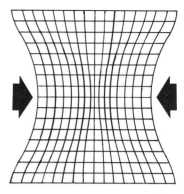

2-7 Enlarged drawing showing the effect of force pushing from opposite directions on a section of metal approximately ½ inch (13 mm) square.

ing action stops here, the damage is not much more severe than a simple bend. If there is sufficient force to drive this rolling action farther into the higher crown, the damage will be severe. This is the case with the buckle indicated by arrow 1 in Figure 2-6. Note that a path of flaked-off paint has been left by the rolling action. This path is referred to as the break-over path because of the breaking or collapsing action that occurs as it forms.

The metal in the break-over path will be upset. The next section deals with the exact nature of upsetting, whether caused by a rolled buckle or otherwise.

Upsets

An upset occurs when opposing forces push against an area of metal and cause it to yield; in yielding, the surface area will be reduced and the thickness increased proportionally. Forces that cause an upset may act only from two opposite directions, as indicated in Figure 2-7, or they may act against a central point from several directions. To identify an upset, remember that one or both of the surface dimensions of the affected area will be reduced.

The effect and importance of an upset will be better understood if one remembers that it usually is restricted to a relatively small area. Figure 2-7 can be considered as representing the same section of metal surface represented by Figure 2-4. Reducing this enlarged drawing to the dimensions of most sheet metal found in the automobile body would indicate a piece about ½ inch (13 mm) square and about 0.037 inch (9 mm) thick. Larger areas of metal can be upset, but the tendency to buckle and relieve the pressure limits the upsetting effect to areas not too much larger than this. The break-over of a severe rolled buckle may be much longer but usually not much wider.

Many drawings of various shapes could be used to illustrate the effect of upsetting. However, each would be similar to the three in Figure 2-8. A represents a small cubical section of sheet metal before the upsetting force application. B represents the same section after

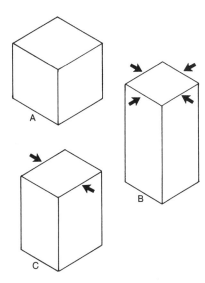

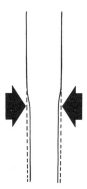

2-9 Upset effect in the break-over path of a severe rolled buckle. The break-over action would reach the point where the solid and dotted lines converge.

2-8 Effect on a small, cubical section within the upset area. In A, the cube is shown before force has been applied. In B, pressure has been applied from four sides. In C, pressure has been applied from two sides.

force application from all four sides. Note that the top surface is shown much smaller, and the height, which would be the thickness, is much greater. C represents the same section after force application from two sides only. Note that only two sides of the top surface are shown smaller, and the height, or thickness, is less than in B.

Upsetting a single section no larger in area than its thickness would not have a significant effect on the shape of a panel. When this effect is spread over an area ½ inch (13 mm) wide and much longer, it is an important factor. The series of photographs in Figure 1-13, showed that as little as 0.005 inch (0.127 mm) would cause an unacceptable bulge in a flat strip. The drawing in Figure 2-7 does not represent any specific upset, but the amount of upset shown would not be uncommon. Considering that this drawing represents an area of metal approximately ½ inch (13 mm) square, the upset shown would be many times more. Such a spot anywhere on the surface of a low crown panel would draw wrinkled-type buckles on each side of it.

Figure 2-9 represents the upsetting effect of most rolled buckles. The offset in the lower section of these parallel lines represents the point reached by the break-over path. The resistance of the adjoining metal tends to force the metal together; lines scribed on the panel before the buckle was formed would have this shape after the break-over action passed between them.

Upsetting is not limited to the effect of the damaging force. The piece of metal shown in Figure 2-10 has had a ridge formed in it by bending and straightening; this is a typical buckle left after any piece of metal has been bent double and then opened up again without work being done directly on the ridge which forms. The section in the center was flattened by hammering it down as it lay on a flat surface. Note that this section has been lowered until it is about level with the metal on

either side. Flattening this section caused far greater upsetting than would be found in almost any rolled buckle. The repairman who does not know that he should avoid hammering sharp ridges will make upsets of this type and add damage to damage.

The metal referred to in this discussion of upsetting is mild steel. Aluminum, being a softer metal, will upset more than steel under the same circumstances. Harder steel would upset less.

Stretches

Stretch, the exact opposite of upset, occurs when an area of metal is subjected to force in tension greater than its yield strength. The result is an increase in surface area. Sheet metal is considered stretched whether the increase of area is caused by an increase of either length or width, or both.

Stretching also can be the result of the improper use of tools, particularly the hammer and dolly block. (These are the repairman's most important tools *if* he will learn to use them properly.)

Stretching occurs under conditions and usually in areas different from those of upsetting because it is the

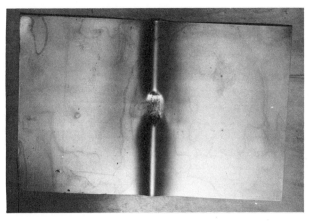

2-10 An upset section of a crease-type buckle, made by hammering the buckle as the piece lay on a flat surface. No heat was used.

result of tension instead of pressure. The most common type of stretching is a gouge. Small, point-type gouges may be seen in the impact area of the dented deck lid in Figure 2-6. A much more severe crease-type gouge is shown in Figure 2-11.

When the exact difference between stretched and upset metal is recognized, the problems of stretched metal become relatively simple. Stretched areas of metal rarely rise above the surface level to cause unacceptable bulges. When they do, they are usually caused by something within the automobile being thrown against the underside of the panel during the collision. The repairman who has learned the proper technique of shrinking metal finds these areas relatively easy to repair. Gouged areas are frequently filled, because the fill can be blended into the surface area easily in most cases. However, the decision as to whether a particular gouge should be filled or straightened by shrinking should not be made without considering the conditions. In some cases, filling is all that is required; in others filling can be a mistake.

False Stretch

The term false stretch refers to a condition often mistakenly considered as stretched metal. It occurs when a severe rolled buckle is straightened without relieving the upset condition in the break-over path. As shown in Figures 2-8 and 2-9, the metal in the break-over path may be squeezed enough to cause upsetting. The incorrect use of a hammer on a sharp ridge can add to the upset. Driving a severe rolled buckle out by hammering on the underside will have a drawstring effect on the undamaged metal adjoining it, similar to that shown in Figure 2-10. We can illustrate this condition by folding a small pleat in the edge of a sheet of paper and mashing it flat. The surface of the paper adjoining the pleat will bulge upward because of the drawstring effect of the pleat. Release the pleat, and the surface will flatten. An upset in the break-over path of a severe rolled buckle, if not relieved in straightening, will similarly affect the adjoining panel surface.

The technique of avoiding false stretch, or at least minimizing it, is explained in Chapter 3 and emphasized in the discussions of straightening procedure in other chapters. The procedure for shrinking unavoidable false stretches is discusses in Chapter 4, along with other shrinking procedures.

VARIABLE FACTORS IN COLLISION

Even though all collision damage is made up of the same basic conditions, few damaged areas are exactly alike. Because the damage from any collision is unique, the repairman is forced to determine his own procedure. He can do this best if he has been trained, or has trained himself, to determine the fold pattern and apply opposite force to reverse the damage. An important part of this training is to learn what to look for when inspecting the damage. The trained eye will see a pattern in what seems a mess to the untrained eye.

Analyzing the job consists of determining (1) the area that received the impact, (2) an approximation of the total force of the impact, and (3) a check on the paths the force might follow to cause related damage at points distant from the impact area. In the analysis he should look for (1) the angle of the impact, (2) the relative speed of the impact object, (3) the size, rigidity, and approximate weight of the impact object, and (4) the construction of the area receiving the impact.

These will be referred to in later discussions as the *variable factors*. They determine the nature of the damage resulting from any collision. It is easy to determine the extent to which each factor has contributed to the total. From this is a simple step to visualize the actual movement of the metal as it folded. The key to good repair procedure is a matter of reversing this movement.

IMPACT ANGLE

The impact angle means the angle at which the impact object collided with the automobile; or, put another way, the angle at which the automobile collided with the impact object. Often, both are moving. Whether or not the impact object is another automobile is of no consequence, except that it determines the nature of the surface which caused the damage. The reason the impact angle should be considered is that it determines the direction of the flow of force from the impact area into the structure, where it may cause related damage.

With everything else equal, a direct impact will cause more damage than a glancing one, because the full force will be absorbed. It was shown in Figure 2-1 that the force that flows outward from a direct impact will be in tension on a low-crowned surface and in pressure on a high-crowned surface. A much more variable situation results when the angle of impact becomes much more oblique, as shown in A, Figure 2-12. The colliding object may either dig into the surface or glance off. If it digs in instead of slipping, it tends to push, or crumple, the surface ahead of it and to pull on the sur-

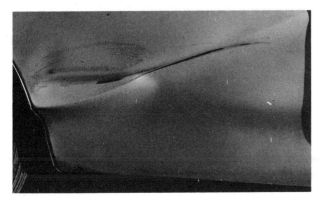

2-11 A crease-type gouge, the result of a high-speed impact by a small, rigid impact object.

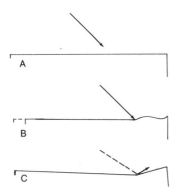

2-12 Showing the effect of an impact from a sharp angle. Figure A indicates the angle of approach. B shows the effect when the impact object digs into the surface, pushing metal ahead of it and drawing metal behind it. C shows the effect when the impact object glances instead of digging in; this is essentially the same as a direct impact.

face behind it, often carrying it along as shown in B. A severe damage of this type can be difficult to straighten. However, when the impact glances off, as shown in C, the damage is usually minor.

Another typical damage result from a glancing impact occurs when the object slips instead of holding, leaving a path of dented, sometimes deeply gouged metal as shown in Figure 2-11. It was pointed out in the section on stretched metal that gouges of this type are stretched, often very severely, because tremendous force has been concentrated on a very small area.

A quite different damage condition occurs when a panel having a combination crown, such as a quarter panel, door, or fender, is subjected to a direct impact on

2-14 A .22-caliber rifle bullet hole in a piece of sheet metal.

one end. In this case most of the entire panel is subjected to pressure that will tend to collapse it. Typically, the smooth areas simply fold out of shape, but sharply crowned areas will crumple, or collapse, accordion fashion, if the pressure is great enough. An example is shown in Figure 2-13.

RELATIVE SPEED OF THE IMPACT OBJECT

The speed of impact should be considered as relative because essentially identical damage results whether the damaged automobile moves against a standing object or is struck by a moving object. When both are moving toward each other, as in a head-on collision, the relative speed equals the combined speed of both.

The speed of impact is important because of inertia. Stated briefly, inertia is the tendency of any stationary object to resist being put in motion, or of a moving object to continue moving. An excellent example of the effect of inertia is shown in Figure 2-14. The hole in this piece of metal was made by a .22-caliber rifle bullet. A hole can be shot in a body panel because of the speed at which the bullet travels. A much heavier object could exert the same amount of force at a much lower speed, but instead of piercing the panel, it would crush the surface. The difference is a matter of time; under the impact of the heavier but more slowly moving impact object, the panel has more time to move inward and spread the effect over a larger area.

A general idea of the speed of the impact is important in analyzing damage, because it indicates the extent to which force has penetrated into the structure to cause related damage. A high-speed impact on the front end of a fender may cause severe damage at the point of impact but not affect the alignment of the fender to the hood and door. Impact by a heavier object traveling a lower speed may cause less damage at the impact area, but may break the fender loose from the cowl, causing the fender to move back against the door. The trained repairman would know, by the appearance of the damage, that he also should check the alignment of the cowl hinge pillar; it may have shifted enough to prevent proper door alignment.

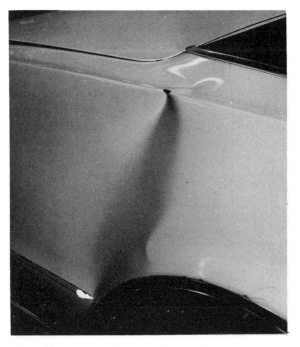

2-13 Buckle formed by the collapse of a section of metal under pressure.

SIZE, RIGIDITY, AND WEIGHT

In addition to the impact angle and speed, the size, rigidity, and weight of the impact object have a great bearing on the type of damage. Again, as in the analysis of impact angle and speed, the repairman need not concern himself with the *exact* size, degree of rigidity, or weight. He is interested only in whether the impact object was large or small, rigid or yielding, or extremely heavy or very light.

The preceding example of the bullet serves as an illustration of the small, relatively rigid, but lightweight impact object. As a contrasting example, consider the effect of a roll-over accident in which the automobile lands on one side in soft earth. It is possible for the automobile to bounce as it continues to roll without causing severe visible damage. However, bends or misalignment may be found in the reinforced parts supporting the panels that received the impact, because the soft earth spreads the impact force over enough panel surface area to avoid severe overloading of any one point. Some of the impact force will be absorbed in displacing soft earth, but much of it will be transferred through the adjoining metal into the reinforcements.

An entirely different type of damage would result if the automobile were to roll into something hard and unyielding, such as a tree stump or rock. The effect would be much more severe, because there would be no cushioning effect. Severe distortion in the impact area would absorb some of the force, reducing misalignment in adjoining sections; force expended at one point cannot travel on and cause additional damage elsewhere.

CONSTRUCTION

The rigidity of the area receiving the impact determines to a large degree the nature of the damage and the extent to which it spreads. For example, a direct impact on the center of a door panel would spread over the entire area, but the same impact on the reinforced pillar section of the same door would probably cover much less area. The reduction in area concentrates the force of the blow. There is no easy way in which the severity of damage in one area can be compared with the other, but it is obvious that greater misalignment would occur from the impact on the pillar section. Similar examples could be pointed out over the entire surface of the body.

In analyzing any damage, it is essential to consider whether the impact has struck an area that is quite rigid or one that will yield readily. The effect on the rigid area will tend to cause severe distortion that spreads over a relatively small area; the opposite will be true of a similar impact on an area that will yield easily. To the untrained observer, however, the larger damage may appear to be more severe because of its size. The trained repairman should never make the easy mistake of judging the severity of damage on the basis of size alone.

TOOLS AND BASIC OPERATIONS

A knowledge of the proper use of the tools of the trade is necessary to understand the procedure of repairing even the simplest dent. Tools of some kind are required for every operation in straightening and preparing a damaged panel for repainting. Some of these operations require tools that normally are classified as shop equipment because of size and cost; others require only such items as may be classified as the repairman's hand tools. Both types of tools require the development of skill in their use. However, skill in the use of shop equipment is primarily in knowing where to use it. For example, comparatively little manual skill is required to set up a body jack, but it must be set up so that it will push against the right spot, or it may do more damage than good. On the other hand, skill in the use of hand tools requires both knowledge and manual dexterity.

This chapter deals with the repairman's hand tools and the basic operations performed with them. The tools are discussed first, then the basic operations in which they are used. This has been done to explain the purpose of the individual tool and what may be expected of it before giving instruction for its use on an actual repair job.

Hand tools may be classified according to basic use, either straightening or metal-finishing. Of course, some tools may be used in both basic operations, but the primary use will be in one or the other. This chapter has been organized with this in mind. The first section deals with the metal-straightening tools and the basic straightening operations, the second with the basic metal-finishing tools and the basic metal-finishing procedures.

METAL-STRAIGHTENING TOOLS

To straighten damaged sheet metal, force is applied to restore it to original shape. This becomes a matter of straightening bends and relieving distortions. Tools used for this purpose are the means of applying the necessary force.

Metal-straightening hand tools apply force by one or more of three ways: (1) striking a direct blow on the metal surface, (2) resistance to a direct blow struck on the opposite side of the metal, and (3) as a lever used to pry against the surface, usually on the inside.

It would be impractical to list every tool available for use in straightening sheet metal, but considered basic may be (1) bumping hammers, (2) dolly blocks, (3) bumping spoons, (4) body spoons, (5) pry or pick tools, (6) caulking tools, and (7) screw-equipped slide hammers.

Development of manual skill in the use of these tools is essential for the student who wishes to become a good repairman. This requires an understanding of the purpose of the tools and practicing to become proficient in their use.

BUMPING HAMMERS

Bumping hammers are made in a wide range of

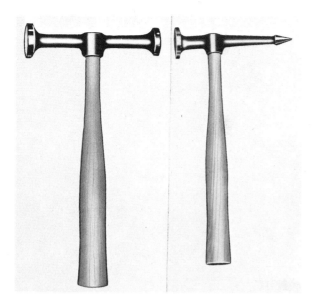

3-1 General-purpose hammer, sometimes called a dinging hammer.

3-2 Combination bumping and picking hammer.

styles, sizes, and combinations by the various manufacturers of body tools. Two very common styles are shown in Figures 3-1 and 3-2.

The distinguishing feature of all bumping hammers is the one head which is quite wide and nearly flat on the working face. The width of this head may vary on different types of hammers, but most of the popular ones will be approximately 1½ inches (38.1 mm). The most common shape for this head is round, but some are made square. Having an exact size and shape of the hammer, however, is not as important as having a hammer that is satisfactory to the person using it.

The large, nearly flat face serves to spread the force of a hammer blow over a fairly large area of the metal surface. This is essential in working with soft sheet metal. A smaller face or one having a high crown would tend to mark the metal when striking a hard blow on a spot backed up by the dolly block. The large, nearly flat face has the additional advantage of taking care of slight errors in aiming the hammer blow. This is particularly important in working on low crown panels.

The shape of the slight crown on the large face is important. The ideal surface is almost dead flat in the center, blending into a crown around the outer edges. This flat center spot may be from ¾ to 1 inch (19 to 25 mm) in diameter. The outer edges should be rounded off enough to prevent making a sharp edge mark when a blow is struck with the hammer turned slightly from the proper angle.

In selecting a bumping hammer, it may be difficult to obtain one that fits this description exactly; if so, it is better to accept one that is nearly flat over the entire area, because it is much easier to round off the edges than to flatten the center. The edges may be honed down with a piece of fine, water-resistant sandpaper wrapped around a stick of wood or a steel strap. Start with 220 or 260 grit and finish with 400 grit paper. A mirror finish can be put on the hammer face in this manner with very little effort. The same procedure can be used to maintain the hammer face when it becomes marked by rough use.

The opposite end of the bumping hammer is almost always different from the large head. The combination hammer (Figure 3-2) is the type most widely used, and is as much a metal-finishing hammer as a bumping hammer. However, the hammer having the smaller round head (Figure 3-1) is an essential tool in straightening panels if its use is properly understood.

The small head is usually not used with the dolly block. It should have a much higher crown than the large head. It is used primarily to work out high spots and ridges in low-crowned panels. Light blows with this head, placed uniformly over the surface of a springy ridge, will straighten it easily. If the face of the hammer is properly polished, it is possible to work out many such areas so that they will require very little extra work to metal-finish.

The same blow struck with the large head will not straighten springy areas nearly so well, because the large head spreads its force over too large an area. Instead of making a very slight bend at the point of contact, the force of the blow is wasted in flexing the surrounding metal. The smaller, higher-crowned head reduces the area of contact enough to do more straightening and less flexing. It is simply a matter of straightening a large area a little at a time.

Much more detail in the use of the bumping hammer will be found in later chapters.

DOLLY BLOCKS

Dolly blocks vary so widely in size and shape that no general description can be applied to all of them. The purpose of all dolly blocks, however, is the same. They are used either as a striking tool or as a back-up tool for the bumping hammer. In both cases, the dolly normally is used on the underside, or inside, of the panel.

Four of the most common types of dolly blocks are shown in Figures 3-3–3-6. Of these, the most frequently

3-3 *(Left)* General-purpose dolly block.

3-4 *(Right)* Low crown general-purpose dolly.

used will be the general-purpose dolly shown in Figure 3-3. This dolly has a variety of curves over its surface, but its primary working face is the broad, smoothly curved upper section. The smaller, rounded lower section has some use as a working face but serves mostly as a hand hold.

The low-crowned, general-purpose dolly shown in Figure 3-4 is similar to the one in Figure 3-3, but its use is more limited. A dolly of this shape is very valuable when repairing low-crowned panels, but the working face will not fit into the shape of higher crowns.

The heel dolly (Figure 3-5) and the toe dolly (Figure 3-6) are both special-purpose tools. Being thinner, both of these may be used in narrow quarters where the larger general-purpose dolly cannot enter. They also provide a smooth, flat surface with sharp, right-angle edges for working flanges and sharp bends. Both of these are convenient tools to have; for various jobs, one will be better suited than the other.

Many other dolly blocks that are not discussed here are available, and many are as well suited to the job of metal-straightening as the ones shown. Preference of a skilled repairman for a particular dolly block is a personal matter. It is much more important that the dolly block be satisfactory to the user than it is for him to use a particular one.

Used as a striking tool, the dolly is essentially a hand-held, handleless hammer. It is good practice to use a dolly in this manner to drive out simple dents. As the metal is brought out, the hammer is then brought into use as needed.

3-5 Heel dolly block.

3-6 Toe dolly block.

Used with the bumping hammer, the dolly is actually much more than just a back-up tool. Its primary purpose is to provide a reaction to the force of a hammer blow. When used properly, the dolly tends to raise the spot of metal that is in contact with its working face. This is true, regardless of whether it is directly under the spot struck by the hammer or a short distance away. These operations are explained in detail in later sections of this chapter.

A very common misunderstanding of the use of a dolly block can be described as the anvil theory. Followers of this theory consider the dolly as a broad, smooth, anvil-like tool to be held on the underside of a buckle so that the metal can be driven down against it. The idea is very similar to the operation of straightening a bent nail by laying it on a flat surface and driving the bend down.

The rather widespread acceptance of the anvil theory accounts for the large number of dolly blocks available that have only one curve to the working face. In the cross direction, the working face will be flat. It is true that some metal-straightening may be done in this manner, but it is not as effective as a properly shaped dolly

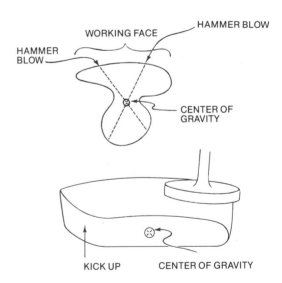

3-7 *(Top)* Balance characteristics of a general-purpose dolly block. A hammer blow on almost any part of the working face will be directed toward the center of gravity.

3-8 *(Bottom)* Balance characteristics of the toe dolly block. A hammer blow on either end will tend to cause the other to kick up, because the center of gravity acts as a pivot.

used correctly. A dolly with the right crown on the working face will result in both faster and better work.

Two factors that must be considered in selecting a dolly block are weight and balance. For normal operation, the weight of the dolly block should be at least three times that of the hammer. This difference in weight is needed because the dolly is at rest when the hammer blow strikes. The weight provides the inertia to resist the force of the hammer blow.

Balance is simply a matter of the distribution of weight. This is illustrated in Figures 3-7 and 3-8. Note that the general-purpose dolly (Figure 3-7) is shaped so that it is in balance regardless of where on the working face a hammer blow is struck. The toe dolly (Figure 3-8) is in balance only when a blow is struck on its center area. A blow on either end will tend to cause it to roll, or kick, so that much of the effect of its weight is lost.

This is not to say that an unbalanced dolly is no good. Such dollies are special-purpose tools to be used where the better-balanced tools cannot enter. In the places where they are needed, they are the best tools available.

SPOONS

The term spoon is applied to so many body tools that it is difficult to define. However, a spoon is usually a bar of steel that has been forged flatter and thinner on one end, sometimes on both ends. It may be bent into a variety of shapes, depending on its intended use. The forged end, or ends, serve as a working face to use against the metal; the rest of the bar serves as a handle.

Spoons serve three basic purposes:

1. To spread the force of a hammer blow over a large area. Such spoons are commonly called dinging or bumping spoons.
2. As a dolly block in areas in which the inner construction limits access to the inner side. These are commonly called body spoons.
3. As a prying or driving tool. Heavy-duty body spoons are usually more satisfactory for this purpose than the lighter dinging spoon.

The use of body spoons has declined as the automobile body has grown more complex in construction and shape. Use of spoons, particularly those classed as body spoons, requires a considerable degree of skill. This has caused many repairmen to rely on filling and panel replacement instead of straightening and metal-finishing panels that would require use of spoons. The acceptance by the industry of methods of working metal from the outside and the almost total use of plastic filler instead of body solder filling has caused many repairmen to adopt the mistaken attitude that spoons are obsolete tools.

The discussion of spoons is limited, because they have become relatively little-used tools. However, it is emphasized that the person who will make the effort to obtain a set of body spoons and learn to use them will be repaid many times in increased skill and productivity.

3-9 Low crown bumping spoon.

His problem may be to find them; he may have to make his own.

The low-crowned bumping spoon in Figure 3-9 is a very valuable tool for smoothing out soft ridges. Its use is shown in Figure 3-36, but it should not be used on sharp ridges of the type shown in Figure 3-37. Ridges such as this should be straightened by other means and the bumping spoon used only in the final smoothing operations.

The primary use of the bumping spoon is on low ridges in fairly stiff combination crown areas. Its purpose is to spread the force of a hammer blow over a larger area than the face of a bumping hammer will cover. It is not particularly well suited to use on nearly flat areas, such as door panels, because it will tend to flex the surrounding metal instead of straightening the ridge. In general, the face of the bumping hammer is a better tool on low crowns than the spoon.

The body spoons shown in Figures 3-11–3-15 are general-purpose tools that deserve more use than they often get. Used properly, they will reduce the number of holes punched for the dent puller screw and often produce a better-quality job with less labor. Although the use of such tools has declined, the reader is urged to investigate and experiment with them as part of his skill development.

Two suggested uses of body spoons are shown in Figure 3-10. The long, thin spoon in A can be used where inner construction prevents the use of a dolly block, as shown here, but it is equally useful as a pry tool. On many jobs the inner construction that makes the long, thin tool necessary also provides a base to rest the tool against for both uses. B shows another spoon of different shape used for the same purpose. Where construction permits, this spoon serves better as a substitute dolly block than the one in A, because its shape provides a better back-up, but there are many uses for both.

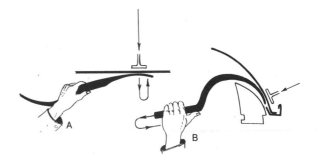

3-10 Balance characteristics of body spoons. A: This spoon has no balance, because the weight does not support the working face. B: This spoon has good balance.

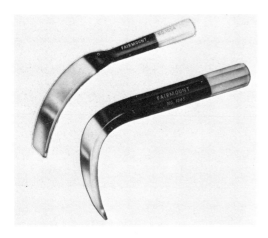

3-11 *(Top)* Pry spoon.

3-12 *(Bottom)* General-purpose body spoon, originally called a turret top spoon.

The spoon in Figure 3-11 is primarily a pry tool, but it can be used as a bumping spoon in reverse crowns.

The spoon in Figure 3-12 is for general-purpose body work. It serves as a pry tool, substitute dolly block, and an offset driving tool (Figure 3-13). It has many uses of this type in various parts of the body and fenders.

The spoons in Figures 3-14 and 3-15 are quite large and heavy. They are excellent tools for both prying and as substitutes for a dolly block in any area where there is room to get them into place behind the inner construction.

The spoon in Figure 3-16 is intended for rough service. It works particularly well as an offset caulking tool.

3-13 *(Top)* General-purpose body spoon. Working face on both ends and an extra length make this spoon particularly useful on door and deck lid panels.

3-14 *(Bottom)* Large offset spoon.

3-15 Rough service spoon.

CAULKING, DRIVING, AND BENDING TOOLS

So many special-purpose tools are used for straightening sheet metal that it would be impossible to list them all. The three tools shown in Figures 3-17–3-19 are typical. Many others are used for the same or similar purposes.

The tool shown in Figure 3-17 is for caulking. It resembles a blunt, wide-bladed chisel, but it is used for reshaping short-radius bends or narrow, flat surfaces. A wide variety of caulking tools is needed to do the various caulking jobs normally found when repairing severely damaged panels. These tools may be of different lengths, and the shape of the working ends may vary from almost sharp to wide and flat.

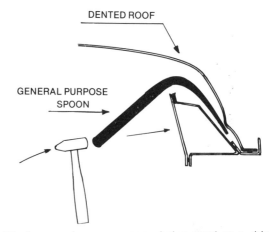

3-16 A general-purpose spoon being used as a driving tool.

The tool shown in Figure 3-18 is a special-purpose caulking tool for straightening flanges. It is particularly suited to straightening the bead section of fenders, but it may be used on any flange that is turned away from the operator's side. In use, one end is hooked into the flange to be straightened, and the other end is held by the operator as he strikes hammer blows on the bar, close to the panel.

3-17 Caulking iron.

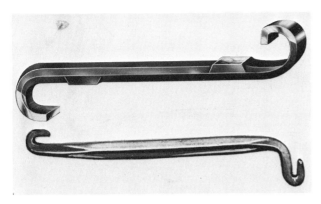

3-18 *(Top)* Special flange straightening and offset caulking tool.

3-19 *(Bottom)* Flange bender, rarely available but easy to make up.

The tool shown in Figure 3-19 is intended for working flanges. This particular tool would not be readily available, but it and the one shown in Figure 3-18 are examples of tools that the repairman can make for personal use, using salvage steel shafts from the scrap pile.

A complete set of pry tools is shown in Figure 3-20. A pry rod in use is shown in Figure 3-21. In this operation, the rod is inserted through an enlarged drain hole, but many panel areas can be reached through open inner construction, particularly the wheelhousing area of quarter panels or doors after disassembling the trim panel. In general, use of pry tools is preferable to the use of the dent puller, described in the following section, on any spot within practical reach and with a suitable fulcrum available to pry against.

SLIDE HAMMERS

Specially equipped slide hammers have several uses in metal work, the most common as a dent puller in panel areas where inner construction blocks access to the under side. These pullers are equipped with a metal screw held firmly in place by a retainer. To use, a hole is

3-21 Use of pry rod through an enlarged drain hole in the lower edge of a quarter panel.

either punched or drilled in the dent, the screw is driven into the hole, and the sliding weight is snapped back against the stop to lift the area. A typical dent puller is shown in Figure 3-22.

It is recommended here that the hole be pierced in the panel with a sharp-pointed scratch awl, instead of drilled. As illustrated in Figure 3-23, the awl makes a depression in the surface, which stiffens the surrounding area. This stiffened area will lift a much larger spot and has less tendency to rise above the correct level (B). A drilled hole does not have anything to stiffen the surrounding metal, so the edge is lifted higher than it should be. The common practice is to grind the paint off of the area after the dent puller has been used. These high edges will be ground off, thinning the metal and enlarging the hole.

Hooks of various types are available or can be made up by the repairman to extend the usefulness of most slide hammers. To use, the screw retainer is removed and the hook threaded to the end of the hammer shaft. One special use is shown with the weld-on pull tabs, shown in Figure 3-24. These tabs are attached to the panel with an electric resistance spot welder and are recommended, instead of the metal screw. The first-time user is cautioned to use care when removing them; they break off easily if twisted as though they were

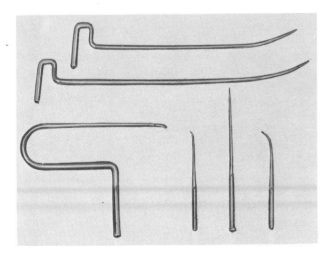

3-20 Set of pry tools.

3-22 Screw-equipped slide hammer, commonly called a dent puller.

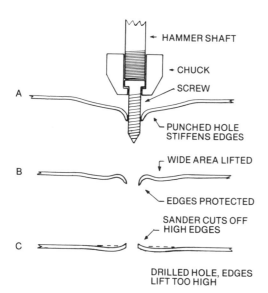

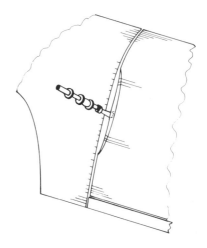

3-25 Slide hammer with wide hook used to straighten forward edge of front door.

3-23 Advantage of piercing instead of drilling holes for dent puller. A, punched hole is stiffened and provides extra screw contact. B, punched hole lifts wide area and edges are protected from sander. C, edges of drilled hole are lifted too high and will be ground off, enlarging hole and thinning metal.

screwed on, but will break a hole in the panel if simply bent back and forth. The procedure for welding these tabs on is explained in more detail in the resistance spot welding section of Chapter 5.

A slide hammer equipped with a wide, relatively thin hook used to straighten the forward edge of a front door is shown in Figure 3-25. These edges can be driven out with a hammer and some type of driving tool by working from the inside, but the repairman cannot see the result. With the slide hammer on the outside, it is easy to align the door edge with the fender.

SPOT WELD CUTTERS

A spot weld cutter kit is shown in Figure 3-26, and Figure 3-27 shows a cutter in use. The various-sized cutters thread onto the end of the mandrel. The sharp-pointed retractable pin extends through the center of

the cutter and acts as a guide. A center-punch mark in the center of the weld should be made to keep the point in place.

In use, the cutter is chucked in an electric drill and pressed against the weld, cutting a circular hole through the upper of the two pieces welded together. The depth of cut can be adjusted by a stop screw in the mandrel, which requires adjustment only when changing from one thickness of metal to another.

The cutter leaves the cut-out piece of the weld still attached to the underpanel. This may be ground off, using a disc sander, or, if the parts are to be rejoined, the slot can be brazed.

WELD-ON PULL TABS

The weld-on pull tabs in Figure 3-24 are a specialty item used only with an electric resistance spot welder and are discussed more in that section of the welding chapter. They are preferable to a metal screw-type panel puller, because it is not necessary to pierce the panel.

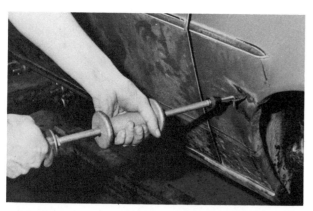

3-24 Slide hammer with hook used with weld-on pull tab.

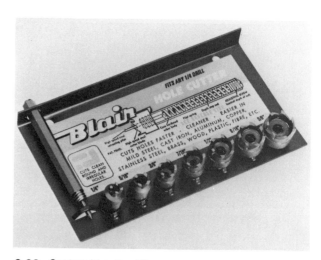

3-26 Spot weld cutter kit.

3-27 Spot weld cutter in use.

They provide a means of straightening many damaged areas enough so that the metal can be finished satisfactorily with plastic filler without removing trim or piercing inner construction to make access to the inner surface.

These tabs can be broken off the surface and re-used, but may require repointing after two or three uses, because the point gets wider with each use. Removal procedure is explained in Chapter 5 on welding.

BASIC STRAIGHTENING OPERATIONS

This section explains and describes the uses of the straightening tools just discussed. The operations are referred to as basic, because they are essentially the same, regardless of the job. For example, the motions of using a hammer and dolly block are very much the same on any panel; the difference in procedure for panels having different damages is in the knowledge and judgment exercised in deciding where and how much to apply the basic operation.

It is suggested that the study of this section extend beyond reading it over once. It is easy for the beginner to fall into the trap of thinking that all he needs to develop manual dexterity is practice. Manual dexterity with his tools is an absolute must, but it is only a part of skill. The other, more critical, part is the knowledge and understanding with which he guides his hands.

Any discussion of the use of the hammer and dolly block should start by pointing out that they should not be abused. The working faces, particularly the hammer, should never strike *anything but sheet metal*. The hammer's working faces should be kept clean and polished with fine sandpaper so that it can be used on a painted surface without leaving marks to mar the reflective surface. Striking a punch or chisel with the hammer will damage it so that it will chop up the paint surface enough to make visual inspection almost impossible. Use another hammer for rough work.

A chopped-up working face on a dolly block may not be quite as bad as the same condition on the hammer, but it is definitely not desirable. Any marks on its surface will be imprinted on the underside of the metal when it is struck a hard on-dolly hammer blow. Many beginning students form a bad habit of tapping their hammer against the dolly block while studying the job. This is an unconscious action, but it should be watched for and avoided because of the damage it can do to both the hammer and the dolly block.

USE OF THE HAMMER AND DOLLY BLOCK

The bumping hammer and dolly block are discussed first, because they are the most important and versatile of the repairman's tools for straightening metal. They are also the easiest to misuse, because the difference between proper and improper use is often very slight. Misuse will cause additional damage. Also, many times it is possible to restore the surface appearance by either picking and filing or building a new surface with filler, even though the proper use of the hammer and dolly would do the same job better in less time. The fact that such work can be done "somehow" often leads the beginner to continue with less than the best methods. It is quite possible for the repairman to have good hammers and dolly blocks in his possession for many years without discovering their full usefulness.

The dolly block is used both with and without the hammer. Alone, it is an excellent tool for striking the inner surface to rough out simple dents or to complete the roughing out of areas being jacked into place. With the hammer, the combination becomes a highly efficient means of smoothing the roughed-out surface.

The dolly, when used with hammer, may be held directly under the spot struck by the hammer face, or it may be held to one side. These procedures are referred to as *hammer-on-dolly* and *hammer-off-dolly*. The dolly position should change as needed between hammer blows.

HAMMER-ON-DOLLY

The first step in learning to use the hammer-on-dolly is to develop the skill necessary to place the dolly under the metal and strike a hammer blow directly on it. This often seems to be an impossible task to the beginner but is actually an easy one to master, if practiced. It is easier for some persons than for others because it is essentially a matter of coordination between the hand and the eye. Even though the hand holding the dolly is out of sight under the panel, the student soon learns to bring any spot on the working face of the dolly into contact with the spot he intends to strike with the hammer. It becomes a reflex action to shift the dolly to the spot on which the eye is focused. Striking the same spot with the hammer should be simple, but the hammer must be held and swung properly.

The proper hammer grip is shown in Figure 3-28. The handle should be held lightly and the grip slackened as the blow descends on the metal. This is easy to do by forming the habit of gripping the handle with only the third and fourth fingers. The thumb aids in starting the blow, and the first two fingers are used to snap the handle back after the blow is finished. The blow starts with a snap action of the wrist rather than a full arm movement. The snap action will be easier if the handle is held at a slight angle to the forearm.

The hammer blow should strike the metal in the center of the broad face, and the contact should be exactly on the spot where the eye was focused in placing the dolly. If the hammer head is allowed to tip in any direction even slightly, the contact will be at the rim of the face rather than the center. Tipping the hammer will cause the blow to miss the intended contact spot by as much as half the width of the hammer face. The result is additional damage, because the edge of the hammer face makes a *chop mark* that must be repaired. An example of both proper and improper hammer-on-dolly

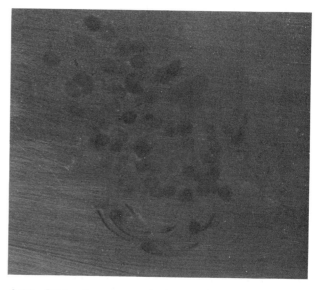

3-29 Proper hammer contact, rounded, smooth spots. Improper, half-moon shaped chop marks at lower edge.

work is shown in Figure 3-29. The surface of the paint was sanded lightly before this work was done so that the hammer contact spots would show clearly. It should be obvious that the round or oblong spots were made by a hammer striking the surface properly and the "half moon" chop marks were made by the edge of the hammer face. The first skill to develop is to place the dolly and aim the hammer so that a smooth contact is made with every blow.

The second skill required is to learn to gauge the force of the hammer blow and the pressure applied to the dolly so that they have the effect needed on that *particular* spot. It may be only a slight smoothing of a small rough spot, using very light hammer blows, or it may be actual stretching and raising, as illustrated in Figure 3-30. Stretching, as the term is used by repairmen, means hitting the dolly hard enough to thin it. Several spots scattered over an area will cause it to rise in a crown because its area has been increased. True stretching would be done by pulling lengthwise, but the effect is similar, so metal is called stretched when it has been crowned by hammering on-dolly.

3-28 Proper grip on hammer and dolly block.

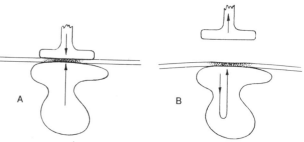

3-30 Action of a hammer-on-dolly blow. A represents the instant of impact. B represents a fraction of a second later when the hammer is moving away and the dolly has rebounded, lifting and stretching the metal.

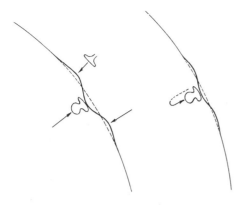

3-31 *(Left)* Using the hammer-off-dolly. The dolly should be held firmly against the low spot before the hammer blow falls.

3-32 *(Right)* The dolly rebounds after the hammer blow, increasing the lifting effect according to the hand pressure applied.

The force of a hammer blow on-dolly can be varied from less than enough to exceed the yield point of the metal to more, sometimes much more, than the yield point. Skill is required to sense just what each blow does to the particular spot struck. For example, a hammer-on-dolly blow on a small rough area, as illustrated in Figure 3-29, should be just short of the yield point if the intention is only to bring the low spot up and the high spot down without stretching. Hammer blows hard enough to cause actual stretching would be used to bring a larger but only slightly low spot up to the level of the adjoining metal. The procedure would be to cover the area with hammer-on-dolly blows in a regular pattern, striking hardest in the deepest area and reducing the force where the low spot blended into the adjoining surface. The harder the blow, the greater the hand pressure that should be applied to the dolly; the extra hand pressure would increase the secondary, lifting effect, as shown in Figure 3-30.

Any repairman skilled in use of the hammer and dolly block will develop the ability to gauge his hammer blows, sometimes without being conscious of it. The beginner who is aware that he should develop the ability and makes the required effort will develop it much more rapidly than if he just waits for it to come. It is partly a matter of feel, transmitted through the hammer handle, and partly sound. If the force does not exceed the yield point of the metal, the hammer blow is deflected almost instantly, with a sharp clear sound. However, any force that exceeds the yield point, causing the metal to stretch, is absorbed in the metal; the deflection of the hammer will be slightly delayed and deadened to some degree. At the same time, the sound will be slightly dulled. These differences would be unnoticeable to an uninformed bystander but very real to the repairman who has trained himself to detect them.

Skill in sensing the effect of the hammer blow and hand pressure on the dolly is important in any straightening operation, but it is critically important in working soft metal, such as aluminum, or mild steel that has been temporarily softened by heating so that it can be shrunk or otherwise worked. This is not as major a problem as it may seem, however, because it is much easier to feel the yield of the softer metal. The thinner but harder steels should present no more problem to the skilled worker than mild steel, because the greater hardness also raises the yield point so they will withstand more abuse.

HAMMER-OFF-DOLLY

Use of a hammer-off-dolly is to lower a high spot and raise a low spot with the force of a single hammer blow. It works because the elasticity of the metal permits an area of metal surrounding a hammer blow to flex inward. The dolly block resists this flexing action if it is in contact with any low spot within the affected area and, when manipulated correctly, returns considerable force to drive the low spot upward. The force returned is provided by reflex muscular action of the hand pressing the dolly against the metal. In effect, the hammer blow triggers a reflex blow by the dolly. These actions are illustrated in Figures 3-31 and 3-32. Note that the hammer is not shown in Figure 3-32 because it would have bounced away by the time the dolly could rebound.

Beginners often think learning to use the hammer-off-dolly is a difficult task because of the need to find and focus attention on two separate spots at one time, but it is really a rather simple problem that can be solved by practice. A person learning to drive an automobile often has a similar problem. At first there is doubt about how far to turn the steering wheel, but the problem disappears with practice.

It is important for the beginner to learn to sense the movement of the metal caused by the force of the hammer blow and rebound of the dolly. The metal moves more freely than when working on-dolly, because it does not have solid support, and the sound is duller. The movement is easier to feel through the hammer because of the greater travel.

The pressure exerted on the dolly is more important than it is when working on-dolly. Not being directly under the hammer, the dolly receives less impulse from the hammer blow. The beginner should learn to relax his hand pressure slightly at the instant of hammer contact, to permit slight travel of the dolly, then snap it back with added force. In this way the hammer will trigger a much stronger reflex action than it would otherwise.

The distance between the spots worked by the hammer and dolly affects the result. If the dolly is too far from the hammer, it does not receive enough impulse to trigger the reflex action needed to make it effective. No positive rule can be given on the maximum effective distance, because it will vary with different metals or even the same metal in different shapes. However, the most effective work will be done when the hammer and dolly are not more than 1 inch (25.4 mm) apart, and better results will be obtained when they are closer. When using a wide-faced hammer, this would bring the dolly

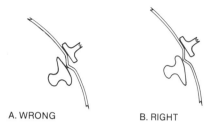

A. WRONG   B. RIGHT

3-33 Wrong and right dolly placement for close-in hammer-off-dolly blow. A is wrong, because dolly will interfere with hammer. B is right, because metal can flex around high crown of dolly.

contact under the outer rim of the hammer face. Whether or not they actually meet in on-dolly contact depends on the force of the hammer blow and the crown of the dolly in contact with the metal. The hammer blow can be gauged so that either it does not have enough force to make actual contact with the dolly, or if it does, it does not strike hard enough to exceed the yield point.

The two illustrations in Figure 3-33 show the incorrect and correct placement of the dolly crown for a close-in hammer-on-dolly blow. The position at A is definitely wrong because the dolly contact is shown in the center area of the working face. The crown is low at this point, and the lip of the dolly is in position to interfere with the hammer. B is correct. The crown of most general-purpose dollies is higher at this point—or at least it should be—and the dolly has been reversed so that there will be minimum interference with the hammer travel. These figures do not show the cross crown of the working face, but any good general-purpose dolly should have enough cross crown to limit the contact to a very small area. It was pointed out in the section on dolly blocks earlier in this chapter that a dolly having only one curve on the working face has limited use; it would be useless here.

A small dent in a combination high and low crown area is shown in Figure 3-34 and, after straightening by the hammer-off-dolly, in Figure 3-35. The only force

applied to the underside of this dent to raise it back to the proper level was a firm hand pressure on the dolly and the rebound action that resulted.

The procedure for straightening this dent is explained in detail, because it is the key to understanding the proper use of the hammer-off-dolly. It is particularly important to note that no hammer blows were struck on the right or left of the dent; all of the hammer work was done above and below it. As it was a combination high and low crown, metal was raised above and below the dent, but the sides were drawn down. Hammer blows would only drive it down further. Instead of accomplishing a repair, hammer blows on either side would tend to add damage to that already existing. A fraction of a second after the hammer blow, reflex action caused the dolly to rebound and strike the underside with considerable force, lifting it toward the proper level.

When this hammer-off-dolly procedure is understood properly, there should be no misunderstanding of the following rule: When using a hammer-off-dolly, a *hammer blow should never be struck except on metal that has been raised above the proper level.* This rule applies in every case. It is even more important to remember in straightening a severe rolled buckle than on this simple dent.

Following this same reasoning, the importance of this second rule should be understood: *The first hammer blows should fall on the high metal farthest from the dent,* and *following blows should work inward progressively.* On the minor dent shown in Figure 3-34, this is simply a matter of closing in from the raised crown areas above and below. When this procedure is used on a long rolled buckle, there will usually be some high metal to be worked in the low crown section, because the overall distortion is much greater.

BUMPING SPOONS

The skill required to use a bumping spoon with a hammer is relatively easy to acquire, compared to that

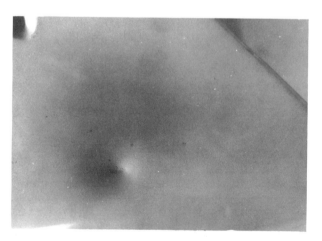

3-34 A small dent in a combination high and low crown section of a fender.

3-35 The dent in Fig. 3-33 after straightening by hammer-off-dolly blows.

needed to use the hammer and dolly block. The primary difference is that the spoon works as a part of the hammer blow instead of providing a secondary reaction to it, as the dolly block does.

The purpose of the bumping spoon is to spread the force of the hammer blow over a much larger area than the bumping hammer face can cover. It is best suited to straightening long, relatively smooth buckles, in which the distortion is comparatively light but is spread over a large area. Straightening could be done by using the hammer alone, but many light blows would have to be spread over the area, and it would be difficult to avoid making damaging hammer marks. The larger contact area of the working face of the spoon is much easier to control, so that such damage is kept to the minimum or avoided entirely. Also, this method is faster on jobs to which it is suited.

The shape, or crown, of the working face of the bumping spoon determines the exact use to which it is best adapted. A flat or nearly flat face is best for high-crowned or combination high- and low-crowned areas. Such areas are quite stiff and require considerable force to relieve the distortion that causes the buckle.

A spoon with a higher-crowned working face is best suited to buckles in low-crowned panels. The metal on each side of such a buckle will be springy instead of stiff, as on the high-crowned panel. The springiness reduces the support that the area provides for the buckle. The high-crowned spoon contacts only a small area, concentrating the force of the hammer blow on it; thus, it actually will straighten such an area better than a flat-faced spoon. The larger contact area of the flat spoon will tend only to spring the entire buckle.

The procedure for using either spoon is essentially the same. Figure 3-36 shows a bumping spoon in position. Note that the center area of the working face is in contact with the metal surface and that the hammer is directly over this spot. Note also that a ball-peen hammer is used instead of the bumping hammer; a good

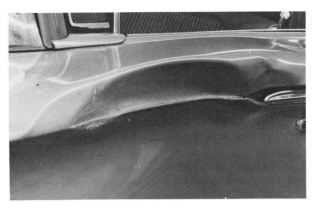

3-37 Ridge which is too sharp for use of the bumping spoon.

bumping hammer never should be used for such a purpose.

The handle of the spoon should be gripped lightly so that the hand does not tend to resist movement. Even though the spoon is being used on metal that is quite stiff, there will be some tendency for the entire area to flex with the hammer blow. The spoon must be free for this movement. If the hand resists downward movement of the handle (Figure 3-36), there will be a tendency to drive the opposite end of the working face down too far. This may cause damaging marks, particularly when using a spoon that has a flat working face.

Most of the damaged areas where a bumping spoon is the proper tool to use are too wide to be corrected with a single hammer blow. It will be necessary to strike a series of hammer blows as the spoon is moved back and forth across the buckle. On long buckles, work progressively down the length in a somewhat zigzag pattern.

In using a spoon on any buckle, start at the point of least distortion. On most buckles that remain after a rolled buckle has been worked out, this point would be as far from the break-over path as distortion could be detected.

The bumping spoon is most effective when used on a buckle under a strain that tends to straighten it. Such conditions will be found occasionally in minor damage on relatively flat panels. The experienced repairman learns to recognize the damaged panel that will snap back to shape after a buckle has been spooned down, leaving only minor damage actually to work out. However, such conditions are the exception rather than the rule. In most cases, the spoon should not be used until most of the unfolding has been completed by other means. Spooning out remaining buckles is very often the final straightening operation.

A very common mistake of the beginner is to use a bumping spoon on a buckle that is too sharp. Metal that has been folded over so that the buckle forms a sharp ridge, as in Figure 3-37, should not be spooned down, because it is too rigid. Striking the top of such a ridge may cause upsetting. After such a ridge has been partly straightened by the proper methods, described in later sections, the spoon would be a very logical means of finishing the straightening operation.

3-36 Bumping spoon in position for the hammer blow.

BODY SPOONS

Skill in the use of body spoons is entirely different from the skill required to use a bumping spoon and in most cases is more complicated. This is because the body spoon is used on the underside of the panel as either a substitute for the dolly block or as a pry tool.

The body spoon is never used for repairing any panel in which a dolly block has free access to the inner surface. Such a panel can be straightened better and faster with the dolly block. The use of the body spoon is made necessary by the inner construction found on many panels, which limits access so that only a relatively long, thin tool may be used. Without such a tool, the repairman would be forced either to cut out the inner construction or to depend entirely on filling to repair damage on such panels. With a good set of body spoons, he can repair many panels faster and with a minimum amount of filling or mutilation caused by cutting out and welding back inner construction.

Exact instructions for the use of the body spoons cannot be given, because the spoons are available in many shapes for use in many different areas and damage conditions. The discussion of procedure must be limited to general suggestions. This is less a handicap than it may seem, however, for the suggestions offered are simply variations of the basic procedure for using the dolly block. It is recommended that the beginner delay his practice with body spoons until he has had enough practice with the dolly block to develop some degree of skill. This should include some actual repair work on simple damage. At that time, the beginner's use of the body spoon will present far fewer problems than if he tries to use it before he develops the basic skill.

The body spoon may be used alone to pry out low metal or with the hammer. Used alone, it serves exactly the same purpose as the dolly block when the latter is used as a striking tool. Usually the main problems are to find a suitable fulcrum to pry against and to avoid making pry marks in the surface.

Used with the bumping hammer, the body spoon serves the same purpose as the dolly block. The difference is that the body spoon is more difficult to use and is less effective. This is because the working face of the spoon extends several inches from the hand; the sense of feel, which helps in locating the dolly block, is almost totally absent. The result is a tendency of the body spoon to wander after each hammer blow against it. This effect is greater from a hard hammer blow than from a light one. Thus an effective limit is placed on the force of the hammer blow, which in turn places a similar limit on the force of the rebound action of the spoon.

A second factor affecting the effectiveness of the spoon as a substitute for a dolly block is balance. This varies with the shape of the spoon, as was shown in Figure 3-10. A spoon having the working face at or close to a right angle to the handle may be in almost perfect balance, so that the only problem is the sense of feel. But a spoon having the working face parallel with the handle will have practically no balance at all. The rebound action obtainable with such a spoon is limited for two reasons: (1), the operator's grip is at a mechanical disadvantage; and (2), very little of the weight of the spoon is under the working face to provide resistance to the hammer blow.

As with the dolly block, the choice of a body spoon is governed by the conditions of the panel to be repaired. Only to a limited extent can it be determined by personal preference. In many areas of the body, a well-balanced spoon would be useless, because its shape would prevent it from fitting into place. If work is to be done in such places, tools to do the job are needed. If it happens that a well-balanced tool can be used, fine; if it happens that an unbalanced spoon is all that can be used, it will be the best tool for the job.

BASIC REPAIR METHODS

It was pointed out previously that the repairman must examine the job to determine his procedure. In Chapters 7 and 8, which deal with much greater damage, this examination had been done by separate discussions on the inspection of the damage and planning the repair procedure. Coverage of this damage is not carried to that length, because it was selected to fit a predetermined procedure.

Careful attention should be given to the details of this damage, as it is essential for the student to learn to examine every one closely. Slight variations from one damage to another may make considerable differences in the procedure to be followed. The ability to recognize such differences and to know how they govern repair procedure may be regarded as an inspection and analysis that enable the repairman to read procedure for doing the job. The beginner may require considerable study to recognize simple features about a job that later will be recognized at a glance.

Whether the inspection of the job is done by a beginner or an experienced worker, it is a matter of looking for the fold lines, displaced sections, and distortions caused by the impact and determining the order in which they occurred. From this information and the knowledge of what may be accomplished with the basic

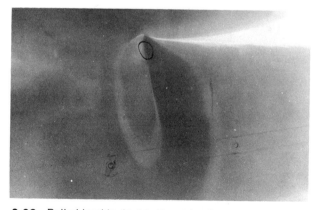

3-38 Rolled buckle dent in the side of a fender.

repair operations, it is a simple procedure to apply force to the damage so that these conditions are relieved.

A quick examination of the dent in Figure 3-38 reveals the following conditions:

1. It has been caused by a relatively light force.
2. It probably has been caused by a direct impact, but it could have been the result of force traveling through the length of the panel from a direct impact on the one end.
3. It is a minor but true example of a rolled buckle. A sharp ridge has formed, pushing a high spot into the high crown of it, but it has not rolled far enough to cause a break-over path of severely upset metal.
4. There has been little or no tension lengthwise of the panel.

This straightening operation is fairly simple—but it falls into two basic steps (called *phases* here and in the text following), just as all other straightening operations do. They are: (1) roughing out, or roughing, and (2) bumping.

The *roughing phase*, in this case accomplished by a few blows of the dolly block, takes very little time, but it is the most critical of the entire operation. When it is done properly, it will be a simple matter to get the high spot at the break-over point down to level. When done improperly, this high spot can be very difficult to remove, even though considerable extra effort is made in the bumping and metal-finishing operations, and it is quite probable that a high spot will show in the finished job.

The starting point of the roughing operation is marked by the black circle just below the break-over point (Figure 3-38). The first blow will be struck on the underside of the circled area; the following blows will be progressively lower.

This procedure is shown in much greater detail in Figure 3-39 in successive stages: (A) before starting, (B) after the first operation with the dolly, (C) almost roughed out, and (D) the completed job. The dotted line represents the original, and the solid line represents the damaged contour.

In A the dolly block, labeled 1, is shown in position to strike the first rough-out blow. Note that it is turned so

that the highest-crowned area of the working face will come into contact with the metal. This is necessary at this point because the blow will strike on the inside of the high-crowned surface. Three or four light blows were struck with the dolly before the action shown in B was started.

B shows the hammer, labeled 2, being used on the high break-over point. Use of the hammer is a follow-up operation. Driving the low metal out with the dolly block has pulled some of the high metal down. It also has left the area under a state of tension. The high spot will drop under the hammer blows until the tension is relieved. It is then time to drive out the surface more, as indicated by the dolly block, labeled 3, in B.

This action should be repeated several times to bring it to the condition shown in C. Each time the dolly is used on the underside, it tends to pull the high spot down. The hammer being used on the outside works with this tendency by driving the high spot down farther and preventing too much tension from building up in the area. If too much tension is built up, it will stretch the metal between the high point and the spot where the dolly block strikes. If this occurs, it will be very difficult to drive the high spot down to the contour shown in D.

Note that in both Figure 3-38 and A in Figure 3-39, the metal in the bottom of the deepest part of the dent is serving as a very rigid brace, or prop, under the highest point. This bracing effect always will be found in any rolled buckle. Instead of unrolling the buckle, hammer blows on the high spot would have caused severe upsetting similar to exaggerated example shown in Figure 2-7. The result would have been a surface very difficult to reshape properly.

It should be recognized that this work was started close to the farthest point that the rolled buckle reached in the high crown and moved progressively into the lower crown area. The result of this first series of steps is shown in Figure 3-40, a close-up view of the area circled in Figure 3-38 and a portion of the sharply buckled area below it; a crayon line has been drawn around the

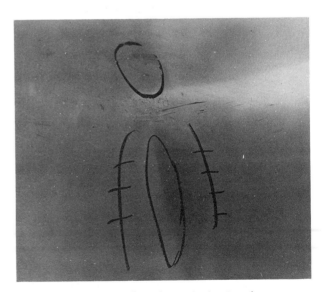

3-40 Close-up view of partly roughed-out surface.

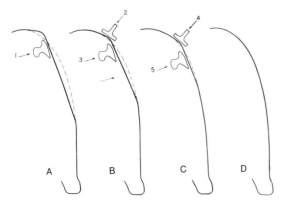

3-39 Four cross-sectional illustrations show the progressive steps in roughing out a simple dent.

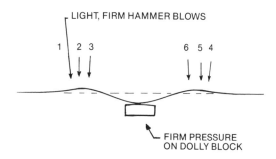

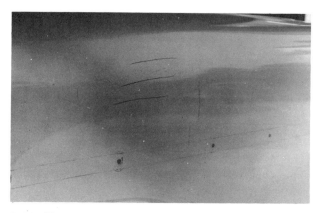

3-41 Cross section showing the pattern of off-dolly hammer blows used to straighten the remaining buckle in Fig. 3-40.

3-42 The straightened buckle, ready for metal finishing.

remaining sharp buckle in the center and two lines with cross marks drawn on the high ridge on each side. Note that the area within the original circle is quite smooth and unmarred, and the crayon line is still clear. This is the result of spending a few seconds polishing the bumping hammer with fine sandpaper.

It should be noted that the lower part of the valley tapers off into a displaced section. If a buckle had formed there, it would have been dealt with in the same manner before proceeding farther. The dashed line indicating original contour is shown higher on B than on A because the few dolly blows have relieved some of the displacement.

The continued action is shown in C. At this point the metal surface is in the condition shown in Figure 3-41. As much as possible of the displaced metal has been released; the remaining area must be worked out with the hammer and dolly block.

The marks on the panel in Figure 3-40, indicating areas of opposed strains, were put on before the photograph was taken. The long curved lines on each side are on surfaces that would spring back down if they were free. The sides of the surface within the long loop would close up and become slightly deeper if it was free for movement. These strains should be relieved by hammer-off-dolly work before driving the valley up farther.

The hammer-off-dolly operation is illustrated in Figure 3-41. Starting at the upper end, the dolly was held firmly against the valley while the hammer was used on each side, as indicated by the arrows. Note that the arrows are at slightly different angles so that the hammer face can follow the slight curvature of the surface. The hammer blows should be light but firm, meaning that the grip on the handle should not be released until the hammer contacts the surface.

The marked area was worked progressively from the upper to the lower end, keeping the hammer and dolly in the same relative positions. The valley was then driven up again, using the dolly as shown in Figure 3-39, and the off-dolly operation repeated.

These operations left the surface reasonable smooth, but some traces of the original ridge remained with low metal immediately below. The hammer and dolly were used spearately to drive the low surface up and the high surface down to restore the final overall contour. Some of the buckled area was worked with on-dolly hammer

blows, using the flattest part of the working face of the dolly. The straightened surface, ready for metal finishing, is shown in Figure 3-42. The crayon marks were made before the photograph was taken to indicate the smoothness of the area. Similar marks on a rough area would appear wavy in a photograph.

METAL-FINISHING

Metal-finishing, as the term is used in automobile sheet metal repair, should not be confused with painting. Instead, it is the work of restoring final surface smoothness to damaged panels after straightening has been carried as far as practical. The primary need for metal-finishing is based on the fact that perfect straightening would require more time and a higher degree of skill than the value of most panels would justify.

The widespread use of plastic filler has led many persons in the body repair field to question the need for a beginner to learn metal-finishing. It is true that there are many workers in the field who have never tried to learn, but that does not prove them to be better mechanics for the lack; it does prove, however, that they are unable to complete even the most simple job without filler.

It is recommended that any beginner learn to finish metal, even though he may not use the skill extensively. Without it, he is starting his trade with a handicap.

Subjects discussed in the rest of this section are body files and their use, the disc sander, sanding discs, feeling for rough or low spots with the hand, and the beginner's problems in metal-finishing.

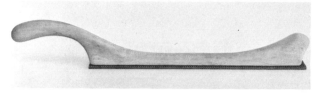

3-43 A 14-inch (approx. 35 cm) body file mounted on a wooden holder.

THE BODY FILE

A typical body file mounted on a wooden holder is shown in Figure 3-43. Practically all files of this type are 14 inches (35 cm) long, have teeth on both sides, and have holes in each end so that they may be bolted to some kind of holder. Both wood and steel holders may be used; it is a matter of which the user prefers. Wood has the advantage of causing less dulling of the teeth on the unused side, which is held in contact with the holder. Some kind of padding material to serve the same purpose is desirable with a steel holder.

Body files, for use on soft metals only, were intended originally for use on mily body sheet metal, aluminum, and body solder when it was in prevalent use. They can be used on most body fillers, but they dull rapidly when so used, because of the abrasive nature of the material.

Special-purpose body files are used, also. The most common of these is the half round (frequently called a shell file), which is used in reverse crowns. Specially bent files and shorter ones have been available, but are rarely seen since the use of body fillers has become widespread. None of the special files present any special problems in learning to use them.

Using the Body File

The beginner is cautioned that his body file should be used for *proof filing* as much as or more than for actual metal removal. An example of proof filing is shown in Figure 3-44, in which all of the lighter areas crisscrossed by file marks are at the proper level. The dark areas between the two large light areas are below proper level so that the file teeth bridged across them. Very slight raising of the low spots and refiling should restore the surface; proof filing has made a very accurate layout of the further straightening to be done.

The key in proper proof filing is in learning to stroke the file properly. If the file had been passed across the surface wood plane fashion, each stroke would have cut a single narrow line. As it is here, every low spot has been outlined clearly with a few file strokes, and very little metal has been cut away.

The technique in proper proof filing is easy to learn, and the beginner should not be permitted, or permit himself, to file in any other manner. The proper file stroke is determined partly by direction on the panel and partly by the shifts made during the stroke.

The direction of the stroke is important because of the differences in lengthwise and crosswise crowns found in almost all panels. The file should lie on the panel so that it has the maximum bridging effect over low spots. If there is any difference in crown, it is obvious that the one nearest to flat will hold the teeth out of the low spots better than the higher one will. This is the reason for the following rule: *The file should be stroked in the general direction of the flattest crown of the panel.*

Cutting a wide area with a single stroke requires two simultaneous shifts of the file. As it moves forward, it should shift either right or left to widen the cut. At the same time, the cutting action should shift from the front end of the file to the rear. These two shifts are illustrated in Figure 3-45, A showing a shift to the left, and B showing a shift to the right to obtain a criss-cross effect. It is not necesary to criss-cross each stroke. In general, an area should be filed one way and then a few strokes made to check surface level.

Note that in both sets the cutting area is outlined at the front of the file at the start of the stroke, and an arrow within the outline points toward the rear. This outline is shown as having moved to the rear at the end of the stroke. Making this shift requires a slight crown in the panel or in the file. Filing in one direction, a combination crown that is dead flat requires a slightly crowned file if the work is to progress rapidly; the crown will permit the blade to rock slightly during the stroke to make the shift.

The beginner may find making the two shifts difficult at the beginning, but it becomes easy with practice. Once the skill is acquired, he will find it *easier* to metal-finish many small jobs than to take time to fill and finish them with plastic.

Any discussion of metal-finishing should include the

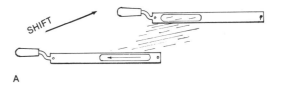

A

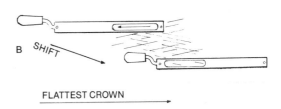

B

FLATTEST CROWN

3-45 Left shift of body file at A and right shift at B. Cutting area, outlined on file, should shift from front to rear on each stroke.

3-44 An example of proof filing to show up low spots.

problems with aluminum and thinner, but harder steels. Both present problems different from those of mild steel, which has always been the standard material of automobile bodies. Aluminum can be metal-finished with no difficulty other than extra care because of its softness. It is not practical to attempt to finish steel that is above a certain hardness, because the file and disc sander will not bite into it enough to make the effort worthwhile. Although metal that hard is not in use on any current body panels, it is reasonable to assume that it will come into use as the pressure for more fuel-efficient automobiles increases. Metal-finishing on such panels will, by necessity, be limited to covering the rough areas with filler.

Picking

Lifting the low spots shown up by filing is commonly called *picking*. It can be done with any blunt-ended tool, such as a pick hammer, the end of the body file, or any type of pry tool in areas where the underside of the panel cannot be reached otherwise. The effect of picking is shown in exaggerated detail in Figure 3-46. A shows a wavy surface before filing. B shows the effect of passing a file across the surface, just cutting the tops of the high spots. In C, the point of a pick hammer is in position to drive the low spots up to proper level to be filed off. Note that these spots are shown slightly above the level of the adjoining filed surfaces; otherwise, the file could not cut them. D shows the surface after the filing has been completed.

Picking, whether done with a pick hammer, pry rod, or other tool, is a precision straightening operation of spots that have been located accurately by filing. The beginner must develop the skill necessary to find the underside of the spot he is looking at and pick it just enough that it will be smooth when filed off. Obviously, picking too much or too hard will cause serious damage when the surface is filed or cut with the disc sander.

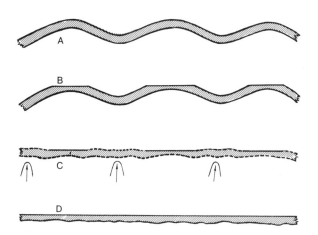

3-46 Cross section showing in exaggerated detail how filing and picking may be combined to produce a finished surface.

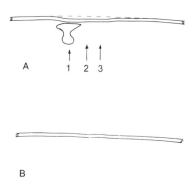

3-47 Dolly block used to raise large low areas instead of pick hammer.

These skills should be practiced on scrap panels before actual repairs are attempted.

The beginner has two problems in locating the underside of a low spot with the pick hammer, or other tool. One is that he is working "blind"; the other is that most people find it awkward to strike a hammer blow toward one's self. Neither problem is serious, but practice is required.

The first step is to position the eye so that light is reflected off the area to be picked; if necessary, rearrange the light. Next, bring the point of the tool (pick hammer or other) out into view and follow it with the eye as it is moved into position under the panel. When the desired spot is reached, or thought to be reached, touch the tool to the underside and hold the position momentarily before striking a light upward blow, and *hold the position*. If the light and eye position is right, the eye should catch the slight upward rise in the surface. The beginner may have to repeat this a few times to find where he *has hit*, but when he finds it, it is simple to move from there to the place he wants to hit. He must hold the position every time he hits, however; if the tool wanders away, it will be necessary to repeat the entire operation. It soon becomes as easy to hit the underside of a spot as it is to hit the side in plain view. The awkwardness of hitting toward one's self is soon forgotten.

The beginner should never work with a sharp-pointed pick hammer; the intention is to raise an area, but not to pierce the surface.

Lifting With the Dolly

A fairly large low area can be lifted with the dolly better than with the pick hammer, as shown in Figure 3-47. This is not practical on small low spots, but larger ones that can be reached with the dolly can be lifted faster and more smoothly than with the pick hammer or any other tool having a smaller contact surface.

The larger surface of the dolly crown raises a much larger area of metal without making a sharp pick mark. The surface can be filed more easily and faster with less mutilation. Note that Figure 3-47 shows the first blow being struck on the deepest point. The following blows should be placed over the area as needed.

THE BEGINNER'S PROBLEMS IN METAL-FINISHING

Almost all beginners at metal-finishing have the same problems, which must be solved before they can expect to make worthwhile progress. In every case the problems are caused by errors in procedure that are to be expected because of the lack of experience. To develop skill, the individual must be aware of the nature of these problems and be willing to be self-critical of his procedure to recognize and correct most of his errors; he cannot expect to correct them all, but he must correct the most glaring ones. Even the most skilled people are not error free. The most common errors made by the beginner metal-finisher are discussed separately in the following paragraphs.

Cutting too soon

The cutting operations, disc sanding and filing, must not be started until the surface has been made smooth enough that it will not be damaged. Either tool will remove very little metal when used on a relatively smooth surface, but will bite deeply into sharp ridges or high points that extend to any height above the surrounding surface. The sander is particularly bad in this respect, because of the speed of cutting. There is no way to set an exact standard of surface smoothness required before the cutting operations are started other than to advise the use of *common sense*. An uninformed casual observer should recognize when a panel surface is too rough to be ground or filed, and it is not unreasonable to expect the beginner to do as well.

Although an exact rule is not possible, a good practical rule is that the first cutting operation should contact at least one half of the total surface area being worked. But, this is a result; the surface must be judged before this operation is performed and the result anticipated before starting.

Picking too hard

After the low spots have been located, it is necessary to pick to raise them. They should be raised just enough to be smoothed off with the minimum cutting with either file or the sander. If the spot is larger than can be lifted with one pick mark, it should be picked several times over the area rather than given one or two harder pick blows. Cutting off excessively high pick marks will cause serious damage; the beginner often makes a good start and then ruins his surface by picking too hard.

Picking too much

Picking too much is, in most instances, the result of not having developed enough accuracy in picking to hit the intended spot quickly. It is important to do the least possible amount of fumbling around in finding the target area or spot. The first pick marks, made to find the target, should be very light so that they will not cause damage if they are off target. Furthermore, each pick mark stretches the surface slightly. Too many pick marks will cause a bulge above the proper surface level.

Filing too much

Each file stroke should increase the finished surface area slightly. When further file strokes do not reduce the unfinished area, it is time to stop filing and raise low spots.

Not following a pattern

When the area to be filed is larger than can be covered with normal file strokes, it is usually better first to proof file the entire area lightly, to detect major low areas, then concentrate the finishing effort on an area that can be covered with one file stroke. In general, this area should be on the highest crown, and the work should move progressively from high to low crown as the individual areas are completed. When working a large area of uniform low-crowned surface, it is desirable to work progressively around the edges so that the final finishing is done in the center area.

Not filing enough

When a low spot has been picked, all of the pick marks should be removed by filing before further picking is done. The beginner who finds the surface growing rougher rather than smoother can be sure that he is either not filing enough or picking too much, or both.

Not correcting bad picking

Any pick mark in an already finished area should be straightened, or put back down, before any filing or disc sanding is done. In high crown areas this can often be done with the small end of a combination hammer; in low crown areas it sometimes helps to make a *very light* on-dolly hammer blow against a flat dolly block surface. Simply cutting the high spot down causes unnecessary and often serious mutilation of the metal.

Locating High and Low Spots

The experienced repairman constantly checks the surface he is working on for high and low spots. The beginner who wants to become experienced should make every effort to develop this ability as quickly as possible. High skill is not involved; it is necessary only to learn two tricks: one is to know how to look at the reflections off of the panel surface, and the other is to learn how to feel high and low spots.

Reflections

Judging the surface by reflection works best when the paint is glossy, but the paint can be quite badly scratched or marred before it becomes unusable. The trick is to position the eye so that light from a spot source—window, ceiling light, or a portable lamp—is reflected from the area in question. By moving the eye back and forth, the spot of reflected light will move along the surface. If the surface is smooth, the movement of the reflection will be equally smooth; if the surface is rough, the reflection will dance around or break up. Even the slightest imperfection can be seen easily by anyone in this manner.

The surface condition can be judged by reflection in the metal-finishing operation even though the paint has been entirely removed. This is discussed in more detail in the section on metal-finishing.

Feel

Fine surface irregularities cannot be determined as accurately by feel as they can be reflection, but such determination is an important skill that the beginner should develop. The hand should be laid flat on the panel so that it contacts the surface lightly from the heel of the palm to the fingertips, and the fingers should be spread slightly. Feeling is done by drawing the hand backwards so that the fingertips trail. The trailing fingertips will feel the rise and fall as they pass over the various high and low spots. The same irregularities can be felt on the forward stroke, but most persons find the sensation is sharper on the back stroke.

There should be little difference in the ability to feel with either hand, but most right-handed persons sue their left hand more than their right for this purpose. It is a matter of personal preference.

Straightedge

The beginner is advised to use a straightedge at the start, but should not become dependent on it. As he learns to look at and feel the surface, he will find that its use will be a waste of time.

METAL-FINISHING ALUMINUM

Aluminum can be metal-finished in the same manner as steel, but much more care is required. As aluminum is softer, small high spots will be cut off by either the file or disc sander. Obviously, the surface must be made quite smooth before any cutting operation is started. A coarse-grit sanding disc used over a rough area to remove paint, as it would be on steel, could leave a similar area of aluminum with multiple perforations. If used at all, the grit should not be allowed to penetrate to the metal. On lacquer-painted panels, lacquer-removing solvent is much safer than sanding, but is hardly practical when large areas of paint must be removed.

Discs coarser then 80 grit should not be used on aluminum. Heavy-duty sanders, if used, must be operated very carefully to avoid grinding through or overheating. A high-speed polisher is preferable to a light-duty sander, because it runs at lower speed. With any sander or polisher, the surface should be watched care-

fully and quenched at the first sign of overheating; on flat surfaces it may be necessary to quench between passes.

The body file will load up quickly with aluminum, making it necessary to clean the teeth every few strokes. Filing should be done in exactly the same manner as on steel, but less pressure can be applied, because the surface will flex under the file more than will steel. Fortunately, a file too dull to cut steel easily will work well on aluminum.

The finished surface can be hand sanded or buffed; a rotary type, air-powered sander should be used, with reduced pressure to slow it down.

Plastic body filler can be used on aluminum in the same manner that it is used on steel, but more care is required in cleaning the paint off rough surfaces, and "cheese grater" planes should not be allowed to contact the metal surface. These planes will not scratch steel, but they will gouge aluminum. Other than these precautions, the procedure for finishing plastic filler on aluminum is exactly the same as on steel.

Obviously, the beginner should develop some skill on steel before attempting to finish an aluminum panel.

THE DISC SANDER

The portable disc sander commonly used in sheet metal repair is shown in Figure 3-48. It operates on the 110-volt, 30-ampere power used for lighting and other power tools. Sanders are available that operate on the higher-voltage power lines, but their use is restricted mostly to industrial operations larger than the average body shop. Air-powered sanders are used by some shops, particularly large ones. They are powerful and lighter in weight for the same capacity, as compared to the electric machine.

Care of the Disc Sander

Proper care is an important factor in the life of any disc sander. Rough handling must be avoided; do not drop the machine or pick an electric one up by the cord. When not in use, the machine should be laid down or hung up so that it does not rest on the edge of the pad, causing it to warp and vibrate in operation.

Overheating is probably the most common cause of

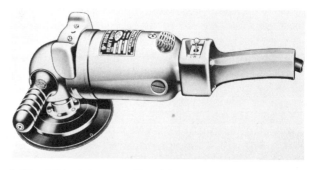

3-48 A 9-inch (approx. 23 cm) heavy-duty disc sander.

serious damage to an electric sander. Although it may be the result of too heavy use of a light-duty machine, it is most commonly the result of clogging the motor ventilating system. All portable electric power tools circulate air through the motor by means of a fan. The air passages in a sander tend to clog more than most electric tools because disc sanding is a dusty operation. Any electric sander should be cleaned periodically.

A sander should never be laid down while the pad is still turning. Serious injury can be caused if any part of the body comes into contact with the still turning pad. Furthermore, an electric sander will pick much more dust from the floor than it does in the operator's hands, because the air vents are close to the layer of grit and dust that the operation has just deposited there. This dust contains bits of metal and sanding grit, both electrical conductors that, if allowed to accumulate in the motor, will cause short-circuiting.

Sanding Discs

Sanding discs used in sheet metal repair work consist of a stiff fiber disc coated on one side with abrasive grit. The grit used almost universally is aluminum oxide.

Several manufacturers of abrasive discs offer their products to the automobile repair trade. These products vary somewhat in special features, but all manufacturers have standardized disc sizes and the method of identifying grit size by number.

Disc size refers to the diameter of the fiber disc. Two sizes are in common use: 7 inch, and 9⅛ inch. Discs of smaller diameter also are used for special purposes, but they usually are obtained by cutting a larger disc down to the size needed. This is much more practical than purchasing smaller sizes, because they can be cut from the unworn center area of the larger size. Smaller diameter discs are available, however, when they are needed in sufficiently large quantities to justify their purchase.

The sanding disc is held in place by means of a special, wide-flanged nut that passes through the center hole and threads either to the hub of the pad or the spindle. Most disc sanders require a ⅞-inch center hole, although some have been made which require a ½-inch hole. Discs are available having either size of center hole, or a special nut can be obtained that will center the larger-size center hole on the smaller spindle.

Grit size of the abrasive material used to coat sanding discs, and many other coated abrasives, is specified by number, such as 16, 24, 36, 50, and so on. This number refers to the size of screen this grit will pass through. Screen size is determined by the number of mesh per linear inch. Thus, a 16-grit would pass through a screen having 16 mesh per linear inch but not through the next smaller size, 24.

The coarsest grit, 16, is intended primarily for paint removal and coarse cutting. It is not recommended for metal-finishing panels because of the extremely coarse swirl marks left by the large grit. However, most paint can be removed by a 24-grit disc, and whenever possible it should be used. The 24 grit also can be used for

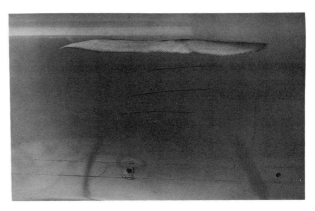

3-49 First stroke with the disc sander, moving from left to right. Swirl marks show up low spots because they follow the flattest crown of the panel.

metal-finishing, but the panel will be left in much better condition if it is finished with a 36 grit. Buffing can be done with a worn 36 grit, but it will be better if a 50 or 60 is used.

Finishing Metal With the Disc Sander

The disc sander has two basic uses in metal-finishing: the first is as a partial substitute for the body file, the second to buff the filed surface to remove deep scratches. Each requires a different stroke of the sander to produce the required results.

To use the sander as a substitute for filing, it is important that the disc be applied to the surface in such a way that it will leave a pattern of grit swirl marks that bridge across low spots. This can be done best by stroking the machine back and forth on the panel, following the direction which is nearest to flat, just as in filing. The pad should be pushed against the metal with enough pressure to cause it to flex, but not enough to cause the machine to slow down. As the disc moves back and forth across the surface, the spindle should be tilted away from the direction of travel just enough to throw the cutting action to the following edge. At the end of the stroke, a fraction of a second is required to stop and start the back stroke in the opposite direction. During this time, the spindle should be tilted to the opposite direction so that the cutting action will switch to the opposite edge, which will become the following edge. The swirl marks this will produce should be in a definite pattern, as explained below.

The swirl marks shown in Figure 3-49 were made by stroking the sander from the left to right. In Figure 3-50, several back-and-forth strokes have been made. Note that the grit swirl marks show a definite crosscut action because of the tilt of the sander on each stroke. Also note that several dark spots show up. These are low spots that the disc has bridged over.

In Figure 3-51, the low spots have been picked up and resanded over the complete area. This surface is smooth enough to be buffed and painted without further work. However, if there had been considerable rough metal, it would have been desirable to file the sanded

3-50 Appearance of several back-and-forth strokes criss-crossed over low area. Low metal shows up as dark spots.

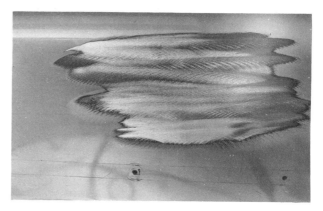

3-51 Appearance of the sanded area after the low spots have been picked up and resanded. This surface should be buffed for the final finish.

area lightly and inspect for minor low areas before buffing.

The position for holding the sander conveniently so that it may be stroked back and forth easily is shown in Figure 3-52. Note that the body of the machine is at a right angle to the direction of travel, but it is not always possible to assume such a position when using the sander on various parts of the automobile. The beginner should start to gain his experience with the sander on a job that will permit him to assume an easy position. As he gains more skill, it will be easy to adapt to the various positions in which the sander must be held without upsetting the pattern of stroking.

Buffing With the Disc Sander

Buffing with the disc sander differs from the finishing operation in the direction of the stroke and the contact of the disc. The stroke should be at a right angle to the finishing stroke so that it follows the direction of great-

est crown instead of the flattest. The machine should be held so that the spindle is straight instead of tilted to one side. This position permits the maximum area of the pad to lie on the panel surface. Figure 3-53 shows the machine being held and stroked in the proper manner. Figure 3-54 shows the finished job.

Best results will be obtained if most of the work is done on the downstroke, relaxing the pressure on the machine as it is raised into position to make the next downstroke.

In many cases where a large area of metal has been sanded to remove the paint and partly to finish the surface before filing, it will save filing to buff the area also. The reason is that the finishing stroke tends to leave ridges between strokes. Buffing off the ridges is just a means of cutting metal with the power tool instead of doing the work by hand with the file.

Use of Star-Shaped Discs

It is difficult to use a round sanding disc in a sharp reverse crown, because the edge cuts a sharp groove in the surface. This can be avoided by cutting the edge of the disc into points, resulting in what is commonly

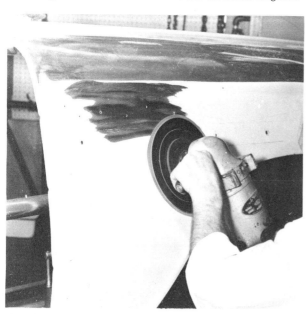

3-52 Proper position for easy stroking with the disc sander used in metal finishing.

3-53 Proper position for easy stroking with the disc sander when used for buffing. The direction of the stroke and the position of the machine are both at a right angle to the direction and position used in metal finishing.

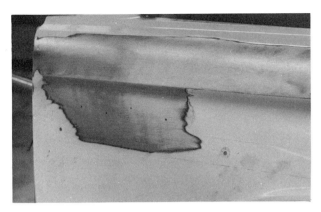

3-54 Appearance of the buffed surface, ready for painting.

3-55 Disc sanding with a star-shaped disc.

called a star disc. The number of points can vary from six to eight or nine. The sharper the radius of the reverse crown, the more points the disc should have.

The action of the star disc is to break the smooth outer edge of the disc so that it does not form the groove. Instead, the outer edge advances and recedes as each point passes a particular spot on the panel surface. The result is a smooth, polished effect that can be repainted easily. Figure 3-55 shows the finished job and the position of the pad. Note that it is being pushed into the work so that the disc is flexed to fit the curve of the panel. This disc will tend to slap the panel if it is not held firmly against it.

The operator never should use a star-shaped disc without full protection for his eyes and face. This disc tends to throw more grit than the round one. Also, it is particularly dangerous to allow the star disc to turn against an edge, because the points can catch and tear off. A flying chunk of a sanding disc can blind an eye or cause a severe facial cut.

Safety Measures with the Disc Sander

The disc sander never should be used without proper eye protection. It throws off particles of grit and metal cuttings at tremendous speeds. The outer edge of a 9-inch (approximately 23 cm) disc driven by a high-speed sander will travel at speeds faster than 1½ miles per miles per minute. Grit thrown at such speeds will injure and can cause the loss of an eye, thus the need for adequate eye protection—either goggles or one of the many available types of transparent plastic face shields.

There is also serious risk of injury if any portion of the flesh comes into contact with the disc while it is in motion. The edge of a new disc will cut a deep gash in the flesh almost as rapidly as a power saw. Such cuts are slow to heal, because the action of the disc removes the flesh instead of making a clean cut. For this reason, the sander should be started or stopped only when it is in the proper working position. It is best to stop the motor before removing the sander from the job. Never under any circumstances lay the sander on the floor or hand it to another person while it is running.

SHRINKING
METAL

Shrinking sheet metal is simply a matter of making an upset where it is needed. The exact opposite of stretching, it may be required on any panel spot where it is necessary to reduce surface area to restore the proper contour. However, not all upsetting should be considered as shrinking. The shrinking is restricted by common usage in the body shop to mean only an operation in which heat is used to soften the metal to permit making the desired upset.

The shrinking operation is performed by heating a spot or an area, working it to shape with the hammer and dolly block, and cooling it. When this is done properly, gouges or raised areas will be brought back close enough to exact contour to be metal-finished. The operation seems simple and easy to someone observing a skilled repairman, but it can be quite difficult for a beginner, particularly if he has not mastered the fundamentals.

The wide use of plastic body fillers has caused many repairmen to avoid shrinking metal as much as possible and, when they do shrink, to do it to a much lower standard than described in the preceding paragraph. They limit the operation to bringing high spots down enough to fall below the level of the filler material and, if done conscientiously, to bring up low areas enough to avoid excessive depth of filler. This type of shrinking, referred to here as *partial* shrinking, is often done in a careless or slipshod manner because, once covered over, it is difficult to detect when the job is first completed. However, it often shows up later as cracks or lifting in areas where the filler has been applied too thickly.

It is recommended that the beginner make every effort to develop reasonable skill in *precision* shrinking. The skill required to restore a gouge or otherwise stretched area to the precise limits required for metal finishing will show up as better and faster technique in less exact straightening operations where shrinking is not involved.

In the following discussion, precision shrinking is intended, unless partial shrinking is stated. To master the shrinking operation easily, the beginner should learn the fundamentals first then develop skill through practice. The fundamentals consist of:

1. Recognition of the types of damage that require shrinking.

2. An understanding of the basic shrinking operation.

3. An understanding of how heat may be used to obtain the required softening and stiffening effect.

4. An understanding of how controlling the rate of cooling by quenching can add to or reduce the amount of shrinking obtained with the individual operation.

In addition, it is essential already to have developed sufficient skill with the hammer and dolly block to be able to use them with precision. The work is done on metal that has been softened by heating. A misdirected hammer blow that would be of no consequence on unheated metal can do serious damage on metal at high temperature.

TYPES OF DAMAGE THAT REQUIRE SHRINKING

Shrinking may be required on almost any area of the sheet metal of an automobile damaged in a collision. The appearance of such areas may vary as widely as their location. However, when shrinking is done as part of any straightening operation, it is to reduce a stretched condition or to blend a condition of false stretch into the surrounding contour. Both of these conditions were discussed briefly in Chapter 2, but a more detailed discussion is required to explain the application of basic shrinking procedure.

It should be noted that the same procedure for shrinking damaged metal can be used in forming metal parts by hand. Although extensive hand-forming operations are outside the scope of this book, the repairman who has leaned the proper use of the hammer and dolly block will find that it is easy to hand-form simple parts needed in rust repair. Shrinking is particularly important in such operations becaue it provides a method of eliminating excess surface area easily.

STRETCHED METAL

Sheet metal is considered stretched when the dimensions that make up its surface area have been changed. The determining factor is whether either length or width has been increased. Usually there will be a proportional decrease of the other dimension of area, length or width.

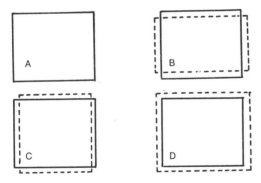

4-1 Typical stretched conditions. A represents an area within a panel of any size. In B and C, the dotted lines show the effect of either lengthwise or crosswise tension; D shows the effect of both lengthwise and crosswise tension. Any combination of these is considered to be stretched metal.

Figure 4-1 illustrates the varying conditions of stretched metal. A represents a small section of a panel surface. This section could be almost any size, from much smaller than shown to several times larger. If such a section could be laid out on the panel before the damage that caused the stretching, the result could be measured afterward. In most instances, the result would be similar to the conditions in B or C, depending on the direction from which the force acted in causing the stretch. If force did act on the section from both sides, the result would be similar to the condition D.

This figure shows that stretched metal may be found in a wide variety of conditions. In many instances there will be some combination of the two conditions represented by B and C; however, it will be the exceptional condition that is exactly uniform, as represented by the dotted lines. Also, these illustrations are simply flat, rectangular drawings on a piece of paper. Stretched metal will be found on the surface of a panel in almost any conceivable shape. Some stretched areas will be driven below the surface level, whereas others will be driven above.

FALSE STRETCH

False stretch is the term used to identify a condition often confused with a true stretched condition, stemming from the similarity of appearance. False stretch may vary from a simple *oil can* condition to a large, raised hump that appears to be stretched. The key to the identification of false stretch is that it will always be a smooth, unworked surface, which pops in and out easily, adjoining an area that has been upset. The raised area is caused by the gathering effect of the upset.

The most common cause of false stretch is failure to relieve all of the upset in a rolled buckle of the reinforced edge of such panels as doors, deck lids, or hoods; however, it can be found in any panel when the conditions are right. Many times, it is difficult to avoid causing a little false stretch, but it is often the result of improper use of tools. Attempting to beat out stiff, unyielding buckles that should be straightened under tension is probably the most usual reason.

A simple demonstration of a condition similar to false stretch can be made by folding a pleat in the edge of a sheet of paper. When the fold is held in place, the center area of the sheet will be raised into a sharp bulge, and when the fold is released, the bulged area will drop back into place.

The ideal method of dealing with false stretch is to avoid it; plan the rough-out procedure to avoid making upsets. Emphasis on such procedures will be found in later sections of the book dealing with the roughing out of actual damage. However, sometimes it is almost impossible to avoid creating some false stretch. In these instances, shrinking is the practical answer.

Shrinking false stretch is a blending operation. When it is done properly, the effect of the upset will be spread over enough area to relieve the appearance of bulging caused by the abrupt change of dimensions. The shrinking effect must not extend into the upset area, but it must blend invisibly with the adjoining metal. This presents a real problem, because in any shrinking operation there is a tendency to overshrink. Unless very close control is maintained, overshrinking will occur, and the upset will be carried farther ino the unaffected metal. This is the condition sometimes described by repairmen as "chasing a stretch across a panel." However, the man who has learned to recognize the difference between stretched metal and false stretch rarely will find himself in this predicament. The actual procedure for shrinking false stretch is described in detail in a later section.

THE BASIC SHRINKING OPERATION

The basic shrinking operation uses the compressive effect of a blow on a crowned surface to make an upset. This is illustrated by the cross section in Figure 4-2. As the hammer blow strikes the crown, it will tend to drive it down to the position of the straight dotted lines. As the crown flattens, it will tend to push outward against points A and B. The compressive effect produced is the result of resistance to outward movement of points A and B.

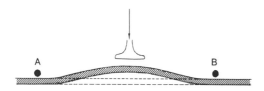

4-2 Showing the compressive effect of a hammer blow on a high crown. Flattening the crown causes outward pressure on points A and B.

If an upset is to be made, the resistance to outward movement must be greater than the resistance to upsetting of the crowned area. The softening effect of heat is required, because without it the crown usually offers much greater resistance than points A and B. The proper application of heat to the crown section will reverse the condition so that it will upset readily. It also will stiffen the resistance to outward movement of the A and B points by expanding the surrounding metal. Thus, heat tends to increase both conditions necessary for shrinking.

The effect of heat is shown in Figure 4-3. In this particular illustration, the temperature range is from 1,400° F. (760° C.) or cherry red at the center of the heated area to normal at, or close to, the A and B points. The expansion resulting from that temperature will raise the crown from the position of the solid line to the approximate position of the dotted line. The result is a low, cone-shaped hump stiffer around the outer edges and softer in the center than the original crown. This new shape offers much greater resistance to the hammer blow around the outer edges, points A and B, and much less resistance to upsetting in the center. Thus, hammer blows on the center area will cause considerable upset because the conditions are right.

4-3 The softening effect of heat. A hammer blow on the heated spot will cause upsetting, instead of forcing points A and B outward.

Because cooling starts the instant the torch flame is removed from the work, the effect of heating is only temporary. Cooling is rapid enough to require that any work done with the hammer be done as quickly as possible. The smaller the spot heated, the more important it is that no time be lost, if the work is to be effective.

This explanation of basic shrinking procedure has been limited to the effect on a single cross section taken through the center of an area of metal raised above the proper surface level. In the simplest stretched condition that would require shrinking, another cross section taken at a right angle to this line would be approximately the same. The four basic steps of shrinking such a spot are shown in Figure 4-4. A represents a cross section of the original spot to be shrunk. Since it is uniform, this may be considered the same as any other cross section taken at any other angle. B shows the application of heat from the welding torch flame to a temperature of about 1,400° F. (760° C.).

The exact temperature and size of the heated area will vary with the conditions of the area to be shrunk. No exact rules can be laid down, except that the temperature should not exceed bright cherry red in normal light and that the area heated should be in proportion to the area of severe distortion. Metal outside the stretched area should not be subjected to high temperature—above the range where discoloration starts—unless the intent is to blend an unstretched area of false stretch into an unavoidable upset. Metal heated to the point of discoloration will be softened enough to upset under the effect of a hammer blow. In fact, many minor shrinking jobs can be done with temperatures well below the red heat range. Many repairmen refer to this as shrinking with "black heat." Temperature variations and the spread of heat are discussed in a later section.

The actual shrinking operation is shown in C of Figure 4-4. The hammer has been used to drive the hot, expanded surface down to a much lower level. Although the hammer is shown in only one position, it would be necessary to strike several hammer blows over the heated surface to flatten the crown to this level. It should be noted especially that the surface is shown with some crown. It would be wrong to drive the surface down so that it is perfectly flat while it is heated, because cooling will cause it to contract and be overshrunk. This slight crown will be reduced as cooling is completed.

The last two steps are shown together in D. The hammer and dolly block are being used to finish straightening the shrunk surface, and the wet sponge is in position

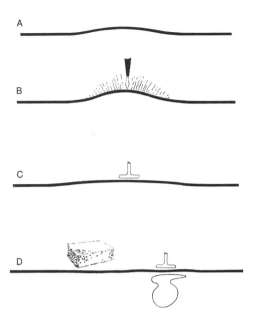

4-4 The basic shrinking operation: A, Cross section of spot to be shrunk; B, the same area expanded and softened by heat; C, the hammer being used to drive down the softened high spot; D, the hammer and dolly block being used to straighten the shrunk area. The wet sponge is used as needed to quench the hot metal.

to quench the hot metal as needed. The hammer is shown on-dolly, which is often necessary to relieve any overshrinking. The hammer also would be used off-dolly to finish straightening any noticeable waves. In this case, the use of the hammer and dolly is not different from that in any other straightening job, except that lighter blows and more care are required, because the heated metal will yield much more readily than unheated metal.

The sponge is not always needed. If the surface has been lowered enough, the rest of the crown will drop into the proper level as the surface cools. If, however, the surface has not been driven down as far as necessary, quenching it with a wet sponge or rag will lower it much more than if it is allowed to cool slowly. Overquenching will cause overshrinking. The problems of quenching are discussed in much greater detail in a later section.

SHRINKING GOUGES

The procedure for shrinking a gouge is similar to that for shrinking an area of raised metal. In both operations the upset is obtained by softening the area with heat and applying force to flatten it. It differs in two respects, however: (1) the gouged area extends below the surface instead of above it, and (2) gouges tend to be stretched more severely than raised areas.

The dolly block plays a much more important part in shrinking the gouge, because force to accomplish the upset must be applied from the underside while the metal is hot. The more severe the stretched condition,

the more important it is that this be done. A very minor gouge can be driven up without heating and then shrunk as if it were a raised area instead. This procedure is recommended for large, lightly stretched areas that have been driven below the surface. However, it is not practical on any but the most minor damage, because it tends to spread the effect over a much wider area. It is a much better practice to use the hammer and dolly block as shown in Figure 4-5.

A represents a cross section through a gouge, with the proper surface level indicated by the dotted lines. In this case, the depressed area is shown as being smooth. Under actual conditions, however, this may be any shape. Quite often the bottom of a gouge shows the imprint of a sharp object. Regardless of the shape, however, the procedure would be the same.

The effect of heat application is shown in B. Expansion has deepened the gouge by causing the metal on the surrounding edges to bulge inward. This is essentially the same as the effect obtained by heating a raised area, except that expansion forces the surface downward instead of upward. Here the temperature required would be relatively high, at least dull red heat and maybe hotter; the more severe the stretched condition, the higher the temperature should be, but *never above bright cherry red*.

The first application of force is shown in C. One or more blows have been struck with the dolly block on the underside of the deepest part of the gouge. This has driven the edges of the gouge above the level of the surrounding metal. On a small, single-point gouge, this high metal will form a ring around the low spot. On a long gouge, several dolly blows should be struck along the

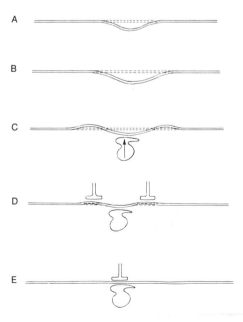

4-5 Basic procedure for shrinking a gouge: A, a cross section through a typical gouge; B, the same cross section expanded and softened by heat; C, the heated area driven up by a blow of the dolly block; D, using the hammer and dolly block to level the high and low spots; E, using the hammer-on-dolly to relieve overshrinking.

heated area so that this high metal will form two lines on each side of the low spot.

The use of the hammer and dolly is shown in D. The dolly block should be pushed hard against the underside of the gouge as the hammer is used to drive the high metal down to level. Usually these two operations will be repeated, often several times. Each time they are repeated, the gouge and the surrounding high metal should be made smaller. Too many variable conditions are involved, however, to attempt to establish the exact number of repetitions. The beginner is advised to try to obtain as much shrink effect as possible from his efforts. It is simply a matter of learning to use the hammer-on-dolly on metal softened by heat.

The last operation is shown in E, with the hammer on-dolly to stretch metal. Sometimes the beginner has difficulty understanding why metal should be stretched immediately after it has been shrunk. The reason is that a line gouge will tend to shrink more lengthwise than across. Covering the area with on-dolly hammer blows will tend to relieve the effect. If allowed to cool without relieving this tendency, the shrunk area will have a drawstring effect on the adjoining surface area, causing large, flappy buckles. This operation is referred to in later sections as *stretching back*.

Probably the most important part of the procedure of shrinking a gouge is in the use of the hammer and dolly block to stretch back as the surface cools. The experienced repairman watches the surface closely and uses his hammer and dolly to relieve buckles caused by too much tension as soon as they begin to form.

Quenching is rarely needed on a gouge, except for final cooling to keep the surface from being too hot to touch. Water should never be applied to the heated metal until the metal has cooled past the point at which steam rises from it.

The procedure described here can be used for any type of gouge, if the heat application and use of the hammer and dolly block are varied to suit the conditions. Shrinking a single spot is the easiest, because only a single spot of heat is required in the deepest part. Shrinking a long, crease type of gouge, such as shown in Figure 4-9, requires that heat be applied along the length, instead of in a single spot. Whenever possible, the entire length should be heated and worked with the hammer and dolly block, but heat should never be applied to more metal than can be handled.

The skill of the individual is the deciding factor in determining how long a section of a gouge can be shrunk with one heat application. The beginner will do well to content himself with fairly short lengths, otherwise he may find that he is doing more damage than good. As he develops skill, however, he will find that he can work longer sections without difficulty. This will improve both the speed and the quality of his work.

THE PROPER USE OF HEAT IN SHRINKING METAL

One of the most important steps in any shrinking opera-

tion is the application of heat. This is true whether the job is relatively simple or quite complicated; however, the more complicated the job, the more important it is that heat be applied properly.

Proper application of heat means that the proper temperature is applied to an area of the proper size. The problem is to apply just enough heat to do the job and no more. If not enough is applied, the metal will not be softened enough to permit the required upset. In this event, the stretched condition will not be relieved, and the surface will be left rough or wavy.

To a limited extent, extra work with the hammer can offset the effect of insufficient heat. Beyond this limit, extra work with the hammer will tend only to spread the crown instead of shrinking it. For example, in Figure 4-2, the tendency would be to push points A and B farther apart instead of making an upset between them.

The effect of too-high temperature is shown in Figure 4-6. This shows the result of heating red hot a small spot in the center of a large, slightly stretched raised area. Instead of shrinking uniformly all over, the hot spot collapses, forming a depression under the hammer. A lower temperature spread over the entire area would have produced a uniform upset and a smooth surface.

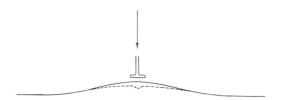

4-6 Effect of overheating a small spot where a much wider area should be heated to lower temperature. The dip in the dotted line represents a collapse on the overheated spot instead of upset.

A common mistake made in shrinking metal is to heat every spot to red heat. No doubt this stems from the influence of the blacksmith. In the early days of the automobile industry, the first repairmen were blacksmiths. An important rule of the blacksmith was that metal never should be forged at any temperature below red heat. This idea was carried over into any work done on automobile sheet metal, and it still persists, even among men who have little or no knowledge of the blacksmith's trade.

Steel such as used in automobile sheet metal begins to soften at the temperature at which the first color forms. The rate of softening increases progressively as the temperature is raised until the dark-blue color temperature range is reached. Past this point, the softening effect is directly proportional to the temperature increase until practically all mechanical strength is lost at bright red heat, close to 1,600°F. (871°C.).

The softening that results from heating to the blue color range is enough to permit considerable upsetting. On large areas that are not severely stretched, heating to the blue range or just slightly beyond will provide enough softening effect to permit the required upsetting as the surface is driven down with the hammer. Figure 4-7 shows an application of heat in the blue temperature range over a wide area. This area could be any size from 1 or 2 inches (25 or 50 mm) in length and width to 5 or 6 inches (125 or 150 mm). Hammer blows spaced over this area will cause uniform upsetting instead of the condition shown in Figure 4-6.

Low-temperature, or "black heat," shrinking, which includes any operation when heat is used below the red range, is not practical if the spot has any degree of work hardening. Severe work hardening requires heat up to the bright-red range to soften it completely. However, such areas also are stretched severely; otherwise, they would not be work hardened. In heating work hardened areas, the high temperature should be confined as much as possible to the areas that are stretched severely, as indicated by Figure 4-8. In a gouge having a cross section similar to this shape, most of the stretched metal, which also is work hardened, would be in the area between the two arrows. Red heat never should extend beyond this area.

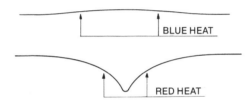

4-7 *(Top)* Showing the approximate spread of low temperature heat over a minor stretched condition.

4-8 *(Bottom)* Showing the approximate spread of high temperature heat over a severe stretched condition.

QUENCHING

Quenching is a means of controlling the rate of cooling. The primary reason for quenching is to retain a greater amount of the upset than would be possible if the spot were allowed to cool slowly after the shrinking with the hammer. After the work with the hammer and dolly has been completed, the sooner the metal can be quenched, the more shrink effect will be obtained.

Quenching adds to the amount of shrinkage by stopping the yield of the heated area to the tension that results from contraction as the metal cools. Quenching is much more effective if the work with the hammer and dolly can be completed before the temperature has dropped below the color range. But it still will have some effect if done while the temperature is above the point at which water will form steam on contact with the hot metal, particularly on relatively large areas. Below that point it is simply a matter of cooling.

Knowing when to quench is largely a matter of experience. The experienced repairman soon learns to judge visually when the surface will cool to the proper contour without quenching. If he sees that it will not, he will pass a wet sponge or cloth across the surface as he watches the effect. When the proper surface condition has been obtained, quenching should be stopped. Many times, quenching will show up minor buckles that can be straightened with the hammer and dolly block; then the surface can be quenched again. This must be done with the minimum loss of time, however. When reaching for the wet sponge, do not lay down the hammer or dolly where it will be difficult to pick up again. The best method is to hold both tools in one hand while the quenching is done with the other; this will avoid fumbling for tools if further straightening is needed.

Only rarely should a repairman quench a shrink spot all the way without looking at what is happening. It is better to move the wet sponge back and forth across the hot spot. The surface action can be watched between passes and the quenching action speeded up or slowed down as needed.

OVERSHRINKING

Overshrinking is the result of shrinking of the temporarily expanded metal in addition to that which was stretched. When this occurs, it will have a drawing or puckering effect on the metal surface surrounding the overshrunk area.

A demonstration showing an effect similar to overshrinking can be made with a piece of cloth such as a handkerchief. With the cloth lying flat on a table top, gather a section in the center of it between the fingers. As long as this section is held, it will be impossible to smooth the surrounding surface so that it will lie flat.

Overshrinking is more likely to occur when shrinking gouges than when shrinking a stretched condition that has been raised above the surface level. It can occur in either situation, however. A slight amount often is desirable, because it will be relieved by the normal picking and hammer and dolly block work that will be done when the spot is metal-finished. If it is too great, however, it will have a gathering effect on the adjoining surface, resulting in the formation of long wavy buckles in the surface. These can be relieved by using the hammer-on-dolly to restretch the shrunk area and, sometimes, some of the area immediately adjoining. When this is done, care should be taken to space the hammer blows over the affected area uniformly and to avoid pressing too hard against the dolly block. The desired effect is the spreading action of the hammer blow against the dolly. The rebound action caused by pressing the dolly hard against the inner surface is not needed. If the surface is low, it should be lifted by striking the underside of the metal with the working face of the dolly.

SHRINKING PROCEDURES ON THE JOB

A typical example of the use of shrinking is provided by the procedure followed in straightening the gouged dent

4-9 Crease in a front door lower panel. The rear end of this crease will require shrinking.

in the door lower panel shown in Figure 4-9. Although the emphasis is on the shrinking procedure, all the straightening operations are explained so that the proper relationship of shrinking to the other procedures can be shown.

This damage probably resulted when this automobile struck a glancing impact against a rigid, sharp object, probably a projection on the bumper of another automobile. However, the same damage could have been caused by another automobile striking this one while it was standing still. Whatever it was, the impact object approached from the front at a very sharp angle, contacting the front door almost at the front edge. As the impact object moved farther back, it dug deeper into the panel. Note that a sharp bend has formed along the lower edge from the center to the rear. The reinforced edges caused the impact object to bounce off the front door and strike the rear, causing another gouge before coming to rest.

The inside of the front door is shown in Figure 4-10, which shows the inside of the outer panel, partly covered with undercoating, and the loading hole. Note that easy access for hand tools is provided by this hole.

Figure 4-11 shows the first operation. The metal was dented and scratched up to the point where the hammer is shown, but not stretched. The dent has been straightened up to this point, using the hammer and dolly, so the area to be shrunk can blend to the correct contour.

4-10 Inside view of a front door, showing loading holes and part of the inner surface of the outer panel.

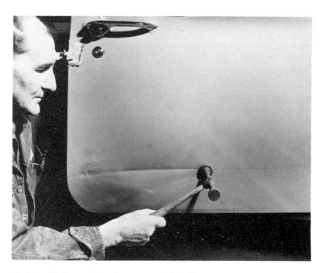

4-11 Using the hammer-off-dolly to straighten the unstretched part of the crease. Most of the work was done off-dolly.

Part of the next step is shown in Figure 4-12. Before the wire brush was used to remove the paint, the surface was scorched with a strongly oxidizing flame. The flame was held almost on the surface of the panel and kept moving rapidly to avoid overheating the metal. By this method, paint can be burned very rapidly so that the brush will remove it easily.

The paint should always be burned on any surface where metal is to be shrunk. It enables the repairman to judge the temperature by color and leaves the surface smooth so that the level can be judged visually much more accurately. Also, if the paint is not removed, the torch flame will burn it, leaving a gummy residue. Particles of this residue will be picked up on the hammer face, making it rough. If the hammer is used in this condition, it will make rough, choppy marks in the hot metal.

The first heat application for shrinking is shown in Figure 4-13. This picture was shot slightly late as the flame was being removed from contact with the surface. The flame first was played back and forth over the general area to spread enough heat to avoid a sharp break-line between hot and cold metal. This was done

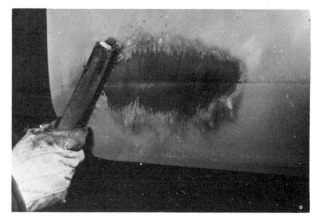

4-12 Using a hand wire brush to remove paint after scorching it with an oxidizing flame.

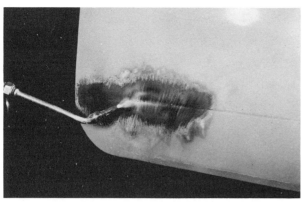

4-13 Heating the gouge before shrinking. A temperature variation from faint color to bright blue was made by changing the speed of the moving torch from fast to slow.

with the tip of the inner cone about 1 inch (25 mm) from the surface. It was then lowered to about ½ inch (12.5 mm) above the gouge at the right end of the burned-off spot and moved steadily to the left to the point where it is shown. Because the stretched condition increases from the right to left, the torch was moved fairly rapidly at the start on the right, but slowed progressively as it moved to the left. This permitted a gradual increase in temperature from right to left. As an indication of the temperature, no actual color appeared in the first inch at the right end, but it had increased to slightly above bright blue at the left.

Shrinking this heated spot was done by using the hammer and dolly in the same manner they were used to straighten the forward section of the gouge where shrinking was not needed (Figure 4-4). As explained earlier in this chapter, only enough heat was applied to permit the required amount of upsetting. In this instance, however, the work had to be done rapidly, because the spot was too small to remain hot long.

The remaining length of the buckle received one more heat application. Because the amount of stretch increased to the left, the temperature was allowed to rise further, up to cherry red in the deepest part. The heating method was the same, however, except that the flame was kept in place longer.

A body spoon and a spoon dolly were needed as the work approached the edge, because the shape of the

facing prevented easy access with the dolly block. These tools and the others used on this job are shown in Figure 4-14. The small screwdriver was used as a pry tool through the drain holes in the lower rear corner.

The end of the shrinking operation is shown in Figure 4-15. This spot has been reheated and is being hammered down again because after the first operation it was left slightly high.

Two steps in the metal-finishing operation are shown in Figures 4-16 and 4-17. In Figure 4-16, a heavy-duty disc sander equipped with a sharp, 36-grit disc has been passed across the straightened and shrunk surface. Paint shows up in the low spots where it has not been burned off, and dark metal appears in the shrunk area. Note that there are few low spots. In Figure 4-17, the low spots have been pried up and filed smooth. After buffing, the surface will be ready to repaint.

PARTIAL SHRINKING

The gouged panel in Figure 4-9 was easy to shrink because the underside was accessible. There are many other areas on doors, quarter panels, fenders, roofs, and so on that can be shrunk and metal-finished similarly. Other, less accessible areas must be worked by other means, usually pry rods or the metal screw-type panel puller. Weld-on pull tabs can be used, but they often break off when used on heated metal. Whatever is used, only partial shrinking will be practical.

Figure 4-18 illustrates the heating procedure for partly shrinking a gouge by lifting with a screw-type dent puller. The notes point out that the screw should be driven in tight to the retainer. This is to protect the hardened threads from the heat as much as possible. In heating, the flame should be directed down the channel of the gouge but away from the thread. The position of the torch should be changed from side to side once or twice so that the heating will be even. As the metal reaches red heat, the flame can be backed up toward the puller, but it is not necessary to have red-hot metal at the screw hole. A means of quick disposal of the torch should be provided so that the hammer can be operated and the metal quenched.

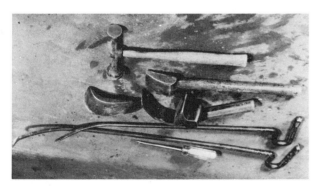

4-14 Tools used in shrinking and metal-finishing the gouge.

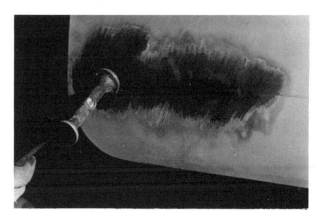

4-15 The final shrinking opertion on a high spot after the gouge has been shrunk to level.

4-16 Appearance of the straightened surface after disc sanding lightly with a sharp, 36-grit disc.

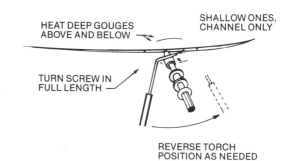

4-18 Heating procedure when lifting a gouge with a dent puller for partial shrinking. Turn screw in all of the way to protect threads and direct flame to both sides away from it. Heat above and below the screw only on extra deep gouges.

As the work progresses from the shallow to the deeper part of the gouge, it may be necessary to heat the sides of the gouge as well as the main channel. This can be done as the torch changes position by playing the flame on the surface well above or below the screw, instead of lifting it off the surface.

A hammer is not shown because, if needed at all, it should be used sparingly and well away from the high-temperature area. Sometimes a light hammer blow above or below the puller will help raise an area, but it must be struck on a part of the surface that is not hot enough to shrink under the impact. Any shrinkage in the outer edges will cause a shallow buckle to radiate outward into the smooth panel area, adding damage to damage.

A deep, point gouge can be shrunk similarly, but the torch flame should be applied in a circular path around the end of the puller. A small tip, adjusted to a small flame, should be used and directed toward the midpoint of the side of the gouge and kept off the end of the puller as much as possible. It is not always necessary to reach red heat. A steady pull should be maintained on the puller as the gouge is heated. The hammer slide may not be needed, but if it is, it should be used carefully.

Pry rods can be used instead of the slide hammer, as shown in Figure 4-19, but a direct lift under red-hot metal should be avoided; instead of lifting an area, it

will simply punch a hole. The rod shown in use has the outer end bent to approximately a 70-degree angle. It is being used upside down so that the curved surface will contact the metal instead of the point. In general, it is better to make several lifts around an area instead of attempting to bring it up with one.

The procedure with weld-on tabs would be much the same as with the metal screw, but the heat must be kept from the weld. If it is too hot, it will break off, leaving a high spot that often has a hole in it.

Partial shrinking is not a precision operation. The purpose is to reduce the depth of fill by folding excess surface, caused by stretching, back into its proper area. It is important to avoid over-upsetting across the gouge. If this occurs, large, shallow waves will be drawn in the adjoining smooth surface when the upset areas cool, adding needless work to a relatively simple job.

SHRINKING THIN SHEET STEELS

Very thin sheet steel requires some adjustment of the procedure used on conventional thicknesses, but it can be shrunk in the same general manner. The difference stems from the way a reduction of thickness of the same grade of steel affects its resistance to bending. As thick-

4-17 The finished panel, ready for buffing. The low spots have been pried or picked up and filed smooth.

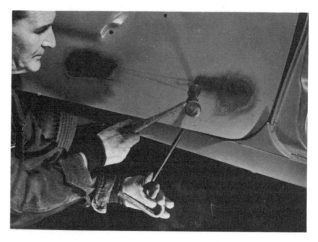

4-19 Using a pry rod to partly shrink a gouge.

ness is reduced, bending resistance drops off to a greater degree. The opposite is true, also: an increase of thickness causes a greater increase in bending resistance. (For the benefit of technically minded readers, bending resistance, technically load-bearing strength, varies as the square of thickness, assuming that length and width are the same. Reducing thickness to one half will reduce load-bearing strength to one quarter. In-between reductions can be calculated from the ratio of the square of one thickness to the other. The formula is $\frac{R_1}{R_2} = \frac{T_1^2}{T_2^2}$, in which R = rigidity and T = thickness.)

The raised area caused by spot heat application bends the metal around the outer edges in two ways: (1) up, to permit the heated area to rise and (2) warp, because the surrounding cooler metal must resist the expansion of the heated area. This action is present in metal of any thickness, but is not a serious problem when heating the thickness for which normal shrinking procedures were developed. It becomes a problem when the thickness is reduced. The problem is affected to some degree by the fact that the thinner steels are usually stiffer, but not enough to make a major difference.

The first adjustment is to reduce the upper limit of temperature. Heat to dull red where bright red would have been used on thicker metal, or, if dull red would have been used, keep the temperature in the black range.

The second adjustment is to avoid concentrating high temperature in a small area. Where it would be safe on thicker metal to heat a very small spot to bright red, it is better to spiral the flame inward over a larger area, making the hottest spot in the center. The result will be a spread of the bending and warping effect over a much wider area.

The third adjustment is that less force can be used with the hammer. The dolly block should be used mostly in the off-dolly positions. Stretching back, to compensate for the extra lengthwise shrinkage along a gouge, should be done largely by slapping the working face of the dolly against the underside. Any hammer-on-dolly blows should be light and the dolly held with a relaxed grip.

The fourth adjustment is the hardest. The thinner metal cools more rapidly, leaving less time to do the work. Safety requires that the flame be shut off or that the torch be handed to another person. Most repairmen learn to regulate the torch valves with the thumb or a finger of the hand holding the torch; this can be done as it is being laid down. The tools should be held ready in the other hand, so that minimum time will be lost. A wet sponge or rag should be in a convenient position, but should be used sparingly.

After that, it is simply a matter of working fast without error. Many experienced repairmen consider shrinking the thinner metal impractical. The time factor adds some validity to the argument, but thin metal can be shrunk by any skilled worker who has recognized the nature of the problems involved and has developed the essential skill.

SHRINKING ALUMINUM

Sheet aluminum can be shrunk in much the same manner as sheet steel, but the procedure is complicated by three factors: (1) it must be done in a much lower temperture range; thus, color is no indicator of temperature, (2) aluminum conducts heat much more rapidly than steel, leaving less time to work the hot metal, and (3) the hammer and dolly block must be used much more carefully, because the already soft aluminum is further softened by heating, so that errors which would be minor on steel will be major on aluminum. It is recommended that shrinking aluminum not be tried until a reasonable degree of skill has been developed on steel.

Heat should be applied with a small tip adjusted to a slightly carburizing flame and held well back from the surface. The size of the area heated should be less than the size of the stretched area, because the heat spreads rapidly by conduction. In general, it is better to underheat and try again than to overheat and burn a hole. The torch flame should be kept moving at all times it is on the metal.

Preparation should be made to dispose of the torch with minimum lost time, so that work with the hammer can be started. Hammer blows should be spaced around the heat-bulged area instead of straight down on the center. As the hammer moves to a new position, the angle should change so that the metal is forced toward the center. The dolly block should be used only to buck up the outer edges. Never strike an on-dolly blow on hot aluminum; it is too soft.

Aluminum requires more care in quenching than steel, because its expansion and contraction rate is greater. A circular pass with the wet sponge or rag should be made around the hot spot, to prevent heat flowing too far into unaffected metal, then quick passes made across it while watching the action carefully. Stop quenching when the surface looks as though it has dropped enough. Overquenching will cause overshrinking. When this occurs, allow the metal to cool and correct it by driving the area up with the dolly block while using the hammer with light off-dolly blows around the edge.

The operation can be repeated if the stretched area has not been completely shrunk. On the second operation there should be little difference in procedure from the first, other than reducing the amount of heat and hammer work to allow for the shrinking already accomplished.

A stretched area of aluminum that has been shrunk properly can be metal-finished the same as a similar area of steel. However, many repairmen will be satisfied to get the high spot shrunk down and complete the finishing by filling. Unless the proper skill has been developed, this may be the safest course, but it is not a substitute for skill.

5

WELDING

In its broadest definition, welding includes most of the processes of joining metal by the use of heat, including soldering. These processes vary widely in method and equipment. The original and the simplest method is that of the blacksmith, who heated the pieces to be joined in the forge until they were plastic and then hammered them together on the anvil. Many modern industrial methods make use of the heat of the electric arc or heat caused by electrical resistance; even heat resulting from friction is used for some special applications. In newer methods, wide use is made of mechanical, electrical, and electronic control systems to make the process completely automatic. Manual methods, such as the oxyacetylene torch and hand-operated electric arc, are still used industrially; however, as progress is made in the development of more efficient mechanized methods, non-automatic welding is becoming more and more restricted to repair and maintenance work.

Welding processes may be classified by whether the metal welded is heated to the melting point, so that it will flow together; heated close to the melting point and joined by the application of force; or heated and joined by diffusion of a molten filler metal into the surfaces of the parts to be joined. The first usually is called fusion welding, because the metal fuses and flows together; it includes both the oxyacetylene and the electric arc processes. The second usually is called pressure welding, because of the pressure applied to make the joint; it includes the electrical resistance and forge welding processes. The most common of the electrical resistance processes is resistance spot welding, used for almost all factory sheet metal welding because of its economy and the fact that it causes practically no heat distortion. The third is called either soldering or brazing, depending on the type and melting temperature of the filler metal used.

The nature of the welding required in sheet metal repair is such that a large part of it is best suited to the oxyacetylene torch processes. These include both the fusion welding of steel and brazing. In fusion welding of steel, the metal being welded is heated to the melting point, and usually a filler rod of similar metal is melted and added to the joint. In brazing steel, the metal is heated only to the temperature at which the brazing rod melts so that it can be deposited on the joint; the brazing material, usually a copper base alloy, flows onto the steel, making a strong joint for most purposes. Brazing requires the use of flux to clean the steel surfaces, but no flux is required for fusion welding mild steel with the oxyacetylene torch. It is essential for the beginner to learn to do both types of oxyacetylene welding in any position, flat, vertical, or overhead.

Some of the welding operations on body and frame repair work can be done better with one of the electric welding processes, arc or resistance. In arc welding, an electric arc provides heat required for fusion and, in two of the three methods, a means of depositing the filler metal in the weld. In resistance welding, heat is generated by flowing an electric current through the metal to be welded, but the weld is made by mechanical pressure applied to the metal when it reaches the correct temperature.

Both basic systems are described in more detail in the following section, but more emphasis is placed on the electric resistance method. It is the basic method used in factory assembly of almost all sheet metal products, particularly automobiles, and has distinct advantages for many body repair operations. The arc welding coverage in the following sections is restricted to the equipment and procedures suitable to the relatively thin steels that the body repairman is required to weld in the normal day-to-day body shop operation.

It is common body shop practice to use the term welding when referring to the oxyacetylene welding of steel with a steel filler rod, because it is the method used most frequently. Other processes are referred to by name, such as brazing, arc welding, and resistance spot welding.

OXYACETYLENE WELDING EQUIPMENT

Although there are several different manufacturers of oxyacetylene welding equipment, all such equipment operates on one basic principle: The flame is produced by mixing the acetylene and oxygen in the proper proportions in the torch mixing chamber and passing them through the orifice in the torch tip, where they are ignited. A steady flame is maintained by adjusting the pressure of both the oxygen and acetylene so that the mixture escapes from the torch tip at the proper speed.

Gas welding equipment consists of the following units:

1. Oxygen cylinder
2. Acetylene cylinder
3. Oxygen regulator
4. Acetylene regulator
5. Hoses
6. Torch, including handle, mixing chamber, and tip
7. Eye protection for the operator, usually goggles or a face shield
8. Spark lighter
9. Hand truck for cylinders

A typical welding outfit, without hand truck, is shown in Figure 5-1.

GAS CYLINDERS

The gas cylinders, sometimes called tanks or bottles, normally are supplied by the company that manufactures the gas. Except in operations where only limited quantities of gas are used, the cylinders are provided without charge for thirty days, after which a demurrage charge is made. Cylinders are also available for limited quantity users on various purchase or long-term lease plans. The exact nature of these plans varies from one manufacturer to another, but in general, the user pays for the cylinders plus the normal maintenance they will require. The user is guaranteed also that full cylinders will be available on an exchange basis when he presents his empties to the dealer. The price for the gas under this plan is slightly higher than for the large-volume user.

Safety precautions require that the cylinders be attached to something that will prevent them from being knocked over. The common practice is to mount them on a specially designed portable hand truck. When portability is not required, they may be chained to something rigid, such as a wall or bench. The use of the hand truck is more desirable, however, because it simplifies the problem of removal in case of fire.

THE OXYGEN CYLINDER

The oxygen cylinder is simply a high-strength steel tank with a specially designed bronze shut-off valve and a safety device to release the pressure under emergency conditions. The standard-size cylinder, shown in Figure 5-2, has a capacity of 244 cubic feet at 2,200 pounds pressure per square inch (psi) at 70°F. (6.9 m³ at 15,158 kPa at 21°C.). Smaller cylinders are also available. One common size holds 122 cubic feet (3.45 m³); similar cylinders of approximately the same size are available from the various manufacturers.

The pressure in an oxygen cylinder varies according to the temperature. A fully charged cylinder will show a pressure of only about 1,780 psi (12,264 kPa) if it is kept outdoors in zero temperature. After it has warmed to

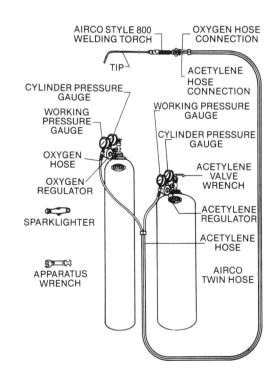

5-1 Oxyacetylene welding outfit.

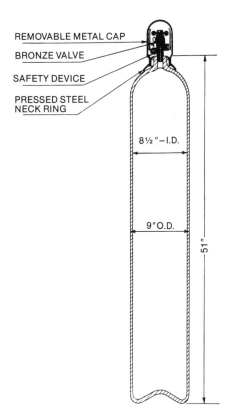

5-2 Oxygen cylinder. Oxygen capacity 244 cu. ft. at 2,200 psi pressure at 70°F. (6.9 m³ at 15,158 kPa at 21°C.).

70°F. (21°C.), the pressure will increase to 2,200 psi (15,158 kPa), and if the temperature is raised to 120°F. (49°C.), the pressure will increase to 2,500 psi (17,225 kPa).

The high-pressure gauge on most oxygen regulators is calibrated to indicate the number of cubic feet of oxygen in the cylinder at 70°F. (21°C.). If the temperature varies from this figure, an allowance must be made to determine the amount left in the cylinder. Although all such calibrations are approximate, they are close enough for ordinary use.

The oxygen cylinder is equipped with a safety cap that protects the valve. This cap should be kept in place at all times when the cylinder, whether full or empty, is not connected to the welding outfit.

Oxygen cylnders are subject to the U.S. Interstate Commerce Commission rules governing containers used for transporting compressed gases. Other countries have similar regulations. These rules are intended to ensure that such containers are safe. The very nature of a container of gas compressed to the pressure normally found in an oxygen cylinder makes it absolutely essential for the user to follow every possible safety precaution. These cylinders should never be stored near heat or highly flammable materials. The National Board of Fire Underwriters has rules for the storage of oxygen cylinders. In many communities, there are also local regulations. These should be followed.

A particular hazard is created when oil and grease are exposed to high-pressure oxygen. A small drop of grease in an oxygen valve can be the cause of a fire and an explosion. Under no circumstances should such material be allowed to get on cylinders or any other gas welding equipment. Other highly oxidizable materials may be equally hazardous. Greasy clothing or gloves should not be used around gas welding equipment.

Oxygen cylinders should never be used to support another object or as rollers to move something heavy. An electric arc should never be struck on the cylinder, because it may cause the cylinder to rupture. The sudden release of oxygen under high pressure would cause tremendous damage; it would probably injure and possibly kill the operator and any other persons in the vicinity.

THE ACETYLENE CYLINDER

The acetylene cylinder differs in construction from the oxygen cylinder, because it is dangerous to store acetylene gas at high pressure in open-space containers. Either heat or shock can cause it to separate into its more simple constituents, releasing tremendous amounts of heat. The fire and explosion hazards under such circumstances are so great that laws and regulations have been established governing the construction of acetylene cylinders.

The problem of storage of acetylene compressed to high pressure was solved by the discovery that it can be dissolved readily into liquid acetone, which can dissolve many times its own volume of acetylene gas. This knowledge led to the development of various porous filling

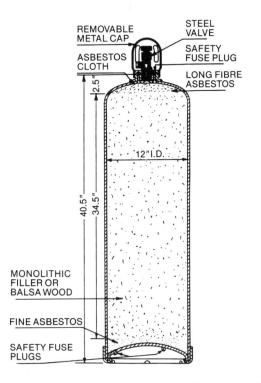

5-3 Acetylene cylinder. Acetylene capacity approx. 275 cu. ft. at 250 psi pressure at 70°F. (7.78 m³ at 1,723 kPa at 21°C.).

materials for the cylinder, serving to absorb the acetone and prevent the formation of open cavities. Thus, all of the acetylene pumped into the cyliner must be dissolved into the acetone. A cross-sectional view of such a cylinder is shown in Figure 5-3.

An acetylene cylinder 12 inches (30 cm) in diameter and 40.5 inches (103 cm) high can store approximately 275 cubic feet (7.78 m³) of acetylene at a pressure of 250 psi (1,723 kPa). Acetylene dissolved in acetone at this pressure in cylinders filled with suitable porous material can be handled with safety. Only a small fraction of this amount of acetylene could be stored safely in an open-space container. For this reason, no attempt ever should be made to transfer acetylene from the proper cylinder to another container.

Safety fuse plugs that melt at 220°F. (104.4°C.) are provided at the top and bottom of the acetylene cylinder. If the temperature of the area in which the cylinder is stored reaches this point, the acetylene will be released into the surrounding air, and the possibility of an explosion will be avoided.

The extreme fire hazard of acetylene dictates rigid safety precautions. The acetylene cylinders should never be used to prop something up or as rollers. Being filled with liquid acetone, they always should be stored and used in an upright position. If a cylinder has been laid on its side, before it is used again it should be allowed to stand upright for at least a half hour to permit the acetone to flow back away from the valve. If not, acetone may be discharged into the welding outfit, causing a void in the cylinder and damage to the equipment.

Pressure variations due to temperature changes are greater for acetylene than for oxygen. Furthermore, because the gas is dissolved in acetone, gauge pressure is not an exact indicator of the amount of gas in a cylinder. The only true indication is weight. 14.74 cu. ft. (0.42 m³) of acetylene gas weighs one pound (0.45 kg). When necessary to determine the exact amount of gas in a cylinder, weigh the cylinder and subtract the tare (empty) weight to determine the weight of the gas. The cubic feet can be calculated by multiplying by 14.74; cubic feet can be converted to cubic meters by multiplying by 0.0283. The tare weight will be found stamped on the cylinder.

THE OXYACETYLENE WELDING OUTFIT

Welding equipment consists of the two regulators for oxygen and acetylene, the hose, and the torch with an assortment of various-sized tips. Goggles or other eye protection, a sparklighter, and a wrench having openings for all of the threaded connections are essential accessories. Most manufacturers offer kits with all these items in one package. The gas cylinders are not considered part of this package because, as mentioned earlier, they usually belong to the company that manufactures the gas. A hand truck for the cylinders is also an essential item, but it usually is sold separately.

The Regulators

The regulators for both gases operate on the same principle, but they are intentionally made not interchangeable, for reasons of safety. The connections to the cylinders are of different sizes, and left-hand threads are used on the connections to the acetylene hose; left-hand threads also are used on the hose connection to the torch handle. This arrangement completely eliminates the possibiity of making a wrong connection anywhere in the system.

A cross-sectional view of a single-stage regulator is shown in Figure 5-4. The important part of the regulator is the valve that controls the flow of gas as it is needed. This is done by the adjusting spring and the compensating spring. In use, the adjusting screw is turned in against the adjusting spring until the desired pressure shows on the low-pressure gauge. This action releases gas to the low-pressure chamber of the regulator, from which it flows through the hose to the torch. As long as the torch valve is open, the flow of gas will continue. Closing the torch valve causes a pressure increase in the low-pressure chamber, which overcomes the pressure of the adjusting spring and closes the valve.

The operation of a two-stage regulator is similar to that of a single-stage regulator, except that the pressure is stepped down in two stages instead of one. The first stage reduces the pressure to a predetermined level, and the second reduces it to whatever figure the adjusting screw is set. The two-stage regulator may be expected to provide more exact control of pressure and to last longer than a single-stage regulator.

The Hose

The hose used in gas welding is made especially for the purpose. It must be flexible, nonporous, and have sufficient strength to withstand the pressure of the gases. Under no circumstances should an air hose or hoses intended for oil be substituted for welding hose, because of the danger of explosion.

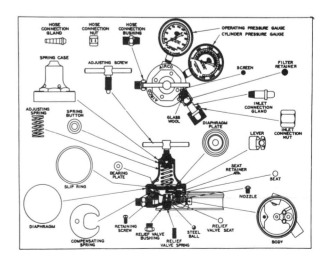

5-4 Single-stage regulator parts.

Separate hoses may be used for acetylene and oxygen, but it is the general practice to use twin, or coupled, hoses because they are easier to handle. Both hoses are of the same size, but they differ in color and the threaded connections with which they are fitted. The acetylene hose is usually red and always is fitted with left-hand threaded connections. The left-hand thread may be identified easily by a groove around the outside of the brass end fitting. The oxygen hose may be either green or black and is fitted with right-hand threaded connections. In replacing these fittings, which is sometimes necessary, it is important to make certain that the correct fitting is used.

Ten feet is about the minimum length of hose practical for work on an automobile. Much less movement of the outfit will be required if a longer hose is used. However, a hose that is to long creates both a housekeeping problem and a safety hazard. In determining the length of hose required, the connections under which it will be used should be considered.

The Torch

Perhaps the most important part of the welding outfit, the torch mixes the acetylene and oxygen in the proper proportions, burns the mixture at the end of the tip, and serves as a means of directing the flame onto the work. To perform these functions, the torch requires connections for the hoses, valves, gas passages, mixing head, and various sizes of tips. The complete unit must be assembled so that a suitable handle is provided for holding the torch as it is manipulated on the work. A torch of the type commonly used in body shops is shown in Figure 5-5.

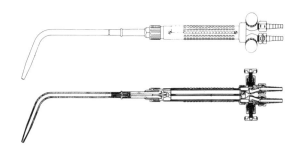

5-5 Oxyacetylene torch assembly.

Most manufacturers of welding equipment design their torches so that they consist of three basic units: the torch handle, the mixing head, and the interchangeable tips. But some torches are designed so that they consist of only two units: the handle and a mixing head combined with each separate tip.

The torch handle includes the hose connections, valves, and gas passages and is threaded on the front end so that the mixing chamber can be attached. Internal and external seats are provided on the handle and mixing head so that a tight connection is made for each gas passage when the mixing head is installed properly.

Most heavy-duty torch handles are designed with the valves at the rear end, and many light-duty torches are designed with the valves at the front end. Not all manufacturers of welding equipment follow this practice, however. Some light-duty torches are made with valves at the rear end, and some of the early heavy-duty torches were made with front-end valves.

The use of a single mixing head with all sizes of tips is an economy measure. For most work it is satisfactory and saves on the original investment. The use of separate mixers for each tip is desirable, if the volume of work will justify the extra investment.

In addition to opening and shutting off the flow of gases, the valves provide a means of making fine adjustment of the flame. The adjustment of one valve is dependent on the other, because the flow of gases must be kept in proportion regardless of the size of the flame.

Common-sense care and a few simple precautions are all that is needed for trouble-free operation from any good torch. Rough handling should be avoided. The torch should never be used as a lever or bar to push metal into place for welding. When not in use, it should be hung up or put in a safe place to avoid accidental damage. Probably the worst abuse that a torch is exposed to in a body shop is laying it on the floor when working on the lower part of the body; it may be damaged either by being stepped on or by heavy tools being dropped on it. Such abuse can bend the valve stems or tip or even do worse damage.

In changing tips, care should be taken to avoid nicking or scratching the mating surfaces of the connection of the mixing chamber to the handle. Mixing chambers not in use, particularly on torches that have them combined with separate tips, often are damaged by not being cared for properly. They should have a storage place where they will be protected. When mixing chambers are being attached to the handle, they should be inspected to see that there is no dirt on the mating surfaces of the connection.

Torch valves should never be tightened so that they are difficult to loosen. To do so will damage the seat. After the seat becomes damaged, it may not be possible to shut off the gas completely even though the valve is turned too tight. The same rule applies to the sleeve nut that holds the mixing chamber in place.

SETTING UP THE OXYACETYLENE WELDING OUTFIT

To ensure safe operation and avoid troubles such as leaks or plugged orifices, a definite sequence should be followed in setting up a new outfit and putting it into operation. Essentially the same steps should be followed in returning an outfit to use after it has been disconnected for some time, or if there is the possibility that dust or dirt could have entered the passages. The sequence is:

1. Place the oxygen and acetylene cylinders on the truck and chain them securely. Or, if a stationary installation is to be used, be sure that the cylinders are fastened in an upright position.

2. Remove the safety caps and put them where they will be available when needed.

3. Inspect the end of the inlet gland on each regulator and the seats in the outlets of both cylinder valves. If any foreign material is found, wipe it off. The eraser on a lead pencil makes an excellent tool for wiping out the seat in the cylinder valve.

4. Open and close both cylinder valves to blow out any dirt or dust that may have entered the valve passage. Close the valves as quickly as possible to prevent the escape of an excessive amount of gas.

5. Connect both regulators. Do not attach hoses.

6. Be sure that the adjusting screws are released, then open the cylinder valves, note the pressure on the high-pressure gauge, and close the valves.

7. Check for leaks by watching the gauge for pressure drop. If time permits, the gauge should be left under pressure for several minutes. If pressure holds steady, ignore Step 8.

8. If pressure drops, it will be caused by one of the following conditions: (a) leaking connection, (b) creeping regulator valve, or (c) a leak in the regulator. Retightening the cylinder connection may stop the leak; otherwise the regulator should be serviced by a competent repairman before being used.

9. Blow out the regulator by turning the adjusting screw in far enough to release a small quantity of gas, then release the adjusting screw.

10. Attach the hoses to the regulators. Do not attach to the torch.

11. Blow out the hoses by releasing enough gas to carry any dust or dirt to the other end.

12. Attach the torch handle without the mixing head.

13. Blow out the torch handle. Open each valve separately to avoid possible fire hazard.

14. Check the hoses and connections for leaks by adjusting both regulators to maximum working pressures (acetylene, 15 psi [103 kPa]; oxygen, 15 to 30 psi [103 to 207 kPa]), then close both the torch and the cylinder valves and watch the gauges for pressure drop. This should also be left under pressure for several minutes. Retighten the connections if the pressure drops.

15. Attach the mixing head; if separate tip is used, leave it off.

16. Blow out the mixing head, using maximum oxygen pressure. Check both gases for smooth flow.

17. Attach separate tip, if used.

18. Light the torch.

This procedure normally would be followed only once, when the outfit is new. It will not take very long, unless trouble is encountered with leaks. If leaks are present, however, they must be eliminated. With a leak, there is more involved than just the loss of the gas— there is the danger of fire or explosion.

When an outfit has been laid aside for some time and is being put back into use again, the need for blowing it out in the sequence listed above is greater than with a new outfit. This is particularly important if there is any doubt as to how it has been cared for. Even though the hoses have not been disconnected from the regulators and the torch, the complete outfit should be disconnected and each piece blown out separately. This will ensure that dirt in the regulator will not be blown through the hoses into the valves and mixing head.

Each time a full cylinder is installed in the outfit, the cylinder valve should be blown out and the mating surface of the gland inspected for foreign material, particularly oil or grease. After the regulator is installed, the adjusting screw should be checked to see that it is loose, then the cylinder valve should be opened and closed to check for leaks. If the high pressure drops without affecting the low-pressure gauge, it is probably because the connection to the cylinder is leaking. If so, it is best to remove the regulator and recheck the mating surfaces of the connection before applying excessive force to pull the connection tight with a big wrench. Most often, the trouble will be surface dirt that has escaped detection. To leave it there and pull the connection tighter may not stop the leak, but it probably will damage the outfit.

In changing the cylinder, it is important to be careful with the regulator so that it will not be knocked around or dropped. It is especially important that the mating surfaces do not come into contact with any material that will contaminate them. Such precautions are only a matter of common sense and awareness of the problem.

LIGHTING AND ADJUSTING THE TORCH

Lighting and adjusting the torch flame is a matter of making a series of adjustments in the proper sequence. Most of the sheet metal welding operations require the flame to be adjusted so that equal parts of acetylene and oxygen are being burned. Starting with an outfit that previously has been shut off and bled, the procedure for opening it up, lighting and adjusting the flame properly is as follows:

1. Check both regulator adjusting screws to see that they are released.

2. Open the oxygen cylinder valve; keep turning the hand wheel until the open seat position is reached. Several turns will be required.

3. Open the acetylene cylinder valve one-half turn.

4. Open the oxygen valve on the torch about one-quarter turn.

5. Turn the oxygen regulator adjusting screw inward until the required pressure is indicated on the low-pressure gauge.

6. Close the oxygen valve.

7. Open the acetylene valve on the torch about one-quarter turn.

8. Turn the acetylene regulator adjusting screw inward until the low-pressure gauge reads the same as the oxygen.

9. Use the sparklighter to light the escaping acetylene.

10. Adjust the acetylene valve until the yellow flame begins to push away from the tip (see Fig. 5-6).

5-6 Adjustment of the acetylene flame before the oxygen valve is opened.

5-7 The neutral flame.

11. Open and adjust the oxygen valve until all but a slight trace of the long, feathery flame disappears, leaving a clearly defined, intense-blue cone of neutral flame burning on the end of the tip (see Fig. 5-7).

The exact pressures to which the oxygen and acetylene regulators should be adjusted are determined by tip size. The reading on the gauge always will be at least equal to the number of the tip, and with some makes of equipment it may be higher. Many welders use approximately 5 pounds of pressure (34.5 kPa) for the tips up to number 5, and increase the pressure to the tip number when larger tips are used. Higher pressures, unless excessive, will do no harm, except to make it more difficult to adjust the torch flame.

The size of the neutral flame produced with any tip can be varied to some degree by adjusting the amount of gases released. The variation in size that can be obtained in this manner is not as great as the difference in size of flame produced by the next larger or smaller tips. For any one tip size, changing the flame size can be done only by changing the speed of the gas flowing through the orifice. If the gas flows too fast, it will blow the flame out, because the gas will be moving faster than the flame can consume it; if it flows too slowly, there will be backfiring, making it difficult to weld.

Some tendency to backfiring is always present in a gas welding operation because of the molten particles of metal that fly from the puddle. When one of these flies into the tip orifice, it extinguishes the flame momentarily by blocking the flow of gas. In most instances, the blocking action is only momentary, because the particle is cooling and shrinking, and gas pressure is building up against it. As the flow starts again, the gas is re-ignited by the molten metal in the puddle. The result will be a minor explosion having sufficient force to blow molten metal out of the puddle; it will make a sound much like a rifle shot. All of this action takes place within a fraction of a second. Occa-

sionally, backfiring will be repeated with almost machine-gun rapidity.

Slowing the gas too much also can permit the flame to enter the tip orifice and follow the passage into the mixing head, making an angry, buzzing sound. When this occurs, the valves should be shut off immediately. It is best to shut the acetylene off first, because the fire cannot burn without fuel. Before relighting, the tip should be inspected for partly blocked orifices and both valves opened separately to be sure that the gas flows freely. The flame should be adjusted so that it is large enough to prevent the condition from recurring, or, if a smaller flame is needed, a smaller tip should be installed.

Adjusting the flame for paddle soldering and some other heating operations is simply a matter of using less oxygen so that a long, feathery flame is produced. The flame may be used at any adjustment that is desired, but it is best to avoid using a yellow flame, because it will tend to deposit soot on the surface being heated.

Acetylene burning alone will give off a large quantity of sooty, black smoke, unless it is forced out of the tip orifice fast enough to mix with the air. The soot will rise into the air and later settle, making a very undesirable mess. This condition may be avoided by opening the valve wide enough to cause the gas to mix with the air and burn clean as soon as it is lighted. It is not uncommon for the beginner to leave the torch smoking while he tries to decide which adjustment to make next. He should be trained to open the valve past the point of heavy smoking as soon as he strikes the light. Proper flame adjustment cannot be made until the acetylene valve is opened to this position, so it is simply a matter of doing it without hesitation to avoid the unnecessary soot.

THE OXYACETYLENE FLAME

The primary characteristic of the oxyacetylene flame that makes it suitable for welding is its intense, high temperature—about 5,850° F. (3,232° C.) when adjusted properly for welding. Temperatures up to 6,300° F. (3,482° C.) can be developed by adjusting the flame to an excess of oxygen; this higher temperature is not suitable for welding steel, however, because of the ill effects it has on molten steel.

The oxyacetylene flame actually consists of two flames: the intense-blue inner cone and the sheath flame. The highest temperature is produced in the blue inner cone. The temperature of the sheath flame, which extends several inches beyond the inner cone, is much lower. The high temperature of the inner cone is used for practically all torch operations.

Three basic torch flames, which may be considered flame types, are made by adjusting the torch valves to vary the ratio of oxygen and acetylene being used: (1) neutral flame, (2) carburizing flame, and (3) oxidizing flame.

The neutral flame is used for practically all welding operations on mild steel. In most instances, either the carburizing or the oxidizing flame will be harmful to steel. Only a very slight resetting of either valve will change the flame from one type to the other. For this reason, it is essential for the beginner to be familiar with the characteristics of all three.

The Neutral Flame

The term neutral flame indicates a flame that has been adjusted so it does not throw off either carbon (from the acetylene) or oxygen to contaminate the molten metal. When the flame is neutral, the torch valves have been adjusted so the volume of acetylene and oxygen entering the mixing chamber is in the exact ratio needed to produce complete combustion. When adjusting the flame setting, this condition can be recognized by the disappearance of the feathery streamers, leaving a sharply defined, intense-blue inner cone.

The neutral flame will produce a clear, clean-appearing puddle that flows easily because the surrounding sheath flame has nothing in it to affect the molten metal. The sheath flame then serves as a protective mantle to prevent burning of the molten metal by oxygen in the surrounding air.

The temperature of the neutral flame, approximately 5,850° F. (3,232° C.) at the tip of the cone, drops rapidly in a very short distance; the midsection of the sheath flame will be about 3,800° F. (2,093° C.) and the outer end will be about 2,300° F. (1,260° C.). Thus, it is obvious that the inner cone should be held quite close to the puddle to obtain rapid melting.

The Carburizing Flame

The term carburizing flame indicates a flame that has been adjusted so it throws off unburned carbon into the sheath flame. The pressure of this condition can be recognized easily by the feathery streamers extending from the tip of the inner cone.

The carburizing flame, by the addition of carbon to the molten metal from the flame, will cause the molten metal to boil and lose the clear appearance it had under the neutral flame. A weld made with a carburizing flame will be brittle when cold.

An experiment to demonstrate the effect of the carburizing flame can be made very easily. Adjust the flame so the feathery streamers extend at least ½ inch (12.5 mm) beyond the inner cone. Then, play this flame on one corner of a piece of sheet metal, keeping it in the position for the neutral flame, so the feathery streamers actually strike the heated surface. While the piece is at bright red temperature, plunge it into cold water. A file test will prove that the metal is much harder because carbon has been added. This experiment can be varied by keeping the carburizing flame on the hot metal for different lengths of time. If the flame is kept on long enough before quenching the metal in the water, the heated spot will become so hard it will snap like a piece of glass.

A slight amount of carburizing may not be particularly injurious to a weld in mild steel, but it is not desirable; if there is excessive carburizing, the weld definitely will be weakened. On some of the nonferrous metals, such as nickel and Monel metal, the carburizing flame sometimes is used without ill results.

Using a carburizing flame to heat metal for the shrinking operation can cause considerable trouble, because hard spots will result. When the file strikes these spots, it will chatter instead of cut and be damaged in the process.

The Oxidizing Flame

An oxidizing flame throws off excess oxygen into the sheath flame. There are no visible streamers, but the flame may be recognized easily by the harsh hissing sound it makes, and the excessive foaming and sparking it causes in the puddle. It can be recognized also as the flame is being adjusted by a shrinking of the inner cone and a purplish color.

The oxidizing flame has no use in welding steel. Excess oxygen will cause the molten metal to burn. Therefore, the slightest trace of excess oxygen should be avoided, because the weld will be weakened proportionally.

The oxidizing flame sometimes is used for heating heavy parts to temperatures below the bright red heat range. It develops temperatures up to approximately 6,300° F. (3,482° C.), which is slightly more than the 5,850° F. (3,232° C.) of the neutral flame.

OXYACETYLENE FUSION WELDING PROCEDURE

The oxyacetylene fusion weld is made by manipulating the torch flame so that a puddle of molten metal is started and carried along the seam. Normally, a bead is built up by depositing molten metal from a filler rod as the puddle moves along. A filler rod is not always necessary, however, if there is enough metal on the edges to be welded so they will flow together and make a bead of sufficient strength without it.

Making a good weld is a matter of manipulating the flame properly and depositing the filler metal in the proper position at the proper time. To do this, the following conditions must be kept under control by the operator: (1) distance of the end of the flame from the work, (2) angle of flame to the line of the seam, (3) rate of travel, (4) side motion (weaving) of the torch, and (5) position of the filler rod end in relation to the puddle and flame.

Each of these conditions is discussed separately in the following sections.

Flame Distance

The distance of the flame end from the work can vary for different welds. In most instances it should be quite close, but it should never touch the molten metal. The approximate distance is shown in Figure 5-8.

The actual distance is determined by the temperature and the spread of heat. The closer the flame is to the work, the higher the temperature will be, and the more it will be concentrated on a very small spot. If the flame is moved back from the work, the drop in temperature is quite rapid. For example, the temperature of the inner cone of the neutral flame is 5,850° F. (3,232° C.), but the temperature at the end of the sheath flame is only 2,300° F. (1,260° C.). When a small tip suitable for welding sheet metal is used, this drop occurs in a distance of 2 or 3 inches (5 to 8 cm).

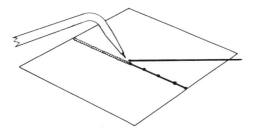

5-8   Angle of the flame to, and its distance from, the work.

In welding sheet metal, it is desirable to raise the temperature of the puddle to the melting point as quickly as possible and also to prevent the spread of heat into the surrounding metal as much as possible. This would seem to indicate that the flame should be held so the inner cone almost touches the metal. However, it is quite difficult to hold the flame in that position without actually touching it to the molten metal occasionally. There is the additional problem of the blast of the hot sheath flame gases that blow against the molten metal in the puddle. A much safer practice is to hold the inner cone away from the puddle just slightly less than its length; thus, a smaller flame would be held closer to the puddle than a larger one. At this distance, the blast effect of the flame is slowed down, and the possibility of accidentally touching the hot puddle is avoided.

Distance affects penetration to some extent. Even on light sheet metal, time is required for heat to flow through from one surface to the other. On heavier metal, time is even more important. By holding the distance about equal to the length of the inner cone, this needed time is provided. If it is held much closer, it may be difficult to obtain full penetration—only the upper surface will be melted.

Greater distance may be required when welding light metal to heavy metal. In such instances, the flame must be directed so that the heavy metal is brought up to the melting point without overheating the light so it melts away. However, other factors as well as distance must be considered when such welding problems are encountered.

Flame Angle

The angle of the flame to the work will vary accord-ing to the job. Actually, two angles must be considered: (1) the angle of the flame to the surface and (2) the angle of the flame to the line of the seam.

In making a simple butt weld on relatively flat stock, the angle of the flame to the puddle (shown in Fig. 5-8) should be somewhere between 30 and 45 degrees and pointed directly down the line of the seam. If increased penetration is needed, the angle should be increased; if less penetration is needed, the angle should be reduced.

Pointing the flame directly down the seam line on a butt weld will preheat both sides evenly. If the torch is turned to either side, that side will be heated more than the other. This will cause unequal expansion and tend to separate the edges even though they are tack-welded together.

On lap welds or when welding light metal to heavy, a different condition will be found. If the torch is pointed down the line of a lap weld seam, the flame will tend to melt the exposed edge of the upper piece faster than it melts the metal it covers. The answer to this problem is to hold the flame so it is turned slightly away from the edge, and to hold the filler rod so it acts as a shield for the exposed edge. This position of flame and filler rod is shown in Figure 5-9. Note that the operator has bent the filler rod so that his hand will be away from the heat of the hot blast from the torch.

In welding light to heavy metal, it always will be necessary to hold the flame so it points toward the heavy piece. The greater the difference in thickness, the more the flame should be pointed toward the heavy piece. It is a matter of experimenting to find the angle and distance from the puddle that will bring both edges to the melting point at the same time.

Rate of Travel

The rate of travel governs the width of the puddle and, to some degree, the depth of the penetration. Holding the flame on one spot without moving it will cause the puddle to grow larger until it melts through; moving it along the seam too fast will not heat the metal fast enough to make a puddle. Obviously, the proper speed is somewhere between these two extremes.

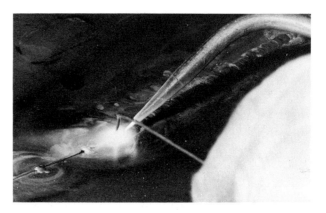

5-9   Position of the flame and filler rod in welding a butt joint. Bending the rod permits the operator to keep his hand away from the heat.

With the torch held at the proper angle and distance, the rate of travel can be adjusted easily by watching the width of the puddle. If it becomes too narrow, travel should slow down; if it spreads too wide, the forward movement should be speeded up.

Lack of confidence many times prevents a beginner from determining the proper rate of travel. Just as soon as the puddle grows a little too large, the novice will pull the flame completely away from the puddle, disrupting everything. All that is needed is to move along the seam a little faster.

Weaving the Flame

Weaving the flame from side to side will spread the heat over a wider path and slow the forward travel. The result will be deeper penetration and more time to add filler metal if a heavy bead is desired.

The weaving motion may be either a straight back-and-forth motion that, when combined with the forward motion, creates a zigzag effect, or it may be a spiral motion. In either case, the result is essentially the same.

When welding the light gauge metal that is found in body panels, it is largely a matter of operator's choice whether the flame should weave or follow a straight line. Mostly, it is necessary only to keep the flame steady and move forward just fast enough to permit the puddle to spread to the desired width. This spreads the heat into the adjoining metal less than weaving will. The result will be slightly faster travel and less heat distortion.

Many welders weave the flame whether it is necessary or not, because they find that they hold it more steadily that way. If so, it is better to weave than to attempt to hold the torch in a straight line.

When welding heavy metal, such as that found in some of the brackets and structural members, weaving is necessary to obtain the required penetration.

Filler Rod Position

The position of the filler rod in relation to both the puddle and the flame varies according to the type of weld being made. In making a simple butt weld, the rod need only be in such a position that the end of it may be melted and deposited in the puddle. Best results occur when the rod is held at a 45 degree angle to the surface and in line with the seam. The end should be kept quite close to the puddle so that as molten drops form on the rod, they may be deposited with a slight downward motion. As the weld progresses along the seam, the rod will describe a continuous up-and-down motion that should never raise the rod above the flame so that the end cools. If the rod melts too fast, it should be held slightly farther from the flame.

The use of the filler rod as a shield to prevent melting away of the exposed edge of a lap weld was mentioned briefly in the discussion on the torch angle. This practice is necessary in many cases where the edge of one piece is exposed more than the other. In making many

such welds, the end of the rod will have to be kept in contact with the edge instead of raising it. In such cases, the filler will be fed into the puddle continuously instead of by a series of drops deposited by raising and lowering the rod.

BUTT WELDING

In learning to make a butt weld, one of the problems is to manipulate the torch and filler rod as described in the preceding sections. It is also necessary to position the pieces to be welded so that the edges are in the proper alignment and spacing, and to tack weld them so they will stay in alignment while the welding operation is in progress. When these steps have been performed properly, making the weld becomes a simple matter of making the weld bead.

Although neither the alignment of the edges nor the tack welding of the seam presents any difficult problems, each is important enough to justify separate discussion. Failure to perform either one properly can result in a very difficult welding problem.

Small pieces of metal have been used in the illustrations in the following section dealing with these subjects, because they they make satisfactory practice material for the beginner.

Alignment of the Edges

Alignment of the edges to be welded means that they should be spaced properly. With sheet metal of the thickness used in body panels, proper spacing is primarily a matter of making certain that the pieces are not separated too widely. Full penetration of such metal is not difficult to obtain when the edges are butted together tightly. Some space between the edges will make very little difference; however, a gap wider than the thickness of the filler rod is difficult to fill because of the tendency to melt back the edges. Extra-wide gaps will result in extra-heavy beads that overheat and warp the surface, plus requiring excessive time.

When welding butt joints in heavier metal, it will be necessary to provide some space between the edges to get full penetration. A good rule is that for metal 1/16 inch (1.6 mm) thick or thicker, the space between the edges should be about the same as the thickness.

The importance of having the edges positioned so that the surfaces are flush is much greater on thin metal, such as body panels, than it is on heavier material. If one edge is much higher than the other, it will be exposed to much more heat. Unless the flame is diverted to heat the lower, less-exposed edge, it will melt the exposed edge away, leaving a hole that will be difficult to fill. Diverting the flame will change the angle so that more heat will be directed to the piece that was low, overheating and expanding it more than the other. The result will be uneven heat distortion that will leave the finished job in a much worse warped condition than if the edges had been heated properly.

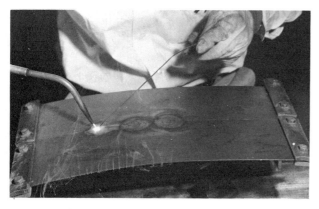

5-10 Tack welding. The flame should be directed toward the tack welds made previously. The smoke is caused by oil on the panel.

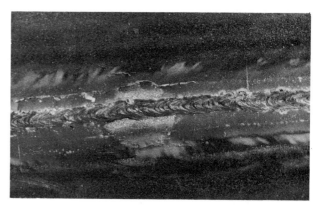

5-12 Rippled appearance of the weld being made in Fig. 5-11.

Tack Welding

Tack welding is necessary for any seam that is more than an inch (25 mm) long. Without tack welding, the preheating effect of the flame ahead of the puddle will cause the edges of the pieces being welded to expand and be forced out of alignment. Depending on the circumstances, the misalignment may be either a wide separation of the edges or an overlap. In either case, the result will not be an acceptable job.

The torch manipulation in making a tack weld is essentially the same as for making a seam weld, except that the torch angle should be more nearly vertical. Tack welding always should be started and carried out so that it causes the least possible heat distortion. In the operation shown in Figure 5-10, the first weld was made in the approximate center, and the third one is in the process of being made. Note that the flame is being pointed so that most of the preheating effect is directed toward the welds that have been made. These welds hold the pieces together so they cannot separate. If the torch were turned in the opposite direction, the warpage ahead of the flame would be much more, because the edges are not held.

Tacking of the other end of this seam will require the angle of the flame to be in the opposite direction. If these pieces had not been held securely in the practice

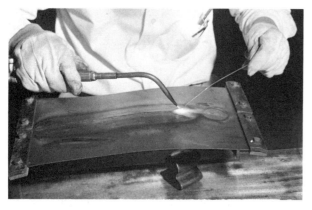

5-11 Welding the tacked seam. Warpage is due to heat.

fixture, it would have been necessary to have tacked the ends first. When tacking an end, the flame always should be directed off the edge, heating the surfaces as little as possible.

The size of the tack weld should be kept as small as possible in order to cause the least possible amount of heat distortion. This is particularly important if the final weld will be finished to a smooth surface. Heat distortion that has been avoided does not have to be corrected.

Controlling heat distortion can be done best with the hammer and dolly block, which were not used in Figure 5-10. They never should be used on a tack until it has cooled well below red heat. Often it is better to wait until the metal has cooled to nearly normal temperature. It is difficult to establish rules to avoid trouble, however, because so much depends on experience. If the tack weld is worked while it is too hot, it will tend to shrink too much; if it is not worked hot enough, it may leave some distortion in the panel. The beginner must learn to judge the conditions for himself.

Welding the Seam

Welding the seam after tack-welding simply involves running a bead to overlap the edges of both pieces. This should be just a matter of maintaining the torch at the proper angle, distance, and rate of travel as the rod is fed into the puddle. No weaving motion of the torch was necessary in making the seam shown in Figure 5-11. Weaving on a seam such as this would only slow the forward motion and heat the adjoining metal more, creating more heat distortion than necessary.

The seam shown being welded in Figure 5-11 was made without stopping. Note that the area of the puddle has bulged upward sharply, and the area at the start of the seam already has started to draw out of shape. This will be warped badly after it finally cools. The warpage could have been reduced considerably by welding only a short distance and stopping so that the metal could cool. The idea would be to avoid excessive heat in the panel by allowing it to escape into the air.

Use of the dolly and hammer to work the area as it

5-13 Underside of the weld shown in Fig. 5-11. The scale is heavier because this side does not have the protection of the flame.

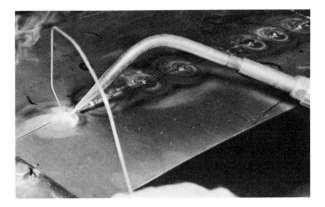

5-14 Using the filler rod to protect the upper edge of a lapped seam being tack welded.

was being welded could have prevented most of the drawing action in this weld. The operation is partly one of straightening and partly a matter of stretching the upset effect of the hot metal. Both are necessary on a weld such as this, if it is to be left in a smooth condition.

Figure 5-12 shows a close-up view of a short length of the upper side of the weld in Figure 5-11, and Figure 5-13 shows the underside of the same section. Note that the ripple action is relatively uniform and raised very little above the level of the surfaces on each side. The cracks showing on each side are in the weld scale; such cracks will be found adjoining any weld. Also note in Figure 5-13 that the weld scale is heavier and more cracked and blistered than that on the upper surface. This condition, also found on any weld, is due to the lack of a sheath flame on the underside to protect it from the oxygen in the air.

The weld bead shown here is a good example of the type the beginner should try to make. Many authorities have recommended that the weld bead should be built up above the surface level as a guarantee against breakage. Such a bead is a disadvantage for a weld that must be finished smooth, even though the final finishing will be done by filling to cover the weld. The experience of most welders is that breaks occur in the metal beside the weld rather than in the bead. For these reasons, it is recommended that the weld beads used on sheet metal be made as nearly flush with the surface as possible. They will be made faster, will hold, and will be easier to finish.

MAKING A LAP WELD

A lap weld is similar to a butt weld in that it requires tacking and a bead to be laid down on the joint. It requires more care and skill to make, however, because tacking must be done more carefully and the upper edge must be protected throughout the operation.

The tacking requires more care because of the overlapped position of the pieces. In a properly aligned butt joint, inward movement of one piece is blocked by the other; in the lap joint, there is nothing to block move-

ment of either piece. The result is that there will be enough movement to change the alignment before the puddle forms. Unless care is taken with the subsequent tacks, this movement will increase with each one.

This tacking problem is so severe that on a long body panel lap weld it is necessary to hold the metal by means of rivets or metal screws before starting to tack weld. If this is not done, it will be very difficult to prevent movement that will affect the shape of the panel. Screws 2 or 3 inches (5–8 cm) apart usually will be sufficient.

The tack welds shown in Figure 5-14 were made without metal screws, but this job is not representative of the problem on a body panel, because the pieces are free on the ends and relatively narrow. This tack-welding operation was done in the same sequence as the tack welding shown on the butt weld (see Fig. 5-10). The only difference is in the flame angle and the filler rod position. Note that the flame is turned toward the exposed edge of the upper piece in Figure 5-14, instead of pointing down the line of the joint, as in Figure 5-10. This flame angle requires the filler rod to be kept between the flame tip and the exposed edge of the upper piece to serve as a shield. If the flame is not held at this angle and the filler rod held in this position, either the puddle will be too far from the edge of the upper piece, or the edge of the upper piece will melt back faster than the puddle can be started in the lower piece. In either case, too much filler rod will be required to make the tack. The result will be a rough weld and excessive heat distortion, because the flame will be kept on the work too long.

In welding the joint in Figure 5-14, the rod is kept in the same position as for tack welding, because the exposed edge of the upper piece must be shielded from the flame continuously. The flame should be turned more nearly down the line of the seam so the puddle will be kept moving forward. most of the time, it will be better not to raise and lower the rod into the puddle, as is commonly done in welding a butt joint. Instead, the rod is fed into the puddle as it melts away. If the rod is raised only momentarily, the exposed upper edge may melt away faster than the gap can be filled.

5-15 Torch and filler rod position for welding an inside corner.

Sometimes it may be desirable to weave the flame slightly in making a lap weld, but usually it will be best to keep it steady as it moves forward.

MAKING AN OUTSIDE CORNER WELD

The outside corner weld is the easiest of all welding operations to make with the oxyacetylene torch, because the angle of the surfaces prevents excessive pickup of heat from the sheath flame. To practice, simply prop two pieces of metal together to form the corner and fuse them together. Tacking will be required on long pieces, but short lengths, up to 3 inches, can be welded without it.

Unless it is desired to build up the bead to keep a square corner, the filler rod is usually not necessary in making a corner weld. The edges will fuse and run together easily, leaving a rounded corner without filler.

The flame should be directed down the line of the seam so that the preheating effect is divided evenly on both pieces. Turning it to either side will cause that side to expand more than the other and separate the edges, making the welding operation much more difficult.

MAKING AN INSIDE CORNER WELD

The inside corner weld is the most difficult to make, because the corner restricts the flow of hot gases from the torch, causing overheating. Unless extra care is taken, the tendency will be to burn through the surfaces on one or both sides of the joint before the puddle can be made and filled in the corner. Because of this condition, it is recommended that the beginner wait to start practicing on this joint until he has developed a fair degree of skill in making the more simple welds.

In most instances, the inside corner will be made with one piece in the flat, or horizontal, position, and the other vertical. It will be much easier to make a smooth, even weld if the torch tip is held at an angle much closer to the horizontal piece, and the end of the rod is held above the end of the flame, as shown in Figure 5-15.

Tacking and welding should be done in approximately the same positions.

Care should be taken to avoid undercutting the upper edge of the bead. The metal at the edge of the puddle will tend to thin if it is too hot. If the thinned section is not filled with molten metal from the rod, it will be left weak. Undercutting does not present a problem on the lower edge of the bead, because the hot metal will flow down and fill any thin spots.

Holding the tip of the flame as close to the puddle as possible without actually touching it will simplify the problem slightly, because the heat will be concentrated where it is needed, deep in the corner. It also will be desirable to use a smaller tip than required for welding metal of the same thickness in a lap or butt joint.

MAKING A "BUTTONHOLE" WELD

A "buttonhole" weld, shown in Figure 5-16, is made by melting a hole in the upper piece of a lapped joint, starting a puddle in the lower piece, and adding filler metal to refill the hole. It requires careful manipulation of both the torch flame and the filler rod. However, the beginner who has learned to make a lap weld should not have particular difficulty in making the "buttonhole."

The problem in making a weld of this type is in preventing the hole from enlarging too much as the puddle is started in the lower surface and the hole is being refilled. Enlargement can be kept to a minimum by using as small a flame as possible and keeping it almost vertical to the surface. The rod should be kept close to the flame as the hole is being melted so that filler material can be melted into the hole instantly when needed. As the hole is being filled, the filler rod should be shifted to shield the edge of the hole at any point where the metal begins to melt away too fast.

Figure 5-17 shows the underside of the welds shown in Figure 5-16. Note that there is considerably less evidence of the puddle than on the upper side. This is the way it should look. If too much metal is added to the puddle, it will only sink through below the surface, where it will do no good.

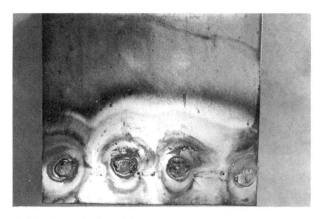

5-16 Buttonhole welds.

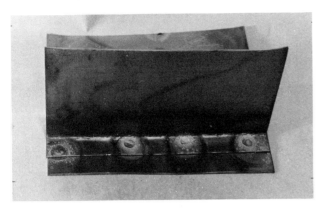

5-17 Underside of the buttonhole welds shown in Fig. 5-16.

BRAZING

Brazing is any metal joining process in which a nonferrous filler material is used to join other metals that have a higher melting point. Brazing and soldering are similar processes but fall into different temperature ranges. Processes using metals that melt at temperatures below 800° F. (427° C.) are called soldering; processes using metals that melt above that temperature are called brazing. The term brazing came into use because the original brazing materials were copper-based alloys, bronze or brass, which were used to join iron and steel. The welding industry has extended its meaning to include a process in which a metal in the brazing temperature range is used to join another metal with a higher melting point. For example, aluminum alloys are produced with a range of melting points wide enough to permit one to melt and flow onto another in the same manner that copper-based metals flow onto steel. This is called aluminum brazing, although there is no brass or bronze involved. Other metals, particularly silver, can be used in the same manner.

In the following discussion the term brazing is used in reference to the use of conventional, copper-based brazing material to join sheet steel.

Braze welding is a term used by the welding industry in reference to a welding operation in which the brazing material is used to fill a prepared open joint or build up a surface. It has little use in body repair operations, but a poorly prepared brazed joint may be simply a braze weld because penetration is not obtained.

PRINCIPLES OF BRAZING

Brazing is made possible by the property of many of the nonferrous metals that allows them to diffuse or penetrate into other metals when the proper temperature and surface conditions are available. The proper temperature conditions are that the copper-based filler material must be melted but not heated above the melting point, and the metal to which it is applied must be heated to approximately the same temperature. Brazing is done only on metals that have a higher melting point than the brazing material; the metal being welded is never heated to the melting point.

To obtain the proper surface conditions, simply clean to remove foreign material, and use flux to clean the surface chemically and exclude atmospheric oxygen while the molten metal is being deposited. Cleaning to remove paint, rust, or other foreign material may be done mechanically by grinding, scraping, wire brushing, or similar means, but it also can be done by means of a strong flux. Usually, such cleaning is done mechanically, because of the problem of neutralizing the chemicals in the flux residue after they have been used. After the surface has been cleaned mechanically, it can be brazed with fluxes that will not cause corrosion after use.

When brazing is done properly, the molten brazing material wets and penetrates into the surface to which it is applied. This penetration is sometimes called diffusion, because the two metals intermix to cause an alloying action at their interface. The alloy thus formed is often stronger than either single metal. Figure 5-18 represents a cross section of a deposit of brazing material on a piece of sheet metal. Arrow 1 indicates the metal; 2, the brazing material; and 3, the alloy at the interface.

The strongest brazed joints are made by reducing the space between the surfaces so that the alloy layers join. The space necessary for this action when brazing steel is from 0.003 to 0.005 inch (0.07 to 0.13 mm). To understand how joints of this type can be made, it is essential to know the action of the flux and capillary action that draws the molten material into the joint.

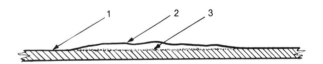

5-18 Cross-sectional sketch of a deposit of brazing material on sheet metal: arrow 1 indicates the sheet metal; 2, the deposit of brazing material; 3, the interface.

BRAZING FLUX

The original brazing flux was prepared in either powder or paste form. The powdered form was used much more than the paste except for very fine work, as in silver brazing. The operator dipped the heated end of the brazing rod into the powder so that a coating of flux would melt and adhere to it. As the filler rod was used to add molten metal to the puddle of brazing material, the flux would melt and run ahead.

Powdered flux has been almost completely replaced by flux-coated filler rod, eliminating the need for constant dipping into the powder can. The quality of the flux used for coating filler rods can vary, but much of it seems to produce better results than was obtained from the powdered type.

Flux can be added directly to the acetylene gas for industrial operations where the torch in in full-time use, but this is not practical for body shop where the torch is used for other welding more than for brazing.

Capillary Action

Caused by the attraction of any surface for any liquid that will wet it, capillary action can be seen in the everyday example of a glass tumbler partly filled with water; a thin film will rise on the sides of the glass about $1/32$ of an inch (0.8 mm) above the level of the rest of the water. This film of water rises against gravity because the surface of the glass attracts it. It rises only a short distance, however, because the attraction of the single surface is limited. A similar attraction will be found on the surface of other liquids in other containers. Molten brazing material will have a similar action in a steel container if the surface is clean and fluxed properly.

Two glass tumblers can be used for an experiment to show how proper spacing of surfaces can be used to fill a weld joint with molten brazing material. The tumblers may be either cylindrical or tapered, but the sides must be straight, and one should be small enough to fit into the other. Put a little water in the bottom of the larger glass and lower the smaller one into it until the bottom just touches the water. Capillary action will draw water on it above the surface level just as it has on the side of the larger one. This is the same action described in the preceding paragraph. Now, press the outside of the smaller glass against the inside of the larger one; a film of water will rise to the top of the smaller glass instantly in the narrow space between the surfaces of the glasses. This occurs because the combined attraction of both surfaces is so much greater than gravity. The action of molten brazing material will be similar in a properly spaced clean joint heated to the proper temperature.

In making this experiment, the effect of different spaces between the two tumblers should be noted. Moving the smaller one away from contact $1/16$ inch (1.6 mm) will permit the water to drop almost to its original level. As the space is closed, however, a point will be found that permits the water to rise almost instantly. This point will be only a few thousandths of an inch away from contact.

A similar result is obtained when brazing is done under ideal circumstances. Figure 5-19 represents a cross section through an ideal brazed joint. The surfaces have been very close together, but not actually touching—0.003 to 0.005 inch (0.07 to 0.13 mm) would be ideal. At this distance, the molten brazing material will flow into the joint just as water can be made to rise between the glass surfaces in the experiment just described.

Figure 5-20 represents the effect on capillary action of wide spacing and uneven heating. Note that this is the same as the joint in Figure 5-19, except for space between the surfaces. The brazing material has been drawn only part of the way into the joint and has fol-

lowed farther on the upper piece than on the lower. This is to be expected when brazing a seam that can be heated from one side only—usually the case with body seams that can be brazed satisfactorily. In many instances, there will be practically no penetration of the seam. This should not be accepted as unavoidable, however, because a good welder will learn to manipulate his flame and filler rod so that he obtains enough penetration to make the joint much stronger.

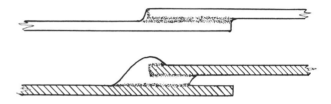

5-19 *(Top)* Cross-sectional view of an ideal brazed joint.

5-20 *(Bottom)* Cross-sectional view through a widely spaced brazed joint, showing the effect of reduced capillary action.

USES AND ADVANTAGES OF BRAZING

The primary use of brazing is in panel replacement to reweld joints originally electric spot welded when assembled in the factory. The advantage is that brazing causes less heat distortion than fusion welding, because the melting temperature of the copper-base alloys used as filler metal is much lower than the melting temperature of steel. Many such welds are located in low crown sections where the extreme heat of fusion welding with a torch flame will cause severe distortion. Most often, more work will be involved in relieving the heat distortion than in making the welds. Brazing sometimes will offer a means of preventing serious heat distortion and save the extra time required to relieve it.

There may be no advantage in brazing on a relatively high crown section that will not distort so readily. Also, it may be better to use proper electric welding equipment, if available, than to use brazing.

Another advantage of brazing is that it can eliminate the need for sealing, if the joint is brazed full length.

Brazing on automobile sheet metal repair should be restricted to overlapped seams. Some materials and methods may be used to make good butt joints, but they are not satisfactory or practical for repairing automobile bodies.

Four joint types suitable for brazing are shown in Figure 5-21. Joints similar to these will be found throughout the body structure of any automobile. A is a true lapped joint, and C is actually a variation of A. Similarly, B and D are variations of the same basic joint in which the flanges extend away from the surface.

To braze joints such as these so that the entire overlapped area is filled is often impractical when using the welding torch. In most instances, the repairman has to be satisfied with a partly filled joint and some build-up

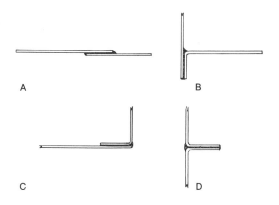

5-21 Four common variations of the lapped joint. Joints A and C are essentially the same, as are joints B and D.

of brazing material on the surface. The problem is to heat both sides of the joint uniformly so that the filler metal will flow by capillary action. If two torches are available, and there is reason to devote the extra effort to the operation, it can be done. Usually, though, only partial penetration into the joint will do.

A brazed joint of the type usually made on sheet metal panels is shown in Figure 5-22. This joint is over-lapped about ½ inch (12.5 mm). It was tested for pene-tration by cutting narrow strips across the joint and pulling them apart. The penetration was approximately one half of the overlap, or ¼ inch (6.3 mm). This amount of penetration would be adequate for any body joint welded satisfactorily by brazing.

The built-up bead over this joint makes the operation a combination of brazing and braze welding. The irreg-ular deposit on the surface of the bead is flux. Although it will do no harm to leave it in place, this may be chipped off if it is on a surface where it is undesirable.

STRENGTH OF THE BRAZED JOINT

Care in fitting up the joint and in manipulating the flame is very important in making a satisfactory brazed joint. Before the pieces of metal are put together, they should be clean, so that flux and molten brazing material can penetrate. It is useless to expect penetration if the joint is filled with sealer, rust, or other material that would prevent tinning.

If everything else is equal, the joint in which the pieces are spaced just wide enough to permit the braz-ing material to be drawn in by capillary action will be stronger than one in which the pieces are much farther apart. This is illustrated in Figures 5-19 and 5-20. Note in Figure 5-19 that the bond between the surfaces is made by the alloy formed on the interface. This mate-rial is much stronger than the pure brazing material that fills the wider space between the surfaces in Fig-ure 5-20.

Proper torch flame manipulation is a matter of watching to see that the temperature is just right to allow the tinning action to be continuous. When it is right, the molten brazing material will flow or spread at

the leading edge of the puddle. If the temperature is not high enough, the molten material will run over the metal much as drops of water will roll over an oily surface. This also will occur if the surface is contaminated, mak-ing the flux ineffective, or if no flux is used. If the sur-face is too hot, the brazing material will be damaged by burning the tin, which is a part of the composition of the copper-base alloys used for brazing.

Appearances are sometimes deceptive, but a good and a poor brazed joint usually can be determined by inspection. The good joint should be smooth and bright, and the edges should blend into the surface of the metal on which it is applied. In contrast to this, a pitted or blistery surface, or an edge that appears to stand on top of the metal, usually is evidence of an unsatisfactory brazing job. An excessive amount of fine, white, pow-dery material on both sides of the joint indicates over-heating; sometimes there will be a considerable amount of such powder, even though the joint does not look as though it were badly burned. This is always evidence of a rather poor job.

EMBRITTLEMENT

One disadvantage of brazing is that the joint, once made, should not be remelted or subjected to melting temperature longer than necessary. Prolonged heating will cause the molten brazing material to penetrate deep enough into the steel to make it brittle. This is not a problem in a normal brazing operation, because the brazing material is molten for a very short time, but long periods should be avoided.

Repairmen often braze a piece of scrap metal to a body panel or frame to make a connection for pulling equipment. When this is done, the piece should not be removed by simply melting it off. Preferably, it should be chiseled off and the excess ground off. When that is not practical, the piece can be removed by taking advan-tage of the fact that brazing material loses much of its strength when it reaches a temperature well below its

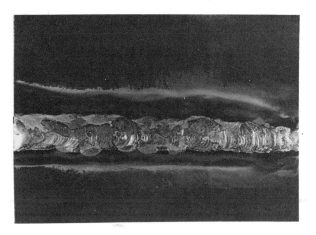

5-22 A typical brazed joint with a low bead built up over the overlap. Testing showed penetration to one half of the depth of the overlap.

melting point. The torch flame should be concentrated on the piece to be removed to heat the entire joint. It will reach a temperature when it can be knocked off with a sharp hammer blow or, if it is thin metal, pulled off with a pair of pliers.

Excessive penetration can be demonstrated by depositing a drop of brazing material on a piece of clean, bright sheet metal and holding it at melting temperature much longer than it would be in a normal brazing operation. If it is held long enough, a faint copperish tint will be seen on the other side. The spot will crack if bent or hit with a hammer. Vibration will cause steel in this condition to crack in normal operation.

RESISTANCE SPOT WELDING

Resistance spot welding is primarily a factory production method of assembling sheet metal parts, but it also serves a useful purpose in the body repair shop. The feature of greatest value to the body shop is the ability to weld long, flat sections of sheet metal with little or no heat distortion. The saving is in time that does not have to be spent in either working out or filling large heat-distorted areas that were undamaged before the welding operation. This welding method is in no way a substitute for oxyacetylene welding, but it is important enough that any competent metal man should understand its uses and limitations and know how to adjust and maintain the equipment. This is essentially a matter of technical knowledge; very little manual skill is involved.

The emphasis of this section is on the use and limitations of resistance spot welding equipment adapted to body repair use. The repair shop has much different problems in replacing a body panel from those of the factory in assembling them on a production basis, even though the equipment used by both operates on the same basic principle. Instead of specialized equipment to do one job repeatedly, the body shop needs equipment with enough flexibility to do a variety of jobs on an intermittent basis. The situation is further limited by economics; the equipment must pay for itself within reasonable time, and it must operate on the power supply that is adequate for other shop equipment.

This discussion is limited to problems of welding sheet steel. Resistance spot welding is used extensively in fabrication of sheet aluminum, but requires special equipment with sufficient power to weld in extremely short periods of time. If such equipment was available for body repair use, the cost would be far out of proportion to the need, so it is not considered further here.

THE BASIC PRINCIPLE OF RESISTANCE SPOT WELDING

Electric resistance spot welding is possible because the resistance of a conductor to an electric current is in direct proportion to the amount of current flowing in it.

A spot on two pieces of overlapped metal can be heated to the welding temperature by placing them in the circuit of an electric current having sufficient amperage to overload their capacity to conduct electricity. The current is applied by electrodes held in contact with the metal surface by mechanical pressure, so that the heat-softened metal will be forced together to form a weld when the correct temperature is reached.

This basic principle is illustrated in very simple form in Figure 5-23. This consists of (1) a step-down transformer, connected to an utility power line, (2) two conductors, large enough to carry the low-voltage, high-amperage current to the electrodes, (3) two blunt pointed electrodes that contact an area of metal considerably smaller than the cross-sectional area of the conductors, and (4) a source of mechanical pressure to force the heated metal together. Two switches are shown: one in the power line to ready the machine for operation and a trigger switch that the operator presses to activate the timer that starts the weld cycle.

This figure emphasizes the difference in the cross-sectional area of the conductors and the spot to be welded. The conductors must be large enough to carry the high-amperage, low-voltage current required to develop welding heat. Power lost by resistance in the conductors reduces the capacity of the machine.

The current must flow only long enough to generate welding temperature in the overlapped surfaces of the joint. The steel in the joint has higher resistance than the conductors, but the point of highest resistance, called the *interface*, is in the contact between the sheets. Heat starts to generate at the interface and spreads to the outer surface very rapidly. When welding temperature is reached, the current is shut off and pressure on the electrodes forces the hot metal together to form the weld. The spot of metal joined is referred to as the *nugget*.

The length of the welding cycle varies to some degree, but it is completed in a fraction of a second. The timer (Figure 5-23) is required for consistent operation, but some relatively low-powered welders operate without one.

A source of pressure is required to force the hot metal together, as indicated by the large arrows. Although pressure must be held slightly longer than the current flow to permit solidification of the nugget, pressure regulation is not as critical as current flow. The

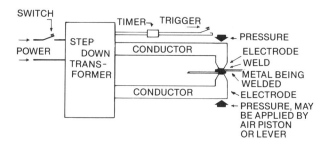

5-23 Basic layout of resistance spot welder using opposed electrodes.

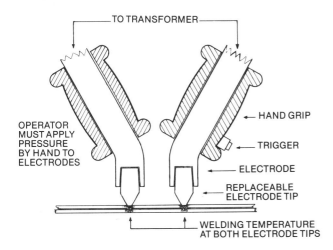

5-24 Hand-held electrodes, used on one side to make two simultaneous welds.

type welder decribed in the next section, designed for body shop use, requires the operator to apply pressure manually.

BODY REPAIR SPOT WELDING

A spot welder equipped with an electrode setup similar to that shown in Figure 5-23 has some body repair use but is impractical for man cause access to the inside surface of many seams is either difficult or impossible. Those that can be reached are usually coated with paint and thick layers of sealer. The problem can be simplified considerably by a variation in resistance welding technique, using both electrodes hand held on the outside, as shown in Figure 5-24. The machines shown in Figures 5-25 and 5-26 are equipped with flexible cable conductors leading to this type of electrode. This system is easy to use and does not require any change in electrode setup for different jobs. The operator turns the machine on, presses the two electrodes against the seam while pulling the trigger, and maintains the pressure on the electrodes briefly after the timer shuts the current flow off. As shown in Figure 5-24, each operation makes two welds.

The machines in Figure 5-25 and 5-26 are equipped with an automatic timer, and one has a power control. The operator must familiarize himself with the proper settings on these, but, once they have been established, they need changing only to take care of different metal thicknesses. The operator soon learns how much pressure to apply, but he must be consistent in applying approximately the same amoung on every weld.

In this system the sheet metal between the electrodes is made a part of the welding circuit. Some of it passes through the high resistance point of the interface and generates enough heat to weld. In a properly made joint, there should be no difference in the welds made at each electrode, if the timer and power setting are correct and the right amount of pressure is applied. How-

5-25 Electric resistance spot welder equipped with timer and hand-held electrodes.

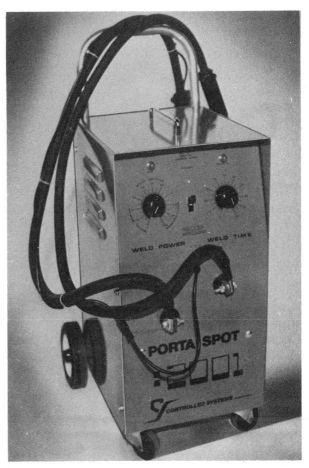

5-26 Electric resistance spot welder equipped with timer, power control, and hand-held electrodes.

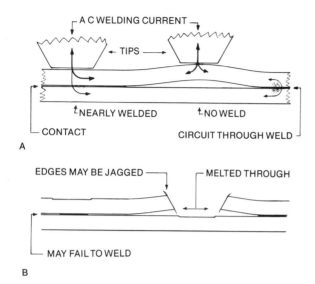

5-27 Cross-sectional effect of attempting to weld without good interface contact.

ever, unless the joint has been prepared properly, it will be impossible to obtain a good weld with these or any other electric resistance spot welder.

WELD JOINT PREPARATION

The joint surfaces must be clean and fit together without buckles of excessive springiness. A welder set up to use opposed electrodes, as shown in Figure 5-23, requires clean metal on both sides of both pieces. The hand-held electrodes in Figure 5-24 eliminate the need to clean the back surface, which is usually the most difficult, but the interface and exterior must be clean and fit together without requiring excessive pressure on the electrodes. This is particularly important on the relatively low-power welders suitable for body repair use.

The effect of attempting to weld with no interface contact is illustrated in Figure 5-27. At A, current flow is indicated by the curved lines extending out of the electrode tips. (Arrows are shown at both ends because the current is alternating.) Some of the current concentrated at the left electrode passes through the interface resistance, but some by-passes through various paths provided by previously made welds, back to the right electrode, as indicated by the curved arrow on the extreme right. All of the current flowing through the right electrode is concentrated in the upper piece, which almost instantly heats to the melting point and allows the electrode to punch through to the lower. Some of the overheated metal is deposited on the lower, but most of it flies out in white hot globs that may travel across the shop, creating a fire and eye hazard. (Never operate a spot welder without eye protection.)

The result of this condition is illustrated in B. The left electrode may make a good weld if there are enough other welds in the area of the right to complete the circuit through the lower piece; the right electrode will

simply punch a hole through the upper piece. There will usually be some crusty "flash" between the surfaces that will extend up around the edges in a jagged, razor sharp fringe.

Opposed electrodes, as in Figure 5-23, will punch a hole in the same way if there are previously made welds or enough other contacts to complete the circuit.

ELECTRICAL CONTACT

The equipment manufacturer's recommended tip diameter is calculated from the ratio of available amperage to the size of the area of contact. The end of the tip, which is in contact with the metal to be welded, must be maintained at this diameter to make satisfactory welds. If it gets too large, the amperage will be spread over a larger area and fail to generate temperature high enough to weld. Figure 5-28 illustrates the result of trying to weld when the contact area is partly covered with any material that does not conduct electricity. Paint is indicated here, but any other material that blocks the flow of current will have the same bad effect.

Figure 5-28 is drawn in direct proportion to the dimensions of a ⅛ inch (3.175 mm) electrode tip contact area being used to weld two pieces of sheet steel 0.035 inch (0.89 mm) thick. The arrow points to paint blocking approximately half of the contact area, so that only a small portion of the tip surface can contact the steel. The entire amperage will be concentrated on this very small area, creating temperatures far beyond the melting point of the steel. The overheated molten metal expands so fast that it actually explodes with enough force to throw out blobs of molten metal that can cause serious burns or ignite flammable material; they will damage paint or window glass on an automobile in an adjoining stall.

The metal thrown out leaves a void in the weld, as shown. A weld in this condition is ruined. Foreign material built up on the electrode tip will often have a worse effect on it than on the metal being welded. Problems of this type are avoidable for the operator who understands the need to clean the metal surfaces properly and to keep the electrode tips in good condition.

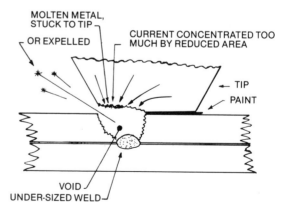

5-28 Effect of attempting to weld with contact area partially covered with foreign material.

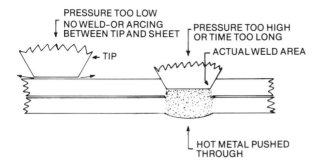

5-29 Effect of attempting to weld with electrode pressure too low *(left side)* and too high *(right side)*.

Electrode Tip Maintenance

Electrode tips tend to spread as well as accumulate non-conductive material on the end. Maintenance is merely a matter of filing or grinding off any foreign material and keeping the end dressed to the manufacturer's specification. A mill file or very fine grit sanding disc is preferable for dressing the contact face, particularly on the relatively small tips normally used in body repair work; coarse scratches limit the contact and will cause premature tip failure and additional maintenance.

ELECTRODE PRESSURE

The effect of too low and too high pressure on the electrodes is illustrated by the cross-sectional Figure 5-29. Not enough pressure, on the left, will make little or no impression on the outer surface in contact with the electrode and, probably, not discolor the lower surface at all. The tip will still complete the circuit (probably by arcing across the gap) so that too much pressure on the other (the right) will penetrate too deep into the surface. This situation is worse when extra-long timer settings are used, because the metal stays hot longer.

The right side shows the electrode tip nearly through the upper piece, leaving only a very thin section of it to weld to the lower. The result is a very weak weld that will break under a very light strain. It is possible to push the electrode all the way through the upper piece, making no weld at all.

This operation involves a degree of skill, but it is simple, compared to many other of the repairman's skills. Any competent worker who recognizes the problems involved and is willing to train himself can learn easily to maintain even pressure.

Electrode pressure is one of the factors of spot weld quality discussed in more detail in the section on Spot Weld Testing.

SPOT WELDING LIGHT TO HEAVY METAL

The capacity of most spot welders practical for body repair use is limited to welding two pieces of sheet metal of the thickness normally used for exterior panels. An attempt to weld thicker metal or one piece of normal thickness to another much thicker will be a total failure if the usual procedure is followed. The technique illustrated in Figure 5-30 will extend the capacity of this type of welder enough to make dependable welds on joints such as the flanges of a quarter panel to the heavier metal of a lock pillar or the seams of a rocker panel. Special preparation is required, but the advantages of spot welding can be retained. The technique is to use a center punch to make small, conical projections on the interface surface of the light piece for every weld. The electrode tips should be oversize when placed against the exterior surface of these projections, where, as shown in A, they serve only as conductors. Each projection becomes an electrode tip for one-time use.

This technique works because the welding current is concentrated on a smaller area than covered by the electrode tip and produces a higher temperature. Higher pressure is required because, as shown in A, the flange must bend slightly as the weld forms. Oversize electrodes are needed to apply pressure over a larger area. There is little risk of punching a hole because the larger tip covers more area than the acutal weld. Also, the heavier metal absorbs the heat faster than does metal of normal thickness.

This technique works best when welding to a heavy piece supported rigidly to withstand the extra pressure. When rigidity is lacking, pop rivets should be installed at 3–4-inch (7.5–10-cm) intervals; otherwise, the joint will slip, and the projection will be expelled. The rivet heads can be hidden by making a weld directly on them. Some rivet heads will leave a center hole, which can be filled by placing a narrow strip of metal between the electrode tip and the rivet and using extra pressure, so that a small piece will be forced into the rivet when the weld is made. A rivet disguised in this manner should not be considered a weld, as it will have no holding power.

Welds made with this projection technique are relatively small, so it is necessary to make at least twice as many as were found on the original seam. After the punch marks are made, the flange should be checked to make sure that the surfaces fit together, as shown in A. After welding it may be necessary to use light hammer blows to drive the outer edge of the flange down between the welds.

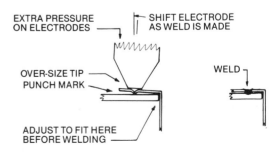

5-30 Technique for welding sheet metal to other metal that is beyond the normal capacity of the machine.

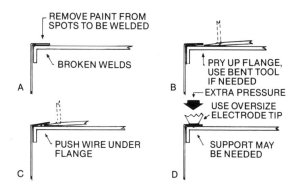

The joint should be prepared carefully when this method is to be used. It is particularly important to avoid blowing holes if it is on a visible surface, such as a lock pillar. If a weld fails but the surface is left solid, the method explained in the next section can be used, but the appearance may not be as good as that of the weld made with the projection.

REWELDING BROKEN SPOT WELDS

A method of rewelding broken spot welds illustrated by Figure 5-31 can be used easily on any joint that has good electrical conduction through the interface. As shown,

5-31 Technique for repairing broken spot welds. Other electrode, not shown, should be grounded to the under piece.

the edge of the flange is pried up to permit a small piece of wire to be pushed into place. The wire serves the same purpose as the punch marks described in the preceding section. A ⅛-inch (3.175 mm) piece cut from a common paper clip is very satisfactory; the steel in the paper clip is similar to body sheet steel.

If the interface is rusted, it must be pried open far enough to permit removing the rust and driven back down again. The flanges should be close together enough to grip the wire. The spring action of the flange is needed to add to the welding pressure.

Some of the weld-through sealers used in factory production may cause trouble after aging. Any trouble can be determined by testing. Some of the sealers remain conductive indefinitely; others are conductive only when wet and *perhaps* will be reactivated by rewetting with water; still others may simply become nonconductive with time. If the seam is difficult to make conductive, it may be necessary to use another method.

The desirability of rewelding broken seams justifies a trial, particularly on seams such as door hem flanges or lock pillars that are quite visible. This method can be used close to trim parts or body sealer to repair broken welds that are causing squeaks or rattles.

Two welds should be made at a time when using hand-held electrodes, but only one is shown in Figure 5-31, because the procedure is the same for both. A welder having opposed electrodes, as represented in Figure 5-23, can be used for this purpose on joints with

both sides exposed, as on a door hem flange, but considerable ingenuity may be required to use it on other joints.

The procedure is explained by the notes on the figures and is not discussed further here except to emphasize that a great deal of pressure should be used on an over-sized electrode. The electrode serves only as a conductor; the piece of wire is the electrode.

SPOT WELD SEALER

Any spot-welded seam on a surface exposed to the weather should be sealed. Conductive sealers are available, so that a weld can be made through them. The material is applied in a continuous bead to one of the interface surfaces before the joint is assembled, and welding pressure spreads the sealer so that the joint space is completely filled except for the area of the weld nugget.

Weld-through sealer is used on all exposed welds in factory production, and some are further sealed with a bead of heat-curing sealer applied to the outer surface. This sealer cures as the body goes through the paint ovens. It is the tough, rubbery material found on door hem flanges and similar seams.

Electric resistance spot welding has not been used widely by body shops, and many body men and body shop managers are not aware that a spot-wleded seam can be sealed. Some seams are easier to seal than others. Those assembled by laying one piece on the other are simple, but a door hem flange presents problems if it must be hemmed with a hammer and dolly block. The hammer blows drive most of the sealer out of the hem. Tools have been made that roll the flange, but they are not used widely.

When a weld-through sealer is not available, an exposed body seam should be sealed on the exposed edge with a high-grade material. If the joint is to last, the moisture must be kept out.

WELD TESTING

Any repairman starting to use a resistance spot welder he is not familiar with should make several welds on scrap metal and test them for strength before using the machine on actual repair work. Whether or not he has had previous experience with other spot welders, he should familiarize himself with the operating characteristics of *that* machine before using it. The reason for this precaution is that, unlike the fusion welding processes, a spot weld is made between two pieces of metal where it is hidden from view. The operator goes through the motions, but he has to learn from testing when he has struck the right combination of time, pressure, and power, if the machine has a power adjustment, to be sure that he is welding. Weld failure can be both costly and embarrassing.

A simple method of testing spot welds is shown in Figure 5-32. For this test the two strips were welded

5-32 Simple spot weld test. A good weld should tear a button out of one piece, leaving it securely attached to the other.

together, using a machine equipped with hand-held electrodes, and the edges were separated to provide a surface to be gripped by the vise and the pliers. Downward pressure on the end of the pliers will provide enough leverage to tear any spot weld apart in metal of this thickness.

A good weld should require enough force to tear a "button" out of one piece. The rim of the button should be nearly as wide as the metal thickness and should have a fresh, grainy surface where it was torn. A button that snaps out easily and has heat discoloration on the rim is an indication that the electrode has penetrated too deep, as illustrated in Figure 5-29, probably because it has been too hot and may have had too much pressure. A weld that separates cleanly on the interface is an indication that either it was not hot enough or not enough pressure was applied. In either case, it is not a weld.

In starting to make a series of test welds the timer—and the power control, if the machine is so equipped—should be set according to the manufacturer's directions. Each weld, or pair of welds, should be tested when made and studied to determine what variations of time, power, or pressure are needed before making another. The metal used for the test should be of the same thickness as that the machine will normally weld.

If the welder is to be used on extra-thin metal, a series of tests should be made on it also.

ATTACHING WELD-ON PULL TABS

Attaching the weld-on pull tabs, mentioned in Chapter 3 and shown in Figure 3-24, is simply a spot welding operation performed with adapters attached to the electrode holders, as shown in Figure 5-33. The adapter shown on the right serves as a ground while the one on the left does the actual welding. The attaching adapter should be installed on the electrode holder having the trigger so that, after one tab has been welded on, the ground can be hung on it as shown and left until the job is completed.

Before starting to install tabs, the repairman should adjust the machine properly. Machines having a power control should be reduced to about one third of the power range; machines having only a time control should have the time reduced proportionally. Welding the first tab to the panel requires a bare spot for the ground adapter. The back of the curved section should be pressed against the bare spot in the same manner it is shown supported by the bracket in Figure 5-33. If a new tab or one that has been reground is being used, welding contact can be made through the paint by twisting the electrode holder. Press the trigger, and the tab is welded on. The ground adapter can then be hung on the tab and others welded on without further concern for grounding.

These tabs are a low-cost, expendable item. They are easily removed after use by twisting, preferably by using a pair of vise grip pliers, but the tip widens with each use. They can be ground down to the correct size point several times before they are too short for further use. If they are not resharpened when ground, it will be necessary to remove the paint before rewelding them.

These tabs can be used individually with a slide hammer equipped with a single hook, or a gang hook-up can

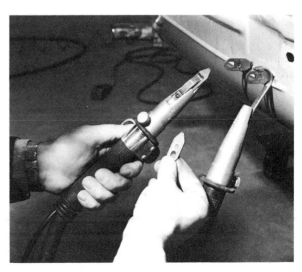

5-33 Electrode holders with adapters to attach weld-on type pull tabs.

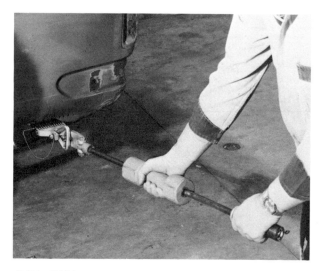

5-34 Weld-on gang hookup with adapter to permit pulling with either a slide hammer or a body machine.

be made, as in Figure 5-34. A slide hammer is shown in use here, but a chain can be connected in the same manner to pull with any type of body machine.

SAFETY RULES FOR SPOT WELDING

Carelessness with any electrical equipment is inexcusable and particularly so when the equipment operates on 230-volt power supply and is portable. Fortunately, the high voltage is confined to the input side of the spot welder; the output is low, usually from 3 to 8 volts. Unless the primary circuit becomes short-circuited to the secondary, there is little electrical hazard to the operator. The following common-sense rules should be followed to reduce electrical accidents to the minimum:

1. The plug-in connection should be removed from its receptacle and the power cord coiled on the machine when not in use.
2. The power switch should be turned off when a delay occurs in the welding operation.
3. The power cord should never be placed where automobiles will run over it.
4. When any damage to the power cord is noted, the machine should be disconnected and taken out of use until repaired.

There is additional risk of personal injury or fire caused by flying sparks. The following rules should be observed to reduce the risk to the minimum:

1. All persons using the machine should wear adequate eye protection.
2. Bystanders should be kept at a distance.
3. The operator should wear gloves and full sleeves.
4. Before starting to weld, the operator should check the area and remove any flammable materials, particularly gasoline, paint materials, or paint-coated masking paper.

ELECTRIC ARC WELDING

The electric arc is used as the source of heat in arc welding. The basis of the method is that an electric current flow can be maintained across an open space after it has been started under the proper current and voltge conditions. Temperatures well above the level required for welding result because of the high resistance of the open space. All arc welding systems make use of this characteristic of the electric arc.

In the original method of arc welding, a carbon electrode was used to maintain the arc, and the filler rod was fed into the puddle in much the same way it is fed into the oxyacetylene puddle. There is still the occasional application of the carbon arc, but is has been completely replaced by other, more efficient methods.

A later development of arc welding was the consumable electrode. In this method, the filler rod is used as the electrode by feeding it into the puddle as it melts off. Bare steel wires have been used for this purpose, but they have been replaced almost entirely by the coated electrode. The coating burns off, creating an inert atmosphere over the puddle area to shield the molten metal from attack by oxygen in the air. The result is a better weld that is much easier to make than with the use of a bare wire electrode. This method is in wide general use for most manual arc welding, particularly repair work. In the following sections, this method of arc welding is referred to as *conventional* arc welding.

A still later development in arc welding has been the use of a shielding gas, which is released through a nozzle in the electrode holder to exclude air from the puddle area. Two methods are in common use, MIG and TIG, with the MIG method much more widely accepted for body and frame repair than TIG.

MIG is an acronym for Metallic Inert Gas, meaning that a metallic electrode is used with an inert gas. The term originated when the only gases used were inert, usually helium or argon. Helium and argon are used in welding many of the nonferrous metals, but carbon dioxide, which is really not inert, is used for welding most steels.

TIG is an acronym for Tungsten Inert Gas, meaning that a tungsten electrode is used with an inert gas. In this system, the tungsten electrode is used in much the same manner as the oxyacetylene torch, and the filler rod is fed into the puddle by hand. Tungsten is used because it does not burn away.

In all arc welding systems, the metal to be welded is made a part of the electric circuit. The arc is produced by contacting the electrode to the work, or *striking the arc*, to complete the circuit and then held slightly off the surface to maintain the arc. The manual skill in arc welding is in learning to maintain and manipulate the arc so that the filler metal is deposited where it is needed and the proper penetration is obtained.

In the following discussion of arc welding, the emphasis is on the conventional system. It is the most widely used in body and frame repair, and the skills required for it are much the same as for the other systems.

CONVENTIONAL ARC WELDING EQUIPMENT

Two basic types of arc welding equipment are in general use: the alternating-current transformer type and the direct-current generator type. Each has its advantages and disadvantages.

The advantages of the alternating-current, or AC, machine are that it is a relatively simple device, costs less, will last a long time, and is adequate for most simple welding jobs. For these reasons, it is the machine most commonly used in automobile repair shops, particularly body shops.

The chief disadvantage of the AC welder is that there are many welding operations for which it is unsuited—for instance, those jobs requiring the use of direct current so that the polarity of the electrode will be either positive or negative. Such jobs cannot be done satisfactorily with an AC machine. However, most such jobs are on alloys or nonferrous metals that the automobile repairman usually is not required to weld. The alternating current of the AC welder is slightly more difficult to weld with in a vertical or overhead position as compared to the direct-current generator type. This is due to the change of polarity of alternating current, which occurs 60 times per second. However, this is not such a drawback to the repairman as it might seem, because he can learn to operate the AC machine in either position with a little practice. Most of his welding will not require work in a difficult position, anyway. A practical AC arc welder is shown in Figure 5-35.

5-35 Alternating-current arc welder.

The advantage of the direct-current generator type welder, or the DC machine, is in its greater versatility, as compared to the AC machine. With few exceptions, the DC welder will do any job that can be done with the AC machine, plus those that either cannot be done or are difficult to do without direct current.

The DC welder normally is driven by an electric motor drawing current from a utility power line. However, it may be driven by any type motor having sufficient power and flexibility to carry the load. Except in rare instances, when other motors are used, they are either gasoline or diesel. The operating costs and maintenance problems of using either motor are much greater than with electric drive, so they are used rarely, except where portability is needed. However, when it is necessary to take the welder to a job where an electric power line either is not available or connection to it would be difficult, the gasoline engine-driven welder provides a satisfactory and efficient means of doing the work. There is no difference in the quality of the work done with either the electric or other type drive.

MIG AND TIG WELDING SYSTEMS

MIG and TIG welding systems are similar, in that they both use gas to shield the puddle, but both the machines and the methods of operation are different. It is possible to adapt a conventional welder to operate on the TIG system because the machine used for both maintains the welding current at a constant amperage level. However, more efficient operation will be obtained from a machine designed especially for TIG welding.

The MIG machine maintains the welding current at a constant voltage level. This difference makes it impractical to adapt a conventional welder to MIG operation. MIG welding is a useful system that has been adopted for many industrial uses, including the body shop industry. When equipped with a timer, it makes a very practical spot welder. A typical maching is shown in Figure 5-36.

The MIG welding gun, shown across the machine, is operated in much the same manner as the electrode holder used in conventional welding, the primary difference being that the filler metal is a fine wire, fed automatically through the gun nozzle, instead of a coated rod that must be hand loaded into the holder.

The operator who has learned conventional welding should be able to adapt to MIG welding with very little trouble. As with any new technique, it is necessary to become familiar with the system, particularly the adjustment of the machine and some other differences, but these do not pose difficult problems.

The TIG system can be used on practically all metals that are considered weldable. The equipment can be adapted to a wide range of thicknesses from thinner than body sheet metal to the maximum that can be welded by ordinary processes. However, it has had limited acceptance by the body shop industry and is not illustrated here.

5-36 MIG welder.

The original shielding gas used with both MIG and TIG systems was helium or argon, hence the I in both names. However, when MIG is used on steel, it is common practice to use either carbon dioxide or a mixture of carbon dioxide with a small percentage of argon. Use of carbon dioxide, which is not an inert gas, makes the term MIG a misnomer, but it is in common use. People in the welding industry prefer to call the MIG system Gas Metallic Arc Welding (abbreviated GMAW) and the TIG system as Gas Tungsten Arc Welding (abbreviated GTAW).

A sample MIG (GMAW) butt weld is shown in Figure 5-37 and a sample spot weld in Figure 5-38. MIG welding is shown being used to assemble the heavy duty truck cab in Figure 5-39. Although this is a manufacturing scene, it is a good example of how MIG welding can be used in rebuilding any sheet metal structure. This same work on a high-production body would be done with resistance spot welding.

AC ARC WELDING GUN

An arc welding gun and special AC transformer is shown in Figure 5-40. When used with the proper electrodes, this outfit makes an arc-spot weld in much the same manner as a MIG spot, but depends on feeding an exact length of the electrode into the puddle instead of being shut off by a timer.

The advantage of this unit is that the equipment is less costly than either resistance or the MIG unit, and it causes less heat distortion than the oxyacetylene torch. It can be used in any position without difficulty, but should never be used without eye protection from flying sparks; if it is used overhead, full face protection should be worn. Colored lenses are not necessary, because the weld is made within the end nozzle.

The transformer produces a lower voltage current than a conventional AC welder, which limits the length of the arc it will maintain. The electrode coating contains iron powder, which aids in starting the arc on contact. The gun is designed to permit a predetermined length of electrode to be fed into the weld puddle. When the feed stops, the arc is extinguished automatically. When the feed length is adjusted properly and the operator learns to push the gun down at the correct speed, these machines will make satisfactory welds with much less heat distortion than can be expected with the oxyacetylene torch. The worst disadvantage is that a much rougher weld is made than by either the resistance or

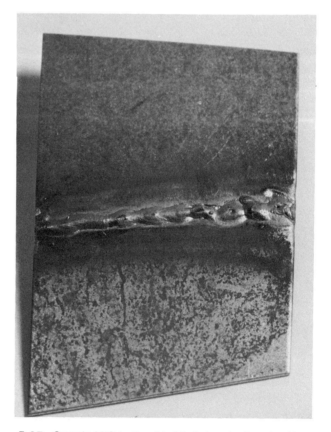

5-37 Sample MIG butt weld. (Made in a trade school.)

5-38 Sample MIG spot weld. (Made in a trade school.)

MIG spot methods and that considerable skill is required to avoid burning holes. The metal to be welded must be in close contact.

USE OF ARC WELDING IN BODY REPAIR

The two types of joints in body repair work on which arc welding (by either conventional MIG or TIG systems) is preferable to the torch are (1) joining the heavier metal used in frame members and some body reinforcements and (2) as a substitute for resistance spot welding on long, overlapped seams. In addition to these, other special uses arise from time to time, often enough that the qualified repairman should develop the skill to use the arc correctly on jobs where it should be used. This is simply a matter of practice, preferably under the supervision of a qualified instructor who understands the basic problems of arc welding in body repair. The skills required for body repair work are but a small part of those involved in the overall arc welding field, particularly in heavy industry or building construction.

ARC WELDING PROCEDURE

The process of learning to arc weld starts with learning to strike and maintain the arc to make a uniform weld bead. It is then necessary to learn to make good weld beads on butt and overlapped joints in various positions. Welding straight down on a flat surface is relatively easy, because both gravity and surface tension tend to keep the molten metal in place until it solidifies; greater skill is required to weld on vertical or overhead positions, because gravity works against surface tension, tending to make the molten metal flow out of position before it solidifies. The repairman should learn to

5-39 MIG welding being used to assemble truck cabs.

weld in all positions, as many of the joints that should be arc welded are on either vertical or overhead surfaces. The type of machine used and the electrode selected are factors affecting the skill required for many welding opertions, particularly those in the vertical or overhead positions. In general, the AC transformer-type machine requires slightly greater skill than the DC motor-generator. However, transformer-type machines are more widely used in body shops, because they are less expensive, and a good one is adequate for the need when it is operated properly.

Electrodes are made in a wide range of sizes and types, some intended for general-purpose use on mild steel and others for restricted use on certain alloys only. They vary also for different types of joints. Some general-purpose electrodes can be used on any position, others are intended for use only on flat surfaces, and still others will weld in any position but work particu-

5-40 Arc-spot welding gun.

larly well in the vertical and overhead positions. The beginner should start using a good general-purpose electrode for practice in the flat position, but when he comes to vertical and overhead joints, the extra expense for electrodes designed to work in those positions may be more than repaid in faster skill development.

The machine used by the beginner should be adjusted properly for his first practice, but it is as important to learn to adjust the machine as it is to use it. The beginner working alone to learn arc welding has no alternative but to study all available technical information and depend on his own interpretation of it. The advice of an experienced welder can be very valuable in such circumstances.

In the following discussion of arc welding procedure for the beginner, it is assumed that he will be dressed properly, for protection against arc light burns, and is wearing suitable gloves, flash goggles, and helmet. The flash goggles should be worn at all times to provide eye protection against an accidental flash while the helmet is raised. The helmet must be in the down position at all times the arc is in operation. Also, the beginner should be aware of his responsibility to avoid exposing other persons in the vicinity without warning.

PRACTICE MATERIAL

The beginner should practice arc welding on steel of the thickness that will be welded on the job, starting with metal no thicker than ⅛ inch (3.175 mm), and should learn to weld seams in all positions. As his skill increases, the practice should be on thinner metal. Long butt or lap seams with a continuous bead are rarely arc welded on body panels. There are many jobs on which arc tacking will serve as a practical substitute for resistance spot welding. The skill level required to make good tack welds is the same as that required for seams.

The pieces used to learn the arc and run beads may be almost any size. The pieces used to learn to weld butt and overlapped joints need be no larger than 2 by 6 inches (5 × 15 cm); larger pieces will often be a waste of metal. When usable metal is difficult to obtain, pieces used for seam practice by one class can be saved for practicing striking the arc and running beads by a following group.

STRIKING THE ARC

To start striking the arc, a piece of the ⅛ inch (3.175 mm) stock should be placed on the bench in a convenient position for the hand, right or left, that the student normally uses. If small, it should be clamped down, and the ground clamp attached if the bench top is not grounded. Before starting the machine, the movements of striking the arc and running a bead should be visualized, and a convenient position to assume should be determined. Then start the machine, load an electrode into the holder, hold the tip of the electrode poised about

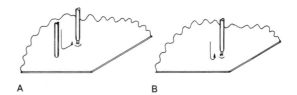

5-41 Striking the arc: A, scratch method; B, touch and lift, the preferred method.

1 inch (25 mm) above a predetermined spot and slanted approximately 20 degrees away from the direction of weld travel, lower the helmet, touch the tip to the surface, and lift it slightly. There will be a flash, which will continue and become the arc if the operation is performed smoothly. If not, either the electrode will stick or the arc will go out.

The correct motion for striking the arc may require a little practice, but it is easily developed. Some beginners find it easier to use a scratching motion at first, as illustrated in A, Figure 5-41. However, the touch-and-lift motion, illustrated in B, is more accurate and should be adopted after a little practice.

With the arc started, close attention will be required to keep it going. Arc length should be held firmly for a moment, to start a puddle of molten metal, then carried forward at a rate that will keep the puddle at a uniform width and build a bead of deposited metal behind it. This can be confusing at first. The electrode must be lowered at the same rate it is consumed by the arc, and at the same time it must be kept in forward motion without changing the angle to the work. Control of the combined motions requires practice but soon becomes a reflex instead of a conscious action.

The beginner is often confused by the answers received to questions about the arc length. Specifications varying from ⅛ to ¼ inch (3.175–6.35 mm) are often given, followed by reference to long and short arcs. Instead of a specification, the arc should be considered as having a range within which it can be varied to control heat. The longer the arc, the higher the temperature. As it gets too long, the color darkens from intense blue to a purple tint, the sound changes from a smooth hiss to a harsh crackle, and blobs of molten metal will form on the tip of the electrode. Past that point it goes out.

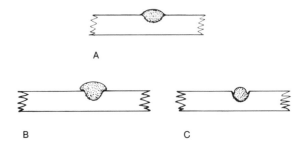

5-42 Cross sections of practice weld beads: A, good; B, weld metal overlaps surface, not acceptable; C, undercut, not acceptable.

If the arc gets too short, it will stick, short-circuiting the entire output of the machine. It should be broken loose or released from the holder before it gets red hot.

The beginner should continue practicing striking the arc and running beads until he can start a predetermined point and make a continuous bead with uniform width and build up, as illustrated in cross section A in Figure 5-42. It is not acceptable to leave an overlay, as shown in B, or excessive undercutting, as illustrated in C. After the slag is chipped off, the bead should have a rippled appearance, much the same as a weld made with an oxyacetylene torch.

BUTT WELDS

A butt joint is simply two pieces of steel joined by a weld bead, but it requires more careful manipulation of the electrode than when making a bead on solid metal. The added factor is penetration. The exposed edges absorb heat faster than a solid surface, increasing the tendency to burn holes.

A good butt weld should penetrate the full depth of the joint, so that the small bead is formed on the lower surface and a much larger one on the upper; the bead should blend smoothly into the adjoining surface. On metal ⅛ inch (3.175 mm) thick, or less, some welders, particularly beginners, feel that they can weld better by weaving the electrode back and forth along the length of the joint or in a circular pattern. Either method will make a larger weld bead than required for the thickness. The beginner may find it necessary to use one or the other of these motions at first, but he should make slight changes in the electrode angle, arc length, and rate of travel to find a combination that will enable him to weld without extra electrode movement.

Four cross sections of common weld conditions are shown in Figure 5-43. The beginner's attempt to avoid burning holes usually leads to piling up too much on the upper surface and not enough penetration, as shown in A. A weld showing traces of the original edges is definitely not acceptable. B represents full penetration with a slight bead on the lower surface and a full bead blended into the upper. C represents the beginning of

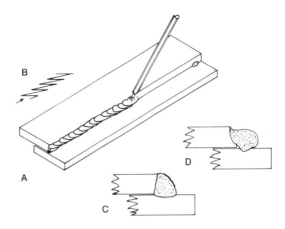

5-44 Lap joint: A, joint layout and electrode position; B, weave pattern; C, cross section of good weld; D, cross section of poor weld, showing excessive undercut, insufficient penetration, and overlap, not acceptable.

undercutting due to overpenetration and failure to fill the puddle completely. The strength of the weld is reduced in direct proportion to the depth of the undercut. Even greater undercutting is represented in D. In any industrial setting where welding is judged by established standards, undercutting is not acceptable. Although strict standards are not enforced in automobile repair work, undercutting should be no more acceptable for it than for any other industrial situation.

The beginner should chip the slag off each practice weld and inspect both sides for improvement. At first, many welds may show all of the various conditions represented by Figure 5-43. However, after reasonable practice, definite improvement should come. Practice should be continued until acceptable welds can be made.

LAP WELDS

Lapped joints can be practiced by using narrow strips, overlapped as shown in Figure 5-44. Strips can be added to either the upper or lower surfaces for additional welds.

A good weld, as represented by the cross section at C, should have full penetration without melt-back of the upper edge or overlay. Unacceptable conditions are shown in D. Here, the upper edge has melted back, thinning the cross section; the inner corner is not fused, thinning the joint more; and molten metal has run out over the surface of the lower piece to form an overlay. A weld with no better fusion than this would break easily if tested, as described in the following paragraphs.

Most beginners will find it necessary to weave the electrode in a diagonal pattern, as suggested by B, to avoid melting too much of the exposed upper edge. Weaving creates a long, narrow puddle instead of a round one. The purpose is to allow the molten metal at one end to solidify partly before adding more. Whatever weave pattern is used, the arc must return to all points before any one cools too much. The pattern in B is only a

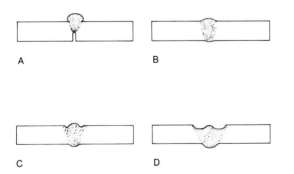

5-43 Cross sections of four common weld conditions: A, not enough penetration; B, full penetration with slight bead on under surface, acceptable; C, undercutting and unfilled gap, not acceptable; D, excessive undercutting and underfilling, not acceptable.

suggestion; each welder must find a pattern that works for him.

Visual inspection is not enough to judge the quality of a lap weld, because the depth of penetration into the inner corner is hidden. Working with small pieces, it is easy to grip one piece in a vise and twist the other around it lengthwise. Almost any lap weld can be broken in this manner by repeated bending, but a good one should stand considerable bending before failing. When the beginner can make welds that seem to pass the bend test, he should saw some of them apart crossways. No traces of the lower corner of the upper piece should be left.

ARC WELDING SAFETY

The problems of safety in arc welding fall into two classifications: protection for the operator and avoidance of fire hazards. Both of these should be considered when doing arc welding.

The operator needs protection from the ultraviolet light given off by the electric arc, against burns from the hot metal, and against the possibility of injurious electric shock. The brilliant light given off by the arc will cause burning, similar to sunburn, on any exposed area of skin if the exposure lasts for more than a few minutes. It will cause serious eye injury in much less time. The eye never should be exposed to the arc for even a fraction of a second.

Protection for the eyes and exposed parts of the face and neck should be provided by a face mask, shown on the left in Figure 5-35, large enough to cover the entire face and neck. It is fitted with a special glass that filters out untraviolet light. If broken, this glass never should be replaced with any other glass without the same filtering characteristics. The shade of the glass is no indication that it is suitable. Many glasses of the same size are available for use in oxyacetylene welding helmets. Use of such a glass is dangerous, even for a short time.

The glass filter in the welding helmet is covered with a piece of clear glass to protect the expensive filter glass. This protection is necessary because the operator must get close enough to the welding operation to see what he is doing. Flying sparks of white-hot metal will strike his helmet and the cover glass, ruining the filter glass very rapidly, if exposed. Replacement of the clear glass with any piece of glass satisfactory for good vision is permissible. However, glass with flaws that tend to distort vision should be avoided.

Protective clothing and gloves always should be worn by the operator. Bare forearms, open shirt collars, or bare hands are an invitation to severe burns. Burning can take place through lightweight clothing if it is exposed to the arc for any length of time. In making a two-minute weld, there is no problem. There is danger, however, if the operation continues for a half-hour or more.

Although the operator receives the greatest amount of exposure because he is closest to the work, protection for a helper or another person working in the area is important. Many times another person will help the operator by holding a piece in alignment. There is usually more risk of injury to the helper's eyes than to the operator's because the helper rarely wears a helmet. Instead, he will usually depend on turning his head or closing his eyes as the operator strikes the arc. It is much better for the helper also to wear a helmet. Better yet, the work should be set up so that the services of a helper are not required.

If arc welding is done in a special area, some kind of screen should be set up so that other persons in or passing through the area will not be forced to look at the light of the arc. This is particularly important in an area where persons not familiar with welding will be exposed to it.

There is little risk of arc burn on the skin for persons who are not actually doing the welding. Under most conditions, such exposure is too short to be of any particular consequence.

There is always a certain element of fire hazard with any welding operation. In general, the risk is about the same for arc and oxyacetylene welding when highly flammable materials are in the area. Under such conditions, welding should be delayed until the materials can be removed or the welding job taken to a safer area. However, around less flammable materials, particularly wood, there is much less fire hazard with arc welding, because it does not release the blast of hot gases characteristic of the torch flame. But it will throw sparks for considerable distance and may set fires the operator does not see because he is blinded by the helmet.

Probably the greatest risk of fire with the arc is in welding a frame in the area of the gasoline tank or the lines. An arc striking a gasoline tank, full or empty, is an almost positive guarantee of a distastrous fire and explosion. Striking a gasoline line with the arc may seem less hazardous than on the tank, but it can be as bad. A small quantity of gasoline burning on the shop floor can heat the tank, causing the gasoline to expand and spew out of the ruptured line to add fuel to the existing flame.

There should be an absolute rule that the gasoline tank must be removed before any welding, by any method, is done on any part of the body or frame where there is risk of welding heat's striking it. Another person standing by with a fire extinguisher is not sufficient protection. Human reaction is not fast enough to stop some gasoline fires. The only safe precaution is to remove the possible cause. When removed, the tank should be stored in a safe place.

The risk of serious injury through electrical shock is always present with any electrical machine, but is much less from the welding cables than from the higher voltage current in the power lead to the machine. This is particularly true when a portable machine is used with a long, plug-in cable. Worn or damaged insulation can expose the conductors; if they come into contact with the metal being welded or even a damp floor, the operator can be injured seriously. Damaged cables should be repaired or replaced immediately.

Filling has always been an important part of automobile body repair procedure. The original filling material was solder, often referred to as "lead," because of its high lead content, 70 to 80 percent instead of the 50 to 60 percent in solders used for most other purposes. In recent years plastic filler materials have almost completely replaced solder for several reasons, the most important being cost and the relative ease of application. In the following discussion of fillers, plastics have been considered the primary materials and have been used in the various repair jobs explained. The directions for applying solder are given because it still has a place in high-quality body repair work, particularly on high-priced sports cars and antique restoration. Many serious students of the body repair trade are interested in reaching the skill level required for such work. They should at least understand how solder should be applied.

Filling is a part of the straightening operation, but it must be emphasized that it is not a substitute for the whole process; it will save considerable time on many jobs, but there are many others that can be done faster, with much less filling than is often used, if the straightening is done correctly. There is a further disadvantage that excessive dependence on filling tends to stop progress in skill development.

6

FILLING

TYPES OF FILLERS

Two types of fillers are used in body repair work: polyester and epoxy resin base materials. The epoxy resins make a better bond to steel or aluminum, but have three disadvantages that have limited their general acceptance by the body repair trade: they are more costly, more difficult to use, and more toxic. Even though the polyester base materials do not bond quite so securely, the bond is good enough to justify their use as a general-purpose filler; many shops use them exclusively.

Hardening

Both polyester and epoxy resins harden by chemical action started by adding a catalyst, usually called a *hardener*, just prior to application. Hardening will be speeded or retarded by high or low temperatures. The manufacturer's directions for the amount of hardener to add are based on use at 70° F. (21° C.). Most brands of polyester fillers can be worked within fifteen minutes, if mixed according to directions. No general statement can be made about the hardening time for epoxy fillers, because different manufacturers formulate their material to different specifications.

Regardless of the temperature of the materials when mixed, heat is generated by the chemical action. Polyester filler applied at normal temperature will grow quite warm to touch in a few minutes. It should be allowed to cool a few more minutes before it is filed or planed. The same action takes place with epoxy fillers, but not necessarily at the same rate.

Shrinkage

Both epoxy and polyester base materials shrink in the process of hardening, polyester more than epoxy. An experiment that can be performed by anyone is shown in Figures 6-1–6-3. For this, two batches of lightweight polyester filler were mixed separately, the left one first, using material from the same container. Six drops of the manufacturer's liquid hardener were added to the left one and twelve to the right. The photograph in Figure 6-1 was taken immediately after the right batch had been deposited on the aluminum foil. The foil is the ordinary kitchen type available from any grocery store.

The photograph in Figure 6-2 was taken when the first signs of buckling began to appear around the right batch, approximately four minutes after it was put in place. The left side is buckled much more, but it has had about three minutes more time to harden.

The photograph in Figure 6-3, taken sixteen hours later, shows very definite buckling around both batches but a little more on the right than on the left. There was *almost* as much buckling a half-hour after the photograph in Figure 6-2 was taken, but a photograph of it was not included, because there was only a slight difference between it then and later. This shows that most of the shrinkage occurs as the material hardens.

The under surfaces of these samples were rounded by the drawing effect as the material shrank. The soft aluminum, 0.001 inch (0.025 mm) thick, was used because it has little resistance to the drawing effect of shrinkage. The sheet steel or aluminum in a body panel has far greater stiffness than the foil; however, the drawing effect is always there. It is enough to pull a large, nearly flat, thin steel panel out of shape when a large section is filled. It can be kept to a minimum by following the manufacturer's directions to build up a deep fill in successive coats, allowing each coat to harden before applying the next. However, if the panel is flat and thin enough, excessive filler will be required to make up for the collapse of the slight crown caused by shrinkage of the filler.

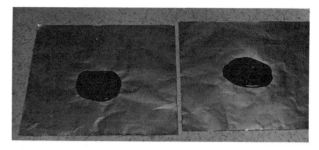

6-2 Photo of batches taken 4 minutes later. Aluminum foil has started to buckle on left batch, but it has had 3 more minutes to harden.

POLYESTER FILLERS

The following sections deal with polyester fillers. The procedures for surface preparation, mixing, applying, and finishing any type of filler are enough alike that, if one is understood, there should be no problem with others. However, when using any new brand or type of filler for the first time, it is only common sense to take time to read whatever instructions the manufacturer provides.

There are many brands of polyester fillers, but only a few manufacturers of the base materials. All contain the fluid resin and a solid to provide the necessary working properties. The two most commonly used solids are talc and tiny glass beads. Glass fiber, flake aluminum, and some other solids are used to some extent, but not nearly as much as the talc and glass beads.

Talc-type fillers are generally cheaper, but they tend to become excessively hard if not finished soon after curing. Talc is moisture absorbent also. The glass bead-type fillers, usually referred to as *lightweight*, will remain workable hours or even days after curing. The glass beads, obviously, will not absorb anything. However, after being painted, the exterior surface is sealed well enough that moisture absorption is not a problem. Any holes in the panel under the fill should be sealed by either brazing or soldering, if the inner surface is exposed to moisture in any way. This statement is contrary to the claims of some filler manufacturers, but it is based on experience.

The type of solid used does not affect the mixing and application procedure.

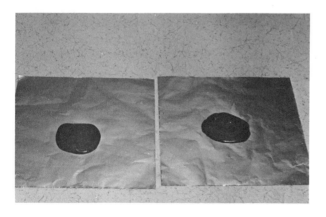

6-1 Shrinkage test of polyester filler. Batch on left was mixed with 6 drops of liquid hardener. Batch on right was mixed with 12 drops approximately 3 minutes later. Photo was taken immediately.

6-3 Photo taken 16 hours later. Right batch, which has had the most hardener, has buckled the aluminum foil the most.

APPLICATION

Applying body filler does not require a high degree of skill, but it should be done properly to obtain a satisfactory fill and to avoid waste. The tools required are (1) stirring paddle, (2) mixing board, (3) wide-blade spreading tool, and (4) disposable wiping cloths.

When first opened, a new container often has liquid resin that has separated from the solids and come to the top. This should be stirred back in to restore the proper balance of resin and solids; *never* pour this off. The stirring paddle can be used to dip out material as needed from the container, but it should not be used for mixing—it may carry hardener back into the container.

Hardener should be added to the batch according to the manufacturer's instructions. However, the exact amount used is not critical to the point that it should be measured. Some allowance must be made for temperature, particularly extremely hot weather. The user soon learns from experience how much variation will be required for different conditions.

Mixing the hardener into the filler should be done with the spreading tool. There is no exact procedure to follow, but good results will be obtained by first scooping material up around the edges and piling it in the center, then working across the pile from side to side with a kneading action. Repeating this several times from different angles should ensure that all of the batch gets mixed uniformly. Mixing is shown in Figure 6-4.

The mixing board may be almost anything with a smooth surface. Molded plastic boards are well liked, because the filler does not bond to them strongly. Pieces of plywood or heavy paper box board are used, but must be cleaned carefully after every use.

Plastic spreaders are inexpensive and easily kept clean. Some repairmen prefer to use a wide-bladed putty knife and accept the extra effort required to keep them clean. The practice of keeping the spreaders or putty knives in a can of scrap thinner should be discouraged, however, because of the fire hazard.

To apply the first coat, the spreader should be held at

6-5 Applying the first coat of plastic filler. The knife is pressed hard against the surface to ensure that no air pockets are left under the material.

a low angle and pressed hard against the panel (Fig. 6-5) to force filler into the depth of the disc sander scratches. These scratches are essential to the bond but, if not filled completely, each one may serve as a tiny, elongated air pocket and pathway for moisture under the fill.

The importance of applying filler in thin coats was emphasized in the preceding section and is repeated here, particularly for the first coat. If the surface is rough, it is best to put on just enough to fill the hollows and allow it to harden before applying more. Hardening, as the term is used in reference to preparation for following coats or final finishing, means that the material has cured enough that it can be filed or planed without gumming up the tools or tearing strips out of the filler. If the first coat has been applied properly, it should be smooth enough to allow application of the second coat as soon as it is hardened, without any finishing; however, any rough, high spots should be planed off first.

The second coat should be applied with firm pressure, but it should be finished with a light touch, holding the spreader at a higher angle, so that the surface can be smoothed without dragging it out of shape. It should then be allowed to harden so that it can be finished.

Sometimes filler will begin to harden before the shaping operation is complete. When this occurs, it is useless to attempt to work it further. Instead of just getting stiffer, it will begin to form into separate large lumps that will roll up on edge, leaving open spaces deep in the fill. This will occur any time that the material is worked too long after mixing, but it will happen more often when the hardening time is reduced by use of extra hardener or because of high temperature. Whatever the cause, it should be allowed to harden completely, then be planed down and refilled.

FINISHING

The tools commonly used to finish body filler are (1) "cheese grater"-type plane, referred to here as the

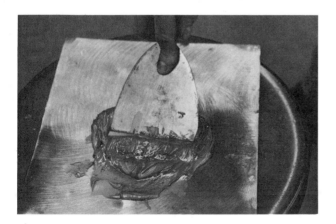

6-4 Mixing plastic filler with hardener. Kneading motion with the broad-bladed knife mixes in less air than a stirring motion.

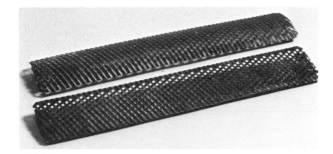

6-6 Flat and half-round plane blades.

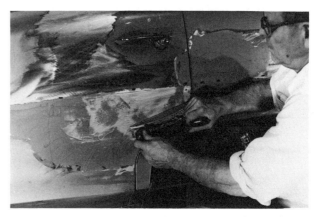

6-8 The start of the rough finishing operation, using a "cheese grater" plane.

plane, (2) air-powered board-type sander, (3) hand board sander, and (4) body file. Rotary sanders are used to some extent, but they make a lot of dust, and it is difficult to control the depth of cut.

The plane consists of a holder and detachable cutting blades, which are available in both flat and half-round shapes (Fig. 6-6). Some prefer to use the half-round blade without the holder for all surfaces, grasping it by the edges, as shown in Figure 6-7. With or without the holder, it should be stroked in a criss-cross pattern similar to the method recommended for use of a body file. The plane is intended for use only when the filler first sets up and is still quite soft. Talc-type fillers will be too hard to plane within an hour or two, depending on temperature and the amount of hardener used; the lightweight, glass bubble-type fillers can be planed much longer, usually after standing overnight.

The plane is a "speed" tool when used to rough-cut the still soft filler, as shown in Figure 6-8. Care must be exercised to avoid cutting too much, particularly when working around the edges of large low spots that will require additional filler. The surface around the low spot should be planed to contour, but care must be taken to avoid cutting it too low, as illustrated in Figure 6-9. This mistake is easy to make, because the toe of the plane tends to drop as it passes over the edge of the low

spot, cutting down the first edge, and the heel drops as it approaches the opposite edge, cutting it down. The result is that the low spot is made to appear smaller when actually it has been made wider than it was at first by cutting away needed material. Large low spots should be refilled, as shown in Figure 6-10.

When a filled area has been planed properly, it should be possible to finish it by sanding down the coarse marks left by the plane.

Either the air-powered or the hand sanding board may be used for the final sanding. The air-powered tool is shown in use in Figure 6-11, being pushed back and forth sideways across the job because its stroke provides the forward motion to do the cutting. The hand board is used in the same manner as a body file on a steel panel. The rough sanding should be done with 36- or 40-grit sandpaper, and then should be final-finished with 80- or 100-grit paper.

The primary use of the body file is on areas too narrow or otherwise obstructed to permit use of the sanding tools. It can serve for the entire job, eliminating all other equipment except fine sandpaper, but is rarely the only tool, because it is too slow and the filler dulls the file blade rapidly.

The job that was filled, planed, and sanded is shown in Figure 6-12. It has been refinished in Figure 6-13.

PROPERTIES OF BODY SOLDER

All lead-base solders differ from almost all other metals in that they melt over a wide range of temperature, instead of changing from solid to liquid at a fixed point.

6-7 Using a half-round blade held by the edges.

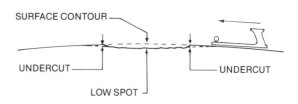

6-9 Undercutting of edges of low spots, caused by careless planing of partly filled area.

6-10 The final coat of plastic, applied after the first coat was roughed planed. This coat refilled the low spots showing in Fig. 6-8.

Other alloys of nonferrous metals have this property, but not to the degree found in solders composed of lead and tin. All of the lead-tin solders in common use begin to soften when heated slightly above 360° F. (184° C.), but the final melting point varies with the lead content. Those with approximately 70 percent lead liquefy at close to 500°F. (260° C.). By applying the torch flame properly, a batch of body solder can be kept within the part of this temperature range between solid and liquid, in which it has the consistency of motar. This permits it to be worked into the desired shape, using an oiled hardwood paddle.

Solder Paddles

The best solder paddles are made of bird's eye maple that has been treated with boiled linseed oil. The decline in the use of solder has made paddles difficult to obtain. If one is made up, it should be soaked at least overnight in boiled linseed oil. A second, but less desirable, choice would be outboard motor oil. If another wood must be used, it should be one of the varieties of hardwood having a very close grain; resinous or open-pored wood is almost useless for the purpose.

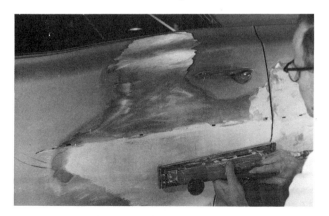

6-11 Final-finishing the plastic, using a straight-line sander.

6-12 The finished surface, ready for repainting.

BODY SOLDER APPLICATION

There are four basic steps in applying body solder: (1) cleaning, (2) tinning, (3) filling and shaping, and (4) metal-finishing.

The procedure for applying solder is essentially the same for any surface condition for which it is a suitable means of repair. The greatest problem for the beginner is to learn to use the torch flame on relatively flat metal, so that heat distortion is avoided. For that reason, it is best for him to practice on higher-crowned surfaces until he has developed some skill before he attempts to apply solder on the more difficult areas.

Cleaning

Any material that will prevent the solder from adhering to the surface to which it is to be applied must be removed. The materials that, under normal conditions, will be on the surface to be soldered are (1) paint, (2) weld scale, and (3) rust.

Occasionally, body sealers, cements, or other foreign matter that has found its way onto the surface by accident also must be cleaned off. The same cleaning methods will be satisfactory for the removal of all types of material.

6-13 The finished job, ready for delivery.

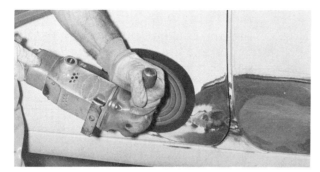

6-14   Removing paint with the disc sander.

6-16   Brushing flux on hot metal; steam indicates proper temperature.

The clean, bright metal surface left by the disc sander is ideal for solder application (see Fig. 6-14). Wherever possible, use the sander to remove paint, rust, or weld scale. However, body solder is used as a finishing material over surfaces that are entirely too rough to be cleaned with the sanding disc; rough welds are an excellent example. Cleaning a panel with a saucer-shaped wire brush mounted on a disc sander is shown in Figure 6-15. Although not satisfactory for removing large areas of paint, the wire brush will clean out either paint or weld scale from sharp depressions very rapidly and without contamination. It is best, however, to avoid its use on any surface where cements or sealers are present, because it will smear such materials instead of removing them. Such materials may be removed much more easily by heating them and scraping.

Acids should not be used.

TINNING

Tinning is the operation of coating with melted solder the surface to be soldered. Flux is required; either liquid or the flux contained in cored solder may be used. With liquid flux, the metal surface should be heated enough to form steam when the flux is brushed on, as shown in Figure 6-16. A small quantity of solder is then rubbed on the hot surface (Fig. 6-17). The flame should

then be played over as large an area as possible without causing heat warpage to bring it to the melting point of solder, so that the applied material can be wiped across it. When done properly, the result is, in effect, a surface painted with melted solder. The wiping cloth, shown in use in Figure 6-18, should be handled as though it was a paint brush; used with a scrubbing action, it will simply rub the hot solder off.

When using flux-cored solder for tinning, the surface should be heated as for liquid flux and the end of wire solder rubbed over it enough to leave patches of melted solder and flux over approximately one fourth of the area. Wiping is the same for either type of flux.

The Torch Flame

Assuming that the work will be done with an oxyacetylene torch, the tip should be selected for the size of the spot to be filled. A No. 3 would be satisfactory for the spot shown. When lighting, the acetylene valve should be opened slightly past the point where it stops giving off black smoke. The oxygen should be opened just enough to remove all traces of yellow. The result will be a soft, blue flame, which should be held 3 to 6 inches away from the surface and kept in constant motion when directed at the surface. When it is lifted away, to permit the tinning and application operations, the operator should be careful to hold it in a position where it will not cause damage or set a fire.

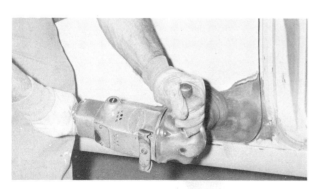

6-15   Using the saucer-shaped wire brush on the disc sander to clean paint out of a deep gouge.

6-17   Applying small quantity of solder for tinning. Note torch flame adjustment and distance from panel.

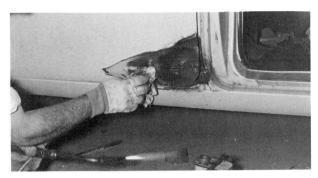

6-18 Wiping melted solder over the surface to complete the tinning operation.

6-20 Paddling the solder into shape.

Adding Solder

Solder is shown being added in Figure 6-19. The operator has held the flame well back from the panel, but directed toward the tinned surface, while holding the end of the bar of solder much closer as about 1 inch (2.5 cm) of the end softened. When the end of the bar began to sag, it was pushed against the preheated surface with a twisting motion, leaving the softened solder joined to the tinning coat applied previously. Note that the flame is directed under the automobile, where it will do no harm as the solder is applied to the panel.

Shaping

The shaping operation is shown in Figure 6-20. The flame has been played back and forth over the entire area to bring the deposited solder to the proper temperature to work. The paddle is being used to push the hot solder into place. It should never be turned on edge, just pressed down as the paddle slides toward the point where solder is needed.

Oil

The paddle was wiped on a freshly oiled rag before the operation was started and was rewiped after every three or four strokes. When solder was in general use,

several good lubricants were available for application on the paddle, but many repairmen used motor oil. Outboard motor oil is the best modern substitute, with automatic transmission fluid second choice. The oil tends to prevent solder sticking to the wood, but it will be necessary to sand the surface occasionally and re-oil it.

Quenching

A container of water and a sponge or rag should be at hand so that water can be dashed on the hot surface as soon as paddling is finished, as shown in Figure 6-21. If the surface is not quenched, some of the swelling caused by expansion may remain as heat distortion in the finished job. Quenching is particularly important on a flat surface, such as this door panel, but should be done on any solder fill job.

Metal-Finishing

The metal-finishing operation is shown in Figure 6-22. The best practice is to blend in the edges before finishing the center. The beginner is usually inclined to file solder too much. It cuts rapidly and tends to clog the file teeth. A sharp rap on the back or edge of the file will usually clean the teeth, but sometimes it is necessary to pick the solder out. A new, sharp file will clog more than one that is duller, because it tends to bury the teeth into the soft solder instead of shearing it off. It is better to use a slightly dull one.

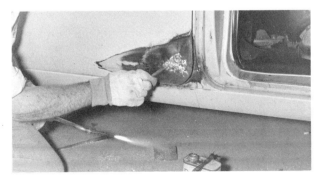

6-19 Applying solder for filling. The torch flame has been used to soften the bar and keep the tinned surface in the plastic temperature range.

6-21 Quenching the hot solder.

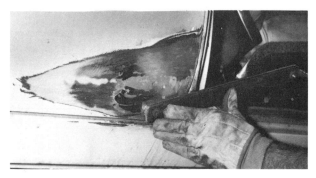

6-22 Finishing the lower edge. The center area will be filed to blend it into the finished outer edges.

6-23 Smoothing the surface with sandpaper wrapped around the file.

Sanding

The finished surface is being sanded for the final finish in Figure 6-23, using a sheet of 80-grit production paper wrapped around the body file. If the surface is not sanded, it will be difficult to hide the file marks when the panel is painted. Sanding should be done with full strokes, criss-crossed as in metal-finishing, and not overdone; sanding too much will tend to cut too much solder out at the blend area, leaving a "river bank" effect. At this point the panel is ready for repainting.

Both door panels, ready for repainting, are shown in Figure 6-24.

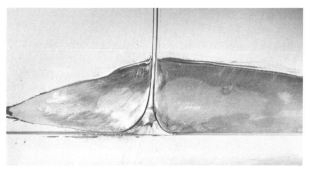

6-24 Both door panels, metal finished and ready for repainting.

In the preceding chapters, the repairman's job was broken down for the purpose of study into separate components dealing with fundamental information and basic operations. The next step is to weave these separate elements into a flexible pattern that the beginner can apply to actual repair jobs as he enters the second phase of his training and begins to do actual repair work. It is recognized that the dividing line between the first and second phase is not clearly defined, but, it is assumed that it has been crossed at this point. This part of the text deals with methods of applying force to various types of damaged panels so that the straightening will be accomplished efficiently and with the least possible distortion. This includes a discussion of the essential equipment and its direct application to the types of repair work for which it is intended. Major repair jobs have not been included.

The discussion in parts of this chapter are about the repair procedure for specific damage panels selected to represent typical repair problems. However, most of it is general rather than specific. At any stage in the progress from rank beginner to fully qualified tradesman, the problem is always how to do the job now at hand. A specific duplicate of a job explained in a textbook may never be encountered in the individual's work experience. General information is all that is obtainable from a lengthy explanation of one repair job. For that reason, most of this chapter is devoted to the type of general information that the repairman must rely on in deciding how to do the various repair jobs encountered daily.

7

BASIC STRAIGHTENING PROCEDURES AND EQUIPMENT

THE PHASES OF STRAIGHTENING

The repair operations on all but the most simple damages can be separated into three groups, or phases: (1) roughing, (2) bumping, or smoothing, and (3) finishing. On major jobs the first phase usually involves *aligning* as well as roughing. Aligning refers to the operations required to shift the reinforcing members back into position to restore the proper fit to door, body glass, and rear lid openings, and it can involve the fit of hoods and fenders. The conditions of the individual job determine whether aligning should be done before roughing or after it, or whether the two operations should be combined. Physical damage appraisers and insurance adjustors usually make a separate entry on the estimate form as a means of evaluating the time required for aligning beyond that required for individual panels.

ROUGHING AND ALIGNING

The terms roughing, aligning, panel, and structural members are defined as they are used here: (1) roughing refers to the operations required to bring a damaged panel from the shape in which the impact left it to an approximation of its correct shape, (2) aligning refers to the operations required to readjust the position of structural members of the body, (3) panel refers to the exterior surface metal only, and (4) structural members refers to the reinforced parts, usually box sections, that make up the body openings and serve as the framework of the body; floor pans can be considered as structural members, because they are primarily reinforcements and appearance is not as critical as for the other surface panels.

The definitions of panel and structural member should not be confused because some surface panels and a part of a structural member are made in one piece. Some quarter panels that have the lock pillar and the deck lid gutter are examples; although made of the same piece, these parts serve separate purposes. On other panels these parts may be stamped separately and welded to the exterior panel. However, these definitions do not apply to part names, as they are listed in the factory part book. Sometimes similar parts are called by different names by different manufacturers.

The estimator and repairman should recognize four types of misaligned conditions: (1) those that should be corrected before the adjoining panels should be either repaired or replaced, (2) those that, when corrected, will relieve a strain on an adjoining panel and allow it either to pop out or to be roughed out with very little additional effort, (3) those that require the adjoining panels to be roughed out carefully as the aligning progresses, and (4) those that will be completely eliminated when the damaged areas are cut out to permit replacement with new parts. These conditions determine the repair procedure and must be considered in the estimator's time allowances.

There is divided opinion among various estimators about whether to make a separate entry on the estimate form for aligning time or to divide it among the various affected parts. In general, both insurance companies that require their adjustors to prepare their own estimates and automobile damage appraisal agencies prefer to itemize alignment separately, because it conveys a better concept of the condition of the damage to interested persons who may never see the automobile. It is of less concern to the shop estimator, but is desirable because it requires closer attention to detail.

ROUGHING

Roughing, sometimes called *roughing out,* is the application of force so that it will undo the effect of the force that caused the damage. This subject is dealt with very briefly in Chapter 3 in the explanation of proper use of the dolly block and hammer. On some minor jobs the simple operations shown there may be adequate, but much more is usually involved when the damage is more severe than in that example.

Skill in roughing out damaged panels is in knowing how to apply force so that it does not create additional damage. A fender or other sheet metal panel can suffer severe damage from force applied in the wrong way or in the wrong place by a well-intentioned repairman. Even though the force that he can apply may be much less than the force involved in a collision, if he is making a mistake, he is likely to concentrate it on a small but vulnerable area where it will cause serious damage that will be added to the original.

There are three basic methods of applying force to rough out damaged panels:

1. Drive the metal back into place, using a dolly block, heavy hammer, or other striking tool. The tool used should not mark or mutilate the metal surface any more than absolutely necessary.

2. Push the metal back into place, using a pry bar, jack, or other means of applying steady force without impact.

3. Pull the metal back into place, using a jack as the power source and some means of attachment to apply tension lengthwise of the member or the panel surface.

Each of these methods has both advantages and disadvantages for certain types of damage conditions; all but the most simple damages will require a combination of two or all three. For the purpose of study, it is desirable to identify the types that are best suited to each method. The importance of being able to recognize the correct roughing-out procedure cannot be overemphasized. A minor mistake makes it necessary to finish the job under a handicap; a major mistake often must be buried under a replica of the panel carved out of filler.

BUMPING

Bumping is a less definite term than roughing because it consists of the hand tool work necessary to prepare the roughed out surface for metal finishing. Highly skilled metal men tend to combine bumping with the roughing operation; this was done in the roughing procedure on the fender repair illustrated in Figs. 7-5 to 7-11. Some others tend to omit the bumping phase entirely and fill areas which should be either straightened and metal finished, or straightened enough that less filling would be required.

Simple Dents

A simple dent in either a high crown area or an area where a combination high and low crown blend should be driven out without use of other means. A good example of this type of dent is shown in Figure 3-41 on the fender pictured to show correct use of the hammer and dolly block. These conditions are illustrated by A and B in Figure 7-1. The important factor is that all of the affected area is free to flex as the sharp buckle is driven out. When the proper conditions exist, roughing out a simple dent should leave only minor surface

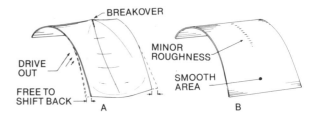

7-1 The type of dent that should be driven out. A, the original condition; B, the condition after roughing out.

roughness in the area of the break-over path, and much of the displaced metal in the low-crowned area should either snap back or require very little effort to bring it back, as suggested by B. Damages of this type, often called *soft* dents, are found in the blend area between a low crown and a combination crowned surface.

The two parts in Figure 7-1 represent the before and after conditions of a rolled buckle in a sheet of curved metal. The dotted lines on the lower sides represent the original positions of the edges before the rolling action caused them to shift to new positions. Roughing out the valley of the rolled buckle properly would permit these edges to shift back and most of the surface not in the break-over path to snap out into almost perfect shape.

The example just given can be considered ideal, in that it is about as simple to rough out as can be found. However, this method is not restricted to use on simple damages. Most damaged panels have two or more rolled buckles extending outward from an area of displaced metal that should be roughed out in this manner. When this condition is found, it should be examined closely to determine on which buckle the roughing operation should start. Sometimes it will make no difference, but quite often one will be holding the displaced metal under a strain that will prevent free movement of the others. When this condition exists, working the wrong buckle first may cause additional buckling of as yet undamaged but displaced metal. Finding the right buckle to start on may be a problem for the beginner. It is a sure sign that the work has been started in the wrong place when new buckles begin to form in areas that have been smooth.

When the start has been made on the correct buckle, it is almost always best to work it only partway before going to the other—or others, if there are more than one. It may be possible to rough it all of the way, but the work should not be carried past the point that new buckles begin to form in the smooth areas. When this happens, *stop and rethink the procedure.*

The best possible sequence to follow in the rough-out procedure would be suggested if it was possible to see a reversed slow-motion picture of the panel or assembly as it yielded under the impact. Even though the motion picture is not available, study of the damage will enable

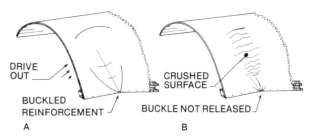

7-3 The error of roughing out buckles caused by a bent or buckled reinforced member. A is the original condition, and B is the effect.

the repairman to visualize the scene well enough to see the sequence in which the various parts should move. It is not practical for one man to work several points at once, as the reversed film idea suggests, but the elasticity of the metal will permit each one to be worked partway before working another. The correct procedure will permit as much as possible of the displaced area to return to normal position without further buckling. The basic idea of reversed motion is discussed in much greater detail in a later section.

The limit of conditions that can be roughed by driving buckles out is reached when the impact of the driving tool batters or crushes the surface it contacts, but causes little or no movement of the surrounding area. Three of the most common causes of this condition are (1) the buckle is folded over so far that it presents a narrow V-shaped ridge to the impact tool, (2) the impact area has been forced into a "knotted" condition that is too rigid to unroll in this manner, and (3) the buckle has been caused by a shift of a stiffer part of the body structure that holds it out of place. This third condition, often called *secondary* or *indirect* damage, must be roughed out along with the straightening of the condition that caused the shift. It is discussed in more detail in the section Jacking Out Dents and Factors Governing the Use of Tension. However, after the condition is roughed out, it would be worked in much the same manner as a rolled buckle caused by a direct impact.

The six cross sections in Figure 7-2 illustrate the difference in the problems of roughing out a shallow and a deep rolled buckle. A represents the forming of the shallow dent at the point where the roughing out would start. The arrows indicate the inward movement as the center is drawn down. Rough-out force reverses the flow of forces, causing the sides to push outward as suggested by the arrows on B. The outward push is most effective when the opposite sides of the buckle meet at the widest angle and have the least curvature. The condition represented here should be straightened with a little more hammer and dolly work to produce the slightly wavy but full-length condition shown in C, which could be finished easily.

When the dent is much deeper (D), the sides will have been drawn in much farther and meet at a much sharper angle. Force applied by a dolly block to metal in this shape (E) meets greater resistance than in the example in A and provides much less outward push. Instead, it tends to spread and upset the area contacted by the face of the dolly and lift the sides above the

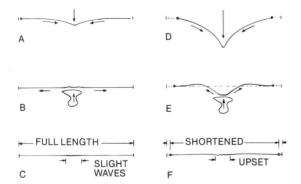

7-2 Cross sections illustrating the effect of driving out shallow and deep valleys of rolled buckles. In A, B, and C the length has been fully restored; in D, E, and F the valley is upset, shortening the length.

proper level, as shown in E. Continued hammering on the ridge will cause further upsetting and batter the contact area out of shape. The final condition would be more like E, upset in buckled area and too short, if the area could be finished, but would probably be filled instead. Being too short, it would distort the overall shape of the panel. The error of driving out a buckled area that has been caused by a bend or collapse in a heavy reinforcement is illustrated by A and B in Figure 7-3. A buckled box member is shown in A with a buckled section of welded-on panel extending above. B illustrates how any rough-out work on the buckle will simply crush the surface if the buckled reinforcement is not relieved first. This would add damage to existing damage. A welded-on box member is shown, but any type of reinforcement that is much stiffer than the buckled metal will have the same effect.

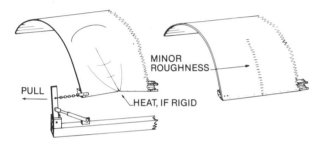

7-4 The effect on a buckled panel when a buckled reinforcement is straightened properly. The method of anchoring the portable machine is not shown, but it would have to bear against some rigid part of the structure.

A and B in Figure 7-4 illustrate how relieving the condition in the reinforcement will relieve the buckled panel so that roughing what remains of the buckle in the panel is a simple operation. A portable body and frame machine is shown in use, but an operation of this type could be done in many different ways on various parts of the body. Portable machines are discussed in more detail in later sections.

When working out a damage that is more than just a simple dent, the procedure must be planned to avoid creating the "horrible" examples, actually a false-

stretch condition, represented by D, E, and F in Figure 7-2. One mistake of this type, involving a very small portion of the surface area, will have a drawstring effect on the surrounding metal, sometimes drawing the entire surface slightly but noticeably out of shape. Although it is not always possible to avoid some false stretch, the wrong procedure can make a major problem out of a relatively simple dent. Most often, it is the cause of excessive use of filler on jobs that could have been done faster with less filler by a repairman who knew how to straighten metal.

The repairman must "read" the conditions of each damage he works to determine (1) the sequence in which each buckle should be worked and (2) whether each buckle should be driven out or a jack set up at a right angle to the main valley to reduce the angle at which the sides of the valley meet. Referring to A and D in Figure 7-2, the sides of A offer considerably less resistance to a lifting force than the sides of D.

DRIVING OUT SEVERE DAMAGE

The dented fender skirt area in Figure 7-5 is a much more complicated straightening problem than the rolled buckles discussed in the preceding section. It was picked from a body shop's scrap and repaired, off the car, by the author to illustrate this section. This is typical damage of the type the beginner should practice on as soon as he has learned to straighten simple rolled buckles.

This fender had been damaged by the glancing blow of a small hard impact object, possibly a projecting bolt end on a bumper. The first impact point is indicated by the arrow on the beaded edge of the wheel opening, and

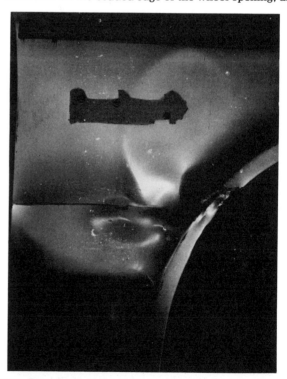

7-6 The effect of the first rough out. A tinner's hammer was used on the inside surface of the bead.

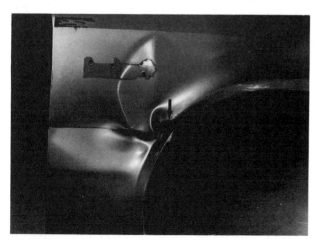

7-5 Damaged fender, obtained from scrap pile. Arrow indicates the first impact point.

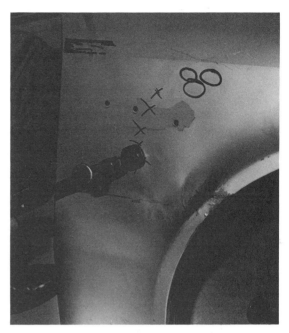

7-8 Relieving the upper ridge with the hammer. O's indicate areas lifted by striking the under side with the dolly. X's indicate hammer blows, working from the upper section down, but without the dolly block.

have been freed, and further movement of the impact area is being resisted by the remaining strains.

The next step, Figure 7-7, was to strike a few hammer blows on the small, semicircular buckle, using the radius-faced hammer and smoothing the bead with the hammer and the lip of the dolly block. This was followed by the operation shown in Figure 7-8. The three circles indicate the lowest part of the upper rolled buckle. The underside of this area was lifted by two or three light blows, using the flattest part of the working face of a general-purpose dolly block. Next, the dolly was held with firm pressure against the lowest point of this area

7-9 The lower area marked to indicate the operation in progress. O's enclosing X's indicate use of the hammer-on-dolly. Open O's indicate areas to be driven up with the dolly block.

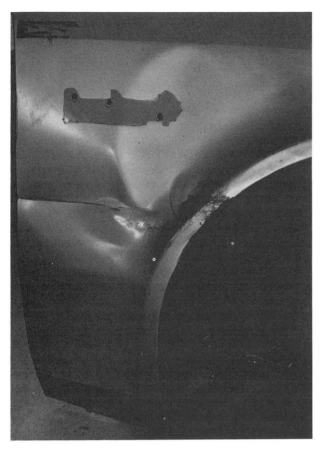

7-7 The effect of a few hammer blows on the sharp ridges adjoining the bea. A radius hammer was used.

a rebound impact has made a minor line gouge across the rear edge. Rebound, or second, impacts are quite common, because both the panel and the impact object tend to bounce off and come back. This one has come back on an area already displaced by the first impact. If there had been no rebound, either there would have been no gouge at all, or the panel would have ripped across its full width.

The displaced metal above and beside the impact area is rolled buckles that have spread from the impact and driven the edge of the fender inward. However, they differ from the simple rolled buckles discussed in the preceding section in that they are held by the knotted condition of the impact area instead of a break-over path at the outer edge. Starting the rough-out procedure at the outer edges would add damage to existing damage. However, straightening the minor buckles in the displaced areas will be simple after the knotted impact area has been *untied*.

The roughing and bumping phases are combined in the repair procedure used on this fender.

The result of the first rough-out operation is shown in Figure 7-6. Three or four solid hammer blows, using a tinner's hammer with a chisel-shaped end, have been struck on the inside of the impact area of the bead, bringing it more than halfway back to position, far enough to make considerable change in the surrounding buckles. Before this, the impact area had tied up elastic strains in the outer area. Now, most of these strains

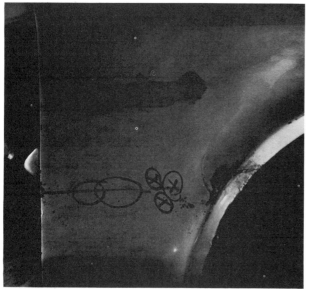

7-10 Rolling out a low area by striking an angling hammer blow under the edge. The hammer and dolly work of the adjoining surfaces has been completed.

while a series of hammer blows were made down the row of X's to the position shown in the photograph. Both the low point and the beginning of the ridge were located by shifting the eye position to see the ripples in the light reflected from the surface. Work with the hammer began at the start of the ridge, and the hammer blows were placed carefully to bring the surface down to level without marking it. In effect, the rolling action

7-11 The result of the first dics sanding operation, using the six-pointed disc shown. The largest low spots were picked up and resanded before this photo was taken. Circles enclose small low spots.

has been reversed to the point where the hammer is shown.

In Figure 7-9 the impact area has been lifted further and smoothed with the hammer and dolly, and the adjoining reverse crown area has been smoothed with the radius-faced hammer and dolly. The open-circled areas have been lifted, using the dolly; some hammer and dolly smoothing has been done in the area with the circle-enclosed X's.

In Figure 7-10 most of the hammer and dolly work has been completed, and the hammer is shown in position to ''roll'' the rear edge where it had been depressed by the second impact. (This operation should have been included with the preceding photograph.) The low point was first driven out with the hammer striking almost at a right angle. This was followed by two or three blows above and below the point with the hammer held at 45 degrees or less to the surface. Blows coming from this angle will lift the surface forward of the edge where it had been tilted down by the impact. This operation must be performed carefully. Striking too hard or trying to raise a low spot that is too deep will drive the edge forward, leaving an ugly wide spot in the door edge gap.

Normally, if this fender was repaired, the work would be done without removing it from the automobile. Done in that position, a light-duty body jack would be used instead of the hammer for the roughing-out operation. However, when panels of this type are obtained for practice material, the work must be done as it was here or using whatever equipment is available to hold it. Working panels off the car should not be considered a handicap because, to become a qualified repairman, one must learn to straighten metal in whatever position one finds it.

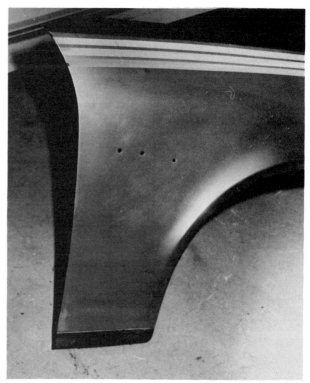

7-12 The painted fender.

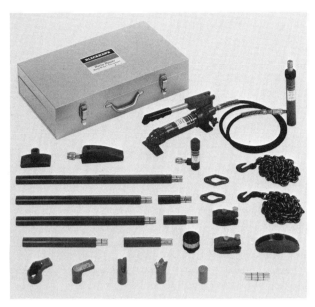

7-13 Four-ton body jack.

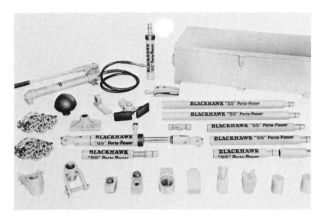

7-14 Ten-ton body jack.

If this work had been done with the fender on the automobile, a slide hammer equipped with a wide hood would have been used on the edge, and part of the rear edge would have been pried up instead of doing most of the work with the hammer and dolly block.

The result of the first disc-sanding operation is shown in Figure 7-11, using the six-sided disc shown on the sander. No picking to raise low spots has been done at this point, but circles and loops have been drawn around spots that need it. These were picked, using the edge of the bumping hammer, because it is more blunt than a pick hammer, and resanded. Enough filling was done to check for undetected low spots, and the surface was buffed with a fine-grit disc for the final operation.

The repainted fender is shown in Figure 7-12.

BODY JACKS

Complete four- and ten-ton-capacity body jack sets are shown in Figures 7-13 and 7-14, typical of most body jacks available in that they are hydraulically operated by separate pump units connected by high-pressure hoses. The pumps shown are hand operated, but air-operated ones can be substituted easily by means of a quick-disconnect coupler. Various types of mechanically operated jacks are and have been available but have never been as popular as the hydraulic, because they are not as easy to operate. This coupler makes it easy to change the pump from one ram to another. However, simultaneous operation of two jacks requires two pumps.

Use and Care of Body Jacks

The manufacturers of body jacks build their equipment to withstand considerable abuse, because of the nature of the work they are required to do. However,

the most rugged jack possible to build can be damaged by careless use and neglected maintenance. The useful life of a body jack can be extended for years by following a few common-sense rules:

1. Offset loads should be avoided as much as possible. When necessary, the jack should be set up as shown in A, Figure 7-15 and kept below its maximum output, if possible.
2. Do not use a light-duty jack on a job that is beyond its capacity.
3. Fittings, whether of the slip-on type or threaded, should never be used in direct contact with a steel surface; protective caps are a part of the equipment and should be used.

JACKING OUT DENTS

Using a jack to push out dents is similar to driving them out but has three advantages: (1) the relatively slow movement of the jack eliminates the impact of the driving tool on the inner panel surface, (2) a buckle can be jacked out partway and held under pressure while other buckles are worked, and (3) a jack or a spreader, which is just another type of jack, can be used in enclosed spaces where there is no room to swing a hammer or a dolly block. It is important to recognize that the emphasis is on the versatility of the jack rather than on its full capacity to push. Applying too much force with a jack can be as damaging as driving too hard with the dolly block, illustrated by D, E, and F in Figure 7-2.

The jack is most effective as a rough-out tool on large panels that have been dented deeply enough to cause two or more severe rolled buckles but little or no misalignment of the body structure. Good examples of this are often found on roof panels that have been crushed in a soft roll-over on flat ground, spreading the impact over a large part of the panel surface. It is not uncommon to find a crushed roof with little or no evidence of a direct impact but two or more severe rolled buckles extending into the corners over the windshield or rear window. The more severe these buckles are, the more important it is to use the controlled movement of a jack to rough them out. The rough-out procedure should start

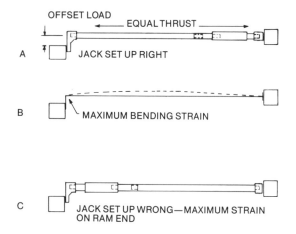

7-15 The right and wrong offset jack setups.

close to the outer end of the break-over path, as explained earlier.

Skill in the use of a body jack is more a matter of knowledge than of manual dexterity. Fortunately, most of the knowledge required is of the common-sense type rather than technical. Some common beginner's problems with the use of a body jack are (1) not providing enough temporary support for the base end, (2) pushing too hard, (3) failure to relieve buckles as an area is jacked out, and (4) failure to allow for the angle effect.

The jack exerts equal pressure, or thrust, at both ends. In almost every use, the jack must be based against an undamaged area to push out damage in another area. There are only a few areas of the entire automobile where the jack can be based directly on body or frame steel without risk of damage. An example would be the underside of fenders where the jack can be based on frame metal. In almost every other place, the safest procedure is to place one or more blocks of wood in position to spread the load over a much larger surface area. This is particularly important on the newer down-sized automobiles that are much lighter in construction than those of the past.

The importance of not pushing too hard may be better understood after studying the discussion of Reversed Motion later in this chapter. The essential part is that any movement of the jack should cause the metal to reverse the movement caused by the impact. When the jack is extended and this reversed movement is not obtained, the setup should be re-examined. *It may be wrong.* Further pushing could add damage to existing damage.

The effect of angle can be ignored in many jack setups, but not all. Jack pressure simply pushes whatever it bears against in the direction in which it offers the least resistance. This is illustrated in Figure 7-16. In A the jack is shown at an angle of approximately 45 degrees between body members. The base could be a rocker panel, and the working end could be a roof rail, but other parts would react in the same manner. Both parts will tend to move in line with the jack, but the stiffer one will force the other to yield. Normally, this type setup would be needed on a roof rail, so the repair-

man should be careful to provide enough blocking to prevent damage to the rocker; it would not be expected to move, but it could be crushed, if not protected with suitable wooden blocks. The effect on the roof rail would be to follow the angle of the jack, which is a combination of both upward and outward. However, the construction of the area affected may offer more resistance to movement in one direction than the other. If lifted too much, welded-on flanges on the underside will be torn loose, as illustrated in B. Or, if forced too hard, the rail might simply be crushed, as illustrated in C.

When damages of this type occur, it is the fault of the operator. The beginner must be aware that a body jack is an indispensable tool, but it must be used with common sense.

The worst possible abuse of a body jack is overloading on an offset load, as shown in Figure 7-15. When set up as shown in cross-sectional illustration A, its precision parts are as far as possible from the point of maximum strain, as indicated by B. In effect, the full length of the jack becomes a lever working against the relatively short L-shaped fitting on the end. When the jack is set up as shown in C, the end of the ram and cylinder are subjected to the maximum leverage. Forethought is all that is needed to avoid this equipment-damaging situation.

It is almost equally destructive to force a jack to the absolute limit of its capacity. There are some straightening operations in heavy truck repair that will require more than the practical output of a 10-ton jack. Very few operations on automobiles will require more than half of that capacity, although some may be beyond the capacity of a light-duty jack. When excessive force is required, the setup should be re-examined; it is probably wrong and should be changed.

REVERSED MOTION

The repair of any sheet metal damage is simply a matter of making the various parts move back where they belong. The idea of a slow-motion picture of a panel

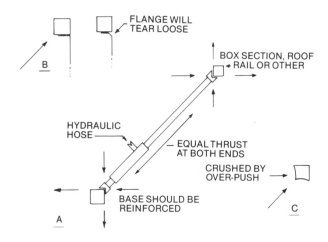

7-16 The effect of too much force.

being damaged, suggested earlier in this chapter to explain the use of a body jack in the rough-out procedure, is expanded here as a very good means of determining the procedure to follow in aligning and roughing out much more complicated damaged assemblies.

This idea is based on two assumptions: (1) that almost everyone has seen a motion picture run in reverse, making broken glass fly back together or a fly ball come from the far outfield, bounce off the bat as it spins the batter in a reverse swing, and bounce back to the pitcher and put him in a reverse windup and (2) that almost all should be equally aware that a slow-motion picture can spread almost instantaneous action over a much longer period to permit time to study it.

Automobile companies and other interested agencies use slow-motion pictures to study the action of staged automobile collisions. These pictures will make a damaged panel seem to drift slowly inward as the effect spreads. However, the spread will be in steps rather than in one continuous movement as pressure or tension builds up on the various points until they collapse and allow the pressure to flow on to the next. At the point of final penetration the motion will stop and spring back to the point where the estimator and repairman find it. Running the picture backward would reverse the motion and bring it back toward the impact point, dropping off sections of undamaged metal until, finally, a fully restored automobile would be seen.

The automobile collision repair industry would not exist as it does if the repair of collision damage was as simple as a reverse showing of a slow-motion picture would make it seem. As the damaging force spreads from the impact area, it sets up new conditions in every bit of metal that it strains past the elastic limit. The repairman's problem is to relieve these conditions methodically so that the reversed action can be kept moving progressively back to the start. The ideal sequence would be suggested by viewing a reversed showing of a slow-motion picture of the damage as it was formed by the impact. However, that is both impossible and unnecessary; the repairman trained to "think backwards" should be able to visualize the reverse sequence, and he will have a better plan than by relying on a set of rules that must be general rather than specific. Visualizing may be slow at first, but will become easy with practice.

Figure 7-17 shows the flow of force from an impact area on a two-door-model quarter panel through the lock pillar into the roof rail and roof panel. The heavy arrow indicates the direction of the impact. The light arrows beside the pillar and pointing toward the impact indicate the pull effect the pillar has had on the floor and the roof. For this discussion it is assumed that the floor has resisted the force, but the roof and roof rail have yielded. As shown, the roof and roof rail would be pulled down approximately 1 inch (2.5 cm) and the same amount inward. That amount of movement would tend to draw the fore and aft sections of the roof rail toward the pillar and affect the door and windshield alignment. Further movement would cause misalignment of both, but probably not affect the rear compartment lid alignment.

A slow-motion picture should not be needed to realize that a lighter impact would damage the quarter panel without affecting the roof or that a much heavier impact would cause damage to spread farther into the quarter panel, roof assembly, and floor.

A slow-motion picture of the damage suggested by Figure 7-17 would show the action start by depressing the impact area of the quarter panel surface, pulling the surrounding metal with it. A few moments later, the shape of the pillar would yield, drawing the quarter panel outer and inner surfaces with it. As the pillar continued in motion, it would pull down and in on the roof structure, roof and roof rail, and pull up and in on the floor and rocker panel. Both would be seen flexing under the strain but retaining shape for a surprisingly long time and at considerable distance from the original position. Assuming that the first yield would be in the roof, a slight ripple would appear in the sharply curved metal just above the drip molding. This would grow rapidly into a severe rolled buckle as the pillar moved downward and the fore and aft section of the roof side moved into the buckle. At this point most of the resistance to further movement of the roof would be concentrated on the very small area of metal in the break-over path; as it went through the rolling upset the paint would fly off, leaving flaky edges. If enough force continued coming, the door and windshield opening would be pulled out of alignment as the fore and aft sections of the roof were drawn together.

The important fact to be learned from the slow-motion picture example is that, even though an accident seems instantaneous, damage spreads in a *series of steps*. Showing the picture in reverse would reverse the steps. The correct repair procedure sequence will follow the steps in reverse order. Correct, as the term is used here, means procedure that is established by the conditions of the specific damage, not a dogmatic set of rules.

Manual skill enters the scene as the repairman begins the process of straightening the damage. The skill with which he releases the various buckles and upsets needed to keep the reverse action moving is as important as the sequence in which they are worked. A few horrible examples, as represented by D, E, and F in Figure 7-2, can ensure that (1) the final result will never

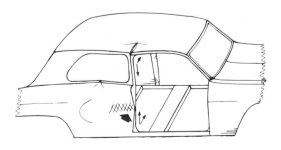

7-17 The flow of force from an inpact area on a quarter panel into the roof.

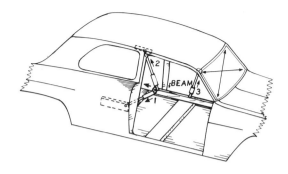

7-18 Typical jack setups to reverse the effect of the flow of force illustrated in Fig. 7-17.

be quite right and (2) more time and material will be used than should have been required.

Figure 7-18 shows some of the typical jack setups that could be used to straighten a damage similar to that shown in Figure 7-17. A wooden beam is shown across the opposite door opening to provide a safe base for the jacks. This may not be needed on every body, but some will crush if not protected in some manner. The safest procedure is to protect the sheet metal with enough wood to prevent unwanted damage.

Jack 1, pushing against the inner surface of the impact area, should be considered the lead. The first step must be to obtain enough reverse motion here to begin releasing the strains that have carried into the roof and floor. However, this is not just a simple matter of setting the jack in place and pushing. The pillar section has been crushed, and the inner panel may block access to the underside of the impact area, depending on the location of whatever holes the manufacturer has provided. It may be necessary to make several different jack setups or to use external pulling equipment to rough the panel out enough to begin relieving its effect on the roof. If external equipment is used, a piece of sheet metal may be brazed or welded to the door opening edge so that a clamp can be attached to it. If the quarter panel is to be repaired, the various areas of the panel should be straightened with hand tools as the work proceeds. If the panel is to be replaced, less care will be required, but the strains should be relieved enough to permit the other areas to be worked.

Jack 2 bears against a piece of wood placed just above the pillar-to-roof joint. As explained in the Use and Care of Body Jacks section, it is both lifting and pushing outward in this position. Both effects will be needed on most damages of this type. Unfortunately, the lift may be more effective than the outward push, particularly if the edge of the roof is buckled severely and the rolled buckle has considerable upset. It was pointed out in the preceding section that the fore and aft portions of the roof tend to move toward each other; the upset metal in the rolled buckle serves as a tie to hold the buckles formed by this movement. If these conditions are not too severe, the use of the jack may be enough to free these buckles. As a general rule, it is best to heat the rolled buckle before the jack is operated so that the metal will be as free as possible to move. As

with any heating operation, the paint should be scorched and wire-brushed off first. Using a small tip adjusted to a neutral flame, heating should start at the tip of the break-over path and kept on it while the jack is extended. Spoons and hammers should be within easy reach so that the buckled metal in the edge of the roof can be worked without delay while the metal is still hot.

These operations will almost always leave some high metal at the tip of the break-over path. A minor amount of this can be relieved by shrinking. However, this is false stretch; shrinking will blend it into the surrounding area to some degree, but the spot will always be high unless the full length is restored to the upset metal in the break-over path by applying tension lengthwise of the roof while heating the upset area. One practical method of doing this is explained in the next section.

Jack 3 is shown in position to shift the windshield opening, which would not be required if the glass was not broken, but is essential if it has been broken by a shift of the pillars. This operation would alternate with the work shown at Jack 2 position. It would not be necessary to use a third jack. The final check on the opening is the fit of the glass; the edges of the pillars should be parallel to the edges of the glass, and the glass should make contact with the metal all around the outer edges.

When alignment has been fully restored, the sequence of further straightening and metal-finishing operations is not important, unless a panel is to be replaced. Then it is best to delay the metal-finishing operations until the panel is welded in place, because unexpected jacking operations may affect an already finished panel.

TENSION

The use of tension offers many advantages over either driving or pushing dents, particularly in panels that may be classified as low crowned. The main advantage is that the tendency toward upsetting is avoided, because force is transmitted through the panel surface

7-19 A typical setup in which a jack and tension plates are used to pull a dent out of a roof panel.

in tension instead of pressure. It is a matter of lifting a dent out by either pulling on each side of it, or by pulling on one side when the opposite side is rigid enough to provide the resistance needed, instead of pushing or striking it on the underside. A typical pulling setup is shown in Figure 7-19.

The trend toward low-crowned, nearly flat panels has tremendously increased the importance of tension in roughing out major damages. As pointed out earlier, the effect of an impact on a low-crowned panel is to pull inward the metal adjoining the impact area. If the impact is strong enough, adjoining reinforcements will be drawn inward, also. The use of tension to pull such damaged metal back to place simply means that force is applied to the already damaged metal in such a way that the least additional damage will be made by the repair procedure.

The difference in the effect of force acting through the surface of a piece of sheet metal in tension and under pressure was discussed in Chapter 2. It was shown that the length of a flat piece of metal makes no difference in the resistance to tension, but it can make a tremendous difference in the resistance to pressure. The limit of tension that can be used is the force required to cause the metal actually to yield. When tension is used properly, however, the yield point never is reached. Almost all damages can be pulled into place with far less force than is necessary to cause yielding, because tension strains the entire area uniformly. The only qualification is that the point of attachment used to apply the tension must be wide enough, at least 2 inches or more, to avoid stretching the metal. Another error to avoid is the tendency toward too much tension.

Tension also can be a great advantage where heat is used to reduce the yield point. This will be discussed in more detail in the descriptions of actual jobs.

In comparison to tension, pushing or driving a dent out tends to concentrate force on relatively small areas, which upset easily. The panel never can be restored to proper contour unless these upsets are relieved. In addition to being a fast method, tension avoids these upsets.

The basic principle of the use of tension, the tendency to produce a straight line, is illustrated in Figure 7-20. The lower line represents a cross section through a typical dent, the upper line the same cross section after it has been pulled out. Note particularly that some of the original bend, which in most cases would be the valley section of a rolled buckle, remains in the upper line. Even though pulling will restore the contour of a dented

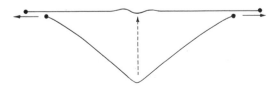

7-20 Basic principle of the use of tension to straighten dents. The lower line represents a cross section of a panel being pulled; the upper line represents the result.

7-21 *(Top)* Jack and clamp setup on bent metal strip to show the limits of straightening by tension alone.

7-22 *(Bottom)* Jack and clamp setup after stretching strip almost to the breaking point. Center arrow points to trace of the original buckle remaining in strip. Arrow at right points to narrow section that is breaking.

flat panel to the roughed-out state better than any other method, it is necessary to do some straightening on sharp bends. Pulling will reduce sharp bends so that they are much easier to straighten, but it will never straighten them completely.

The need for some straightening is illustrated in Figures 7-21 and 7-22. In Figure 7-21, a strip of metal with a sharp bend in it is shown set up so that it can be pulled by means of a jack and two parallel jaw clamps. The bend was made by folding the metal over double and then opening it enough by hand to reach the clamp jaws. In this condition it represents a typical cross section through a typical dent that should be straightened under tension.

In Figure 7-22, the strip has been stretched almost to the breaking point. Note the narrow spot in the right end. Also note that the bent area has retained almost its original width, but the rest of the strip has narrowed enough to make this wide point noticeable. Work hardening, resulting from the bending, has strengthened this bent area enough to cause almost all of the yielding to take place elsewhere. Also, a slight trace of the original bend remains. If the intention had been to straighten this strip, instead of using it as an example of what not to do, it should only have been pulled tight and the buckle worked with the hammer and dolly block.

FACTORS GOVERNING THE USE OF TENSION

The procedure for straightening any damaged panel must be determined by examining the conditions existing on it. Such an examination will determine whether the damaged area should be driven, pushed, or pulled out. On panels where the use of tension is indicated, it is necessary to determine the exact points of attachment for applying tension, how hard to pull, and to form a

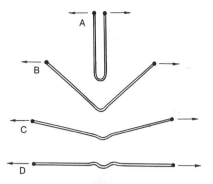

7-23 (A) First of four illustrations showing the loss of leverage as a bend is straightened. A full 180° has the maximum leverage.

7-24 (B) Loss of leverage as a bend is straightened.

7-25 (C) Progressive loss of leverage as a bend is straightened. Note the indications of outward bends beside the original inward bend.

7-26 (D) Loss of leverage as a bend is straightened. Slight buckles remain, but all leverage has been lost.

general idea of the step-by-step procedure. This problem is not as complicated as it may seem at first, if the factors governing the use of tension are understood. Such an examination then becomes an intelligent analysis that will result in a practical answer to the problem.

Of the basic factors that must be considered in using tension to pull dents out of low-crowned panels, the most important are (1) leverage angle, (2) lift reaction, (3) work hardening of the buckled area, (4) variations of surface crown, and (5) alignment with the crown of the panel.

These factors are discussed and explained separately.

Leverage Angle

The leverage angle is the most important factor in determining the effectiveness of any pull on any panel. This is illustrated in Figures 7-23–7-27. In these four illustrations, the metal on each side of the sharp buckle is considered as two levers. When tension is applied to them, they open in much the same manner as the handles of a pair of tongs. The leverage angle is the angle made by two lines connecting the two points of tension application to the lowest part of the dent. The lines that form this angle will become a straight line when the panel has been straightened.

In Figure 7-23, the two lines forming the leverage angle are in a 180-degree fold. It is rare in any panel repair that a full bend such as this is encountered. However, such a bend will provide the maximum leverage angle.

In Figure 7-24, the outward movement of the two surfaces has started to open the bend and draw it closer to a straight line. As the angle between the two surfaces becomes wider, the leverage they can exert against the stiffened bend decreases proportionally. A leverage

angle as small as this, however, is larger than is commonly encountered in most repair work.

In Figure 7-25, the outward movement of the two surfaces has increased the angle and made a further decrease in the leverage as the depth of the dent has been reduced. Note that typical outward bends are shown on each side of the original inward bend. These outward bends usually form because the original bend is stiffer, due to work hardening, than the adjoining metal. If the dent were being driven out from the underside, these bends would form in exactly the same manner, except that they would be sharper because of the resistance to movement of the adjoining metal.

The position shown in Figure 7-25 is more nearly typical of a cross section through a dent suitable for straightening under tension than the conditions shown in the other illustrations. The remaining leverage is much less than with a smaller angle, but there is still enough left to be very effective.

In Figure 7-26, the metal on each side of the original bend has been drawn almost to a straight line. Note that some of the original bend is seen, as are some of the outward bends formed in straightening. Further tension will not pull these out, because there is no leverage on them, and they are the strongest metal between the two points of tension application. Whatever remains of the original bend will require straightening with hand tools.

In the discussion of leverage angle so far, no consideration has been given to the size of the dent and the overall length of the panel. It is not uncommon to have a condition such as represented by the cross-sectional illustration in Figure 7-27, which represents a small, fairly sharp dent in a relatively long panel. The dotted lines connecting points AA and BB represent the leverage angles that could be used. Pulling from points BB would provide a more effective angle than pulling from points AA, because the angle is sharper. The sharper angle provides greater leverage.

7-27 Different leverages to be obtained by pulling from points close to or at a distance from a shallow dent in a long panel.

Another factor, lift reaction, must be considered before deciding whether the attachment to pull out a dent should be made close to the damage (points BB) in Figure 7-27, or at the extreme ends.

Lift Reaction

An understanding of the term lift reaction requires knowledge of one of the basic laws of physics. This rule is: For every action there must be an equal and opposite reaction. This can be demonstrated in many ways. If explained in terms of lifting an object off the ground, it means that when enough force is applied to lift it up, there also will be an equal amount of force exerted against the ground. If explained in terms of applying force to straighten a panel, it means that when enough force is applied to raise the dent, there also must be an equal amount of force applied in the opposite direction somewhere on the panel surface to support the lift.

Sometimes a person who has not made a study of the basic sciences has difficulty in understanding this law, because he is accustomed to thinking of a force application as involving motion. This is not necessarily true; force can be applied without motion. A table standing on a floor is exerting a downward force, and, likewise, the floor is exerting an upward force. The fact that there is no motion simply indicates that the forces are in balance, so the objects involved, the table and the floor, remain at rest. However, if enough weight is added to the table, its downward force may be increased until it is greater than the floor can resist. In that case, the table would push its way into the floor, bending or breaking it.

Applying this reasoning to the problem of lifting a dent is simple if the directions of force application are recognized. An upward force under the dent is required to raise it. It is still an upward force, whether it is applied directly to the underside or indirectly, by pulling on the metal on opposite sides of the dent. For this force to act, an equal force must be acting in the opposite direction. If the dent is being pushed out, the opposite force would act on whatever supports the panel. If the dent is being pulled out, it will act on the points to which tension is applied. This is the lift reaction.

The points to which tension is being applied are referred to hereafter as the attaching points. In the following discussions, lift reaction on the attaching points is considered as a downward force, because it is the opposite of the lifting action.

Lift reaction is illustrated in Figure 7-28. Arrows pointing outward at each end of the curved line indicate tension being applied to lift the dent. The arrow pointing upward in the center indicates the lifting action on the dent. The arrows pointing downward at each end indicate the lift reaction. The combined lift reaction on both attaching points must always be equal to the force required to lift the dent.

This illustration and the discussion accompanying it should make it clear that the force exerted outward to pull, or lift, the dent is not the same as the force exerted downward by lift reaction. When the dent has been pulled up to the proper level, lift reaction will drop to nothing. However, any amount of force, even enough to tear the panel, could continue to be applied in tension on the already lifted surface.

The importance of lift reaction is that it must be con-

sidered in selecting the points of attachment to which the tension will be applied. If these points are not rigid enough to resist the reaction to the lift, they will collapse instead of lifting the dent.

Thus in repairing any panel, attaching points should be selected that are rigid enough to support the load. Many times there is no problem. For example, in pulling a dent in a door panel, simply attach clamps to the edges. The edges, being rigidly supported by the facings, provide far more support than is needed to lift the load. In other instances, there is a real problem, because one or both of the desirable attaching points will not provide sufficient support to lift the dent. It then is necessary to do one of two things: (1) compromise by shifting to a more rigid though less desirable point, or (2) provide extra temporary support for the point.

It would be impossible to detail all of the conditions under which each of these alternate methods would be employed. Common sense will dictate when they should be applied.

An example of shifting to a stronger though less desirable attaching point will be found in most damaged door panels on which the dented area is close to one edge. On many such panels, a large part of the surface will not be forced out of position by the damage. The ideal attaching points would be one edge, using a clamp, and the center area of the panel, using a tension plate. However, the practical methods would be to use two clamps, one attached to each edge of the panel. This would increase the length of the pull and leverage angle, and slightly decrease the effective leverage, but the loss would be offset by the simpler hookup and the much greater support under the edges.

Temporary support should be provided only when the problem cannot be solved by shifting to a stronger point. Usually such conditions will be found on deep dents in long panels, such as roofs and quarters. One means of temporary support is to set a jack under the attaching point; this works particularly well with roof panels because the underside usually is open. Another method suited to quarter panels is to extend the jack tube to some rigid point and block up under it.

The important point is to prevent the collapse of the attaching point, because this only complicates the damage. There will be no difficulty if the basic law of physics is understood and applied to the job at hand.

Effective Angle

The effective angle should be considered on some large area panels but may be ignored on heavy box members. Usually the area to be pulled is approximately 1 foot (30 cm) wide. Tension should be applied on a line that will cross that area. However, tension applied to a wide, nearly flat surface spreads into the area instead of being concentrated in a straight line, as illustrated in Figure 7-29. Applied tension will be much more effective at point B than at point A. The force lost reduces the reaction of the area being pulled and, if the distance is great enough, will cancel it completely, caus-

7-28 Lift reaction. End points will be subjected to down thrust equal to the resistance to lifting offered by low point in center.

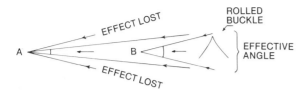

7-29 Loss of effectiveness of tension as point of application moves away from buckle.

ing the entire area to move instead of unfolding the buckle.

It is not always possible to apply tension from a point close enough to a buckle to provide the most effective angle, but when compromises must be made, the application point should be as close as possible to the buckle.

Work Hardened Metal

Work hardened metal in the buckled area is the direct result of the working that occurred as the panel unfolded under impact. Such hardening cannot occur without some changes in the dimensions of the affected area. Most such changes are upsets instead of stretches. The repair problem is to rework this metal back to the original dimensions. Except when heat will be used, reworking will add to the already slightly hardened condition. This is normal; if it does not prevent the panel from being restored to original contour, there is no reason to be concerned if an area of metal is slightly harder than the adjoining metal.

The need to rework the hardened metal to proper shape accounts for most of the work of final smoothing and metal-finishing of a damaged area after it has been pulled. It is the repairman's problem to determine how to do this so that the dimensions are restored. When they are restored, the panel surface will be restored, also. If there is access to the underside so that the dolly block can be used, the hammer and dolly block will be the best means of working the area. When they cannot be used, it is necessary to resort to spoons, pry tools, or any other means available.

Regardless of the method used to rework an upset area in a panel that has been pulled, as much of the area as possible should be reworked before the tension is released. The reason for this is simple: the work done on any upset area should tend to stretch it back to full length. If it is under tension while this work is being done, the tendency to return to full length will be much greater. This is illustrated in Figure 7-30. The arrows at each end indicate that tension is acting on the metal represented by the line. The wavy section of the line in the center represents the remaining part of the original bend, which in most cases would have been a rolled buckle. The rougher this wavy part of the surface, the more it will tend to shorten the panel, causing loose, springy bulges in the adjoining surface that often are mistaken for stretched metal. By holding the entire area under tension, whatever length is lost in the curved sections will be regained when they are straightened.

Holding tension on the panel during as much of the

final straightening operation as possible also removes any spring-back tendency caused by adjoining reinforcements. A common example of this often is found on a door panel that has been pushed in so far that the facing has been pulled far out of line. Pulling the panel back to shape also will pull the facing with it; but when the tension is released, the facing will tend to spring back toward its position when bent. This spring-back action is illustrated in Figure 7-31. Note the arrows at each end pointing inward. Pressure acting inward on a section of metal that is not finally straightened will tend to resist the flattening action when hand tools are used on the remaining buckles. Such an area will tend to rise in a bulge instead of blending with the level of the adjoining metal. Sometimes the springy action of such an area will be enough to be noticed by an experienced repairman.

In considering work hardened metal as a factor in determining the procedure in the use of tension, it must be recognized that each individual job differs. On some it will be so minor that it may be ignored; there is no problem with work hardened metal on a panel that pops back into shape when about half pulled. On others, it is a major problem, and, if ignored, may require excessive labor to work it out.

Sometimes the metal may be work hardened so severely that heat is needed to relieve it. Examples of this are given in the repair procedure section. Heat is used when the work hardened area has been upset so much that it is causing a serious bulge in the adjoining surface. The heat softens the metal so that it can be stretched back to, or close to, the original length.

As with the other factors, good judgment will determine whether allowances must be made for the effect of work hardened metal. Releasing the tension before the panel has been restored to final smoothness may cause a spring-back action that will make final straightening very difficult on some panels, whereas on others it may not.

Variations of Surface Crown

The surface crown must be considered when analyzing any damaged panel to determine where tension should be applied. The crown of almost every automobile panel varies from all others to some degree. Many of them vary from a relatively flat crown over a large part of the surface area to combination high and low or

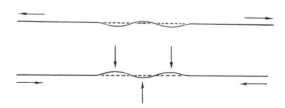

7-30 *(Top)* The desirability of straightening the remaining buckles under tension.

7-31 *(Bottom)* How pressure from adjoining area can resist straightening of remaining buckles.

reverse crowns along the edges; others may include every possible kind of crown on the various areas of the surface.

The variations in the details of the damage that can be found on different panels are almost without limit. Regardless of the details, however, all damage can be reduced to five basic conditions: (1) simple displacement, (2) simple bends, (3) rolled buckles, (4) stretches, and (5) upsets.

These basic conditions were covered in detail in Chapter 3, so they will not be discussed here except to point out that they will be relieved when damage is repaired properly. To repair any panel, force must be applied so that it does the most good. This means relieving the bends and rolled buckles so that the simple displacements can snap back into place and the upsets and stretches can be worked out with minimum effort.

The best results will be obtained from tension when it is applied where it has the greatest effect, and that is on conditions that tend to shorten flat crowns. These include practically all rolled buckles and any other damage in which adjoining areas tend to be drawn together. An excellent example of the latter condition is the folded-over door lower edge shown in Figure 7-32; this is similar to a rolled buckle, even though it is actually only a combination of simple bends in the outer panel and the facing.

Rolled buckles are found most frequently extending into a combination high and low crown area adjoining a relatively flat area. The severity of the rolled buckle is determined by the amount of break-over path that it has formed. When break-over paths have been formed, they usually will extend well into the high crown area. The more severe the break-over path, the more important it is that tension be applied close enough to it that it will be subjected to as much of the pulling force as possible. This, then, is the first rule: If there are severe upsets in the high crown area, tension should be applied to it as close as possible.

The ideal approach to unrolling many rolled buckles would be to make the first pull just below the highest point. As the high point rolled down to the line of tension, the attaching points would be dropped and

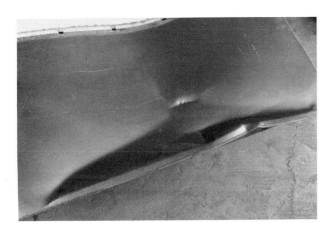

7-32 Folded-over door edge that should be straightened under tension and heated to relieve the upset.

another pull made. In this way, it would be necessary to make several attachments to unroll a single buckle. This is the ideal procedure, but a more practical solution usually demands compromise; a single pull made at the point where the high and low crowns blend is often almost as effective as though several pulls had been made by starting much farther into the high crown and working progressively back to this position.

When working a damaged area such as the folded-over door edge shown in Figure 7-32 tension should be applied directly to the edge. Here this would mean applying the greatest amount of force to the strongest part of the damage. The flanged door edge welded to the facing is much stronger than the panel adjoining it. Furthermore, if upsets are left in the door edge, they will have a gathering effect on the adjoining flat metal. In many cases such as this, it is desirable to use heat on the buckles while they are under tension to restore full length. Only a few thousandths of an inch of upset in this edge will cause severe gathering of the adjoining metal; this would be the condition called false stretch in Chapter 3.

Alignment with the crown of the panel must be correct if the desired results are to be obtained from the use of tension. The problem of determining proper alignment of the pulling setup with the crown of the panel is simple; the answer is based on the fact that tension tends to produce a straight line. Therefore, the tension setup must be aligned with the flattest surface line of the panel. If this rule is followed, no problems should arise due to improper alignment of the pulling force with the panel surface.

Many beginners have not been taught the importance of this rule and are often tempted to use a diagonal pull on a panel that has considerable crown in one direction. However, a diagonal line across the surface of such a panel would describe a curve instead of a straight line. Applying tension diagonally across such a panel would flatten or distort it by tending to make a flat surface where it should be crowned.

There are exceptions to this basic rule, but they apply only where a limited amount of force is needed. An example is minor damage of the pop-out type that probably would not be severe enough to warrant the use of tension.

TENSION ALIGNMENT

Tension alignment must be considered when making a heavy pull using any type of equipment, portable or fixed installations. Figure 7-33 illustrates the tendency of tension to produce a straight line between the two points from which the force is applied. The straight line includes the chains or any other linkage between the anchor and pull points of the machine in use. As shown, there is always a tendency either to lift the machine or to cause the body to drop if there is any difference in the heights of the anchor and pull points unless the chains or other linkages are hooked up on this line.

This tendency can be neglected on light pulls, but

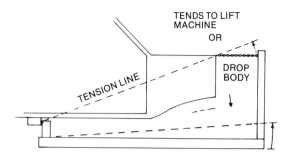

7-33 Tension will cause either the machine to rise or the body to drop, to form a straight line through the body from the anchor to the point of attachment to the machine.

heavier ones may require extra tie-downs or blocking to obtain the effect desired. Several examples are shown in Part 2 of the next chapter.

This same line is formed when pulling and anchoring from points on the same level but is not a problem, because the hookup is on or very close to the tension line.

SHOP EQUIPMENT

PORTABLE BODY AND FRAME MACHINES

One typical portable body and frame machine with accessories is shown in Figure 7-34. The accessories consist of: (1) two pairs of special support stands with tubular crossbars, shown behind the machine, (2) a crossbeam, which can be clamped to the main beam for twist setups, (3) chains, shown coiled beside the hydraulic pump, (4) a bolt-on plate, to attach to frame horns for chain connections, (5) anchor clamps, shown on each side of one chain in the lower left, (6) a self-contained

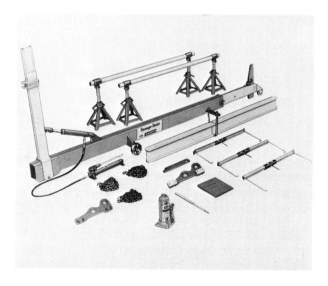

7-34 Typical portable body and frame machine.

hydraulic jack, in the left front, and (7) a set of self-centering gauges, in the right front.

Other manufacturers make similar equipment that operates on the same general principle but may vary widely in construction details and special features. Equipment of this type is adequate for most of the needs of the average small body shop, particularly for work on conventional frame construction, but it is limited to a single pull when used alone. This reduces its utility to some extent, because of the obvious trend toward smaller automobiles of unitized construction that tends to require more multiple hookups. However, enough operations still can be performed with the portable to make it essential equipment, particularly as it can be used anywhere in the shop. Its utility can be expanded greatly by the addition of one of the many systems of anchoring and pulling from floor *anchor pots.*

The basic use of portable equipment, with and without extra anchoring systems, is explained in Chapter 8, Part 2.

MULTIPLE HOOKUP EQUIPMENT

Equipment manufacturers have recognized the need for machines that have the capability of anchoring and pulling from more than one point at the same time, and many designs have been made available.

The manufacturer has two basic choices in the essential design of the machine. One is to take advantage of the rigidity of the concrete floor, which all shops have, and the other is to build an entirely self-contained machine, usually referred to as a drive-on machine. Both have advantages and disadvantages. The big advantage of in-the-floor equipment is less expense and that, when not in use, the space can be used for other activities. This partly is offset by the fact that some jobs will require more time than necessary for the self-contained unit. The big advantage of the drive-on unit is versatility. However, when installed, the space it occupies cannot be used for other activities. The later is not a disadvantage if the shop has sufficient volume to keep the machine busy.

In-the-Floor Equipment

Two systems of in-the-floor equipment are used: anchor pots, often called tie-down or floor pots, and a steel frame set in the floor.

The anchor pots have the advantages of being relatively inexpensive and that they can be installed in an existing floor or can be preset in new construction. Installing a few, to be used in conjunction with a portable machine, will extend the shop's capability to handle major wreck work. However, a complete installation, including one or more power units designed for the purpose, is a more productive setup. It is quite practical to install a few in each working stall in the most advantageous positions and a complete setup in one stall. This will enable the shop crew to handle most of the work in

7-35 Body and frame equipment designed for use with anchor pots, set up to align rear door opening. Anchors are out of view on opposite side.

7-37 The machine shown in Fig. 7-36 setup on van body.

the individual stalls and route only the big jobs to the fully equipped one.

The system shown in Figure 7-35 features a large number of anchor pots and two compact power units. In the setup shown, pulls are being made on the center and rear lock pillars. Both operations would be required before the door could be fitted into the opening. It is not possible to show the anchors in a photograph taken from the position of this one, but an experienced repairman would know that they would be on the opposite side, preferably two, one at each end of the midsection and attached to the frame.

7-36 Body and frame equipment designed for use with anchor pots, featuring built-in floor jack and extra height.

The system shown in Figure 7-36 uses anchor pots also, but has two special features, the built-in floor jack and the extra height. The jack is a convenient feature for setting an automobile on safety stands, but is not intended to support it while making a pull. The extra height is very desirable for work on the upper parts of vans and recreational vehicles, as illustrated in Figure 7-37.

Steel beams set in the floor, as in Figure 7-38, provide almost unlimited versatility to pull or push from any angle and at any level. An anchor or power unit can be set in the exact position it is needed and, if necessary, changed slightly with very little lost time. Equipment of this type has the capacity to handle heavier work than normal automobile body and frame straightening.

Drive-On Equipment

Many different types of drive-on equipment have a wide variety of special features. However, all of them

7-38 Body and frame equipment featuring in-the-floor steel beams.

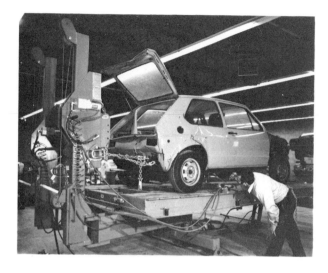

7-39 Drive-on type body and frame machine, featuring four swinging power heads; only two heads show.

consist of a heavy steel frame, or base, large enough to surround the automobile and provide a runway for it to stand on. Added to this is a means of anchoring and various types of power heads to pull, and sometimes to push, from various angles. The machine shown in Figure 7-39 features four swinging power heads, one equipped for vertical lifting, and a winch to pull incapacitated automobiles onto the runway.

Evaluating Equipment

The equipment in this chapter is shown without recommendation. Each has its special advantages and disadvantages. Also, each shop has its special problems,

such as volume of business, space, skill level, and many others. Equipment that would be highly desirable for one shop might be inadequate for another and beyond the needs of a third.

The human factor must be considered along with equipment when evaluating any system. The equipment has the capacity to do the work if it is used in an intelligent manner, but it is only a means of putting the operator's skill to work. It is not uncommon to find a competent repairman doing high-quality work with inadequate equipment while another, using the best equipment available, fails to satisfy his customers.

FRAME-CHECKING EQUIPMENT

The final checking of a straightened frame or the corresponding parts of a unitized body should be done with a frame tram or a set of centerline gauges, sometimes both. Preliminary checks before straightening are rarely required, because there is almost always other visual evidence on the automobile to indicate a frame condition requiring straightening. Door and front-end sheet metal alignment and the condition of bumpers or other parts of the body and suspension systems are reliable indicators of frame damage serious enough to require repair.

Frame tram gauges are used to make diagonal measurements across sections of the frame of the type represented by the diagonal lines on A in Figure 7-40. They are sometimes used to make three-point checks for raises or sags and are essential when it is necessary to check track and wheel base.

Frame Tram Gauges

A frame tram is simply a long bar that has at least two, and should have three, parallel pointers extending

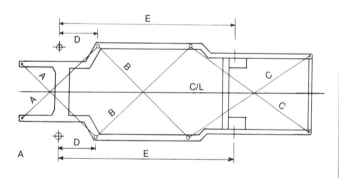

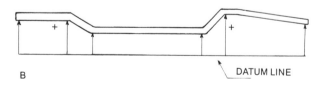

7-40 Typical frame layout. A, diagonal lines represent pattern of cross-checking. B, typical datum line specifications available from shop manuals or independent sources.

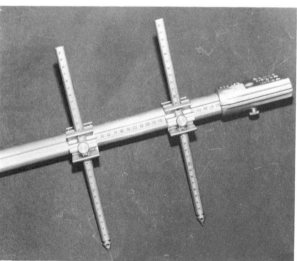

7-41 Tram gauge with attached tape. Extra pointers and bar not shown.

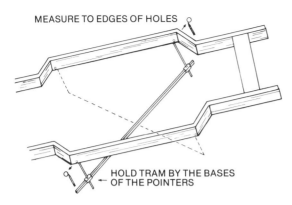

MEASURE TO EDGES OF HOLES

HOLD TRAM BY THE BASES
OF THE POINTERS

7-42 The two positions for making a cross-check. The tram must be held in the same manner in both positions for accurate measurements.

at a right angle and attached so that they can be moved to any position along its length. Preferably, the pointers should be designed so that the distance they extend above the bar is adjustable, and at least one should be removable. A close-up view of one end of a tram gauge is shown in Figure 7-41. The bar consists of sections that snap together, so that it can be set up to the desired length, and is equipped with an extension tape, enclosed in the handle; the pointers are calibrated in inches. The extra bars and third pointer are not shown. The third pointer is used only for three-point checks.

Careful handling of any tram is required to obtain accurate measurements, particularly when measuring over long spans. It should be held at opposite ends by two persons, preferably at the base of the pointers, as indicated in Figure 7-42, except when making very short measurements. When changing to the opposite measurement, each person should change over to the corresponding reference point and take a position that will permit viewing it from the same angle; never change reference points. One should hold his pointer on the reference point while the other makes the adjustment.

When making a three-point check, the pointers should be set to make contact on the undamaged side. The accuracy of the settings can be checked by holding

one end in contact while the other end is raised slowly into position. If the adjustment is correct, the center contact will be felt at the same time as the end touches. On a long span the center pointer may bump two or three times as the bar vibrates up and down. On the other side one person places his pointer in contact, and the other raises his pointer until the first contact can be felt. If all three pointers contact at the same time without flexing the tram bar, there is no raise or sag. However, if there is a gap at either the end or center, it is necessary to determine from the available evidence which point is too high or too low.

Figure 7-43 shows the setup position above and the checking position below on a typical frame without the body. In this case, a gap is shown at the outer end, assuming that the body was there. If the door above the center pointer fitted properly, it would suggest that the outer end of the frame rail was too high. If the door dropped appreciably when opened or was jammed shut so that it would not open, it would suggest that the rail was sagged under the cowl.

The frame tram can be used to check *track* and *wheelbase* when there is reason to suspect that they are not correct and that the normally used reference points may be damaged. Track refers to the alignment of the rear axle to the front wheels and suspension. When it is correct, the center line of the rear axle will be on and at an exact right angle to the overall centerline of the automobile. The rear wheels will then follow the front ones in the same tracks. A track check is illustrated in A of Figure 7-44. No attempt has been made to show the persons holding, but two are required, one at each end. For uniformity when changing from side to side, they should not change ends.

In making a track check, the tram is used to project a line from the rear wheels to the end of front wheel spin-

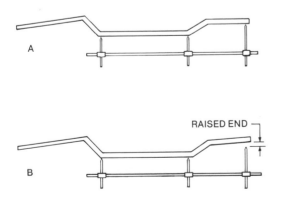

7-43 Making a three-point check for raises or sags. A, setting up on one side with all three pointers in contact. B, comparing the first setting to the opposite side. Tram must be held without strain.

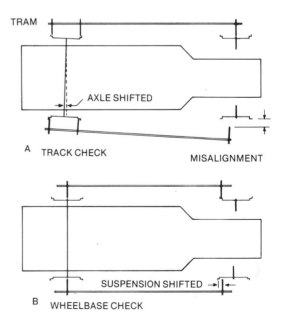

7-44 A, Track check. B, Wheelbase check. Rear axle must be known to be in alignment for this check to be accurate.

dle. When it is correct, the tram set to the two points on the rear wheel and the one on the spindle should fit the corresponding points on the opposite side exactly. When it is not correct, the difference will show up in the gap between the end of the pointer and the spindle, as indicated at the lower right (Figure 7-44).

Making a track check requires some preparation. The front suspension system must be in good condition and the steering wheel turned to the straight-ahead position. Both rear wheels must be checked for lateral runout (wobble) and, if any is found, the point of maximum runout must be turned to either the top or the bottom. There should be no dents or bends in the narrow flat surface of the rim the two pointers will contact. The tram should be held in contact with these two points while the third is adjusted to the end of the front spindle. When moved to the opposite side, pointers will fit the same if the rear axle is in alignment, or track. However, if there is a gap at the front pointer, it indicates that the rear axle or frame is out of alignment. The actual misalignment will be one half of the gap, because the front pointer had to be set back an amount equal to the misalignment on the opposite side. If the first gap shows up at the front pointer on the rear wheel, the tram should be reset on that side and the reading taken on the other.

A wheelbase check is illustrated by B, Figure 7-44. This check will reveal whether the suspension is holding the front wheel in position, as indicated at the lower right, but not why. That must be interpreted by the persons taking the check after considering all the other available information.

A wheelbase check cannot be accurate unless the rear axle is in correct alignment and the front suspension is fully assembled and has no obvious bends. Before taking it, the front wheels should be set in the straight-ahead position as accurately as possible. The check should be taken from the center point of the rear axle shaft to the nearest point on the front wheel rim, as shown. The fore and aft positions of this point will be affected much less by slight variations from straight ahead than the outer end of the spindle.

A track or wheelbase check is rarely needed, but

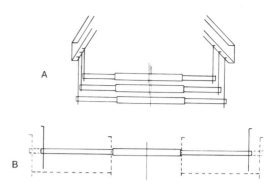

7-46 Typical features of centerline gauges having adjustable horizontal bars. A, checking accuracy of the gauges by hanging them close together between parallel supports. B, showing the approximate range of extension of most gauges of this type.

both the repairman and estimator should understand them. They are a last-resort check when an automobile has been rebuilt after serious frame and suspension damage and there is reason to doubt the reliability of the reference points used to check alignment. Sometimes an automobile that has been damaged previously and rebuilt improperly will be in such condition that the dependability of the normal reference points is questionable. Confronted with this situation, the repair shop can be sure that the automobile will operate properly if the other front-end alignment adjustments are correct and track and wheelbase check out properly. If they are off to an appreciable degree, particularly track, trouble can be expected, because the automobile will tend to run in a circle, requiring the driver to turn the steering wheel to one side to go straight ahead.

CENTER LINE GAUGES

There are two types of center line gauges. The type shown in Figure 7-45 consists of a center unit hung in the frame by chains. The other, illustrated in Figure 7-46 and with Figure 7-34, consists of an adjustable base with upright arms on each end. These arms on most gauges are adjustable for height so that the gauge can be set to datum line specifications when necessary. Both types of gauges have an upright center pin to indicate the center line of the automobile at the point in which the gauge is located. The chain type is centered by using equal lengths of chain on both sides. The adjustable-base types have a mechanism to maintain the pin in center position as the opposite sides move closer together or farther apart. Either type is a practical tool when used properly.

Center line gauges are used in sets of three or sometimes four units. A minimum of three is required. They can be used to check both center line and sags or raises. In use, one gauge is set up in the end of the frame being checked, two more are set up at the opposite end, if it is used. Checking is simply a matter of sighting the alignment of the center pins for center line and the level of the crossbars for raises or sags.

7-45 Centerline gauge set with chain attachment.

To check center line, the eye should be moved back and forth so that the pins can be seen from both sides. If correct, the clearance between the pins will appear the same from both angles. To check for raises or sags, the eye should be raised or lowered to a position from which the alignment of crossbars can be seen. If correct, they will appear parallel. Any out-of-parallel area will be indicated by a wedge-shaped space between the edges. Assuming that the automobile has been damaged on the end being viewed, if the near and far gauges are parallel and the center one low, a sag is indicated at the center position; or if the center and far gagues are parallel and the near one high or low, the near end of the frame is high or low.

The primary value of the center line gauges is that they provide a quick, one-man check for most of the common frame problems. They are much easier than a tram check but are not a complete substitute for the tram, because they do not do everything. They are intended primarily as a final check on the finished job, rather than a preliminary check to determine if repair is needed.

Any set of center line gauges should be checked for accuracy occasionally, as shown in A, Figure 7-46, by hanging them close together on parallel supports. This will make any misaligned condition of any of the gauges obvious. B shows the usual range of adjustment of the horizontal bars of that type of gauge.

REPAIR
PROCEDURES

PART ONE

This chapter is divided into two parts. The first deals with the three-step approach to planning and performing the repair procedure for specific jobs. However, that is pursued only far enough to demonstrate the importance of making and following a plan for every job. The emphasis is on job analysis rather than hammer-blow-by-hammer-blow directions. The second part moves from that aspect to a broader viewpoint in which the general types of damage are related to the construction involved and the general repair procedures that may be used. This is actually a step into the future, as the beginner learning his trade will earn his living on repair jobs that do not exist yet. In fact, if he spends a lifetime at his trade, most of the automobiles he can expect to work on will be built after he has become a skilled repairman.

THE THREE-STEP APPROACH

All of the procedures on actual damage in the following sections have been organized in a three-step approach:

1. Inspect the damage area to determine the type of damaged conditions present and the basic repair procedures suited to them.
2. Determine the general repair sequence to be followed. This is an application of the idea explained in detail in the Reversed Motion section of the preceding chapter.
3. Do the job, following the sequence decided on but watching for situations where trouble will develop, particularly on complicated jobs.

The available equipment must be considered in both the second and third steps. Ideally, everything needed should be available; actually, this is not possible. Also, the planned procedure must be flexible. Even the most experienced repairmen find it necessary to alter the planned procedure at times. Minor changes are to be expected, but when major ones are needed, the job has not been analyzed properly.

DETERMINING REPAIR PROCEDURE

After the inspection has been completed, the next logical step is to determine how to proceed to straighten the damage. In some instances, this may be such a simple process that practically no thought at all is required; in others it may be so complicated that it is difficult to decide where to start. In either event, the only information to guide the repairman in applying his skill is what he reads from the panel surface. His problem is to visualize the folding action that took place as the damaging force was applied and to find the best way, or ways, to apply force to accomplish the opposite effect.

One of the worst possible mistakes is to start the job

without any particular plan. This is even worse than to have analyzed the damage incorrectly and started with the wrong plan, because, with the wrong plan, it will soon be seen that the desired results are not being obtained. With no special plan, there is also no pattern of results to be expected.

An excellent way to plan the repair procedure is to find the answers to such questions as the following:

1. Where should the start be made?
2. Should it be made by driving, pushing, or pulling?
3. What will the shape of the damaged area be as the result of the first step?
4. If there is more than one impact area and related damage, should one be completed before the other, or should both or all be worked together?
5. Where should the next step be taken after the starting and each of the following steps be completed?
6. What methods should be used as the work progresses through the various steps?

General questions such as these can be applied to any damaged panel. The answers, of course, will vary widely from one panel to another, because the damages vary. The value in finding the answers is that intelligent thought is applied to the problem before starting to work. The ideal result of such thinking would be to change the repair of any damaged panel from a problem to a series of simple steps to be carried out in predetermined sequence.

DOING THE JOB

Doing the job is putting the planned procedure to work. If perfection could be obtained, this stage would be no more than just a specified amount of labor. This is rarely the case, however, because the almost infinite number of variables make it necessary to be on the alert for undesired results. This means that the repairman should be constantly inspecting and analyzing the results of his various steps so he can modify his procedure as required.

1. Inspect the damaged area to determine the types of damage conditions present and the basic repair procedures suited to the conditions.
2. Determine the exact repair procedure to be followed.
3. Do the job.

This approach is recommended for any job and to any worker, beginner or experienced. The amount of time spent in the first two steps no doubt will vary widely for the beginner and the experienced man, because the beginner may be forced to study to learn facts about a job that the experienced man can see at a glance. However, the amount of time spent in deciding how to do the job is not in itself an indication that the job will or will not be done properly. It is much more important that the correct procedure be followed than it is to get started in a hurry. A few more minutes spent in getting all of the facts so that the job is started properly may avoid mistakes that will require hours to correct.

INSPECTION

In making the inspection, certain specific information must be learned about the damaged panel. This can be done best by forming the habit of following a definite pattern or sequence of examination. It is also essential to know what to look for. The following list of inspection steps, arranged in the sequence to be followed, includes the information needed:

1. Location of the point, or points, of impact.
2. If two or more impacts are invovled, determine:
    a. Are they equal, or should one be considered as the major and the others as of minor importance?
    b. The exact areas of secondary damage related to each one.
    c. Will the repair of the damage from one impact be related to the repair of the others, or are they independent?
    d. If they are related, which one should be started first so that it will reduce the severity of conditions in the other, or others?
3. The exact nature of the various damage conditions—upsets, stretches, rolled buckles, hinge buckles, displaced metal, and so on—that make up the total damage and determine which are the most severe.
4. Relate each of the damage conditions to the repair method best suited for roughing it out.

An inspection of the damage on an automobile will reveal many facts about the collision that caused it. The information that is of particular interest to the repairman has to do with the nature of the other object involved and the action that took place. Speed, size, rigidity, and direction of motion of the impact object all leave telltale marks that serve to reveal the exact nature of the damage.

Failure to observe that the desired results are not being obtained accounts for more wasted effort and substandard jobs than any other cause. The reason for this is easy to understand. The use of force is required in every step, and the forces must be enough to bend, upset, or stretch the affected metal in some way in each step. If the wrong results are being obtained and the repairman continues to work, the damage will be compounded.

The three-step approach outlined here is nothing more than the thought processes of a skilled professional put into words. Such thinking is essential to analyze any job before it is started. As skill is developed, much of the thinking becomes automatic. Automatically or painfully slowly, however, the repairman must know what he is going to do before starting to do it.

DENTED FENDER

The fender dent shown in Figure 8-1 is relatively minor damage. It has been selected for discussion because it is a typical example of a dent that can be straightened easily and quickly by proper use of the hand tools, even though access to the underside is partly blocked.

8-1 Minor dent in the side of a fender. Note that there are no severe distortions.

The question arises as to whether or not a job such as this should be filled. In this case, it is possible to use a dolly block and a pry rod on the underside of the metal, even though the access is limited. It would not be possible to finish the job with filling alone, because of the high ridges above and below the impact point of the molding. These ridges must be lowered before the shape can be restored by filling. Just a little more care in the use of the hand tools in doing this necessary straightening will leave no place to fill. The extra time to do this straightening is minor, less than would be required to apply and finish the filler.

This same dent farther forward on the fender would probably require filling, unless a lot of extra time was used on it, because it would be much more difficult to reach the underside. In that case, the procedure would be considerably different from that discussed in the following pages. It would then be a matter of prying it out to rough shape and filling the rest.

Inspection

Inspection of this damage reveals the following information:

1. There are no severe distortions.
2. Most of the dented area is under only an elastic strain and should pop out when the buckles in the ridges are relieved, leaving only minor roughness.
3. Limited access to the underside is provided by the construction of the fender and cowl. In Figure 8-2, it may be seen that the underside can be reached for limited use of the hammer and dolly block, and all of the area can be reached with a pry rod.
4. The curved buckle above the molding is the most severe. Less severe buckles are at the lower edge, following the line of rub marks, and vertically at the rear edge where the metal has bent over the inner reinforcement.
5. A minor concave buckle can be expected under the crushed molding. In the undamaged condition, the upper edge of this molding follows a convex crease stamped in the side of the fender. This crease line will have to be restored as a part of the straightening procedure.

Repair Plan

The repair of this damage should be planned to take maximum advantage of the elastic condition in the center area. The more nearly it can be made to pop out to shape, the less additional work will be required to finish the job. The upper ridge and the concave buckle under the molding are holding the area out of shape more so than the lower buckle. For that reason, the lower buckle will be left until the upper area has been worked out.

If space under the fender permitted, the concave buckle under the molding could be driven out by striking with the dolly block. As this is not practical, the dolly can be hold against the underside and stiff pressure exerted against it while the ridge is worked out with the hammer. Reaction to the hammer blows will cause the dolly to drive out much of the low metal.

Additional work with the dinging spooon and the hammer and dolly should smooth the area so that it can be metal-finished.

Repair Procedure

The first repair operation is shown in Figure 8-3. The repairman is reaching through the door opening to the underside of the fender to hold the lip of a general-purpose dolly block against the crushed crease line, indicated by the line of elongated oval marks. Stiff hand pressure is being applied to the dolly block while the hammer is used on the upper ridge, here indicated by a long line with short crossmarks. This operation reduced most of the ridge and allowed much of the displaced metal to snap back to shape.

After most of the ridge had been removed with the hammer, the dinging spoon was used as shown in Figure 8-4. This would not have been practical for the first operation for two reasons: (1), the original ridge was too sharply formed to work with the dinging spoon; and (2), the reaction of the dolly block on the underside would have been lost. After this operation was completed, additional work on the crease line was done with the hammer and dolly block.

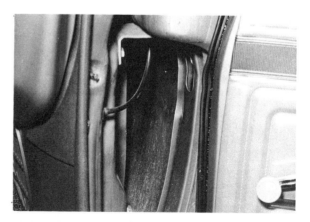

8-2 View of the underside of the fender from the rear end with the door open.

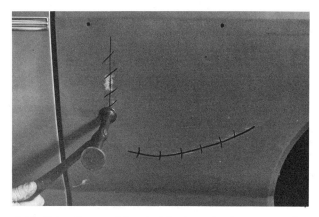

8-3 Working out the dent with the hammer and dolly block. The lip of the dolly is being held under the area of the elongated oval marks and pushed outward with as much pressure as possible.

8-5 Using the small head of the bumping hammer on the vertical ridge. The small head is more effective on springy metal than the large one.

In Figure 8-5, the small head of the hammer is shown being used on the vertical crease. It was used also on the lower ridge. The small head was used because both these ridges are in areas that are springy, making it desirable to reduce the area of hammer contact as much as possible. Using the large head or the dinging spoon will not work in areas such as these as well as the small head.

The worked-out area, shown in Figure 8-6, is relatively smooth, and most of the original crease line above the molding has been restored.

The result of the first sanding operation is shown in Figure 8-7. The sander has been stroked over the area in the back-and-forth motion used for finishing metal. Note that a few low spots are indicated by the black primer remaining in them, but the overall surface is in good condition. An overlay of dust from the sanding operation can be seen on the paint above and to the right of the area that has been sanded. This is normal.

The sanded area has been filed, showing up the remaining low spots in greater detail, in Figure 8-8. The file strokes are parallel to the flattest crown of the fender, except at the lower edge where it was necessary to slant them downward to avoid interference with

the reverse crown on the edge of the fender. No picking has been done on the filed area, but enough filing has been done to show sharp outlines of the low spots. This is the method of filing discussed in Chapter 3. In effect, it is in part a smoothing operation and in part an inspection operation. The overall area was near enough to final smoothness before the finishing operation was started so that the larger areas of smooth filed metal can be considered finished. All that remains to do is lift the low spots slightly so that they can be filed to blend into the adjoining areas.

The repairman is in the process of prying up low spots in Figure 8-9. The upper hinge is being used as a fulcrum for the pry rod as the point is shifted from one low spot to another. Note that he is pointing with one finger toward the spot being lifted. This is not necessary, but many repairmen find that it helps them to locate the spot they wish to pry. The principal caution to observe on an operation such as this is not to pry too hard. It is better to pry the same spot several times than to pry it once too hard.

The filed-off panel, ready for final sanding, is shown in Figure 8-10. The time for this filing operation was very short, only a few minutes—less time than would have been required to fill and finish the surface.

The result of the final sanding operation is shown in

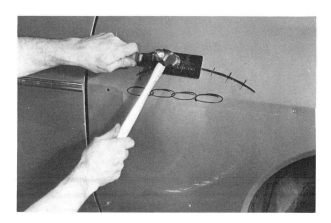

8-4 Using the flat spoon on what remains of the high ridge.

8-6 The straightened area, ready to start metal-finishing.

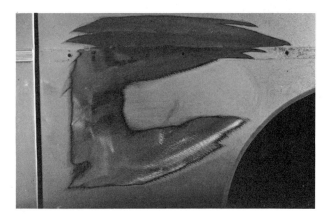

8-7 The result of the first sanding operation. A little paint remains in the low spots.

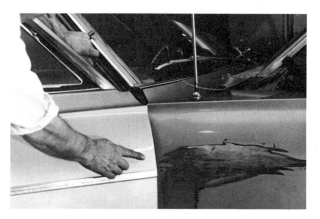

8-9 Using a pry rod on the low spots through the rear end of the fender. Some doors do not swing out of the opening to permit this operation.

Figure 8-11. This sanding was done with a buffing stroke, as described in Chapter 3. For this buffing operation, the sander pad was held so that the swirl marks run as near as possible to the lengthwise direction of the panel, and the machine was stroked up and down instead of back and forth. A worn 36-grit disc was used, and the pressure on it was very light because the intention was to buff, not cut.

Note that a little less attention was paid to the metal that would be covered by the molding than to that in the other areas. A slight low spot, which will be covered by a molding, will not be a problem, because it cannot be seen after the automobile is reassembled.

The final, repainted fender is shown in Figure 8-12. It is in excellent shape, and it was done very quickly. The repairman took advantage of the construction features of the automobile and the nature of the damage and made them work for him. Not all makes and models are so designed that easy access at the rear end of the fender is provided. On some automobiles, different procedures would be necessary. The important point is that the construction features of the automobile must be considered when planning the repair procedure and the maximum advantage taken of those that simplify the job.

UNITIZED FRONT-END REBUILD

The damaged front end on the small automobile in Figure 8-13 has been selected for discussion because it represents some of the types of problems that repairmen can expect in the future. Although not new, it conforms to the trend to obtain maximum stiffness with minimum weight. It differs from many current models by having the fenders and front panel welded instead of bolted in place. Regardless of design differences, some of the repair problems of the future will be on much lighter construction than the body repair industry has dealt with in the past.

Inspection

This front end appears much worse than it actually is because of the condition of the fender and front-end panel. Apparently it has collided with a small, rigid object that approached from an angle of 35 to 40 degrees. Whatever it struck, or struck it, has driven the fender and side panel back against the forward edge of the cowl (see Fig. 8-18), ripped the welds joining the

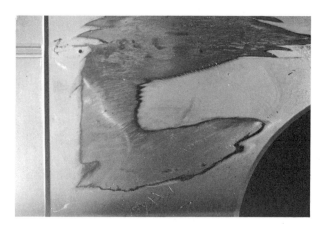

8-8 The result of the first filing operation, showing the remaining low spots in much greater detail than they appeared in the ground surface.

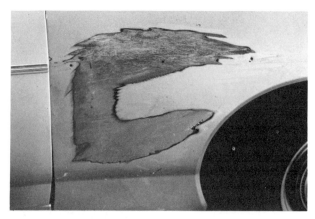

8-10 The surface after filing off the pried-up spots. Low spot in molding line will be covered after molding is replaced.

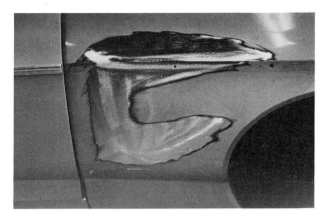

8-11 The finished surface, after buffing, ready for repainting.

front end of the fender and front panel, bent the bumper bracket, crushed the right corner of the hood, and pushed the entire front end sheet metal assembly to the left. Additional parts damaged include the headlight assembly, side marker light (folded out of sight), right parking light, and grille. Under the hood the right side panel is buckled and pushed back, the heater assembly is crushed between the fender and the engine, and some of the flexible ducts are broken. There is no serious mechanical damage. The frame structure and right suspension seem intact, but the right wheel alignment should be checked.

The amount of side shift of the front-end sheet metal is indicated by arrows on the rear end of the fender and hood in Figure 8-14. The fender has twisted enough to cause a small buckle at the upper rear end, indicated by the large solid arrow, and broken the welds that join it to the cowl at the position of the two opposed small arrows. The rear end of the hood is bent down between the two open arrows. This bend can be seen from the inside in Figure 8-15, which shows a sharp buckle in the inner diagonal brace as well as the outer panel. The right hood hinge was bent as the hood shifted, but it is not shown in detail, because it is only a simple straightening job.

The back thrust on the cowl has tipped the hinge pillar slightly, allowing the door to drop at the lock pillar,

8-13 Front-end sheet metal damage on unitized construction automobile.

but not enough to prevent opening and closing. This would not be expected on most past model unitized construction bodies, but should not be ruled out for future models.

Repair Plan

Four essential steps should be completed before pulling the right side panel back to position: (1) remove the damaged right fender, (2) pull the twist out of the left side of the front-end panel, (3) realign the left fender and reweld it to the cowl, and (4) rough out and fit the hood to the realigned fender and cowl. With these steps completed, the side panel can be pulled into position and fitted to the hood and the replacement fender fitted to both it and the cowl.

A parts problem developed after the job was started and complicated the repair plan slightly. The owner (the author did this job, but is not the owner) had purchased

8-12 The finished job.

8-14 Left side view of the automobile shown previously. Large solid arrow indicates buckle. Opposed solid arrows indicate broken weld and open fender to cowl joint.

8-15 Setup to pull twist out of grille opening.

8-17 Straightening left rear corner of hood, using improvised tool.

this automobile from a salvage dealer and was rebuilding it for his own use. A salvage fender and front-end panel were part of the deal. Normally, salvage parts would simplify the parts replacement, because the fender and front panel are already welded together and could be replaced as a unit. After starting, it developed that the parts were for a past model that had a different bracket in the lower part of the front panel for the bumper bracket attachment. As new parts would be additional expense for the owner, the brackets were stripped out of both panels so that the replacement could be fitted to the original. Otherwise, the parts could be made to fit and match in appearance after shrinking out a pressed-in depression in the lower section below the headlight. The shrunken spot can be seen in Figure 8-24.

Repair Procedure

Pulling the twist out of the front panel is shown in

Figure 8-15. A heavy duty C-clamp was used as a hook in the right corner of the grille opening. No attempt was made to protect the panel, because this part is to be cut away later. This was a diagonal pull, but most of the effect was to the side instead of forward, because there was less resistance to movement in that direction. The machine is anchored by the chain to an opening in a bracket on the frame that supports the lower control arm. The same anchor was used for the next operation, but, as both were light pulls, there was no risk of front end misalignment.

The fender has been removed, and a strap is being used to pull the fender into position in Figure 8-16. A light force was applied to swing the fender to the right just far enough to make a uniform gap between the rear edge and the cowl. The fender was then welded to the cowl edge by brazing. Before brazing, the joint was cleaned by scorching the paint with a oxidizing flame and wire-brushing it bright. This simplified the problem of making the brass flow down into the joint, leaving the upper edge with normal appearance.

The operation on the front of the fender is not shown,

8-16 Strap setup to pull left fender back into alignment with the body.

8-18 Close-up view of dent in cowl top panel.

8-19 Using dent puller on cowl dent.

8-21 Anchor setup for lengthwise pull.

but the clamp used was left in place. The fender flange had been pushed in slightly by the hood. This was given a light pull while the machine was in place.

The straightening operation of the rear corner of the hood panel is shown in Figure 8-17. Two holes were drilled in the corner reinforcement and a heavy metal screw threaded into them for the slot in the pry bar (an old spring leaf). The diagonal bracket was heated and the buckle lifted out while it was in the red heat range. The locking pliers held the pry bar from twisting to the side. No measurements were taken, because an experienced eye can judge when a part such as this is in shape. This is a good example of the situation in which the repairman must improvise with what is at hand.

A close-up view of the dent in the cowl top panel is shown in Figure 8-18. This was made as the cowl and fender were driven back by the impact. A scrap of the fender is still attached to the cowl, but it has been completely removed from the side panel; note the circular spot-weld cutter marks.

In Figure 8-19, the side panel has been pulled for-

ward, and a dent puller is being used on the cowl dent. This area is completely boxed in so that it is impractical to drive it out from the inside, leaving the dent puller as the only practical method to use.

A hookup to pull the upper part of the side panel is shown in Figure 8-20, using a special clamp intended to be attached by bolting through holes in the panel. The chain is attached to the piece that is hidden by the panel. The fender bracket, just forward of the clamp, made it necessary to install the chain piece inside, but it is effective either way. One bolt was put through an existing hole, and a new hole was drilled for the other.

The method of anchoring for the lengthwise pulls is shown in Figure 8-21. The clevis is attached to a shipping bracket, put on by the factory to tie the automobile

8-20 Pulling upper edge of side panel.

8-22 Pulling lower part of side panel.

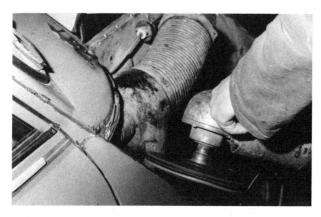

8-23 Grinding pinch weld flange.

down in transport. It was fortunate that this was in place, because the automobile has very little under-construction rigid enough to withstand a hard pull.

The setup for the main lengthwise pull is shown in Figure 8-22. The clamp is attached to a reinforcement where there is little chance that a piece will pull out instead of moving the panel. At this point, the machine is under slight tension, but most of the pulling remains to be done; note the buckle next to the reinforcement. The panel will be pulled and shaped to fit to the hood, which has been installed.

Most of the damaged section of the front panel has been cut away. The upper bar of the grille opening has been measured and trimmed to length; the lower part at this time has been rough-cut with the torch. The replacement piece will be laid over the lower section and clamped in temporary position so that the length of the grille opening can be measured carefully. The old section will then be marked and trimmed to fit to the replacement piece. Trimming can be done here with a pair of aviation-type tin snips.

The operation is not shown, but a light-duty body jack was set up inside the door to aid in realigning the opening. Wood blocks were placed against the wheel housing

and the working end of the jack placed against the cowl hinge bracket. This may not have been necessary because the pull in Figure 8-20 should have tipped the cowl forward. However, doubts about the rigidity of the anchor made it seem desirable to limit the force applied. Setting up the jack required far less time than would have been needed to repair the damage if the anchor did pull loose.

The old flange had to be ground off the pinch-weld that joins the rear edge of the fender to body side panel, as shown in Figure 8-23. Unlike most spot-welded seams, the welds in this one are very close together, almost overlapped, making an almost continuous weld. The only practical way to separate it is to cut the old fender as close to the flange as possible and grind the rest away. The replacement panel required the same operation, because it was salvage. However, this was not a major operation, because the seams are short.

In Figure 8-24, the replacement panel has been clamped in place and tack-welded at the upper and lower edges of the grille opening. Unfortunately, the torch hose almost totally hides the lower weld. This should have been noticed when the photo was taken, but was missed. The space between the front ends of the fenders was held by the tack-welds in the upper bar of the front panel, but the straps and turn buckle were needed to draw the rear end tight to the cowl top panel. The clamps on the pinch weld hold the fore-and-aft position.

It was mentioned in the repair plan that a depression in the lower section of the front panel was shrunk out.

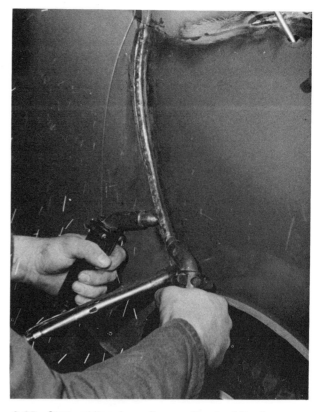

8-24 Replacement fender tack welded, clamped, and strapped in place.

8-25 Spot-welding hem flange. Short white lines are sparks, thrown off by left electrode.

8-26 "Buttonhole" welds in fender flange.

This is the blackened spot directly below the head light opening.

Spot-welding the pinch-weld flanges is shown in Figure 8-25. The short, white lines in the lower left are sparks thrown off by the left electrode. This was a two-step operation. In the first step, welds were made about 2 inches (5 cm) apart from the top to the lower end. In the second stop, closely spaced welds were made along the full length of the seam.

Note that the electrodes are held apart instead of directly opposite. This has two advantages: it speeds the operation because the machine has the capacity to make two welds, and it eliminates the possibility that variations of pressure could cause the electrodes to penetrate the surfaces and come into direct contact. The second advantage is particularly important on this

8-28 the finished job, ready for reassembly and repainting.

seam, because the previous welding and grinding may have left thin spots. However, hand-held electrodes should be used in this manner on any seam that can be welded from both sides.

The inner surface of the fender flange would have required excessive grinding to prepare it for spot welding, so it was torch welded, as shown in Figure 8-26. These are "buttonhole" welds. Many shops use brazing for this type of joint. Either is satifactory.

The right front and left rear corners of the hood were filled, because inner construction prevented access for hand tools. A hand-held half-round plane blade is shown being used to finish the fill in Figure 8-27. This same photo is shown in Figure 6-7.

The panels have been finished, ready for repainting, in Figure 8-28. Note the paper over the right side of the windshield. This was to prevent flying grit from marking the windshield glass when the disc sander was used on the fender.

The refinished automobile is shown in Figure 8-29.

8-27 Finishing filler on hood, using hand-held half-round plane blade.

8-29 The completed job.

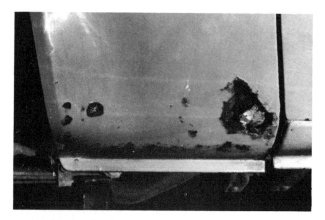

8-30 Typical fender rust damage.

RUST REPAIR

Rust repair may be done by welding in metal or by several non-metal methods, and to various standards of quality. All of the non-metal methods use some form of resin to provide adhesion and stiffen a fibrous material. It should be obvious to anyone interested that the larger the hole in the panel, the more it is important to repair it by welding in metal to restore physical strength.

Rust repair by any method cannot be expected to restore an automobile to new condition. It is not economically practical to disassemble welded sheet metal assemblies to clean out every trace of rust and restore the treatment of the inner surfaces applied in the factory prior to painting. The repaired automobile must go back into service under the same conditions that caused the original metal failure, but carrying the handicap of inadequate inner-surface protection. A high-grade undercoating should be applied, but it is not the equivalent of factory pretreatment of the metal. The result is that the life of the automobile will be extended, but will rarely be doubled unless the car is operated in very dry climatic conditions.

The rust that perforates body panels works from the inside. It almost invariably starts in the lower sections of the body where dust will settle and muddy water will accumulate in wet weather. The water dries by evaporation, leaving whatever soil it contained added to the

dust. The deposit accumulates and is rewet by wet weather or in washing operations, particularly the commercial installations that flood the automobile with hundreds of gallons of water in a very few minutes. If the vehicle is operated on icy roads treated with salt to provide traction, rusting will be accelerated by the addition of salt to the accumulated deposit.

The rusted area on the inner surface is almost invariably larger than it appears on the outer. This is often hard to explain to some owners who see only a small hole and bring it to the repair shop to be repaired before it gets any larger. The lower section of the fender shown in Figure 8-30 is a good example. This is a four-wheel-drive vehicle operated on all types of roads under very difficult winter driving conditions. It seems to be just one large hole and several smaller ones along the lower edge. When tested with the hammer, light blows made holes out of the dark spots where the hammer is shown and dented the metal easily in the bead section above that point where the paint seems to be good. An uninformed owner would be surprised to find the damage as extensive as it is, as shown in Figure 8-31.

Any rust damage should be tested with the hammer as shown here, preferably in the owner's presence and *with his or her permission.*

Patching this fender is complicated by the rather deep reverse crown at the wheel opening. It could be patched by laying several strips in the reverse crown area, wrapping a flat sheet around the straight part, and welding the whole thing together. Instead, a piece of scrap metal, cut from a salvage hood top panel, was shaped to general contour, welded on, and finished with body filler. No attempt was made to shape the patch perfectly, because the economics of the situation limit the amount of time that can be spent on a job of this type. However, when conditions do justify the extra time, flat metal can be shaped to an exact contour by the general method shown here. An example would be high-quality restoration work on special-interest or antique automobiles, where appearance, inside and out, is more important than cost.

The rough-cut patch is shown clamped to the wheel opening in Figure 8-32. The rear end has been trimmed to fit to the shape of the door opening, but the lower edge still has to be cut to fit to the fender flange, and the

8-31 Hammer test, to determine extent of inner rust damage.

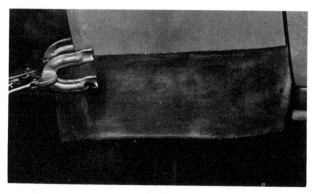

8-32 Fitting the lower patch.

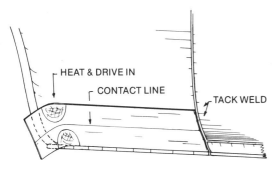

8-33 Method of fitting patch to contour of fender. The flat patch should be bent so that it fits on the contact line in the center. Metal above and below will be heated to permit stretching.

front end is too long. The paint has been removed from both sides by searing, using an oxidizing flame, and wire-brushed off.

Figure 8-33 shows the preparation of the patch for forming to the shape of the fender. The first step was to bend the front end (left side in the photos) to fit to the reverse crown. This should be done carefully so that the center (marked contact line) is in contact with the old metal, or where the old metal should be if it is entirely rusted away.

The next step was to align the rear end of the patch to the door opening and tack-weld it into place. If the intention had been to shape the patch to exact contour, it would have been tack-welded only in two places, approximately 2 inches (5 cm) apart, so that it could be removed for final shaping. This was welded securely, because it was intended to stay in place.

With the panel secured at the rear, the lower edge was tack-welded at the rear end and center. The spots marked on the illustration were heated and driven in, as shown in Figure 8-34, using the handle part of a general-purpose dolly block. A No. 4 torch tip was used to heat a large area so that the effect would spread instead of concentrate on the contact line. The piece tended to twist when struck, but excessive twisting was

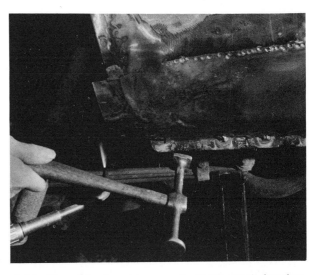

8-35 Use of heat and hammer to finish rough forming. Brazing could have been used to weld the upper and lower, but the spot weld is preferable for the upper.

prevented by the tack-welds, locking pliers, and the hand-held steel bar on the lower edge. The action is shown on the upper, but both upper and lower were worked in the same manner. The process was continued until a reasonably close fit was obtained.

After the general shape was established, it was welded as shown in Figure 8-35 and the final shaping completed with the hammer and torch. This is a shrink-

8-36 Forming the flange by shrinking with hammer and long, thin palm dolly.

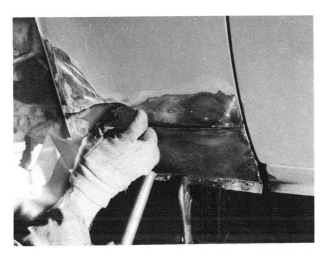

8-34 Driving the heated metal into shape. For precision work, this would be done with a block of hardwood and hammer.

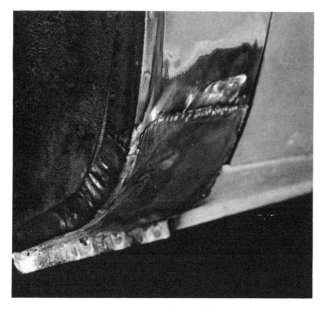

8-37 The finished flange. Welding is complete except at rear edge.

8-39 The patched area, partly filled and rough planed.

ing operation, essentially a shortcut. The exact shape could have been contoured at this point by breaking the spot welds so that the piece could be worked with the hammer and dolly block. Some shrinking would have been required, because it would be quite difficult to avoid some buckling on the contact line. Lighter welds would have been made if removal had been planned.

The flange of the patch was heated and shrunk down to the fender flange, as shown in Figure 8-36. This could have been done to any degree of smoothness. It was shrunk enough to avoid overlaps, as shown in Figure 8-37.

In Figure 8-38 an extension has been added to cover the weakened metal shown up by the hammer test. It

was spot-welded in place and shrunk down in much the same manner as the lower but, obviously, required less effort.

The first filling coat has been applied and rough-planed in Figure 8-39. Filling has been completed and finished in Figure 8-40. The repainted fender, ready for delivery, is shown in Figure 8-41.

A patch of this type can be made to exact contour by varying the procedure, if the conditions justify the much greater time required. The flat piece would be fitted to the contact line, but attached so that it could be removed for hammer and dolly work. Assuming that here is enough good metal left to weld to, which this fender had, the rear end would be pushed against the

8-38 Upper patch, welded in place and partly formed.

8-40 The completed fill job.

fender enough that two light tack-welds could be made approximatley 1 inch (2.5 cm) above and below the contact line. At the front end, two cuts, approximately ¾ of an inch (19 mm) apart, and centered on the contact line, would be made. These cuts would extend to the start of the reverse curve to make a tab that could be bent around and clamped to the fender flange; sharp corners would be heated for an exact fit.

The patch would be heated and worked in the same manner, except that a piece of hardwood, such as the large end of a broken ball bat, would be used instead of

8-41 The repainted fender, ready for delivery.

the dolly block. It would work better and absorb less heat, although it would smoke and smell. When worked into rough shape, the piece would be removed and clamped to something rigid for final shaping with the hammer and dolly. Some shrinking would be required, because some buckling would be difficult to avoid.

Although beyond the scope of this text, there are many methods of hand-making specially formed patches for use on high-quality automobile restoration projects.

PART TWO

The discussion of repair procedures in this section is from the dual viewpoint of the repairman and the estimator. The dual viewpoint may surprise some repairmen who do not write estimates on the incoming repair work. However, most of them do more estimating than they realize, some from only a critical viewpoint, but many others actually participating in the estimating process, either as advisors or as writers.

The repairman and the estimator have a common interest in repair procedure. The former must read his procedure from the job; the latter must have already read the same procedure from the job and determined essentially the same general procedure to allocate a fair time allowance. If he does not, either the customer is overcharged or the repairman is asked to do more than practical within the time allowed.

The beginner expects the estimating to be done by a more experienced person. Although the estimator's duties vary widely from shop to shop, the alert beginner should see the estimating assignment as a first step into promotion or, if he is interested in starting his own business, as an important step in qualifying himself to become a shop proprietor. Unfortunately, many beginners fail to realize the need for a broad viewpoint until they are well past the point when they can be considered beginners. This is emphasized here in the hope that at least some of the students starting the trade will develop attitudes that will make them promotable, either within their employer's organization or in their own enterprises.

The emphasis in the following sections is on the type of damage in which the alignment of the overall structure is involved. It is arranged in the sequence of frame and frame problems, body shell alignment, and some body panel problems. Body problems include some suggestions that apply to the replacement of complete panels or sections. Only enough has been included to provide general coverage. It would be impossible to make a complete list of all possible damage variations.

General suggestions about the factors that govern the time required for most of the repair problems are included because, as stated previously, this portion of the text is intended for both the repairman and the estimator. Both have, or should have, an interest in the subject. However, there is no way or formula by which specific times can be established. An estimated repair time will reflect the personal opinion of the person who set it.

FRAME TYPES

Three types of frames are used in automobile construction. They are (1) ladder, (2) perimeter, and (3) unitized body and frame. These are broad types; frames built by different manufacturers may be of the same type but vary widely in design detail.

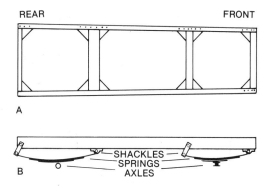

8-42 Basic layout of ladder-type frame. A, top view; B, side view, with spring and axle positions shown.

LADDER FRAMES

The ladder frame is so called because of its resemblance to a giant ladder. Its principal features are two lengthwise beams and at least four cross members. (The term rail is used in this text to refer to side parts of all frames. It is common practice throughout the automobile industry to call frame crosspieces *members*.) The ladder-type frame was used in all of the early automobiles and is still in wide use in trucks, including some pickups and four-wheel-drive vehicles. Figure 8-42 represents a simplified ladder design.

The primary disadvantage of the ladder-type frame for automobiles is that the passenger compartment and whatever load-carrying capacity it has must be above the level of the side rails. This is essential for heavy trucks that require a platform to support the load, or other vehicles that require high ground clearance, but a distinct disadvantage where streamlining is desired. It has another disadvantage in that there is little bracing between the side rails, so that an end impact will tend to shift one in relation to the other (called *diamonding*). This is discussed in the section dealing with damage and repair procedures.

PERIMETER FRAMES

The perimeter frame (Fig. 8-43) is actually a ladder frame redesigned to eliminate some of its worst features. The center section is made much wider, so that the passenger compartment floor can extend into the space between them. In effect, the lower part of the body is within the perimeter of the frame instead of on top of it. Lowering the floor permits lowering of the roof line and a lower center of gravity. Both contribute to stability to reducing the tendency to roll over.

The side rails of most perimeter frames are set out far enough to be in line with the front and rear wheels. This requires offset, or compound bends at the corners of the passenger compartment section, because the rails must be higher and closer together in both the front and rear sections. The front section does not require as much height as the rear, but rails must be set

in farther to provide clearance for the wheels to swing in steering. The rear section rises higher to permit up-and-down movement of the axle assembly.

The amount of offset in these bends requires quite rigid construction, because they are subjected to a twisting effect at all times. It also causes a tendency to collapse under an end impact. The needed rigidity is provided by joining two C channel sections for a single box section. Bracing from side to side is provided by one, or sometimes two, heavy front cross members. In most instances the front cross member provides the support for the suspension parts.

The rear offset sections are of similar but lighter construction than the front. They tend to collapse in the straight part over the axle rather than farther forward in the compound curved offset. However, the forward section will collapse under sufficient impact force.

Automobile engineers seem to prefer the perimeter-type frame for larger-sized automobiles. It is relatively flexible, so that it tends to absorb noise and road shock better than earlier designs. However, as the trend toward lighter, more fuel-efficient automobiles continues, it will probably be replaced to a large extent by the unitized design.

UNITIZED FRAME AND BODY

In unitized construction the frame and body are combined in one unit. The term unitized is applied by the automobile industry to any type of construction in which the side structures are stiffened so that they can serve the same purpose as the side rails of the ladder- or perimeter-type frame. The heavy lines around the door openings and front and rear sections in Figure 8-44 represent the stiffened areas. The exact design varies widely from one manufacturer to another, but in all designs the side structure becomes, in effect, a truss resting on the front and rear suspension.

Unitized construction is used for most of the smaller automobiles where light weight and economy are the prime considerations. It has less flexibility than the perimeter-type frame, but this is not a severe disadvantage for an automobile having a relatively short wheel base. However, the rigid construction causes damage

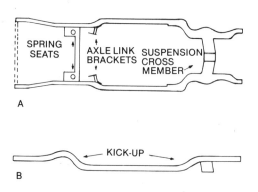

8-43 Basic layout of perimeter-type frame. A, top view; B, side view.

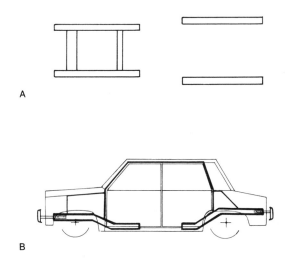

8-44 Basic layout of unitized body. A, position of front and rear frame rails; B, body layout with reinforced areas represented by heavy lines.

patterns that differ from those caused by similar impacts on either a ladder- or perimeter-type frame. The generally lighter parts tend to crush more at the point of impact instead of acting as force paths into the adjoining sections to cause damage there. Another reason is that the lighter the automobile, the less inertia it has to an impact. In any collision, the automobile struck tends to resist movement until it absorbs enough force, by crushing under the impact, until its inertia has been overcome. Once set in motion, it can absorb more of the remaining impact force only by moving faster. It then acts in the same manner as a kicked football; it may strike another object, skid, or roll over and receive further damage in new impact areas, but the damage in the first impact area is complete when the inertia is overcome.

It is difficult to predict future design trends, but it seems reasonable to assume that the use of unitized construction by all manufacturers will continue to increase. The trend toward more fuel-efficient automobiles is fixed by law, but would be an economic necessity even without the legal aspect. It is well suited to front-engine, front-wheel-drive construction, because it permits better use of space in both the engine and passenger compartments. It also seems reasonable that it will go through several evolutionary changes. A relatively high kickup section in both front and rear is shown on the sketch. The adoption of front-wheel drive and independent rear suspension will tend to reduce the front kickup height and could eliminate it altogether in the rear.

TYPICAL FRAME DAMAGES

Frame damages may be classified in several basic types, directly related to the type of accident in which the automobile has been involved. Also, each type of

damage can be related to a suitable repair procedure. The time to do the job is simply the accumulated time required for the individual steps required to complete the procedure. The estimator's problem is to visualize these steps and allocate sufficient time to do the work.

In the following discussion of frame damages, the sequence is from relatively simple to more complex conditions. A suitable repair procedure is suggested for each one, but there is no intention to present the suggested procedures as the *correct* procedure. There are many ways in which most frame-straightening jobs can be done; some will be better than others, but which is correct is usually only a matter of opinion of an individual.

Body parts have been omitted in the figures showing repair procedures on separate frame and body construction. Sometimes it is necessary to work the body and frame together, but most frame repair work should be done first to relieve whatever effect it has on body alignment.

SIMPLE BENDS

Most simple bends are found in combinations of at least three in most damaged frames, because movement at one point of the structure requires at least two others to yield. An exception is on a protruding member such as a frame horn, which is a section of the front side rail that extends forward of the suspension cross member to support the bumper assembly and sometimes the front-end sheet metal parts.

Figure 8-45 represents two typical horn damages. The inward bend, A, is probably the most common and the easiest to repair. In estimating this type of horn damage, the estimator should determine whether the repairman can simply place a jack between the indi-

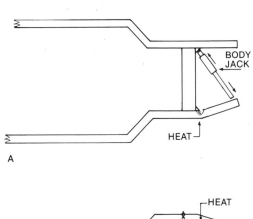
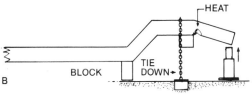

8-45 Simple frame bends. A, jack setup to straighten bent-in frame horn; B, jack with tie-down and block to straighten bent-down frame horn.

cated pressure and anchor points, or if an external setup will be required because other parts block access for the jack. The use of heat is indicated, but in some cases of very minor damage it may not be needed.

A bent-out frame horn is not illustrated, but the same procedures apply except that a pull jack would be substituted for the conventional push jack where construction permits its use. External equipment would be used more often on it than on the bent-in horn.

A down-bend, illustrated by B, occurs less frequently than the in-bend, but is quite common when a heavy impact has caused other damage farther back on the side rail. The setup to straighten this, as suggested by the arrows, could be as simple as a chain across the top of the frame and attached to a ring in the shop floor for the center anchor and blocks at the rear. Usually the use of heat will be required. A down-bend combined with other damage almost always will require an equipment setup to apply fore-and-aft tension.

A minor sag, usually under the cowl section of the body, can be considered a simple bend, if the other parts affected by it are not strained too severely. Figure 8-46 represents this condition. This could be caused by a roll-over in which the automobile has landed hard on its roof. Or the repairman might find the rail still sagged after pulling a collapsed side rail to length. When it is found with no other frame damage, there will almost always be plenty of evidence to suggest that the frame should be checked. A V-shaped gap between the door and fender edges, or a door that drops sharply when opened may be considered such evidence.

A sag under the cowl section tends to twist the suspension cross member of a perimeter-type frame, but usually the twist effect is within the elastic limit. Sometimes it is necessary only to tie it down in two places and jack it up into place. The tie-downs can be as simple as the two pots shown in Figure 8-46, or whatever method is provided by the equipment being used. However, selection of the tie-down points on the frame is important. The front chain should be over the top of the suspension cross member, not out on the end of a projecting horn. The rear should be at the reinforced rear end of the center section. In general, heat should *not* be used; this means that is will be necessary to push the rail well past the desired level to overcome the tendency to spring back, usually twice the distance actu-

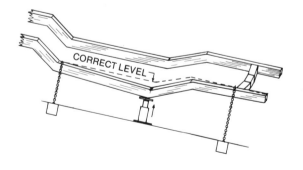

8-46 Jack and tie-down set to straighten frame sag in cowl area.

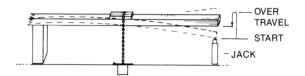

8-47 Approximate amount of over-travel needed to straighten frame or other reinforced member without using heat.

ally gained. The problems of spring-back are explained in more detail in the discussion of twist and illustrated in Figure 8-47.

A sagged rail should not be confused with one that has been raised on the end. Any appreciable lift at the front end will strain the suspension cross member much more than would the same amount of movement in a sag under the cowl. A very minor condition may not cause strains beyond the elastic limits of the cross member and the opposite side rail; such a condition can be straightened with the setup for a sag. It is sometimes difficult to determine whether a frame is sagged under the cowl or if the front end is raised. This will not make a major difference in the time required, but it is essential that the repairman identify the condition properly. If the front end is lifted enough to twist the cross member but he simply jacks up the cowl enough to realign the door, the frame will be left in a twist.

SPRING-BACK

Allowance for spring-back must be made in any cold bending operation because of the elasticity of the metal. Slow-motion moving pictures have been made of automobiles being crashed under various circumstances. The first-time viewer of one of these will be impressed by the extreme deflection the various parts of the automobile go through at the instant of collision. The slow-motion pictures will show that most of the damaged parts have been distorted much more at the moment of impact than they are an instant later.

Spring-back works both for and against the repair operations. It is important to recognize the elastic strains in damaged areas that will spring back in the repair operation when the buckles holding them are released in the repair operations. The repairman also finds many parts of the automobile will withstand considerable flexing before actually yielding to applied pressure; this often uses up a large part of the travel of his body jack ram before getting enough strain on a flexible member, such as a frame side rail, to make it yield. Sometimes enough over-travel is required to cause damage, usually buckles in large smooth areas, before the required mend is made.

Figure 8-47 illustrates the problem of over-travel to offset spring-back. The total travel is shown as about twice the amount of actual gain. This will vary with the shape and construction of the part being worked, but it is common to find at least that much required. A plain box member is shown here, but the problem would be similar on almost all cold straightening operations.

A bend that has been heated as it is straightened will spring back much less than one straightened cold. However, when a sharp bend is heated to straighten, the corrective force must be applied at considerable distance from the spot actually heated. All of the metal between the force application points and the heated area will be subjected to elastic strains. When the force is released, the elastic strains will spring back, but the spring-back in the heated area will be relatively little.

SIDE SHIFT

A ladder-type frame is shown in Figure 8-48, because this type is more apt to shift in this manner than the others. However, any type of frame will side shift under the right circumstances.

A side shift is almost always the result of a side impact at the extreme end, front or rear, acting against the inertia of the automobile. The bumper assembly and cross members, if any, serve as force paths to carry the impact to the opposite side member; these members may collapse, adding to the total damage.

A direct impact in the midsection will bend the automobile lengthside, making much more severe damage than a simple side shift. If repairable, the procedure would be much more complicated than the procedures for side shift discussed here. This problem is discussed in a later section.

Some of the common indications of a side shift are (1) door edge spaces, or gaps, too tight on the side to which the frame has shifted and too wide on the impact side, (2) when sighting through windshield and back glass, front or rear end appears out of alignment with center of body, and (3) the known tendency of the particular make of automobile either to side shift easily or to resist shifting. Often, the evidence of shifting is enough that further inspection is needed only to determine that additional damage—crushed members, twists, and so on—are not involved.

An accurate check for the amount of side shift is difficult if either the cross member or the side rail has collapsed. These members should be straightened first.

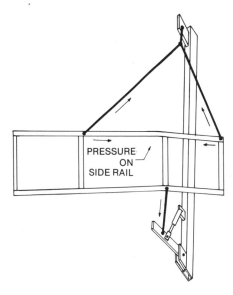

8-49 Basic "bow and arrow" hookup to straighten a side-shifted section. V-shaped anchor connections develop compressive pressure on side rail.

Some minor side shift is almost always involved in any collapsed condition. However, the estimator should determine whether the extra setup will be needed and, if so, allow time for it.

The two anchor points and the place to pull to correct a simple side shift are indicated in Figure 8-48. This is a relatively easy setup to make on any type of straightening equipment that permits multiple hookups, drive-on, or in-the-floor installations. Pulling at the end is suggested in the figure to avoid shifting the other end of the vehicle, but the same effect would be obtained by pulling on the other points.

A portable frame and body machine can be used to straighten a side shift, as shown by Figure 8-49, but it has a distinct disadvantage when compared to the direct action of the multiple hookup type of equipment. This setup requires two pull lines, usually chains, connected to separate points on one side and a third line pulling between them on the opposite side. It is important that the two lines on the one side be long enough to form a narrow angle where they meet to avid excessive pressure on the side rail between the attachment points, as noted in Figure 8-49. This pressure can be enough to collapse a light side rail if the lines are too short. However, a competent operator can use this hookup safely, if he exercises good judgement. All connections should be made where there is a cross member connecting the sides or a temporary connection should be made.

This hookup is often called a *bow and arrow*, the frame being the bow and the machine the arrow. Some operators prefer to use the machine diagonally across the shifted section. This works if all the bends that permitted the shift are within the section being pulled. However, it has little mechanical advantage over any bend effect that extends into the adjoining section.

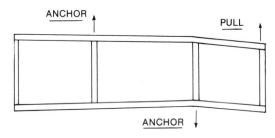

8-48 Appearance of a side-shifted frame section. Arrows indicate where the anchors and a pull should be applied to shift the section back.

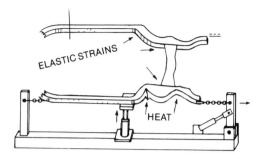

8-50 Portable frame machine set up to pull a minor collapsed side rail on a perimeter-type frame. This arrangement should not be used if center section has been driven back.

COLLAPSED SIDE RAIL

Figures 8-50 and 8-51 represent a minor and a severe collapsed side rail on the right front side of a perimeter-type frame; each includes a practical setup to repair the damage. These are typical damage conditions that any experienced estimator or repairman knows to look for when an automobile having this type frame has been involved in a hard front-end collision concentrated on one side rail. The examples shown would be the result of a straight-on impact. An impact coming at an angle from either side would complicate the damage by adding side shift to the collapsed side rail.

The first concern when inspecting a damage of this type should be to determine whether or not the impact has driven the center section out of square. Referring to Figure 8-51, the diagonal measurement A will almost always be slightly longer than measurement B, because the front section is pressed back against it. This may be only an elastic strain that will be relieved when the front section is straightened. On more severe damage, the center rail may have been forced back far enough to affect the kickup and cross member over the axle. Two telltale signs of this condition are (1) a semicircular rim of freshly exposed surface beside the rear body bolts and (2) cracked road film on the surface or an actual buckle in the offset curve of the opposite front side rail. However, the safe procedure is to cross-check the center section before establishing the time allowance.

It would be impossible for one side of the front section to be driven back far enough to cause buckling back of the suspension cross member without putting a strain on the entire frame. In moving back, the cross member acts as a lever on the opposite side rail. These strains may or may not exceed the elastic limits of the affected parts. When they do not, the result is a rather simple repair job, as represented by the sketch in Figure 8-50, which requires only the use of suitable equipment and careful heat application to pull the buckle back to shape. When done properly, this operation should relieve the elastic strains in the frame and make some improvement in the before and after diagonal measurements in the center section. However, if they are still

out of tolerance, the job has been misjudged, and a hookup similar to that shown in Figure 8-51 will be needed to pull it into alignment.

The hookup in Figure 8-51 places the entire frame under a diagonal stain without pulling diagonally. Equipment permitting multiple hookups is required. Anchor pots are shown here, but other equipment will do the same thing, and some is easier to use. (It would be possible for a skilled operator, using an extra-long, heavy-duty machine, to pull diagonally from the front cross member to the anchor point shown on the opposite side; however, there is risk of damage to the equipment, and it may be difficult to avoid bending the anchor point outward.) With the hookup shown, force will be applied to both sides from the correct angle. The two side anchors prevent the vehicle from swinging into diagonal alignment with the main anchor points. Use of the anchor for the machine eliminates the risk of bending its horizontal beam.

The procedure for both setups (Figs. 8-50 and 8-51) should be to apply enough to put a light load on the deep buckles on the right side. At that point the torch should be applied to the sharp part of the buckles to relieve them. From then on, it is a matter of proper torch manipulation and extending the machine to *maintain* tension on the frame. *The worst possible mistake would be to pull too hard.* The force applied should never exceed the minimum required to keep the buckles unfolding as they are released by the heat. As the job progresses, the force required will increase, because some of the mechanical advantage is lost as the rail straightens, but it should never increase to the total capacity of the machine. (Very few automobiles having this type of frame have ever been built that would require the total output of straightening equipment powered by a 10-ton jack.)

As the work progresses on the main buckle, it is essential to keep close check on the center section diagonal measurements, the length of the collapsed side rail, and the overall center line. A skilled operator can usually bring all three out together. However, when the job appears to be nearly right, it is best to stop, release

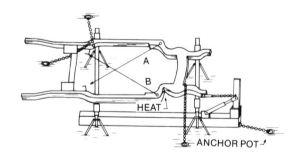

8-51 Portable frame machine and anchor pot setup on a perimeter-type frame to pull a collapsed side rail. This hookup should be used when the center side rail has been pushed back but changed back to the arrangement shown in Fig. 8-50 when the side rail has been moved enough that length A equals length B.

the machine, and check the conditions. Almost always it will be desirable to make some changes in the hookup. An extra jack is shown in place to lift the center in Figure 8-50. This may be needed if the front end is high. Or it may be necessary to tie the center down, shift the jack to the rear, and raise the hookup on the machine to lift the front. If there has been a buckle in the opposite side rail, it may require heating to permit the front to swing into center line. Heat should be applied while the frame is under full tension. Nothing would be gained by heating before the frame was nearly straight, because there would be very little strain on it until then.

The center section should be cross-checked as the work progresses. If it checks correctly before the main buckle in the front side rail has reached full length, the anchor should be changed from the opposite to the buckled side—left to right in the illustration—before making the final pull. When the rail has been pulled to full length, the final checking can be done with the center line gauges.

CREEP

Any large structural area that has been straightened without heating can be expected to *creep* back slightly after the straightening operations are completed. The tendency to creep varies with the construction. Frame members or other long box sections made of relatively heavy metal will creep more than panel assemblies, making it primarily a frame rather than a body problem.

The amount of creeping to be expected on a particular job is hard to predict, but some should be anticipated on the type of job described in the preceding section. Knowing that it will occur, the repairman should carry the straightening operations a little past the point of full correction, so that at least a part of whatever creep that occurs will be an improvement rather than a loss of alignment.

Creeping is due to the fatigue of temporary strains set up in the metal by the straightening operations. A change large enough to affect tolerances may be found in some frames within an hour or two after the last jack has been released. Further but slight change may occur after the autombile is put back into use. However, the total is rarely enough to affect overall alignment if the straightening operations have been carried slightly past

the center point of the tolerances; alignment can be affected if the operations are stopped when the measurements just reach the point of specified minimum tolerance.

DIAMOND SHIFT

Figure 8-52 represents a very simple example of a frame damage condition called *diamond shift*. It was not uncommon with the simple frames used in the early years of the automobile industry, but it is almost unknown on automobiles built in recent years. It can occur on some heavy truck frames, but few beginning body men or estimators will be confronted with this type of damage, unless they get involved with heavy truck repair.

The name diamond grew out of the elongated appearance of the normally square section of the frame, which to some persons suggested the facets of a diamond. Although not a common condition, it is explained here because many repairmen still use the term diamond or diamonded in reference to the condition in which a part of a frame rail has been pushed out of diagonal squareness with the other side. The center section of the frame condition described in the Collapsed Side Rail section is an example. The term is sometimes used in reference to other units, such as core supports, windshield or rear window openings, or door openings.

BOTH FRONT RAILS COLLAPSED

When both side rails are collapsed, two similar hookups are required, essentially doubling the job of repairing one rail. However, the estimator should consider the repairman's problem of making the final check. When the opposite rail is undamaged, he can simply make comparison checks to it, using a tram to measure length and the center line gauges to check height. When both rails are damaged, he may be able to get by with a guess or he may be forced to take time to consult the specifications and work to length and datum line measurements. Such problems should be reflected in the estimator's time allowance.

The estimator should be alert to detect damage that is not severe enough to be readily noticeable, particularly on separate frames. Sometimes badly crushed sheet metal parts will tend to conceal the fact that both frame rails have been pushed back just enough to cause misalignments when the job is rebuilt. It is much better to find such conditions first.

It is desirable to use equipment that permits multiple hookups when straightening both rails. When a portable machine must be used on two badly collapsed rails, it is best to alternate from side to side, pulling each partway. Attempting to pull one side all the way will leave it under a strain from the cross member. When the other side is pulled, the strain is removed and the first side moves farther. By alternating sides, the strain is kept within controllable limits.

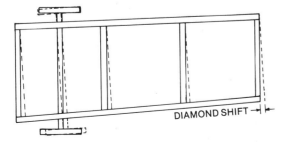

8-52 Basic diamond shift.

TWISTS

The basic condition of twist is illustrated by Figure 8-53, together with the setup to correct it. This is simply a matter of tying down and lifting at opposite corners. Two jacks are shown, because twist must be straightened cold, requiring the assembly to be pushed far past the desired point to allow for spring-back. The full travel of one jack will often be needed to load the assembly so the other one can begin to be effective. It should make no difference which jack is extended first or if they are worked together.

The construction of the automobile involved governs the tendency to twist, but almost any will twist to some degree. Those having the greatest resistance to twisting are usually the hardest to straighten when they *are* twisted.

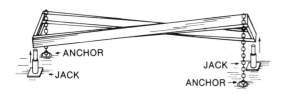

8-53 Basic twist, with four-point setup to straighten.

Twist is not always the simple, overall condition shown in Figure 8-53. Usually it is combined with localized bending, which makes a more complicated repair problem. One simple example of combined twist and bending is shown in Figure 8-54. A conventional frame will bend in this manner when the automobile is involved in a roll-over and comes down hard on a front corner. The side member is subjected to a direct bending strain at the junction of the front and center sections. As it lifts, it has a twisting effect on the suspension cross member. Depending on the construction and the amount of force involved, the cross member and the opposite rail may be only under an elastic strain or they may be actually twisted; if they were bent to a noticeable degree, it is unlikely that the job would be considered for repair.

If the cross member was only under an elastic strain,

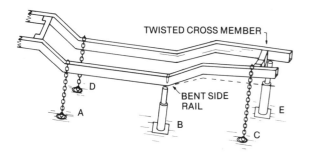

8-54 Basic setup to straighten up-bend in side member combined with a twisted cross member on a perimeter-type frame.

the two tie-downs, shown at A and C, and the jack shown at B would be all that was needed to straighten the damage. When the center was lifted enough to be back to proper level, a center line gauge check would show no twist.

If the cross member and opposite rail are actually twisted, only straightening the right rail would leave the entire frame in a condition similar to that shown in Figure 8-53. The extra tie-down and jack, shown at D and E, would be required to relieve the twist. This makes a setup similar to the one shown, except that the jack on the right side is at the midpoint of the frame instead of the rear. It should be kept there; otherwise, the buckle straightened by it may come back. Extending the jack at E will release the tension of the chain at A. The chain could be used on the other side, if necessary.

A conventional frame was chosen as an easy example to illustrate this condition, but there are many other parts of both conventional and unitized construction that will have similar damage. It will always occur where a fairly long member has moved as it bent, or buckled, and applied a twisting effect to adjoining construction. It is not uncommon for damage of this type to require enough over-travel in the straightening operation to cause buckling of undamaged panels. It is quite important for the estimator to be alert for this condition, or the probability of it. Sometimes the actual condition is hard to predict, if there has been no previous experience with a new model or a make that the shop rarely repairs. Once the job is accepted, it must be repaired regardless of the extra time required to straighten a previously undamaged panel.

REAR-END DAMAGE—PERIMETER FRAMES

Rear-end damage to perimeter-type frames tends to follow typical patterns, which are enough alike that a few general procedures will apply to almost all straightening operations. Although there is some similarity in the general shape of the front and rear ends, the rear is much lighter and has higher kickups. This, plus the fact that the body absorbs much of the force of almost all rear-end impacts, tends to reduce the severity of rear-end damages; straightening the body will often be a larger operation than straightening the frame.

Figure 8-55 is typical of the rear-end construction of some of the down-sized perimeter frames in current use. In comparison to former designs, the weight of these frames has been reduces as much as possible: the metal is thinner and harder, and some parts have been eliminated entirely; for example, the rear cross member has been eliminated because the rear end of the side rail bolts directly to a relatively heavy cross member in the trunk floor.

When subjected to a direct rear-end impact, this type frame is most apt to buckle at the points indicated on Figure 8-55: (1) the high point of the kickup, (2) between the high point and the rear end, sometimes at the end of the bumper shock absorber, and (3) the front curve of the kickup, where it swings out to join the center sec-

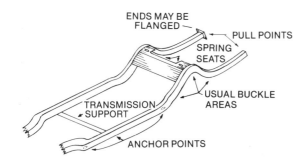

8-55 Perimeter-type frame layout showing areas where a rear-end impact usually causes buckles and the points from which hookups to anchor and pull can be made.

tion. All these areas will be strained under a rear-end impact, but the most leverage is concentrated at the high point, so it often buckles without apparent damage in the other areas. However, all will buckle if the impact force is great enough.

Most rear-end damages on this type of frame can be straightened conveniently with a portable body and frame machine. However, multiple hookup equipment may be needed for the body damage. The estimator should determine whether the body and frame can be pulled together or if separate hookups will be required for each before setting the time allowance. Some minor damage may not affect the body at all, so that it can be ignored. On more severe damage, it is often necessary to make separate connections to both body and frame for both anchoring and pulling. If not anchored securely, the body may slip on the forward hold-down bolts when force is applied, throwing it out of alignment with the fenders and hood. If multiple hookup equipment is used and the body bolts in the damaged section are not pulled out or bent, it is usually best to make separate hookups to the body and frame and pull them together. If the bolts are damaged or pulled out, it is often better to remove them, straighten the frame to proper length and shape, and pull the body to fit to it.

As with any other sharp buckle, heating will be necessary on the buckles in the kickup section. Fire and safety hazards are greater at the rear than at the front, because of the proximity of the gasoline tank and lines, wiring, body sealer, hydraulic brake lines, and body trim. The job should be examined carefully to determine what parts will have to be removed and replaced to permit heating, and, preferably, these should be listed separately on the estimate. If not specifically directed to do so, some repairmen will be tempted to take a chance and not remove parts or take other safety precautions. This is always done at the risk of fire, serious injury, or loss of life.

SIDE DAMAGE—PERIMETER FRAMES

The severity of a side damage in the center section of a perimeter frame can vary widely. Most often, repairing the body will be a bigger problem than repairing the

frame. As shown in the cross-sectional view in Figure 8-56, the side rail is enclosed on three sides by the floor pan and rocker panel, inner and outer. Unless the frame rail is caught by a very low-impact object, the rocker panel and floor must be crushed before the rail is damaged.

When the center section of a side rail has been driven in no more than an inch or two (2.5–5 cm), the repair operation is just a matter of restoring appearance. However, when it has been driven in to a depth of 5 or 6 inches (13–15 cm), the front and rear sections on that side will be drawn together enough to affect both track and wheel base. Checking with center line gauges would show a definite curve instead of a straight center line. This plus the body damage may cause the automobile to be salvaged. However, if it is rebuilt, it is essential that the procedure followed will restore the full length to the side rail. Otherwise, it may be difficult or impossible to restore correct wheel alignment.

The effect on the body will be similar. The door pillars will be drawn and the entire floor pan affected by crushed rocker panels. There wil be additional damage in the panel, or panels, which received the direct impact: door, quarter panel, center pillar, and so on.

It will be necessary to remove the damaged outer rocker panel, and often the inner, to get access to the frame. The straightening operations should start on the frame. On minor damage, it may be possible to complete the frame before working the body but, if the damage is severe, it may be necessary to use multiple hookup to straighten both together.

A repair setup to restore full length to the side rail is shown in A, Figure 8-56. Full tension should be maintained on the side rail throughout the operation.

Selecting the wrong anchor and pull points for the lengthwise tension could damage the frame. They are shown connected directly to the ends of the center section; pulling from the outer ends of the frame will not be as effective, because some of the force will be absorbed in the kickups and offsets in the front and rear sections; connecting to the extreme rear end would be particularly bad, because the construction is much lighter.

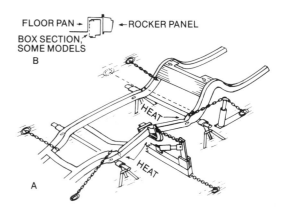

8-56 A, Multiple hookup to straighten side damage in the center section of a perimeter-type frame; B, cross section showing floor pan, rocker panel, and frame construction in the center section.

The anchors for the cross pull are shown connected at the cross members. It may not be practical to connect close to the cross member over the rear kickup on some automobiles. If the connection must be made farther forward, it may be desirable to connect the two side rails by means of a chain and a toggle-type chain tightener. The positions for these connections are shown by the dotted lines on Figure 8-56.

The operation should be started by applying lengthwise tension while watching the movement of the indented rail. It should move freely at first, but resistance to further movement should built up rapidly. Any sharp buckles should be heated to bright red to prevent cracking. Three buckles are shown in the figure, but there may be fewer, or sometimes more. The cross pull should be put in operation as soon as further heating does not cause additional free movement. At this point, both jacks should be operated together to maintain tension on the lengthwise pull as fast as it is relieved by the cross pull.

A steel pad is shown between the hook and the inner surface of the rail. This would be difficult to put in place until after the rail had been moved away from the crushed floor section by the lengthwise pull. If the side rail has been crushed too badly, it might not be completely effective. Another method would be to weld pull tabs to the upper and lower outside corners and not use the hook. Any breaks should be welded securely and the rough spots smoothed as much as possible. It may be necessary to open a "window" in the side or lower surface of the rail, but this should be done only as a last resort.

An open channel side member will require less heating than the box section. The steel pad should be the right width to fit into the channel. Most commercially available hooks have extensions that will reach into the full depth of the channel. If necessary, additional steel can be added to fill the inside. Usually the edges of the flanges must be shrunk, but this should not be done until measurements indicate that the full length has been restored.

The straightening operations on the body will be similar to those required on similar damage to a unitized body but slightly less critical, because wheel alignment is not involved. Some variation of the distance between door pillars can be made up by door adjustment. Doors should be hung in place and fitted before the outer rocker panel is installed. If the floor damage has been severe, it may be necessary to hold the floor pan under lengthwise tension while the rocker panel inner and outer is welded.

FRONT-END IMPACTS

Similar minor impacts on the front ends of conventional and unitized construction bodies can be expected to cause similar damages. Any differences would be caused by the different construction of fenders, hood, front-end panels, and so on. Similar major impacts, great enough to penetrate to the frame structures, will cause different types of damage, because the unitized construction has much less flexibility. For this reason, the effects of hard impacts on conventional and unitized bodies are discussed separately. The removable exterior sheet metal parts are not considered.

FRONT-END SHEET METAL PARTS

Part for part, the exterior sheet metal parts of conventional and unitized construction automobiles correspond, although they vary in size and design. All hoods, most front fenders, and whatever front parts support the grille are separate units that bolt together. A few front fenders on some unitized models are welded in place, but this is the exception rather than the rule. Whether severely damaged parts are bolted or welded on is an important factor to be considered by the estimator when deciding whether to replace or repair them.

The situation is entirely different with the inner sheet metal parts that support the outer. The primary inner part on conventional construction is the radiator core support that holds the complete front-end sheet metal assembly together on conventional construction. It is a bolt-on part supported on the front end of the frame, but insulated from it by rubber-padded hold-down bolts. The inner sheet metal parts on unitized construction are an important element of the structure that serve as the frame in the front section.

HOODS

Hoods are less exposed to nicks and dents than most body panels because of their high location. When damaged, it is usually a part of the overall damage pattern in which the other front-end sheet metal parts are affected. Hoods that extend to the grille are more exposed than those that close behind a front-end panel. However, damage limited to the front end is usually relatively simple, as compared to that which extends to the center or rear sections of the panel.

Hoods that have been bent out of alignment are often replaced for these reasons: (1) the inner panel, used on most hoods, prevents tool access to the under surface, (2) the metal is quite flat, making it difficult to work, (3) the flat shape makes surface irregularities quite noticeable, and (4) replacement requires only a very few minutes.

When inspecting any hood with structural damage thought repairable, the following conditions should be considered as well as the condition of the outer panel: (1) the metal may be aluminum and more difficult to work than steel, (2) the hinge attaching surfaces may be pulled out of shape, (3) wide separation may exist between the inner and outer panel, indicating that the plastic bonding between them is broken, (4) there may be broken welds, and (5) there may be evidence of previous repair.

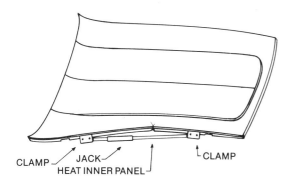

8-57 Jack and clamp setup to straighten buckled hood flange.

A jack and clamp setup to straighten a very common but repairable type of structural damage is illustrated in Figure 8-57. The hood is the type with the inner and outer panel joined with a flange that extends downward. A similar setup can be used on hoods joined with a hem flange, but the clamps would extend outward instead of down.

In the setup shown, heat should be applied only to the inner panel. Softening the inner panel reduces its resistance, allowing most of the tension to work on the outer panel. The hammer, or hammer and flat spoon, should not be used until the buckle has been pulled as far as it will go without excessive force, and then used carefully; the hammer work should start at the beginning of the buckle and work toward the edge. When disc sanded, a fresh, sharp disc should be used to avoid excesive frictional heat that could cause heat distortion. Completed properly, this operation should restore the full length to the outer edge and avoid leaving an area of false-stretched metal in the adjoining area.

A buckle of this type often extends into the adjoining deep rib-type reinforcement pressed into the inner panel to stiffen the side and provide a mounting surface for the hinge. If the buckle is minor, it can be worked with a panel puller while the outer edge is under tension. Or, with the ends supported firmly, it can be heated and hand pressure applied to push it out. A more severe buckle may require a setup to pull it out; if so, it should be done before the outer edge is worked. No setup is shown, but the jack can usually be based against the hinge at the rear. At the front, a solder-on tension plate is ideal, but, lacking that, a piece of scrap metal can be brazed or screwed to the panel for use with a clamp.

A hem-flanged hood should always have the reinforcement straightened before the outer edge.

RADIATOR CORE SUPPORT

Radiator cores vary widely in design, but almost all consist of a rigid frame for the core with side extensions to support the fenders and air baffles. Most modern supports have the radiator section lowered between the frame horns, so that the shape is similar to that in Fig-

ure 8-58. Heavy rubber pads isolate the assembly from metal-to-metal contact with the frame at the hold-down bolts. Oversized holes for the rubber mounting pads provide a wide range of fore-and-aft and side-to-side adjustment. Shims can be added on each side to raise the support, and some are factory-equipped with a shim pack so that the assembly can be raised or lowered by adding or removing.

A major collision may directly damage the core support, but they are more often damaged by forces transferred through the fenders, front bumper, or hood. In addition to any obvious direct impact damage, the support should be examined carefully when the condition of the outer sheet metal suggests the possibility of damage. Conditions to look for are (1) back or side shifts on the frame, (2) diamonding of the core opening, (3) twists, and (4) torn-out and hold-down bolts. Most of this is visual inspection; it may be necessary to use a creeper to look up at the underside of the hold-down bolts for semicircles of bare metal indicating shifts, but the conditions of the core will reveal most of the other conditions.

It is policy in many shops to replace the core support if it has been damaged in any way. This policy is based on the assumption that the hood and fenders cannot be aligned properly if the support is not perfect. But this assertion is open to question for two reasons: (1) minor damage is relatively easy to repair, and (2) the appearance of the core support is not critical, because much of the assembly is hidden from view. Some minor misalignments can be corrected by shifting the position on the frame. A body jack can be set diagonally in the core opening to correct most diamond conditions. It is much better to base the decision, when the decision is to replace or repair, on a comparison of the costs of both.

CONVENTIONAL FRONT-END CONSTRUCTION

Figure 8-59 represents a cowl that has been tipped back in a front-end collision and a practical repair setup to correct it. When inspecting any severe front-end damage, look for three signs of this condition: (1) a door which is either jammed tight against the lock pillar or drops noticeably when opened, (2) a wide gap between the door edge and roof rail at the upper corner of the windshield, and (3) a buckle in the roof over the lock

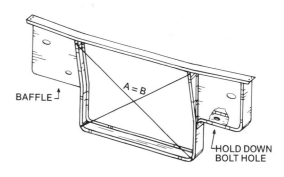

8-58 General features of the radiator core supports used on conventional construction.

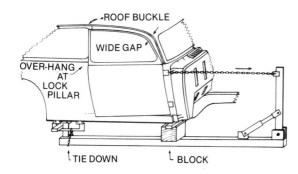

8-59 Typical hookups used to pull tipped cowl side back into alignment. Shown on conventional construction, but sometimes needed on unitized.

pillar. If the door is jammed shut, look for separated hem flange welds on he door hinge facing. There may or may not be additional dents, gouges, or collapsed sections on the cowl top, side, or fire wall and edge damage on the door. These latter conditions vary widely, so no attempt has been made to show them on Figure 8-59.

On older models it was safe to push most tipped cowls back into place with a body jack set either diagonally in the opening or based against the bracing for the rear seat. There is risk of crushing metal at either or both ends of the jack on more present-day bodies by using it in that manner. No doubt the risk will increase with the trend toward lighter construction and thinner metal. It is a much safer procedure to use some type of external pulling equipment, portable or stationary. Any frame straightening should be done first. Allowance should be made for spring-back by slight over-correction, because this is a cold bending operation.

Whatever type of equipment is used, the rear end should be tied down and a block used under the cowl so that the bending strain will be concentrated under the base of the hinge pillar. It is usually safe on most bodies to let the frame rail bear against the block, but a few may require extra support between the lower edge of the rocker panel and the block to prevent floor damage. The operator should watch this point carefully as the work progresses.

The connection to pull is shown on the door pillar at the upper hinge. This position must be well-reinforced on all bodies. A plate can be put under the bolts on bolted-on hinges or welded to weld-on ones. However, some hinges are attached to the pillar crossways instead of fore and aft, making it necessary to use another method of attachment. Usually something can be bolted or welded to the same general area, because it must be reinforced to take the strains from the hinges when the door is open and during operation on a rough road. Some cowls have a forward extending flange that serves as the weld joint between the fire wall and the outer panels. Most of these have a brace (not shown) extending from the hinge pillar to the front edge of the flange, making a safe position for the use of a clamp.

The estimator must be alert to catch any damage to the inner bracing of the cowl. Both upper and lower hingers require rigid bracing to withstand the strains of

normal operation. A front-end collision is more apt to damage the upper braces than the lower, but both can be affected. Some may straighten easily, but others may require removal of the side panel to gain access. If the panel is removed, the door opening should be checked for fit before it is replaced.

UNITIZED INNER FRONT-END CONSTRUCTION

The manufacturers of unitized bodies have many different designs of front-end construction, but all are combined with the body to form a rigid structure. Figure 8-60 shows the general construction features, but does *not* represent any specific make or model. Shock absorber towers, usually referred to as *towers*, are shown, because they are typical of the MacPherson-type suspension systems used on many unitized automobiles. No attempt has been made to show other suspension parts of the means of attachment, because there are too many variations for any one to be considered typical.

Almost all unitized front-end parts are made up of three major assemblies: two side panels and a front-end panel. The side panels are rigid members, welded securely to the front end of the cowl so that they become extensions of the body side frame. They have a relatively light box member welded to the lower edge, corresponding to the conventional frame side rail, but its primary purpose is to support the bumper assembly and the lower control arm and strut of the front suspension. The side panels are relatively heavy, as compared to body panels, with reinforcements on the upper edge. On some designs, the reinforcement extends full length, whereas on others it extends from the cowl section to the front suspension area.

The front panel is reinforced at both top and bottom, but is not usually as rigid as the side members, because it is subjected to much less strain than the side members.

Front-end repair problems vary too widely on unitized construction to establish a typical damage condition, making it impractical to show a typical repair setup. Instead, the typical problem areas are num-

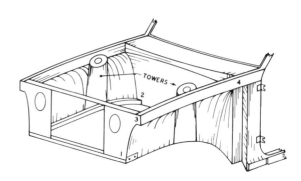

8-60 General features of the front end of unitized construction bodies. Numbers indicate areas most frequently damaged in front-end collisions. Not representative of any specific make or model, but similar to most.

bered, to provide a reference to the discussion of a variety of typical repair problems.

The lower front corner, marked 1, is exposed to more collision damage than the other parts, because the bumper is attached to it. It also provides the mounting points for the lower control arm and strut of the front suspension system. It is important that any collapsed condition in this section be restored to full length. For minor damage this may be as simple as anchoring to the rocker panels and pulling with any type of equipment. The problems of connecting to the front end vary with the construction. On some, it is as simple as bolting a plate onto the bumper attaching point; on others, it may be necessary to use weld on clamps or improvise a special bracket. The harder the pull, the greater this problem becomes, because metal used in this area is relatively light.

Direct impact on the bumper section has less tendency to drive the rail section back into the floor of the cowl (2 on the left side) than a conventional frame has to bend in the same general area for two reasons: (1) the tendency of the forward section to collapse and (2) the rigid bracing in the cowl area. When it does, however, the side panel assembly must be pulled back to position either as part of the repair operation or in preparation for replacement. In either situation, the length must be restored for wheel alignment. Pulling on the old panel is simply a matter of using it as a means of applying force to the damaged section of the cowl. It is also the best assurance that, when the old assembly is removed, the new one will fit. There may be a few exceptions to this general rule, but it will apply to almost all damages affecting the cowl.

Higher impacts, in the top area marked 3, or farther back, do not affect the structure of the shock towers and usually require only a light pull to straighten the side panels. If the front panel is crushed badly enough to require replacement, it is usually best to remove it first to simplify straightening the side panel.

A high impact hard enough to drive the side panel back into the cowl (4) or cause door misalignment is uncommon. However, then this does occur, a variation of the hookup shown in Figure 8-59 should be used. Instead of connecting the pull chain to the hinge section of the door, it should be applied to some part of the side panel assembly, often to the top of the shock tower or the forward edge of the cowl. The anchor clamps should be attached to the rear end of rocker panels to raise the line of tension as high as possible. This is explained in detail in the Tension Alignment section in Chapter 7 and illustrated in Figure 7-33.

Side impacts on the front section have less tendency to cause a side shift than those on conventional frames, because of the lighter construction. The tendency is to collapse the cross members instead, concentrating the effect on the side receiving the impact and crushing the cross members. Whatever the damage condition, it should be pulled back into general position, either as part of the repair operation or in preparation for replacement.

Side pulls are generally more difficult to make than

on conventional frames, because the unitized construction provides fewer rigid anchor points and those that are available are usually less rigid. Equipment manufacturers are beginning to make anchor systems in which the rocker panel lower flanges are held rigidly against movement in *all* directions. Lacking such equipment, the repairman is often forced to weld on or improvise special brackets for the purpose, usually spending extra time in the operations.

Center line realignment is more critical on unitized construction than on conventional frames because of its rigidity. The only provision for side-to-side adjustment of fenders is made by oversized holes for the bolts that hold the fender flange to the upper edge of the side panel. Any misalignment great enough to shift the front section off center line beyond this narrow range of adjustment must be corrected. A cross-check across the top should be the final step of any straightening operation and should be used in aligning any new side panel assembly before it is welded in place securely.

When making a preliminary inspection of a severly damaged unitized front end, the estimator and repairman should first look at any undamaged exterior sheet metal parts for evidence of serious misalignment. Doors that open and close properly are evidence that the cowl structure is not affected seriously. The hood, even though damaged, may still be in alignment with the top of the cowl and possibly one fender, indicating that the center line is not affected. The distance between the top of the shock towers should be checked against specifications. When these conditions are correct, the repair job will probably be a matter of straightening the front end of the side panel, or panels, and straightening or replacing the front panel. However, when any of these areas are misaligned, it is probable that a multiple hookup will be required to restore alignment before the straightening or replacement operations can be completed.

When the suspension has had a direct impact, it is particularly important to check the control arm bushings for evidence of twisting or torn metal. This applies also to the anchor bracket that holds the control arm strut. These points should be restored to exact position, as specified by the manufacturer.

UNITIZED BODY REAR-END REPAIR

A in Figure 8-61 represents a typical repair setup on a unitized body that has relatively minor rear-end damage. It is shown with part of the damaged quarter panel, rear-end panel, and floor pan cut away to reveal inner construction. This is not intended to suggest that these parts, when damaged, should always be replaced; the decision to replace them should be based on the condition of individual panels and sometimes on whether removal is necessary to permit access to other panels.

Only general statements can be made about the repair of rear-end damage on unitized bodies, because they vary in construction. However, almost all of them

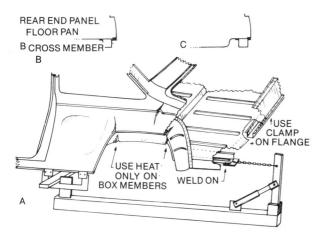

8-61 A, typical repair setup on unitized body having minor rear-end damage; B, typical cross section of rear of floor having no flange convenient for clamp attachment; C, variation of detail B, which further complicates problem of attachment.

have flanged U-shaped channels welded to the underside of the floor pan to serve as frame rails and rear-end cross members. The result is a relatively rigid body, as compared to conventional construction.

When alignment is involved, it is necessary to use some type of pulling equipment on almost all rear-end damages because of the lighter construction of unitized bodies. An attempt to use a jack inside the body will often cause more damage to the base it rests on than it corrects. Minor damages of the type represented by Figure 8-61 can usually be straightened with a portable body and frame machine if the floor pan is not damaged seriously. The condition is different if the floor pan is crushed so that it ought to be pulled from two different angles. There are some exceptions, but it would almost always then be better to pull one setup partway and hold it under tension while pulling the other. Working this way, each setup would tend to relieve the strain on the other; doing this with a portable machine would

require changing the machine and the advantage of holding one hookup under tensions while operating the other would be lost.

Before allocating repair time for a rear-end repair, the estimator should determine what problems will be encountered in making and using the connections to pull and anchor. Connecting can be as simple as attaching a clamp to a convenient flange, as indicated at the rear end of A. Other methods are needed, however, when there is no flange. Some rear-end panels are connected to the floor by a flange that extends inward instead of outward, as shown in B. This construction would make it necessary to remove the rear-end panel before a clamp could be attached to the flanged edge of the cross member and floor pan. The problem is further complicated when the floor pan is depressed below the level of the cross member, as shown in C. With the rear-end panel removed, this could be pulled only enough to straighten the cross member, assuming it is not damaged badly enough to require replacement.

Sometimes a pull connection can be made by bolting to the holes for the bumper attachment, usually at the point of attachment for the bumper shock absorbers, although some bumper shock absorbers are rugged enough to withstand a direct pull on the outer end.

A welded-on connection is shown in A. Sometimes this is the only practical method, but it should be considered as the last resort, because it takes extra time and the welding burns the protective coating off of the metal. The two views in Figure 8-62 illustrate a good method of doing this to the lower surface of an upright U-channel. Welds should be made only along the sides so that they can be cut cleanly with a cutting torch. This method is not satisfactory for U-channels that have the open side facing either outward or inward.

Brazing is not as desirable as welding for frame attachment, because of the risk of embrittlement when the piece is removed. When brazing is used and the piece is removed by heating, the flame should be kept on the attached piece, heating it uniformly until it is close to the red heat range. At the right temperature, it can be knocked off with a sharp hammer blow. The remaining brass should be ground off. Melting if off will guarantee embrittlement, particularly on thin metal.

Anchoring for a rear-end pull can usually be done by attaching a set of anchor clamps to the lower flanges of the rocker panels. However, many anchor clamp sets designed for use on conventional bodies may damage lightweight rocker panels when subjected to a hard pull. As illustrated in Figure 8-63, the clamp assembly tends to rotate around the point of force application; the

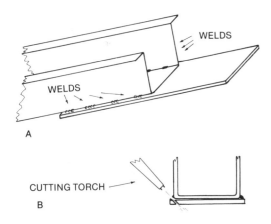

8-62 A, method of welding temporary pull plate to lower surface of upright U-channel frame rail. B, use of cutting torch to remove temporary plate.

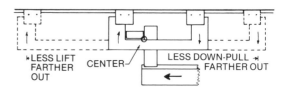

8-63 Extra-long anchor clamps will reduce the risk of damage to rocker panel lower edge.

clamp position forward of this point pushes upward, tending to crush the lower side of the rocker, and the rear clamp position tends either to strip off or tear the flange. These tendencies are greater when the clamp positions are close together. Some equipment manufacturers have designed anchor clamp sets that are much longer and have multiple clamps to spread the load enough to avoid crushing the rocker panel. The trend is toward clamps that grip full length and can be anchored in all directions.

The use of heat is essential in straghtening any sharply buckled metal, particularly the lighter metal used in unitized construction. Otherwise, buckles will break or tear instead of straightening. More care is needed in heating light metal than on the heavier material used in conventional frame construction. The note on Figure 8-61 emphasizes that heat should be applied only to box members. If the member has two or more bends that must yield at the same time, they must be heated at the same time. On complicated jobs, it is often worthwhile to have a second torch and a temporary helper so that some buckles do not cool while others are being heated. This is particularly important on thin metal, which cools relatively rapidly.

UNITIZED BODY SIDE DAMAGE

Figure 8-64 represents a suggested repair procedure for deep impact damage on the side of a unitized body. The seriousness of this type of damage is directly related to the depth of penetration into the side of the body. If deep, it must be repaired properly to restore wheel alignment. Penetration of the impact to an appreciable depth will draw the front and rear sections together, reducing the wheel base on that side and bending the entire automobile lengthwise. A center line check will show a curve instead of a straight line. If this is not fully restored to the straight line condition, the automobile will tend to travel in a long curve instead of straight ahead.

Severe damage of this type is a test of ability for both the estimator and the repairman. The estimator is apt to under-estimate the damage unless he is familiar with the problems involved, and he must know that the shop crew is competent. The repairman who spends most of his time straightening body panels is accustomed to have his work judged primarily on appearance. On this type of job, accuracy is as important as appearance.

The importance of restoring a side-damaged conventional frame is explained in an earlier section. This type of damage presents the repairman with a more difficult problem because, instead of a single, heavy box member, the side of the body is made up of several pieces of light metal that join at right angles. The movement under impact tends to stretch the lengthwise parts, particularly the inner and outer rocker panel, and crush the floor and its reinforcements.

Two important steps must be taken before any attempt is made to pull the damage out with a cross pull: (1) the crushed sections of the rocker panel, and sometimes the whole panel, must be removed, and (2) the lengthwise pull must be set up to exert the maximum tension it is safe to use.

The complete outer rocker panel is shown removed, with the added note to remove the crushed sections. Whether to remove all or only part should be determined by the condition of the floor cross braces at the front and rear. If they are bent or crushed, the panel should be removed. On severe damages, it is usually best to remove the complete panel.

The inner rocker panel is shown still in place. This is not always practical, but is desirable when possible. When removal is necessary, it is best to remove as little as possible. Unless mangled severely, the cut-out section can be straightened and welded back in place as easily as a new piece can be installed. The cut-out section has the advantage of fitting.

Welding in a complete inner rocker panel requires considerable labor, particularly if the oxyacetylene torch must be used. The problems of replacing rocker panels are discussed in the next section.

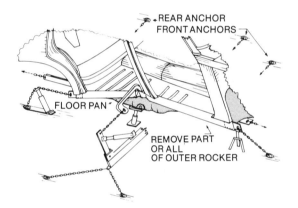

8-64 Multiple hookup on side damage in the center section of unitized bodies. Similar hookup may be needed on conventional bodies.

In operation, the cross pull will relieve the lengthwise tension. It is good practice to operate both jacks together so that the tension is never allowed to slacken. The various buckles in the floor pan should be watched carefully so that elastic strains can be relieved as they form. Bent floor reinforcements must be dealt with, as they come under strain as the work progresses.

The cross pull is shown anchored by two chains so that it can be shifted along the side as needed. The hook would be used as much as possible, but clamps will be needed to connect directly to the edge of the floor pan in areas where the inner rocker panel has to be removed because the welds holding it in place have broken. On severe damage, it may be necessary to reposition the side pull unit several times.

A separate jack is shown in position below the bulged-down floor pan. This would not be needed at the start of the operation, but will be necessary to finish it. The floor will begin to unroll easily as the lengthwise tension and the cross pull are applied, but it will build up resistance until at some point the movement will stop. The lift jack should then be extended enough to apply an elastic strain to the floor. From that point on, it should be gradually extended to maintain the elastic strain, but never forced enough to push the floor up faster than the other operations are pulling it into shape.

Finding suitable points from which to pull and anchor can be a problem on many unitized bodies. This problem has increased with the trend toward small, lightweight automobiles in which much of the steel is thinner and harder. However, it varies from one make to another, so that specific rules cannot be made. In some makes it may be as simple as attaching a clamp to a conveniently placed flange; on others the repairman may be forced to improvise special brackets or resort to welding on.

Two methods of connecting for the lengthwise pull are shown. The direct connections to the inner rocker panel are preferable for the straightening operations when the rocker panel can be used. After these operations have been completed, tension should be released and the side measured for length. Often the floor pan will draw back enough to leave the side short, unless it is held under tension while the rocker panel is welded into place.

Holding the floor under tension while welding the rocker panel may require changing the connections. On some automobiles, it may be practical to pull the rear end by attaching to the rear axle link; other automobiles may not have one. The next best approach is usually to weld on to a rigid part of the structure. Unless a flange is convenient at the front, welding on may be the only choice.

Three anchor points are shown on the opposite side for the crosswise pull, one at the rear end of the center section and two at the front. At the rear the repairman may have no choice other than to weld on. At the front it is usually possible to make a connection to a rigid part of the structure to which the front suspension parts are attached. If so, the forward anchor would be used. If not, a more convenient attachment may be possible at the junction of the front and center sections by either welding or a clamp. A clamp would be anchored to a point farther back.

The importance of wheel alignment on this type of job makes it desirable to recheck the measurements of the entire automobile, front, center, and rear sections, after the rocker panel has been tacked in place enough to hold. When the welding has been completed, a good grade of undercoating should be applied to the inside of the rocker panel and the outside of the floor.

ROCKER PANELS

Rocker panels are long, narrow box members, usually made of heavier metal than the rest of the exterior panels of the body. Both shape and construction limit the repair possibilities to what can be done from the outside or by piercing holes for pry or pulling tools.

Sometimes a crushed section can be pulled out by welding or brazing a piece of metal to an edge for a clamp. However, when damaged severely, the outer rocker panel usually will be removed to permit access to straighten the floor pan.

Because of complicated construction, it is common practice to replace only the damaged section instead of the complete panel. The hinge and center pillars sit on top of the rocker and are welded to it. This causes the upper flange to be sandwiched between inner rocker and the pillars. The problem is further complicated on some two-door models by the quarter panel welded to the outer edge of the top surface; this joint is welded in the factory before the body shell is assembled, but it is almost totally inaccessible on the assembled body.

When the areas under the pillars, and some two-door quarter panels, are undamaged it is common practice to make a straight-across butt joint within the door opening instead of removing the entire panel. This is a simple joint to make if the proper welding procedure is followed, but weld draw will warp the outer surface up or down if the joint is not aligned and tack-welded properly.

The welding procedure is illustrated in four progressive steps in A, Figure 8-65. After the panel has been cut and fitted, the procedure should be (1) weld the upper and lower flange to the inner panel, (2) tack-weld the outer edges and check the alignment, (3) add tack welds as needed in a skip pattern, and (4) complete the seam, welding no more than ½ inch (13 mm) in one place, allowing it to cool slightly and moving to another. A small flame should be used if welding with an oxyacetylene torch. Shielded arc with a cored electrode is a better method, if available.

Two butt joints are required when a section is welded into a door opening. If the piece is less than 1 foot (30 cm) long, the first and second steps should be completed for both joints, but the third and fourth should be completed on one weld at a time. Each completed weld should be allowed to cool before going to the next. If the welds are much closer together, it is better only to clamp the piece to the inner rocker panel, using vise

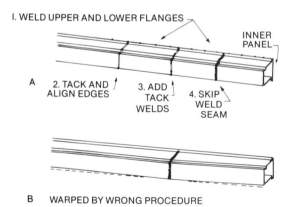

8-65 A, the progressive steps to butt weld a rocker without causing warpage. B, warpage caused by improper welding procedure.

grip pliers on both flanges, and complete one weld. Then weld the flanges and complete the other, following the procedure described. This way, weld draw from the first will not affect the second weld.

B in Figure 8-65 illustrates what can happen if the joint is welded without concern for heat control. The outer surface is shown warped down, but it can go either way, depending on how the welding was done.

Extra care is desirable when welding in a new inner rocker panel. The accumulated weld can be enough to shorten the wheel base on one side of unitized construction if the welding is done carelessly. The floor pan should be held under tension, as shown in Figure 8-64, and a skip-weld pattern used to avoid getting any section hotter than necessary.

The time allowance should be based on what actually has to be done. When the entire side of a body has to be replaced, rocker panel replacement is relatively simple. It can be a much greater problem if the rocker is damaged from end to end but the other panels are not. However, putting a section in a door opening is relatively simple. Sometimes a short damaged section can be cut out, straightened, and put back in place to make a satisfactory repair more economically than a new part can be installed.

HINGE PILLAR AND COWL SIDE PANELS

A hinge pillar, cowl side panel, and their reinforcements make up a complex sheet metal structure that is relatively difficult to repair. It is often necessary to remove a damaged hinge pillar to provide access to straighten the inner parts. However, many damaged pillars can be repaired more economically than they can be replaced, leaving much of the original factory welding and sealing intact.

Use of a body jack diagonally across the cowl to push out a damaged pillar is not practical on most automo-

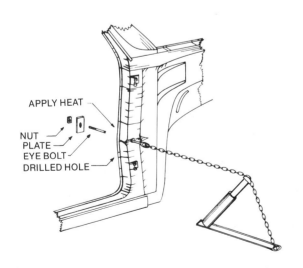

8-66 Use of eyebolt to straighten bent hinge pillar; method of anchoring not shown. Requires hole to be drilled and later filled.

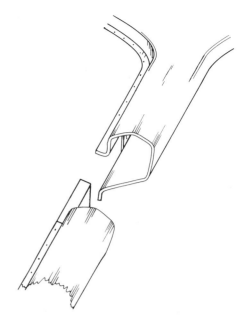

8-67 Offset joint in windshield pillar should be used to avoid continuous butt joint.

biles, because of the risk of damage to the opposite side by the base of the jack. The setup shown in Figure 8-66 is more practical. The method suggested is to drill a hole for an eyebolt in the heavy metal of the pillar; the hole must be welded shut or otherwise plugged later. The plate should have a hole of suitable size so that it can be placed over the bolt on the inside, making a positive connection when the nut is screwed on. The buckle should be heated because it is much stiffer than the rest of the structure. The flame should be kept off the eyebolt as much as possible.

No anchors are shown in this hookup, because method of anchoring will vary widely from one automobile to another. However, the anchor bar of a portable machine should *not* be used against the inside of the opposite rocker panel. This pull will require enough force almost to guarantee damage to the rocker panel. The anchoring problem should be checked before setting the time allowance, particularly on unitized construction.

This hookup can be used at any point, high or low, on the pillar. When used where the pillar is enclosed by a welded-on inner panel, it will be necessary to drill through both the outer and inner. When this is done, the plate should be large enough to cover the flanges of the outer; otherwise, the plate will be pulled into the pillar.

When replacing a hinge pillar that is not damaged in the upper end, it is common and acceptable practice to make the joint in the windshield opening instead. However, an all-around butt joint should be avoided by cutting the inner and outer at different positions, as shown in Figure 8-67. This way, each weld is reinforced by an uncut section of the other piece.

This method has two additional advantages: (1) the flanges can be clamped before welding and the opening adjusted to an exact fit for the glass before any welding is done, and (2) weld draw will be almost entirely eliminated if the flanges are tacked before the butt joints are made. The butt joints should be skip-welded, never straight across without stopping.

WINDSHIELD OPENING MISALIGNMENT

Windshield opening misalignment is almost always a part of a pattern of roof damage caused by either a side impact or a rollover. Some misalignments are obvious, but others may be missed by both the repairman and the estimator unless checked carefully. If the glass is cracked, broken, or popped out of its rubber channel, the opening is probably misaligned. The glass serves as a brace for the pillars as long as it is properly installed, but the pillars tend to bend at the upper and lower corners of the opening when the bracing of the glass is lost. They rarely bend in the midsection of the opening unless they receive a direct impact.

Three types of windshield misalignments are common: (1) one pillar bent inward without affecting the other, usually causing the header to raise away from the glass, (2) both pillars pushed to one side approximately equal amounts, and (3) the header collapsed, sometimes with part of it too high and part driven down into opening. Most windshield damages have a combination of two and sometimes all three of these conditions.

A jack is shown in Figure 8-68 set up diagonally from the right rocker panel to the left upper pillar. This will push the left pillar outward and draw the roof and right pillar with it. This setup can be made quickly and used for both the first and second condition, but the technique varies for each. For the first condition, the header will almost always be raised above the opening and the header buckled. The procedure is to heat the buckle before extending the jack, causing the buckle to drop instead of pulling the opposite pillar out of alignment—or, if the opposite pillar has shifted outward, not to pull it past the point of correction. The technique is to balance the heating and the jack operation so that the

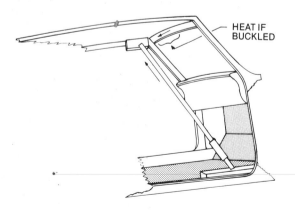

8-68 Jack set up to shift windshield pillars to the side. Header, if buckled upward, should be heated to aid reshaping.

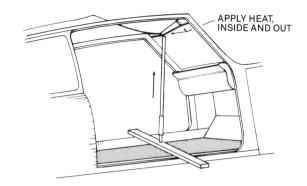

8-69 Jack set up to raise windshield header when collapsed into opening. Buckles, inside or out, should be heated as jack is operated.

header drops into position as the pillar moves outward. Not enough heat will draw the opposite pillar too far inward; too much will allow the heated area to stretch, making a mess out of the header.

It is better to make two or three tries, checking the opening between each, than to carry the operation too far. Diagonal measurements across the opening will provide a rough idea of the alignment, but the final check should be made with the glass set on the flanges. Before use, the glass should be taped around the edges both for safety and to reduce the risk of breakage. It may be found necessary to use a block of wood and a heavy hammer on the pinch weld flange on an area of the header that is hard to make drop into place. However, this should be avoided as much as possible, as it can make more problems than it solves; the block and hammer should *never* be used on the outer edge of the roof and used on the pinch weld *only* when the header is under tension.

When the block and hammer are used for the latter condition, both pillars shifted approximately the same amount, care must be exercised not to allow the header to flatten too much, a tendency always found in any curved member under tension. If the misalignment is minor, this tendency may be ignored. However, when the misalignment is greater, the pillars should be tied together in some manner, usually using clamps and either a pull jack or a turnbuckle.

When the header has been collapsed into the windshield opening, a sharp buckle will always be formed in the outer edge of the roof panel. This buckle will extend well back into the panel and usually form a high ridge in the midsection. Also, there may be a buckle on the inside of the header, caused by a portion of the windshield staying in the opening.

The header should be lifted back into general shape before correcting any sideshift. The jack setup shown in Figure 8-69 and the proper use of heat on the buckle (or buckles, if there are two) should raise the header and relieve most of the roof buckle at the same time. The jack should be equipped with a wide-blade-type fitting, to bear on the underside of the pinch weld before setting it in place with just enough pressure to hold it while the buckles are heated. A small torch tip should be used

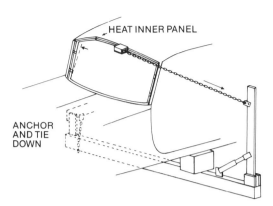

HEAT INNER PANEL

ANCHOR
AND TIE
DOWN

8-70 Portable frame machine set up to shift windshield pillars and straighten header. May be combined with use of jack, as shown in Figs. 8-58 and 8-59.

and the heat concentrated on the sharp creases. When the buckles are red hot, the jack should be extended rapidly so that the heat-softened metal will unfold with the least possible resistance.

In this operation, the roof buckles may usually be ignored until the header is back into position. However, if any valley buckles extend to the sides, it may be desirable to rough them out so that they do not interfere with the free movement of the roof panel.

The outside hookup shown in Figure 8-70 is not normally needed but is well worthwhile when one side of the header has buckled and the other side flattened, causing severe misalignment of the opening. When the proper position is selected on the pinch weld flange, this hookup will tend to draw raised areas down and push low areas up. Jacks can be used with this as needed. When an area has been raised quite high, it may be necessary to set up a jack diagonally to oppose the pulling action and concentrate more force on the buckle on the inner surface of the header.

This hookup is shown using a portable frame machine, but it can be done as well or better with any type of multiple hookup equipment. The body must be supported and anchored as shown, or the pull will simply tip it over. The dotted lines show the machine bearing against the inside of the opposite rocker panel. If this is done, the operator should watch the operation carefully. Most bodies have enough reinforcement in this area to withstand a light strain; the pillars and roof will not offer great resistance. However, another method of anchoring should be found if this area begins to crush. A block of wood of the right size should always be used between the anchor beam and the rocker panel.

CENTER PILLARS

Center pillars are rigidly reinforced by a heavy steel stamping that extends from the base to the midsection of the window. When this reinforcement has been driven out of shape by a direct impact, it is usually best to replace the pillar.

Center pillars are often bent in or out at the belt line without other serious damage. Either condition is relatively easy to straighten. An in-bend can be pushed out with a body jack based against the opposite rocker panel as shown in Figure 8-71 or pulled out with an external setup. Most out-bends can be straightened with a large C-clamp and a piece of wood, preferably 4 × 4 (10 × 10 cm), and the approximate length of the pillar. A smaller piece of wood should be used under the clamp at the belt line to protect the sheet metal. The piece of wood is placed upright against the inner surface of the pillar and the pillar drawn against it with the clamp.

A center pillar will occasionally be bent fore or aft by a door being driven against it or twisted by a rear door that has been struck from the rear while open. A fore or aft bend will usually be part of a damage pattern that will require other fore or aft pulls, with the pillar being pulled at the same time. The estimator can make a quick check for these bends by sighting across to the opposite pillar for an out-of-parallel condition.

Flat-rate time allowances for pillar replacement usually show two operations. One for replacement of the complete pillar, the other for cutting the pillar between the top of the reinforcement and the roof. The latter should be used unless the upper part is actually damaged or the roof is being replaced. The welds in the inner and outer should be staggered, as shown in Figure 8-67. Cutting the pillar in the reinforced section is not considered practical, because the reinforcement is completely covered by sheet metal, blocking access for welding.

8-71 Jack set up to push out bend in center pillar.

QUARTER PANELS

For the purpose of repair, the two-door quarter panel has three sections: (1) front, forward of the wheel opening, (2) center, over the wheel opening, and (3) rear. Each has different repair problems that vary to some degree by make and model, but in all the primary problem is access to the inner surface. Four-door models do not have the front section, but the problems in the center and rear are essentially the same as for the two-door models.

It is common practice to use panel pullers and filling to repair minor dents in all areas of the quarter panel. This is much more acceptable in the front and center sections, but not acceptable in the rear, where most of the inner surface is exposed to view when the trunk is open. Where it is practical to use hand tools or pry rods, they are preferable to the panel puller. Where the puller is used, the holes should be sealed, preferably by brazing. Weld-on pull tabs are acceptable in any area.

Probably the nearest to a typical problem is repairing major damage in the front section is re-establishing alignment of the pillar section to the front door. If door damage is involved, the repaired or replacement door should be installed and fitted to the rest of the opening so that the panel can be roughed out to fit. This is equally important if the panel is to be replaced.

A particular method or roughing out front-section damage cannot be recommended for conditions that vary widely. However, a repairman who understands rough-out procedures should be able to avoid serious problems in this area.

The rear section is exposed to both direct impact and secondary damage caused by frame impact on the rear end that carries through to the floor pan, quarter panel, and often the wheel housing. Repair procedures vary for conventional and unitized types. The greater flexibility of the unitized construction often permits the frame and body to be done separately. The lesser flexibility of the unitized body usually makes it necessary to straighten all of the damage as a single unit. The alternative is to remove the quarter panel, or portions of it, and straighten the rest of the structure so that a new panel can be fitted.

Quarter Panel Replacement

No attempt is made here to establish guidelines to follow in determining whether a damaged quarter panel should be repaired or replaced. However, it is emphasized that, when the panel is obviously repairable, the quality of the repair job may exceed the quality of the replacement when judged in terms of durability. It is desirable to retain as much of the original factory processing as possible. Welding, pre-paint processing, paint priming, paint curing, and sealing operations can be done in the repair shop, but not to the standards of quality obtainable in factory production. When the panel is judged not-repairable, it is still desirable to retain as much of the original factory processing as pos-

sible. For this reason, it is recommended that, when the damage is all within one section, only the portion of the new panel actually needed should be put in.

There is an occasional cost saving when the unused portion of a panel can be used on another job. However, this happens less often than might be expected. The most common saving is obtained when it is possible to replace the rear end of a two-door model with a less costly four-door panel. The rear-end section of some makes are identical in shape on two- and four-door models, but this is not true of all. If not known, this should be checked carefully before ordering parts. When there is a difference, it is usually enough to make alterations impractical.

Quarter Panel Sections

Some of the more common ways that a quarter panel can be sectioned are illustrated in Figure 8-72 by the dashed lines. This is not a copy of any particular panel, but is similar to many. The locations of dashed lines indicating where cuts may be made are intended as suggestions; variations of shape and window design will determine the exact location.

The rear section is the most commonly used. A cut in the general area indicated by line A will require the least labor and mutilation of the original structure. However, the shape of the side panel and the welding method to be used must be considered. Broad, nearly flat surfaces are more difficult to weld and finish smoothly than those with a fairly high crown, particularly if the welding must be done with a torch. Resistance spot welding in an offset joint is preferable. A skip pattern should be used if either arc-spot or brazing is used. A few skilled repairmen can butt weld a joint of this type and peen the weld smooth, using a hammer and dolly block, so that little or no filling is needed except at the ends. Whatever type of joint is used, the ends should be fusion welded.

When only the front section is needed, the panel can be cut in the general area indicated by line B. This requires cutting the window frame, preferably in the general area of the lines marked B, C, and D. Cutting the

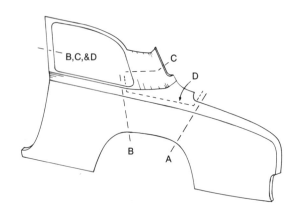

8-72 Various sections of a quarter panel that may be used when the complete panel is not needed.

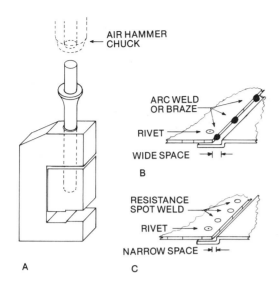

8-73 A, offsetting tool for use wth air hammer; B, spacing of offset seam desirable for either arc welding or brazing; C, close fit of offset seam desirable for resistance spot welding.

panel at either line C or D will permit putting in the complete lower section without disturbing the roof area; at C is preferable if the rear window must be removed for other purposes. If not, it is usually better to drop below into the general area indicated by line D. Line D may be the choice when the roof has a vinyl cover and the rear glass is unbroken. When the glass must be removed for other purposes, it sometimes is better to strip a vinyl roof cover back so that the weld joint will be in a covered area, particularly on a four-door model that does not have a quarter window.

Weld joints in window corners should be avoided, because they require considerably more time and effort to align and finish.

In general, the rest of the quarter and the adjoining panels should be aligned before cutting out the damaged section. However, strains in the damaged section may prevent re-alignment of other areas until cut away. Alignment problems must be solved according to the existing conditions.

Before any cutting is done, the lines to be cut should be laid out on both the damaged and the new panel. When more than one cut is to be made, the layout for the first one should be completed on both panels before going to another. The extra length for overlap seams should be on the new panel so that an air hammer-driven offsetting tool, as shown at A in Figure 8-73, can be used without interference. As shown at B, the gap between the panel edge and the shoulder of the offset should be wide if arc tacking or brazing will be used in welding the joint; this will keep the arc puddle away from the shoulder and permit better penetration of brazing metal between the surfaces. If resistance spot welding is used (C), it is better to leave as small a space as possible so that the weld spots can be staggered instead of kept in a straight line.

Before using the offsetting tool, the sharp crease lines should be notched slightly as shown in Figure 8-74, leaving that section to be butt joined, preferably by fusion welding. The offsetting tool may be used on fairly short radius curves without any problem, but attempting to use it across a sharp crease, as shown in the center section, will cause a high spot that will project above the surface.

The panel should be clamped in place and the alignment checked carefully. A few tack-welds may be required in the door or deck lid opening, but these should be kept to the minimum until *all* of the joints to be welded are in alignment. Removing the panel to correct a previously unnoticed misalignment is simple at this stage, but can be a real problem if extensive welding has been done.

When the alignment is correct, the overlapped seams should be drilled and fastened with pop rivets or metal screws, but not welded until the panel has been welded around the outer edges, making sure that enough spots are fastened securely enough to prevent any shifting due to weld draw. The butt joints at the ends of the overlapped seams should be welded before welding the seam. This is particularly important when the oxyacetylene torch will be used, because these joints will tend to draw the seam slightly. While it is still joined only by rivets or screws, the panel retains some flexibility to permit the surfaces to slip slightly as the butt welds cool and tend to draw them together.

The overlapped seam should always be welded in a skip pattern, if either arc or brazing is used. In quite flat areas, it is desirable to cover the edges of the seam with water-soaked asbestos if brazing is used, but this is not necessary for arc spotting. The important point is never to let any area get hotter than absolutely necessary. As a general rule, it is better not to quench welds, but it may be necessary if heat distortion is allowed to get out of control.

Brazing the full length of the overlapped seam may cause excessive heat distortion in the flat sections. This can be reduced by making short tacks, leaving approximately one half of the length unbrazed. Small spots, approximately ¼ to ⅜ inch (6–10 mm) long, are preferable to longer welds and gaps.

When using resistance spot welding, heat distortion is not a problem, but the seam can be misaligned by the pressure applied with the hand-held electrodes if

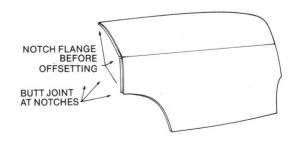

8-74 Notching of crease and sharp break-lines for offset seam.

enough rivets or screws are not used. In flat areas it may be necessary to place these no more than 2 inches (5 cm) apart to prevent slippage.

The finished seam should be checked for high spots before being finished with filler. If the seam is in an exposed area of the trunk, the rivets or screws should be removed. The offset seam should be sprayed with undercoating—normal procedure for any repair operation. Filling and finishing is the same as for any other repair operation.

The problems of welding reverse crowns are not mentioned in the preceding discussions, because very few are found in current styles, and the demand for weight reduction should prevent their return. However, any joint *across* a reverse crown should be offset unless the curve is too short for the upsetting tool. Those that cannot be offset should be butt welded. A lengthwise seam of a shallow reverse crown should be offset, but when the curve is short, a simple lap is satisfactory.

This discussion is limited to general information about (1) the basic sheet metal construction of passenger compartment doors, (2) weatherstrip sealing of door openings, (3) hinge operation and adjustment, (4) lock operation and lock striker adjustment, (5) door alignment procedures, (6) removing and replacing the door assembly, (7) major damage repair, and (8) outer panel replacement. No attempt is made to explain specific service procedures that vary from one make to another. The best and only reliable source of such information is the manufacturer's shop manual or service bulletins.

Although this discussion is limited to passenger compartment doors, much of the information applies to the other hinged assemblies, hoods, deck lids, hatchback lids, and station wagon tail gates. These other parts differ in detail but, with the exception of the two-way swing station wagon tailgates, service problems on them are less complicated than on doors. The two-way tailgate should present no serious problems to the repairman who understands the basic adjustments of hinges and door lock strikers.

DOORS

DOOR CONSTRUCTION

Some of the important features of door construction are shown in detail in Figure 9-1, illustrating a front door;

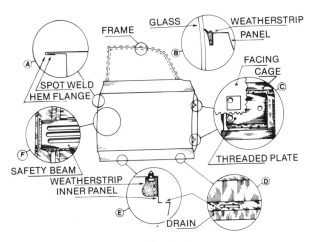

9-1 Typical door construction features.

rear doors have similar features, except that many have fixed instead of movable glass. The details are representative of doors in general, not intended to show the exact construction of a particular one. The design can vary considerably and still accomplish the same purpose.

A spot welded hem-flange is shown in detail A. Although keyed to a single spot weld, this flange extends the full length of the front, lower, and rear edges of the outer panel and is welded at intervals of 3 or 4 inches. When the panel is stamped, the flange is left standing at a right angle to the surface so that it can be hemmed over in the assembly operation. When an outer panel is replaced in the repair shop, the hemming operation is done with a hammer and dolly block. In factory assembly, the inner panel is placed into the outer and the flange is folded down by a hemming die. It then goes to a welding press that holds the assembly rigidly against another die while all of the welds are made simultaneously.

Welds made in the press join only the hem-flange to the flange of the inner panel facing. This is desirable for both the factory production and the repair shop situations. If they appeared on the other surface, it would be necessary to finish the surface before it could be painted in the factory. In the repair shop, it becomes a relatively simple operation to remove the outer panel by grinding through the edge, using a disc sander held at a right angle to the panel surface. Sometimes additional welds at the upper corners must be cut or broken; often the outer surface can be lifted off after the edge is ground, leaving the edge exposed so that the rest of the hem-flange can be broken off easily. Repaneling is described in more detail in a later section.

The detail of the upper flange and one method of sealing the space between it and the window glass are shown at B. Some flanges have a reinforcing piece welded to the flange, but many are as shown here. The rubber weatherstrip is attached to this flange, sometimes by screws, but more often by clips. This weatherstrip, not to be confused with the weatherstrip that surrounds the door, makes sliding contact with the door glass to seal out most of the weather. Ideally, it should seal out all air or water, but this is difficult to accomplish in practice. Drain holes provided to dispose of water and ventilate the inside are shown in detail D and will be explained later.

A similar weatherstrip is used on the inner surface of the glass. It is usualy attached to the upper edge of the door trim panel. Without it, there would be excessive air flow in or out of the body, depending on wind conditions and the direction of travel into or out of the wind. Other materials have been used for this weatherstrip; whatever is used, it must make sliding contact with the glass without scratching or too much friction, and it must provide good sealing.

The construction that permits the adjustment of bolt-on hinges is shown in detail C. The essential feature is fairly heavy steel plate, drilled and threaded to accept the hinge bolts, and held in place on the underside of the facing by a welded-on cage. The cage is large enough to permit the threaded plate to shift the full range of adjustment permitted by the oversized bolt hole in the facing, usually approximately 5/16 of an inch (8 mm). The usual practice is to shape the hinge so that the attachment to the pillar is at a right angle to the attachment to the door facing. Thus, the door can be shifted fore or aft on the pillar and inboard or outboard on the facing. An up or down adjustment can be made on either attachment.

A growing trend in automobile body design is to weld the hinges in place permanently in factory assembly. This requires very precise holding fixtures; otherwise, the doors would be difficult to align after installation on the body. The only possible adjustment for a welded-on

hinge is that which can be obtained by bending. When the hinge facing of either a door or pillar is damaged in collision, welded hinges complicate the straightening job, because very precise alignment must be restored.

The position on the dramin holes in the lower edge is shown in detail D. Only one hole is shown, but another would be located in the corresponding position at the opposite end, and some have a third hold in the center. These holes are located below and outside the weatherstrip so that water draining from the door goes to the outside. The position of the weatherstrip in relation to the drain hole is shown in the cross section in detail E. The arrow on the bent line leading from D into E indicates the drain hole position.

The weatherstrip in E is shown held in place by a plastic retainer. Holes for these retainers are spaced around the facing at suitable intervals, and matching holes are molded in the weatherstrip so that installation is simply a matter of pushing the retainers through the holes after they have been snapped into the rubber weatherstrip. The sealing action of weatherstrips is explained in a later section and illustrated in Figure 9-3.

The approximate position of the safety beam is shown in detail F. These beams, required by safety regulations in all passenger compartment doors, are made of heavier metal than the inner and outer panel and welded securely to the facings over the lock assembly. Safety regulations require door locks to remain securely attached to the striker and the striker to remain attached to the pillar when subjected to almost any strain caused by collision impact. Prior to the adoption of this type of lock and safety beams, it was not uncommon for a door to be driven through the opening into the passenger compartment by a relatively light impact. This construction has saved many lives and reduced the severity of many bodily injuries. Safety beams are required on the two-door-model quarter panels, but would serve no purpose on deck lids and hoods.

HINGE FACING REINFORCEMENT

The hinge facing is subjected to much more strain in normal operation than any other part of the door. It must be rigid enough to support the full weight of the door assembly and resist the twisting strain applied when the door is forced open as far as it will go. Some method of stopping travel is required on all doors; otherwise it could swing around and damage the adjoining panel. Whether the *stop* is built into the hinge or a separate link is used, it must be only a relatively short distance from the hinge pin. The opposite edge of the door is much farther away and has a proportional mechanical advantage over the much shorter leverage of the stop. The result is that the hinge pillar and the hinge facing of the door are subjected to tremendous forces when the door is pushed open against its stop.

One method of reinforcing the hinge facing is shown in the cross-sectional drawing in Figure 9-2. In this case

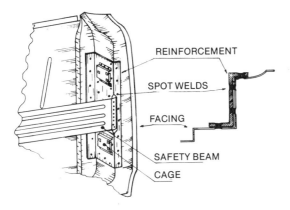

9-2 Inside view of typical door lock facing with reinforcement and safety beam. Cages allow threaded plate to shift up, down, in, and out.

the reinforcement is simply a liner stamped to fit into the inner surface of the inner panel and welded securely in place. The wide flanges and heavier metal provide sufficient rigidity to withstand any normal strain.

Other methods of reinforcement have been used by the various manufacturers. The one shown here is similar to methods in common use, but not representative of any particular make or model. All are rigid enough to withstand normal operating strains, but can be seriously damaged by a severe impact.

WEATHERSTRIPS

The sealing action of a door weatherstrip is shown in the cross-sectional view in Figure 9-3. At A the door is in the off-latch position, so that the weatherstrip is expanded to its full thickness. At B the door is latched. In this position the space between the door facings and body surfaces is less than the thickness of the soft weatherstrip, compressing it between the surfaces. In effect, it becomes a gasket to seal the opening.

The plastic retainer that holds the strip to the door is shown in C. The T-shaped head is installed in a cavity, molded in the weatherstrip, through a small hole by stretching the rubber over it.

Weatherstrips for doors that have an upper window frame are usually made in one continuous piece. Doors that have the glass edge exposed, however, require a separate upper weatherstrip attached to the body opening instead of the door. The lower section would be unchanged, except for provision to seal the section at the base of the window opening where the upper and lower meet. This usually is done by vulcanizing specially molded pieces of sponge rubber to ends of the lower section.

The weatherstrip shape shown in cross section in this sketch is not intended to represent any particular make or model, but is similar to some in use. Many others are used by the various manufacturers. On many, the shape varies in different sections of the same weatherstrip. However, whatever the shape, they all seal in the same manner—by compressing the soft sponge rubber.

The pressure on a weatherstrip should be uniform, or very nearly so, all around the perimeter of a properly aligned door. Too much pressure at any one point will make the door difficult to latch; too little pressure will cause air and water leaks. In theory, the pressure should be correct when the door outer edges are spaced evenly in the opening and the surface is flush with the adjoining panel. In practice, variations are often found, sometimes due to a faulty panel, but more often due to improper straightening of a sealing surface.

Weatherstrip pressure can be checked by closing the door against a sheet of paper laid across the contact surfaces, as shown in Figure 9-4. The weatherstrip should grip the paper enough to require a definite effort

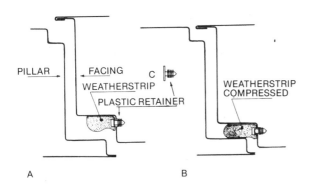

9-3 Weatherstrip attachment and sealing details. A, door open; B, door latched, compressing weatherstrip to seal opening.

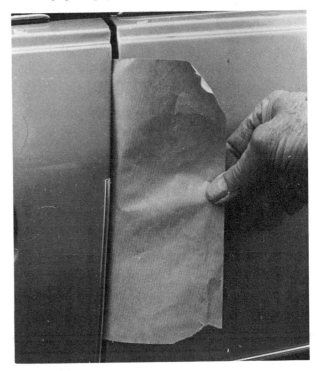

9-4 Checking weatherstrip pressure by withdrawing a sheet of paper with door latched. Pressure should restrict movement, but not enough to cause paper to tear.

to pull it out, but not enough to tear. If the paper is gripped too hard, the cause should be determined and corrected. It may require adjustment of one or both hinges or the striker, or it may be necessary to rework the contact surfaces.

Any weatherstrip will not retain its original shape, as shown in Figure 9-3 at A, after it has been in use for several months. Whether the automobile is in use or parked, the weatherstrips are almost always under pressure, because the doors are kept closed most of the time. The rubber tends to deform into the shape in which it is held. This will not affect sealing under normal circumstances. However, if the door is removed and replaced, the repairman should be careful to put it back in the original position. Even more care is desirable when a used door is removed from one body and placed on another immediately. There is usually enough difference in the two body surfaces to make some difference in sealing. Time will take care of such conditions, unless they are unusually bad, because the rubber will gradually expand to its original shape when the pressure is light.

HINGES

The obvious purpose of the hinges to to provide a pivot to permit the door or other hinged assembly to open, but most manufacturers add devices to limit the distance the door can open and a means of holding it open. How-

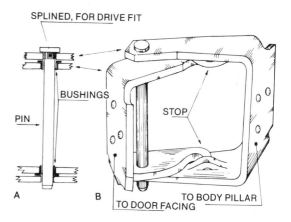

9-6 Mate to hinge shown in Fig. 9-5. A, details of hinge pin and bushing; B, hinge assembly with built-in stop.

ever, a few use separate devices for these purposes, usually a link between the hinge pillar and door facing that serves both purposes.

A photograph of a hinge with a built-in hold-open device is shown in Figure 9-5. A hinge of similar design, except that it has a built-in stop, is shown in more detail in B, Figure 9-6. The construction features of the pin and bushings are shown in A. The pin is splined under the head so that it is a drive fit in the bracket that attaches to the body pillar. The bushings, which are press fitted into the bracket that attaches to the door, provide a good bearing surface for the pin. The bushing material may be either bronze or plastic. If plastic, it is important that the hinge not be subjected to heat, which would melt the plastic.

The view of the hinge in B is from the angle of the passenger with the door open against the stop. Bolt holes are shown, as this one is intended as a mate to the door in Figure 9-5. However, similar hinges can be installed by welding simply by omitting the bolt holes and running a weld bead along the upper and lower corners of both brackets.

Figure 9-7 represents another type hinge used by

9-5 Typical bolt-on hinge with built-in hold-open device.

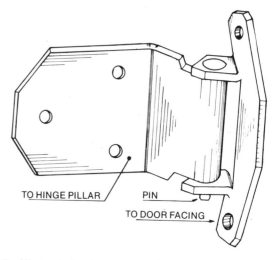

9-7 Hinge similar to some used on compact models.

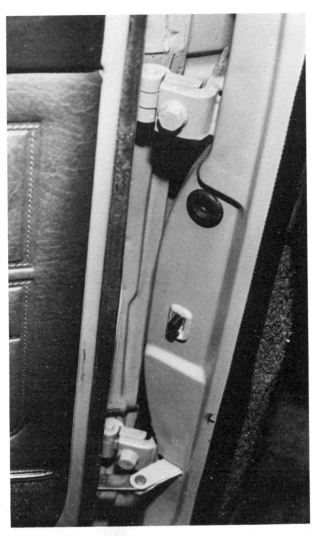

9-8 A pair of weld-on hinges that have a bolt-on feature in the hinge pillar bracket.

some manufacturers, usually on relatively small automobiles. Bushings, if used, would be installed in the bracket that attaches to the hinge pillar, and the pin would be a drive fit into the bracket that attaches to the door facing. One or both brackets of this hinge can be attached by welding along the edges, but it has mostly been used with bolt-on attachment, as shown.

A photograph of a pair of weld-on hinges of entirely different construction is shown in Figure 9-8. This rather simple and quite practical hinge has a bolted joint in the bracket that attaches to the hinge pillar but requires a separate check link to stop and hold the door open. This door can be removed easily by disconnecting the check link and removing the two bolts in the hinge brackets.

Many other hinge designs are in use by the various automobile manufacturers, and others will come in the future. From the viewpoint of the repairman, the design of the hinge is important only insofar as it affects the problem of re-aligning the door after it has been misaligned either by collision or, sometimes, by normal

wear. Hinges that have a full range of adjustment are easier to adjust than those that are welded on and can be adjusted only by bending. However, an adjustable hinge *must* be re-adjusted every time the door is removed. The separate pieces of welded-on hinges must be located very precisely on the door and pillar facings so they will mesh and the pin can be inserted when the door is installed on the body, in factory assembly. Unless damaged severely, they do not present severe realignment problems. These problems are discussed more fully in the following Door Alignment section.

DOOR ALIGNMENT

Door alignment, or aligning, as the terms are used here refers to whatever operations are required to position a door properly within its opening. Some aligning may be needed as a follow-up to a major straightening operation, particularly if the door has been removed and replaced, the outer panel replaced, or a new assembly used. Each job must be analyzed to determine what is needed. The skill involved is mostly a matter of experience and good judgment; the manual dexterity required is relatively simple.

To be considered in alignment, a door should meet four conditions: (1) it should be centered in its opening so that the spaces between its edges and the adjoining panels are uniform, (2) the surface should be flush with the adjoining panels and continuous lines should match, particularly sharp creases or narrow ledges at the belt line or lower edge of the window opening, (3) all parts of the weatherstrip should seal against the contact surfaces of the adjoining panels, and (4) it should open and close easily without lift or drop as the striker enters the lock.

The space between the door edges and the adjoining panels is referred to in the following discussions as *edge gap*. When the edge gaps are acceptable, weatherstrip pressure and effort required for opening and closing will usually, but not always, be acceptable. When differences are found, they are more often caused by damage to one or both of the weatherstrip contact sur-

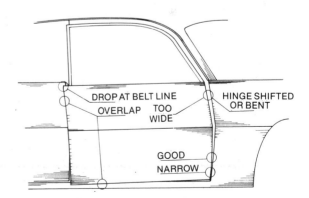

9-9 Effect of bent or shifted hinge. Other hinge serves as a pivot point, so that all points move in direct proportion to the distance they are from it.

faces than by variations in the panel caused by the manufacturing processes. Hard closing will almost always be caused by too much pressure on some part of the weatherstrip at some point.

The effect of a bent or shifted upper hinge is illustrated in Figure 9-9. The typical conditions are: (1) a V-shaped edge gap, narrow at the lower end and too wide at the upper, (2) a drop-off at the belt line on the lock pillar, (3) overlap on the adjoining panel, quarter or rear door, and the rocker panel.

When the position of one hinge is changed, the movement causes the entire door to tend to pivot around the other hinge. Thus, all points on the outer edge of the door move in direct proportion to the distance they are from the pivot point. This pivot action is shown in Figure 9-10. Although the movement is only a fraction of a degree, it should be considered as rotation around the other hinge, in this case the lower. Four radius lines are shown from the lower hinge: to the upper hinge, to the lock pillar belt line, and to both lower corners. Obviously, any movement at the upper hinge will cause much greater movement at the rear belt line and lower rear corner, but much less at the lower front.

The illustration shows the effect of shifting of the upper hinge, but a similar shift of the lower hinge would have an exactly opposite effect. This could be shown by turning Figure 9-10 upside down.

Correcting a misalignment due to a bent or shifted hinge is simply a matter of shifting it back to position. Bolted-on hinges can be loosened and moved, if not already at the limit of the adjustment range. When this occurs, either the attaching surfaces are bent, or the opening is out of alignment. Welded-on hinges can be adjusted only by bending.

INSTALLING AND ADJUSTING BOLT-ON HINGES

The correct procedure will simplify the adjustment of bolt-on hinges, whether they have been completely disassembled or only a slight shift of one hinge is required. One problem is that every time a hinge is loosened, the weight it supports is transferred to the other hinge, causing it to flex slightly and allow the door to drop in the opening. If the hinges are loosened and retightened alternately a few times, the door will drop the lowest part of the vertical adjustment range.

Some trial-and-error adjustments should be expected when replacing a door after the hinges have been completely disassembled. When replacing the door, it whould be set well above the proper vertical position to take advantage of the tendency to drop as the hinges are loosened in making adjustments. This is particularly important when installing a new door that has no hinge marks to aid in positioning the hinges. When reassembling the original hinges on the original door, it is best to position them to hold the door slightly high, because it is easier to lower it than to raise it.

To lower a door in the opening, (1) adjust the door facing bolts so they are snug but not tight, and (2) drive

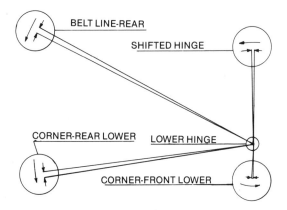

9-10 Movement of various points on door around other hinge, as shown in Fig. 9-9.

each hinge up on the door facing, using a block of wood and light hammer blows. To raise it in the opening, (1) place a support under the lower edge of the door close to the hinge pillar, and (2) drive each hinge down in the same manner. The support should be just high enough to hold the door an inch or two (2.5–5 cm) above its proper level; the support will reverse the strain on the hinges so the weight of the automobile will aid the shift. If the adjustment is made on the pillar instead of the facing, the hinge should be driven in the opposite direction.

After an adjustment has been made, the hinge bolts should be drawn up to the high limit of torque specified by the manufacturer. It is not practical here to give a torque specification that would apply to all hinge bolts, because of the wide variations from one make to another. Manufacturers specify torque for most of the bolts on their products. Their specifications should be followed.

When making a simple fore or aft shift at the upper hinge without changing the height of the door, the hinge bolts should be slacked off and the hinge driven into place. Before retightening the bolts, the hinge should be driven down slightly to pick up at least part of the weight transferred to the other hinge as it moved.

A hammer and a block of wood should be used to drive hinges either fore or aft, or up or down, if possible. However, this is not always practical when a front door hinge must be moved rearward while the fender is still in place. A slide hammer equipped with a hook should be used in such cases.

Hinges should never be driven into a "cocked" position. The upper and lower pins must be on or close to the same center line, or they will bind when the door is opened or closed, and the bushings will wear excessively. Fortunately, the elasticity of the metal will tolerate a reasonable amount of misalignment of the center line, and excessive misalignment can be avoided by use of *common sense*.

SHIFTING WELDED-ON HINGES

Welded-on hinges can be adjusted only by bending.

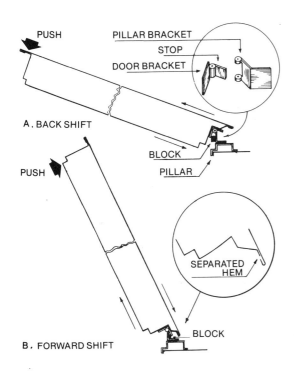

9-11 Cross sections showing blocking hinges to shift weld-on types in opening. A, shifting rearward; hinge detail shown in circle—typical but not a copy of any specific hinge. B, shifting forward; this operation is always done at the risk of separating the hem-flange, as shown in circle.

However, unless damaged, they should stay in alignment. The parts are located very precisely on the pillar and door facing in factory assembly and need very little further adjustment, unless they are bent or dislocated in collision. All doors with hinges of any type can be adjusted rearward (aft), as illustrated in A, Figure 9-11, and most welded-on hinges have a stop designed so that it can be used for a forward shift, as illustrated in B. To shift either way, an obstruction is placed in the hinge and the door forced against it.

This operation must be performed carefully to avoid breaking the hem-flange spot welds. When shifting aft, the outer panel pulls against the hem-flange, as shown by the arrows on A. There is risk of breaking the welds, but the flanges will not separate. When shifting forward, the outer panel pushes against the welds so that, if they break, the flange will separate, as shown in the detail linked to B.

A method of rewelding broken spot welds, using electric resistance spot welding, is explained in Chapter 5. Arc welding or brazing can be used if the resistance welder is not available. The separated flanges can be put back in place by blocking the hinge in the opposite direction. If the edges are fully separated, it is best to pry the hem up first, so there will be no interference. Sometimes the flange can be rewelded without removing the door.

Broken welds left unwelded are almost sure to cause annoying squeaks and will cause the facing to break if left long enough.

When the misalignment is more than just a slight condition, the exact cause should be determined. It may be that the opening is distorted. If so, the opening must be re-aligned before door alignment is attempted. Check the opening by measuring between the hinge and lock pillars on both sides of the car for comparison, at the points shown in Figure 9-12. The measurements can vary slightly, but a difference of more than ⅛ of an inch (3–4 mm) may be necessary to correct the opening before the door can be fitted.

These measurements will often save considerable time when re-aligning a door opening that has been damaged in a front-end collision. The measurement from pillar to pillar at the belt line must be reasonably close before the door is re-installed. This measurement will almost always be too short, because the pillar is often driven back but rarely driven forward.

Assuming that pillar-to-pillar measurement is correct, the measurements between the upper and lower hinges and the lock pillar, as shown, should be quite close to similar measurements taken either on the other door or on another automobile.

Use of a hammer and a block of wood to drive a welded-on hinge forward is shown in Figure 9-13. This is always better procedure than blocking a hinge for a forward shift, because it avoids the risk of breaking the hem-flange welds. However, this should not be done if the measurements shown in Figure 9-12 are correct, which indicates that any misalignment must be in the door facing.

Door facings are often driven inward at the upper hinge by the cowl and hinge pillar when the automobile has been involved in a front-end collision. In such cases the hem-flange welds will be strained and may be broken. If broken, the facing flange will move at least enough to crack the sealer, and it may separate from the hem-flange completely. This is the condition that should be repaired by forcing the door closed against a blocked hinge, as shown in A, Figure 9-11. However, if there is complete separation, the hem-flange should be pried open to permit free movement.

Any broken spot welds should be rewelded, but only after completion of any other alignment operations to be performed on either the door or the opening.

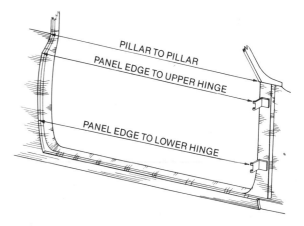

9-12 Measurements to check door opening alignment.

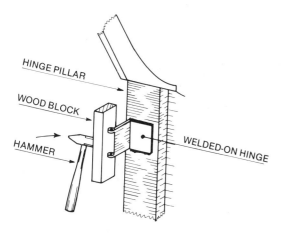

HINGE PILLAR

WOOD BLOCK

HAMMER

WELDED-ON HINGE

9-13 Driving a welded-on hinge forward. A safer method than blocking, as shown in Fig. 9-11.

A door facing can be pulled outward at the upper hinge by a hard side impact or a crushed roof that forces the hinge pillar forward. This condition can be determined visually, because the hinge will be bulged well above the rest of the facing. If the outer panel is to be replaced, the bulge can be straightened by blocking, as shown in B, Figure 9-11, because the welds will have to be broken anyway. If the door is to be repaired, it is much better procedure to straighten the bulge as shown in Figure 9-14, using a hammer and a block of wood. The rapid impact of the hammer blow is much less apt to break the hem-flange welds than the steady push used when blocking the hinge. The risk of hem-flange separation can be reduced further by welding it first, as shown. Oxyacetylene welding will make it necessary to repair the paint, but there is usually other damage that will require repainting; if not, it may be preferable to risk the separation and omit the welding. If rewelded by the electric resistance method, several welds will be required.

The probability of misalignment of the upper and lower hinge pins is less than with the bolt-on type, but it can happen if the repairman is careless in straightening a hinge pillar or has used too much force in the operation shown in Figure 9-11. Removal and replacement of any door equipped with weld-on hinges is done by removal and replacement of the pins. The small ends of most pins are tapered so that they can be installed easily if the hinge is slightly misaligned. Any misalignment great enough to prevent the pin from entering easily should be corrected.

INSTALLING WELDED-ON HINGES

The two hinge brackets, or *halves*, are assembled to the door facing and hinge pillar in manufacture and are not fitted together until the door is assembled to the body. In that operation, the factory door hanger fits the two halves together and inserts the pin. It is common practice for the upper pin to be inserted from the under side

and the lower from the top. A spring retainer clip may be used.

Although rarely required, when replacement of a welded-on hinge is necessary, it must be aligned exactly with the other hinge. The safest procedure is to drill and bolt the hinge in position on the facing and pillar temporarily so that alignment can be checked before welding. Depending on construction, it may be necessary to make an estimate of position off-the-body but, if possible, the door should be installed on the undamaged hinge and propped in alignment in the open position. If only one half is being replaced, it should be assembled to the other by installing the pin, and then drilled while in position if possible. If not, the position should be marked carefully before the hinge is removed for drilling. The drill used should be the tap size for the bolt that will be used, unless the inner surface can be reached to install a nut. After drilling, the hole in the inner surface should be tapped, and the outer one enlarged with an oversized bit to permit a degree of final adjustment.

Welding should be delayed until the final alignment has been established and the door opens and closes properly. If possible, welding should be done with the door in place, but, if it is necessary to remove the door, extra care must be taken to avoid shifting the only temporarily aligned hinge. Hinge construction varies too widely to specify exact welding procedures, but arc welding is usually best, if available.

In general, the construction of door facings and hinge pillars designed for welded-on hinges is not rigid enough to permit substituting bolts for welding.

It is rarely necessary to replace both hinges, because the door would probably be damaged enough to justify replacement, which would include the two hinge halves.

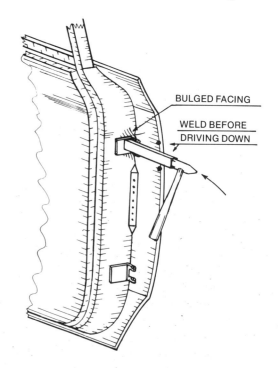

BULGED FACING

WELD BEFORE DRIVING DOWN

9-14 Straightening a bulged-out door facing with a hammer and block of wood.

However, if both hinges must be replaced, both halves of one hinge and one half of the other should be installed with temporary bolts. The general procedure outlined above would be followed from that point on.

LOCKS

In common usage, any mechanism that holds a hinged assembly in the closed position is called a lock. The locks on passenger compartment doors, deck and hatch lids, and station wagon rear gates serve two purposes: (1) they hold the unit in the closed but unlocked position, and (2) they lock to prevent entry without a key. A better term for the first purpose is *latching*, and that term is used in the following discussion of lock operation, except where the reference is to actual locking.

Any lock system consists of two primary units: the lock assembly and the striker. As stated in an earlier section, any lock and striker combination used on passenger compartment doors must conform to safety regulations: (1) the lock must not unlatch under sudden shock or strain, (2) the striker and lock must not sepa-

rate under tension, and (3) the latching mechanism must have two steps, so that the door will be held securely even though not quite fully closed. In effect, these regulations require that a door, when latched, must stay latched, unless the latching mechanism is literally torn apart. In addition to safety regulations, there are the obvious use requirements that, when latched, (1) the lock and striker should not rattle or cause other undesirable noises and (2) should open and close easily.

Many possible designs can meet the safety and use requirements for locks. One of the most common is the *fork bolt*. (In reference to locks of any type, the term *bolt* refers to whatever secures the striker; it has no reference to a threaded bolt.) In this type lock the striker is engaged by a fork-shaped bolt that holds the striker against a sliding wedge so that there is no movement in any direction. An outside view of one lock of this type is shown in Figure 9-15 in the unlatched position. In this view the ends of the fork bolt are labeled 1A and 1B, the tip of the arrow labeled 2 indicates the pin that serves as the pivot for the fork bolt, and the plastic wedge block is labeled 3. This plastic block is placed so that it will be pushed back against spring pressure as the striker reaches the latched position. The spring action wedges the striker securely between the fork bolt and the plastic block.

In Figure 9-16 the striker has been removed from the pillar and latched in place in the lock. It is held securely so that there is no possibility of movement to cause rattles or wear, whether the door is properly fitted or not. However, it will rattle in the safety position, because the striker will not be far enough into the lock to engage the wedge.

Unlatching is simply a matter of lifting a pawl, hidden

9-15 Typical door lock, as seen from the outside. 1-A and 1-B, ends of the fork bolt; 2, location of the fork bolt pivot; 3, plastic wedge block, with spring on wedge block hidden.

9-16 Striker, removed from pillar and latched in place in lock. One washer is always used; the second serves as a shim, when needed, to align the bolt to the striker assembly.

inside the lock, so that the fork bolt will be free to turn back to the unlatched position. This particular lock has no spring on the fork bolt to return it to the unlatched position, but one is not needed. Weatherstrip pressure will cause slight movement, but the person opening the door will push it away from the lock.

Locks built by other manufacturers operate in much the same manner, but differ in detail. Some have two fork-type bolts, one above and one below the striker. Others have a striker that consists of a loop of metal welded to a plate. No doubt, additional designs will be introduced but, whatever the design, the basic requirements will remain the same.

There are no adjustments on door lock assemblies, and parts are not available. If bent or otherwise damaged past the point of repair, the entire assembly must be replaced. Repairing should be limited to straightening minor bends in the lock frame. If the internal mechanism is damaged, replacement is justified for safety reasons.

An adjustment range of approximately ¼ inch (6 mm) up or down and in or out is provided for the striker by a threaded plate retained loosely be a cage, similar to the cage and plate provided for bolt-on hinges. In theory, the striker should be removed while the hinges are adjusted to hold the door in its proper postion; the striker should then be installed so that it enters the lock without causing the door either to lift or drop and holds the panel surfaces flush. In practice, it is not necessary, except when a major re-adjustment is needed. If the door seems in alignment but either lifts or drops when unlatched, it may be necessary only to re-adjust one of the hinges so that the door will meet the striker properly.

One heavy washer is always used under the base of a striker of type type shown in Figure 9-16 to provide rigidity. Sometimes extra washers are added to shim the head of the striker forward so that it does not make contact with the fork bolt as it enters the lock. The proce-

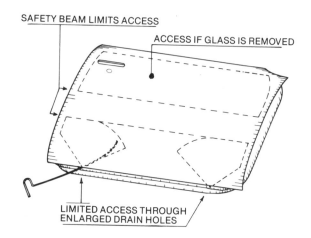

9-18 Areas of door that may be worked easily with pry rods inserted through enlarged drain holes.

dure for striker adjustment is essentially the same for any type of lock.

REMOVING AND REPLACING DOORS

A hydraulically operated door jack, of the type shown in Figure 9-17, will avoid the need for an extra man to help lift a door assembly while removing or replacing it. When a door is strapped in place on this jack (the straps do not show in the photo), it can be wheeled into place and held at the proper height, leaving both hands free to install the bolts or hinge pins. It has the additional advantage of reducing the chance of paint damage during the operation.

DOOR OUTER PANEL DAMAGE

Door panel damages that may be considered repairable can be classified into two broad groups: (1) simple dents, gouges, bent edges, and so on, which can be repaired with hand tools, and (2) major damage that has distorted the shape of the door so that it does not fit the opening. The latter usually requires a setup with pulling equipment to restore shape. Doors damaged more severely will require either repaneling or replacement.

SIMPLE DOOR DAMAGE

Access to the under surface is a problem on almost all doors. Although accessibility varies on different makes and models, it is the reason many repairmen rely—perhaps excessively—on the dent puller for repairing most dented panels.

Accessible dents often can be straightened with hand tools faster and better than with the puller, as shown in Figure 4-5. many late-model rear doors with fixed window glass are more accessible than the one in this

9-17 Hydraulic door jack, holding door in position for installation on the body.

example. Other areas, not accessible for hand tools but within reach of pry rods, can often be straightened as fast or faster without piercing the panel. Areas that can be reached easily are shown in Figure 9-18. If availble, weld-on tabs may be used in almost any area, but they require a resistance spot welder for application.

If quality workmanship is required, any hole pierced in the outer panel should be sealed shut and the entire repaired area undercoated with a good quality material. Moisture will attack the exposed edges of the holes and the underside of the filler material. Some fillers are claimed to be moisture resistant, but it is only common sense to avoid exposing the repaired area many more than necessary.

Holes can be either soldered or brazed shut, with brazing recommended here, because acid in the solder flux is difficult to neutralize. Traces of acid on the surface will cause rusting under the filler coat. There is no apparent problem with brazing done with flux-coated rods. The old-style dip-type brazing flux will leave lumps that should be chipped off. Holes can be brazed with very little heat distortion in most straightened areas, if a small tip is used.

The inner surface should be undercoated, using a high-quality material. Although both closing the holes and undercoating the panel are usually neglected, failure to do so is poor shop practice and is evidence of inferior work. In addition, an unprotected repair may quickly deteriorate, and come back to the shop at the repairman's expense.

MAJOR DOOR DAMAGE

Major door damage, as discussed here, includes conditions too severe to be repaired with hand tools. However, there is no attempt to establish the limit of repairability; that must be decided by the persons involved for the particular door.

Excepting deep, long gouges and torn metal, most major damage will involve crushed facing as well as the outer panel. Facings must be straightened properly to prevent an area of false-stretched metal in the adjoining panel section. An attempt to drive out a deeply crushed facing of the type represented by A and B in Figure 9-19 will upset the hem-flange and adjoining metal in both the outer panel and facing. These problems can be avoided by roughing the dented section out under tension and applying heat to permit the hem area to be pulled back to full length.

A is shown below the area of the safety beam where it would present the least straightening problem. A severely crushed facing in the safety beam area may require removal of the outer panel to permit straightening, creating the choice between repaneling or replacement. The crushed lower edge, shown in B, poses essentially the same problem, but straightening it can be more difficult, because the section is flat. The opposed arrows at the lower left-hand corner of A and B indicate edges drawn in by the crushed area.

Welding the hem-flange is indicated by notes on A, B, and C. There is always a problem of hem-flange separation on this type of damage. Before any straightening is started, the edge of the hem should be welded securely to the facing at the deepest point of the dent; if a long section is affected, additional welds should be made about 2 inches (5 cm) apart. The best results will be obtained by making a short weld bead, using the oxyacetylene torch and a steel rod. Brazing is not satisfactory; the sealer in the hem will probably prevent good penetration, and the metal may become embrittled.

Almost any practical means of applying tension is satisfactory. Clamp positions are shown in A with a double-pointed arrow to indicate that they should be pushed apart. Normally, the facing has some vertical crown, so it is desirable to place the clamps as close together as the conditions of the damage will permit. A body jack can be placed between them; alternatively, clamps that attach directly to the ends of a jack are available.

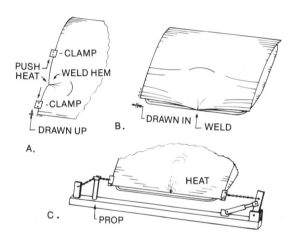

9-19 A, typical crushed door facing; B, typical crushed lower facing; C, tension setup, using portable body and frame machine; prop supports door at convenient height for easy working.

The sharply creased areas of both the outer edge of the panel and the facing should be heated as tension is applied. Hand-tool work may be needed on the facing but must be avoided while the metal is hot. The progress of unfolding should be watched carefully and hand-tool work delayed as long as the overall unfolding continues. As various buckles develop resistance to further unfolding, they should be relieved, usually by light hammer work on the outside. During the roughing-out process, there will usually be less need to lift low spots than to work ridges down. When lifting is necessary, careful work with a pry rod is preferable to use of a panel puller. However, not all areas can be reached with pry rods, so some work with the puller may be necessary.

A setup of the type shown in C for the lower edge is preferable to the use of a jack between clamps, as suggested for A. The anchor chain is supported by a piece of jack tubing with a V fitting on the upper end holding the lower edge of the door in level position and at a convenient working height. This would not be needed if an anchor beam with sufficient height was available. No support is shown under the upper part of the door; anything of convenient height is satisfactory, because the door is held rigidly as long as it is under tension.

There are many other ways of applying tension. Any method that will maintain steady, controlled tension to pull the panel and facing into shape is satisfactory. It is particularly important to have the capacity to apply considerable force for the final pull. Sometimes a severe buckle may need an extra setup with a jack and pair of clamps; most of the adjoining area should be relatively smooth, but, if any area of false stretch appears in the panel, it will be due to *unrelieved* upset in the hem area. Heat and tension should relieve the upset. The process should be continued until the bulged area of false stretch disappears.

Do *not* quench an area heated for this purpose, and do *not* release tension on a heated area until it has cooled far below the red heat range.

The effort and time spent in properly roughing out door damages of the type discussed here should be more than regained in the finishing process. Assuming there are no long tears or deep gouges, excessive effort to metal-finish or a deep build-up of filler should not be required.

A good-quality undercoating should be applied to the inner surface of any panel that has been repaired, particularly to areas that have been heated in the process of repair.

DOOR OUTER PANEL REPLACEMENT

Door outer panels, often called "skins," are available for many makes and models. Because the cost for a skin is considerably less than for a door assembly, many shops consider it normal procedure to replace a severely damaged outer panel if the inner and safety beams are either undamaged or easily repairable. Many insurance adjustors insist on using an outer panel in those circumstances. However, there is no uniform practice; some that should be replaced are repaneled, and other that could be repaneled easily are replaced.

There is a valid argument against repaneling doors on nearly new automobiles. The new door assembly has been through the factory processes of weld-through sealing, welding, phosphate coating, and primed with bake-on-type primer. The outer panel has had the same paint pre-preparation and priming, but the repair shop must break the primer to weld it to the inner panel. Also, many shops omit any sealing between the surfaces. Some repairmen further complicate the problem by not turning the hem-flange properly, and then find it necessary to use filler on the outer surface of the new panel to fill rough spots caused by poor workmanship. When done in this manner, the only rust protection for the bare metal in the seam is whatever sealer is applied to the hem-flange. The inner surface is exposed to any

moisture or chemicals, usually salt, that enter through the glass opening.

This argument can be largely offset by applying a bead of good grade sealer to the inner surface of the outer panel, preparing the hem-flange for welding, turning the hem-flange properly, and using good welding technique. When the door is installed properly and the hem-flange is sealed, the quality of a repaneled door is close to that of the original.

Any repair work required on the inner panel or safety beam should be done after removal of the outer panel—with one exception: A bulged-out hinge facing should be straightened by blocking the hinge, as shown in Figure 9-11, while the edge is held by the hem-flange welds. This will be quicker than straightening it afterward. If the hem-flange welds break, it is no real loss, because they are to be broken anyway.

Most doors require complete removal of glass, trim, and weatherstrips for repaneling. However, a few have no welding across the upper edge, making it possible to repanel them without disassembly other than of the weatherstrip. When this is done, the upper edge and flange should be painted and the weatherstrip installed before the panel is put on the door. Lacquer can be used for this if enamel paint is to be used. The color should be close, but a match is not necessary, because any exposed paint will be repainted.

The steps in repaneling are (1) remove outer panel, (2) if it is damaged, straighten facings and safety beam, (3) if facings or safety beam have been straightened, rehang inner panel in opening to check fit, (4) prepare hem-flange surfaces for welding, (5) assemble inner and outer with bead of sealer between surfaces, (6) turn hem-flange, (7) weld, and (8) seal hem-flange.

A disc sander should be used to separate the outer panel from the hem-flange, as shown in Figure 9-20. When held at a right angle to the surface, a sharp disc will cut through the exposed edge rapidly, leaving the hem-flange still attached but easy to remove. Separating it across the upper edge will require breaking any

9-20 Grinding hem-flange through with disc sander.

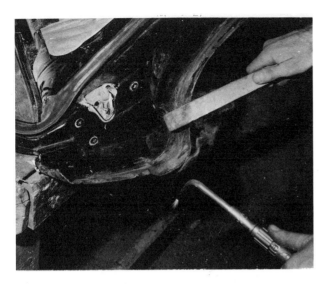

9-21 Wire-brushing sealer after scorching it with an oxidizing flame.

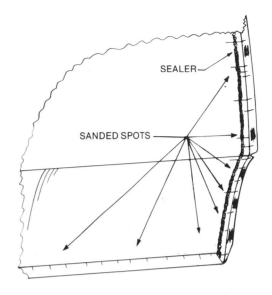

9-22 Preparation of new panel for brazing or spot welding.

welds found. There is too much difference in makes and models to give exact instructions.

Crushed flanges can be straightened much easier with the outer panel removed. Careful work with the hammer and dolly is all that is needed on most, but it is important that the alignment should be checked by hanging the inner panel back in the opening in the latched position. At this point it is very simple to make any needed corrections of the outer flange if it is not flush with the adjoining panels or the edge gap is either too wide or too narrow. Allowance should be made for the thickness of the outer panel in checking both. If the panel is welded on before making any needed corrections, correcting them will be a major operation that could have been avoided.

When the facings or safety beam have not been damaged, or the door twisted, checking is not necessary.

Cleaning the inner-panel flange requires removal of the old hem-flange and sealer. Some of the hem welds will separate by raising the end of the flange and twisting it back and forth; those that do not break readily should be ground off after breaking or cutting most of the flange away. It is best to avoid breaking the weld button out of the flange.

Before grinding the weld buttons, the old sealer should be removed; otherwise it will smear the disc and later interfere with the welding operation. Part will scrape off, but most should be wire-brushed, as shown In Figure 9-21, after scorching with an oxidizing flame. The flame should be kept in rapid motion to avoid overheating.

Brazing requires removal of the primer from the inside of the hem-flange, and electric resistance welding requires it to be removed from both inside and out. Hand sanding is much safer than using a disc on the inner surface; the disc may catch on the narrow flange and hurl broken pieces at high speed in any direction. For brazing, spots should be selected a few inches apart, as indicated in Figure 9-22, sanded clean and

marked on the outside so that they will not be lost when the flange is turned. For resistance spot welding with twin, hand-held electrodes, the spots should be selected in pairs; if preferred, an oscillating sander may be used on the outer surface. A high-speed disc sander may thin the edge unevenly and make it difficult to make a smooth hem joint.

A small bead of good grade sealer should be laid close to the hem-flange along its full length. This is shown in both Figure 9-22 and A in Figure 9-23. Excessive sealer should be avoided, because it will spill out into the hem-flange and interfere with welding if either brazing or arc welding is to be used. However, if resistance spot welding will be used, a small amount of weld-through sealer should be applied. Sharp corners should be notched out.

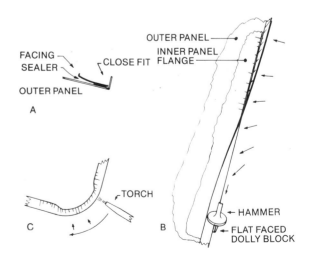

9-23 Assembling the panels. A, cross section showing proper fit; B, turning the flange; C, heating curved flange to avoid wrinkling.

The hem-flange can be turned, or hemmed, so that the edge of the outer panel will require very little finishing, if done properly. The technique (Fig. 9-23, in B) is to avoid stretching the edge of the hem by driving it down a little at a time. The door assembly should be placed on a padded bench, outer panel down, and positioned so that the outer edge can be backed up with a flat-faced dolly block. As shown, the flange should make a long, sweeping turn by using the hammer back and forth along the edge and changing the angle to follow the movement. The arrows along the right side represent a series of progressive hammer blows, each of which should be backed up by the dolly. The flange should be driven down until the three surfaces are in contact, but *no more.*

A piece of heavy-duty jack tubing or a round steel shaft may be used to back up sharp reverse crowns. This is not illustrated, as it would be essentially the same as other areas. It is best to use a hammer with a suitable radius on these crowns, but the high crown part of dolly block may be used as a hammer instead.

When a door has a rounded corner, that should be hemmed last. As shown in C, the adjoining edges should be hemmed as close as possible without causing buckles. Then, the oxyacetylene torch, adjusted to a small flame, should be passed around the corner just fast enough to heat the upper edge red hot. The edge should be driven down in much the same manner as on the straight sections. When heating, the flame should be kept away from the outer panel surface. Reheating may be necessary.

When hemmed, the assembly should be turned over and the edges welded.

WELDING HEM-FLANGES

The hem-flange should be welded to the facing without warping the outer panel and causing an unnecessary repair on a new panel. This is no problem using an electric resistance spot welder, but brazing and arc welding must be done carefully. Brazing is the most commonly used and the most apt to cause warpage.

Brazing

The tip used should be small, preferably No. 1, adjusted to a small, neutral flame, and the rod should be flux coated. The torch and rod positions for the start of the operation are shown in Figure 9-24. The flame is directed on the facing close to the edge of the hem-flange. The end of the filler rod is placed very close to the surface, where it will protect the edge of the flange while it heats. The double arrows on both rod and torch indicate in-and-out motion but no weaving. The rod should be withdrawn if it reaches melting temperature before the facing is hot enough. The torch should be withdrawn if the edge of the hem flange gets too hot before the facing is ready. Weaving to spread the heat

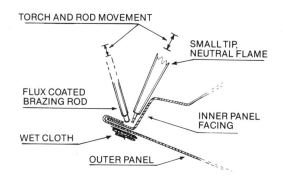

9-24 Correct torch position for brazing the hem-flange.

will only guarantee warping the outer panel. When this is done properly, one drop of molten brazing metal will be deposited next to the edge and will flow into the joint by capillary action. The flame should be removed instantly.

Further build-up of filler rod will add practically no strength to the joint, but the extra metal will hold heat and increase the tendency for warpage. A folded wet cloth is shown on the underside to absorb heat. It can be held in place with a locking welding clamp. Use of a cloth is not as important on the crowned part of the front and rear edges, but it is desirable. It should always be used on the lower.

Arc Welding

Skill and equipment are important factors for welding the hem-flange with the conventional arc method. A skilled welder, using a small electrode and a good machine having fine control in the low power range, can weld a door flange easily and quickly. Only a very small tack-weld is needed to join the edge of the hem-flange to the facing. A larger weld is both unnecessary and an almost sure guarantee of heat distortion in the new panel.

Any build-up of weld metal should be ground off. However, this should not be a problem to a welder having the required skill. No one should try arc welding a door hem-flange without having had enough practice tacking sheet metal, using the same equipment and electrodes, to feel confident of his ability.

MIG and TIG

Both the MIG and TIG methods are well adapted to this type of welding. Assuming that the equipment is available and has the capacity to work in the sheet metal range, either is a very good method on hem flanges. Many MIG machines are equipped with a timer for spot welding; if available, this should provide more consistent results than doing it manually.

Whatever method is used, conventional, MIG, or TIG, if it is done properly, the final sealing will conceal it.

FINISHING THE PANEL EDGE

Some finishing will be required around the outer edges of the new panel, but this should be a relatively simple job, if the flanging and welding have been done correctly. The lower edges should be checked with a straightedge and the high and low spots straightened. This will be simple *if* the edge has not been hammered too much in the flanging operation. All the edges should be examined both visually and by feeling, and straightened as necessary. It should be possible to do most of the finishing with a few passes of a fine-grit disc on a conventional sander.

Sealing and Undercoating

A sealer that can be painted should be applied to the hem-flange between the primer and color coats. It should be smoothed enough to restore the original appearance, which should be no problem if no built-up welds are projecting through it.

The inner surface of the new panel should be sprayed with a good grade of undercoating. It may be necessary to do this after the painting operation is complete, if heat is used to dry the paint; otherwise, the undercoating may run down to the lower part of the door and clog the drain holes.

BODY SHOP MANAGEMENT

This chapter discusses basic information about body shop management that anyone earning a living from the body repair trade should know, whether he is employed as a repairman, is the manager of a large body shop operated by an automobile dealership, or is the proprietor managing his own independent shop.

It is beyond the scope of this text to provide complete instruction in body shop management, as that would be a complete book in itself. This chapter is intended to make sure that the reader is aware that his services as a repairman are valuable only to the extent that they contribute to the continued operation of the business organization in which he is a part. It is hoped that those whose ambition is either to seek a management position in a large automobile service organization or to set up their own shop will seek further business training.

This chapter consists of two main sections: management and estimating. Discussed under management are: starting the business, day-to-day operation, office procedures, and long-range planning. Estimating is actually a part of the day-to-day operation, but has been set out in a separate section because of its importance.

STARTING THE BUSINESS

The repairman who decides to start his own shop has made his first managerial decision. When he does so, he should be aware that he is casting himself in the role of proprietor and manager. From that time on, his future success will depend as much on his ability to manage as on his ability as a repairman. Most repairmen start in business intending to do at least some of the repair work. However, as the business grows, they find that management problems make increasing demands on their time, leaving less and less time for repair work. Somewhere in the process the proprietor finds that he has fully assumed the role of manager and can leave the production work to his employees.

This generalization should be qualified by recognition that there are some persons who wish to be independent but are not particularly interested in building up a large business organization. The man who fits this category often prefers to keep his business small so that he has few or no employees and will be satisfied with what he can earn from his own efforts. Such a person should be respected as a solid citizen able and willing to take care of himself.

Whether the plan is to build up a big business or to stick to a one-man operation, the beginner should not start before giving serious thought to such problems as his financial situation, the local market for the services he has to offer, the location of his shop, the amount of sales promotion effort needed, and how to handle the *record keeping* part of the business. The term record keeping has been substituted for bookkeeping because most repairmen-turned-proprietor tend to limit their part of the operation to keeping records to turn over to someone more experienced as a bookkeeper.

MARKET SURVEY

A market survey is often made by a firm planning to set up in business in a community. The purposes are to estimate expected sales volume and find suitable locations before making the final decision to proceed. The method and depth of the survey will be governed by the type of business and the size of the planned operation. A large retail sales firm would study in depth such factors as population density, income level, traffic flow patterns, the number and sales volume of competing firms, and so on and be guided by the findings. Most body repairmen planning to set up their own shop will have at least some of the pertinent information about their own community, but a careful analysis of local conditions could discover a special need that local shops are not filling.

The prospective proprietor should know the number of existing body shops in his community, the type of work they specialize in, and the general state of the body repair business at present and over the past year or so. Although he should be concerned with all, he should pay particular attention to the larger, well-established shops to determine if their business is slack or if they are working to capacity.

The body repair business in almost all communities can be divided into two types: major wreck rebuilding and appearance reconditioning. Major wreck rebuilding is usually considered the most desirable type of business and is usually the most competitive; as compared to appearance reconditioning, higher skill is required, and a larger capital investment is needed for equipment and operating funds. Assembling a staff of competent repairmen may be more difficult, but the level of skill for painters is the same for both types of work.

Appearance reconditioning, as the term is used here, applies to the repair of minor dents and scratches, spot or complete refinishing, and sometimes trim repair. In most instances the work is paid for by the owner. It is sold both retail and wholesale. The retail market is to the private owner for his or her personal automobile, and wholesale to such buyers as new and used automobile dealers and fleet operators. Whether or not it is a less desirable business is a matter of opinion for the individual to decide. Its advantages are that less equipment is required, fewer funds will be tied up in parts and supplies because payment is usually on delivery for retail work, and the skill level for repairmen can be lower. A disadvantage for volume work is that space requirements can be relatively large.

THE FINANCIAL SITUATION

The repairman considering a venture into business should give careful consideration to two important questions. One is how large is the necessary capital investment? The other is how will he budget his hoped-for income after he gets the business in actual operation?

Capital

Capital invested in property, building, and equipment, as well as the cash needed for operating expenses, are considered together because they represent the total amount of money needed to get the business started. The proprietor probably has already acquired some equipment and perhaps a suitable building, and has saved some money for his start. He will be well advised to make a careful estimate of the total needs and compare it to what is currently on hand. The estimate should be very realistic, because the probability of failure increases drastically when any business venture is under-financed.

Past experience qualifies most repairmen to determine their needs for shop equipment and floor space better than it does to forecast the cash needed for operation. Equipment and space in which to use it has been part of the repairman's daily routine, and it is quite probable that he has urged his employer to obtain various pieces of equipment he saw a need for in doing his work. However, his employer paid for it, paid him regularly, and took care of all operating expenses. His experience as an employee has not required him to be concerned with having ready cash for operation.

Any rule by which the exact amount of capital needed to start a new body shop would be impractical, because of the many variable factors. Even the personality of the individual is important, because some are willing and able to make a greater effort than others. The type of work to be sought is also important. For example, less equipment is required to do used-car appearance reconditioning than for major wreck rebuilding, and the building location is not as important. Furthermore, the used-car work is usually paid for on delivery, whereas the major wreck job will require considerable cash investment in parts, and payment may be delayed for several weeks. The only possible rule is that the beginner should have enough to permit operation through an expected "lean" period when he starts.

Budgeting

The repairman just starting in business must recognize two important facts: (1) his need for ready cash for operating expenses will increase as his volume increases, and (2) his capital investment will depreciate with use. Mismanagement of his finances will cause these basic realities of business life to become serious problems.

The business represents a separate entity with first claim on gross income for the cash needed to keep it solvent. It belongs to the proprietor but, if he takes more out of it than good business judgment dictates, he risks failure. It would be unrealistic to expect the owner of a newly opened body shop immediately to start budgeting for future needs before the business has shown any pattern; quite often the problem is to obtain enough income for survival. As soon as the business becomes self-supporting, however, future problems should be considered.

The repairman's previous experience as an employee may not have required him to manage financial matters other than his own wages, and they were all his for his personal and family needs. As a businessman, he should consider himself an employee of his own business and draw a salary from it that will not be enough to affect continued successful operation. Tax laws favor this method, and it has the advantage that ready cash can be accumulated for operation, some being set aside for replacement of capital equipment as it wears out or becomes obsolete.

The cost of capital equipment can be calculated on a daily basis by establishing its useful lifetime and prorating the total investment over that period of time. For example, a $10,000 investment that can be expected to be useful for ten years will cost $1,000 a year or $5 per day for 50 weeks of 40 working hours. Because of inflation and an increase in equipment sophistication, its replacement cost will be much greater, and the successful businessman will anticipate this by accumulating funds for future purchases.

The methods of handling equipment replacement funds, special accounts, investment, and so on are beyond the scope of this text. As stated at the beginning of this chapter, it is desirable for the repairman planning to go into business to take at least some business training. However, it should be pointed out also that many body shops are operated successfully by repairmen with no business training other than common sense.

LOCATION

Often the prospective proprietor has acquired land and a building as a part of his preparation, so that the location of his shop is fixed. If not, it is to his advantage to make as good a choice as possible within the limits of what is available and his financial ability. Very successful shops have grown from a start in a one-car garage in the proprietor's backyard, but better quarters are liklier ingredients for success. Other successful starts have been made in ideal buildings and locations. The situation is too varied to make worthwhile recomendations other than the advice to avoid heavy mortgage or lease commitments until the wisdom of the venture is proven.

Zoning regulations must be considered first in seeking a suitable location for a body shop, before either purchasing or leasing property. These regulations vary from one community to another, but almost all organized or incorporated communities have laws or ordinances that restrict commercial and industrial operations to selected zones. A new business cannot be started in an area zoned for residential use only. Businesses existing at the time zoning regulations went into effect are permitted to remain as "existing nonconforming uses," but usually only for the lifetime of the owner—and he is not permitted either to sell or expand it in most instances.

Local electrical and plumbing codes and health regulations must be considered, also. Many communities require a license before a business can operate and refuse to issue it if the building and premises are not up to standard. These conditions can be corrected, but often at considerable expense. The prospective proprietor's concern with these should be more than just bare conformity with codes, particularly the electrical wiring. Efficient operation requires adequate lighting and convenient electrical outlets. The cost of correcting any of these conditions should be considered before entering into any agreement either to lease or purchase any building.

Assuming that two or more suitable locations that meet all legal requirements are available and within an acceptable price range, the following conditions deserve consideration in making a final selection: (1) local competition, (2) exposure to the public's view, particularly passing traffice, (3) location of parts and supply sources, (4) fire protection, and (5) local industrial or community conditions or proposed changes that could have adverse effects.

The importance of considering local competition should be obvious. A new shop can expect rough going in a community in which the existing shops are scrambling for business. The chances of survival are best for a new business when it fills an existing community need. If the local shops are suffering from a lack of business, it may be wiser either to look elsewhere or wait until conditions improve.

Any new business venture has the problem of letting the public know that it is there and its services are available. A location on a busy street or highway, where the shop can be seen by the traveling public, provides valuable and continuous advertising. But a less conspicuous location is not in itself a sign of impending failure, for some very successful shops operate in almost hidden locations. The shop in the less conspicuous location usually has the advantage of operating on lower-priced real estate if it is either being purchased or rented.

The nature of body shop work makes consideration of fire protection an absolute must in choosing a location. Few businesses have the combination of welding and use of highly flammable materials found in the average body shop. A serious fire can deal a crippling blow to any business, particularly one struggling to get established. The prospective proprietor should check the fire protection available and the rates. Fire insurance rates vary according to the available protection, with the highest rate where the protection is least. Other factors may outweigh fire protection, but common sense indicates that it should be considered seriously in choosing a new location.

Local industrial or community conditions may seem an unnecessary concern, but it is an undeniable fact that some industrial areas are not attractive to the general public. Starting a shop in an area which many people prefer to avoid may be assuming a handicap that is difficult to overcome. A similar handicap can develop as the result of a major change in a community, especially a major highway relocation that will alter local traffic patterns.

This discussion must be limited to some of the general disadvantages to try to avoid in choosing a location for the start of a new shop. Any location considered will have both advantages and disadvantages that must be weighed in making the final choice, which will be a compromise in almost every case.

ADVERTISING

The proprietor of a body shop must sell his services just as any other retail business, grocery store, or gasoline station must. He can stay in business only as long as his sales—the work he takes in—produces enough gross cash income to pay the expenses of operation and provide a satisfactory net income. It must be assumed that any body man who seriously can consider starting his own shop must also be fairly well informed about the local business conditions in the body shop field. He probably has what is often referred to as a "following"—people who know him for his work. This would include personal acquaintances, customers of former employers, insurance adjustors, automobile dealers, or others with whom he has contacts. This following is an intangible asset that may or may not have considerable value. It can be over-estimated.

Rather than depend entirely on his following, the beginner should consider some form of sales promotion when he first sets up shop. Whether he should continue with this promotion or drop it after a while would be determined by the existing situation; some shops find sales promotion unnecessary, and others find it worthwhile. Two common methods are advertising in the local media and direct solicitation. The shop should also have an attractive sign.

Media Advertising

Media advertising is directed at the general public and can be very effective for selling some types of body shop service and less effective for others. Newspaper, radio, or television advertising will bring in people who are interested in repaint jobs or minor body repairs, work that the owner buys and pays for. However, large collision jobs are normally covered by insurance and paid for either wholly or in part by the insurance company's claim department. The choice of shops may be made by the owner, but more often it is decided by the insurance adjustor, who usually selects the lowest bidder. Media advertising in general is less effective here than it is on the direct sale to the owner.

Direct Solicitation

Direct solicitation by the body shop is usually an effort to obtain a source of repeat work rather than just one job. Insurance company claim departments are often solicited for business because of the large volume of claims they authorize. Other firms that may provide a source of repeat work are automobile dealers, new and used, for their used-car appearance reconditioning.

Automobile rental agencies, taxicab companies, bakeries, utility companies, or other firms that operate fleets of automobiles are also good candidates for direct solicitation.

The Sign

The Sign is essential to identify the shop so that customers can find it. It should be a full-time advertisement as well. It should be in good taste, placed where the passing public will notice it, and designed so that its message can be read at a glance.

The sign conveys more information than just the message spelled out on its surface. The bad impression caused by such things as crude lettering or neglected appearance may be all the passer-by knows or wants to know about the business.

Customer Satisfaction

Customer Satisfaction is the most powerful advertising that the shop can conduct. No other factor affects the future success of a body shop as much as its reputation for quality work and fair dealing. Human nature being what it is, the dissatisfied customer is very much inclined to tell one and all about his complaint and to warn others not to patronize the place of business. Unfortunately, the satisfied customer will be less forceful in spreading the message, even though he or she can be expected to remember when service is needed again.

The repairman's "following" has been mentioned in a previous section. Whether or not he has a following will soon be apparent when he starts his own business. Small or large, the group of people who believe in him are one of his most valuable assets. In the final analysis, all of his sales efforts must be directed toward building up his following. Few beginning shop owners can expect enough following to keep them in business without further sales effort, but, as they become established, many will find that a reputation for satisfied customers is all the sales effort they need.

EQUIPMENT

Equipment includes everything used in production other than the repairman's personal hand tools. Adequate equipment is required for efficient operation. Although some jobs can be done with hand tools alone, most will require equipment that represents considerable capital investment. A good test of the proprietor's managing ability, particularly when he is starting his business, is in how well he selects essential equipment and avoids over-investing in items which his business volume does not justify.

Some equipment items are basic. It would be almost impossible for a body shop to operate without a disc sander, body jack, floor jack, welding outfit, air compressor, and paint gun. The addition of a few safety jacks, vibrating sander, and an electric drill would make it possible for a proprietor working either alone or with one or two employees to get by if the business were limited to appearance reconditioning. An alert proprietor will soon recognize the need for many additional items to save time and improve efficiency. Needed equipment should be acquired as finances permit.

An indisputable rule in all business is that an investment should show a satisfactory return, or it is not justified. Justification can be on the basis either of improving efficiency or the addition of a new service that the shop has not been equipped for previously. For example, sanding to prepare an automobile for painting can be done by hand, but much of it can be done with a relatively inexpensive power sander in much less time. Another example would be an improved welding method that would save considerable time in installing body panels. Examples of additional services are the addition of heavy-duty frame straightening and front-end alignment equipment to a shop that previously had sublet such work.

The following list should provide enough equipment to permit a small shop, one to three repairmen, to work efficiently doing a combination of appearance reconditioning and major wreck rebuilding, but would require subletting of all but minor frame work and front-end alignment:

1. air compressor, with at least 1 horse-power motor
2. air transformer
3. two air hoses, approximately 20 feet long and equipped with snap fittings
4. two paint guns, one used exclusively for primer
5. polisher, for lacquer
6. vibrating or oscillating sander
7. heavy-duty disc sander
8. sander-filer, used primarily for finishing plastic body filler
9. heavy-duty hydraulic body jack with attachments
10. light-duty hydraulic body jack
11. oxyacetylene welding outfit
12. lift jack
13. safety jacks (at least four)
14. air wrench
15. creeper
16. electric drill, (¼ inch)
17. mechanic's extension light
18. work bench with vise
19. pneumatic hammer and chisel kit
20. heavy duty chains, (2 or more)
21. caulking gun

Other items, which some persons may consider hand tools, are needed to supplement the above list. A few of the most important one are:

1. tap and die set
2. cut-out knife for removing adhesive caulked body glasses
3. molding and door handle removing tools
4. spot weld cutters

Some repairmen may prefer to buy their own items in this list, and a few may buy items in the first list, but it is customary in most businesses for the shop to furnish them, particularly the ones essential for certain jobs.

If and when business volume permits, most proprietors will feel the need for additional equipment either to improve efficiency in operations already being performed or to add an entirely new service. A shop specializing in appearance reconditioning would be interested in such items as

1. custom-built spray booth
2. steam cleaner
3. sand blaster
4. drying ovens
5. sewing equipment for trim repair

The shop doing mostly major wreck repair would be more interested in such items as

1. frame-straightening systems, either portable or the drive-on type
2. front-end alignment systems
3. arc welder
4. electric resistance spot welder
5. MIG arc welder
6. hoist
7. wrecker truck.

Some equipment items used in the body shop, particularly electric power tools, are available in both heavy- and light-duty grades. Purchase of cheaper, light-duty power tools for use in body shop production is usually false economy. Increased working life and dependability of the heavy-duty power tool will almost always offset the difference in original cost. Equipment items or systems intended specifically for body shop use are usually available from local supply houses. Many factors affect the selection of such equipment, but probably the most important one is versatility—which, however, must be weighted carefully against the problems of the individual shop's operation. The capability of a machine or system to perform operations that the particular shop may rarely use is of doubtful value.

Safety

Safety should always be given first priority. Human nature being what it is, people as a group tend to demand that safety practices be adopted, but as individuals they tend to ignore them. Body repairmen are not different in this respect, but the nature of their work makes strict adherence to sensible safety rules a must. Probably the greatest hazards in the body shop are found in the areas of fire, eye protection, and working under automobiles.

The following common-sense rules will reduce the probability of fire, but not eliminate it altogether: (1) welding should not be premitted in areas where either painting is done or paint materials stored, (2) a gasoline tank should be removed and stored in a safe place before welding or heating is done close to the tank position in the automobile, and safety cans should be available for storage of drained-out gasoline, (3) fire extinguishers should be serviced immediately after any use, (4) all portable electric tools should be equipped with three-wire, grounded power cords, and (5) all plugged-in electric cords should be removed from the receptacles at the end of the day.

The need for adequate eye protection in any welding or grinding operation cannot be stressed too strongly. Suitable goggles or shields should be available, and whomever is in charge of the shop should insist on their use without exception. Masks or eye shields should be provided and their use established as a condition of employment.

Body repair does not require a lot of work under the automobile but, when it is done, the automobile should be supproted on non-tippable safety jacks. Also, absolutely no person should be permitted beneath an automobile while it is under strain from any type of heavy-duty straightening equipment.

Most of these rules, and many others that could be added, are included in various local, state, or provincial safety codes. Safety problems do not arise from the lack of adequate codes; they arise from failure to use common sense. When safety codes are analyzed, they are seen to be only common sense enacted into law.

RECORD KEEPING

A trap many repairmen fall into when setting up in business is failure to recognize the need for an accurate accounting system to record their business transactions. The system is usually referred to as *bookkeeping* or the *books*. Neglect or confusion of the bookkeeping system can cause the business to fail just as quickly as lack of sales or inefficient production in the shop. Unfortunately, in many cases the individual's personal likes and dislikes that led him toward the trade also lead him to avoid the paper-work side of business as much as possible.

The beginner who recognizes the need for a bookkeeping system and develops a good one is fortunate. There are several ways to meet the need. The important point is that the beginner should start prepared. Preparation means that he should have a well-thought-out plan by which he will either do or have his bookkeeping done.

Without question, any person without previous experience who plans to set up his own business should enroll in a business course to learn as much as possible about bookkeeping and business management. By keeping his own books until the business grows large enough to justify hiring a full-time office staff, he will save considerable money and have a better understanding of business procedures. However, it is recognized that the existing situation or the personality of the individual may make this impractical. Many mechanics find paper work difficult and disagreeable to the point that they will either do it poorly or neglect it, either of which will guarantee trouble and probable business failure. The following suggestions are intended for the individual who has made an honest appraisal of his interests and

capabilities and wishes to avoid the task of bookkeeping.

Few body shop businesses are started on a scale that will justify hiring a full-time bookkeeper. The alternative is to use the professional accounting services available in almost all communities for a fee. These range from well-organized firms that specialize in bookkeeping for many small firms, to the semi-retired accountant who is available on a part-time basis. Either can relieve the proprietor of most of his bookkeeping task.

Whatever system of bookkeeping he uses, the proprietor cannot expect to free himself completely of the responsibility, because he must keep the records of his transactions, which the professional will record in the books. Unless he has someone full time to do it for him, he must record every transaction, money paid out or received, money owed or due, or anything else that will affect profit and loss. The bookkeeper cannot start until this record is available.

The records kept by the proprietor can be quite simple. The exact manner in which they are kept would be determined by agreement with the person doing the actual bookkeeping, but the least the proprietor can get by with is to keep all receipts for money spent and make out duplicate receipts for all money received. It is much better practice for him to keep, in addition to all receipts, a daybook or journal in which he writes down each transaction as it is made. In bookkeeping language, a journal is a book in which daily transactions are recorded. It can be as simple as a pad of columnar forms, as shown in Figure 10-1. Entering every transac-

10-1 Daily journal.

tion, purchase or sale, on a form such as this provides a check against loss of an important receipt and sums up the day's activities.

The form is intended as a suggestion; the proprietor and his bookkeeping service will have to determine the exact type of journal that suits their specific purpose. Note that separate columns are used for cash and charge purchases, for the cash and uncollected sales, and for sales tax. The uncollected sales applies particularly to the body shop, because so much of the work is billed to an insurance company after delivery to the owner.

Computerized Record Keeping

Minicomputers have been an important development in developing record-keeping systems. They enable a person who understands the basics of operating a business to perform at least four important accounting tasks: (1) general ledger, (2) accounts receivable, (3) accounts payable, and (4) payroll. Without the computer, the professional accountant must perform these tasks by hand. The availability of minicomputers enables the proprietor (or his accountant) to perform these tasks more quickly and save money. Whether or not such a machine is within the price range a new business proprietor can consider, only he can answer. If not, it deserves consideration in his future plans. The general subject of computer use is discussed more fully in the Long-Range Planning section of this chapter.

The computers referred to here are the type available to the general public from computer retail stores. Mainframe computers are intended for large business firms and are much too costly and sophisticated to be practical in a small body shop.

Business Forms.

Many small businesses operate successfully without investing in special business forms by using standard ones available from almost any stationery store. However, few firms that attain any appreciable volume of business find this satisfactory; specifically designed forms become a necessity for efficient operation. Furthermore, the public expects an established business to use individualized forms and are inclined to suspect the permanence of a firm that does not have them.

A body shop should start with repair order, estimate, and receipt book forms. Standard forms are available from specialty printing firms, and almost any local printer has samples that can be supplied in the relatively small lots a new business would need.

The Repair Order

No job should be started without the owner's signature on the repair order. This authorizes the shop to have possession of the automobile and obligates the owner to pay for the repairs made or, if insurance is involved, to pay whatever portion of the bill is to be charged to him or her. Many insurance companies issue their own order to the shop to authorize whatever part they are to pay. It is usually itemized, so that all parts and labor operations are spelled out clearly, and states what part they are to pay. However, this does not change the fact that the shop is dealing with the owner and should have his or her authorization before proceeding with the repairs.

Although very few repair bills are disputed in court, it is good practice to have each entry on the repair order written so that it makes a clear statement of what is to be done. Both the owner and the shop need the protection of such information. When it is stated in detail on the repair order, the owner's signature is evidence of his or her agreement. In effect, the repair order is a contract.

The repair order forms used in most shops are prepared in three- or four-sheet packs with interleaved carbon paper, ready for use. The first sheet will be used as the invoice when the job is completed and the bill totaled, the second (and third, if used), is for accounting purposes, and the last is usually made of stiffer cardboard for use as the shop copy. Forms of this type are available from large printing firms that specialize in business forms of all types.

The operators of many small body shops do not feel that the volume of their business justifies purchasing repair order forms in large quantities. Almost any job printing shop can make up smaller quantities of suitable forms and usually have samples from which to choose.

10-2 Estimate form.

The combined estimate and repair order form described in the next section, The Estimate Form, is an example.

The Estimate Form

It is common practice to prepare estimates on a printed form on which the word ESTIMATE appears in large letters across the top, along with the shop name, address, and phone number. It is quite common for the proprietor's name to be included in the heading if it is different from the shop name. These may be prepared by any printer.

Most estimate forms are printed on standard 8½ x 11 inch paper. As most estimates are written by hand, the forms are ruled horizontally, with vertical columns for entry of labor operations, time allowances, parts and material prices, and sometimes sublet operations. The exact format is a matter of choice. A typical form is shown in Figure 10-2, but many operators of small shops prefer the combined repair order and estimate form shown in Figure 10-3.

The form in Figure 10-2 has this statement in the lower left corner: "This is an estimate, not a definite contract. Parts prices subject to change." Some proprietors feel that a statement of this type is needed to protect them against bearing the cost of unpredictable parts price changes or hidden damage. Some others add a time-limiting statement, usually for a period of 30 days.

It can be a convenience to have the labor column subdivided into three separate columns in shops where the repairmen are paid on an incentive plan, but subdivision is less essential when they are paid on an hourly or other fixed-sum basis. Similarly, the paint materials column is convenient for listing the totals needed for various panels. Flat rate manuals and independently published sources of such information list dependable paint materials allowances with the various paint labor operations, making it relatively easy to copy figures for each panel and add them for the total figure. An item that will be sent to another shop is entered in the sublet column.

Receipt Book

A standard receipt form, available from stationery or office supply stores in pad form, is satisfactory, but a form with the business name on it is more impressive. The owner's copy of the completed repair order serves as a receipt in usual circumstances; but there other are other occasions when a receipt is needed, and some type of form should be used.

PRODUCTION

Production is measured in the dollar volume of jobs performed for the customer. It provides the gross income

that sustains the business. Without sufficient gross income, the proprietor will not have any profit left after paying his expenses. The profit margin should be large enough to provide sufficient funds to pay operating expenses, budget for future capital expenditures as the business expands, and pay the proprietor a fair salary. Thus, production is the primary activity and should be the manager's prime concern. This is especially true for the proprietor who is managing his own shop during the early phases of getting started.

There are no simple secrets which, once learned, will provide the manager with all of the answers to the problems of keeping production up to a satisfactory level. However, many of the problems can be avoided by exercising foresight in two general areas of operation: (1) job planning and follow-up and (2) employee-employer relations. Job planning and follow-up is a matter of making sure that a job entering the shop will not be delayed by lack of parts or supplies because essential equipment is either in use or not working properly, or a repairman is not available to do the work. An alert manager should foresee such possibilities and take action to avoid them before they become problems. Employer-employee relations can be more difficult than job planning. The manager must compete with other shops for the services of skilled people or train them himself. After acquiring the services of competent employees, he must be aware that keeping them depends largely on the working conditions he provides. This is partly a matter of income, but other factors are

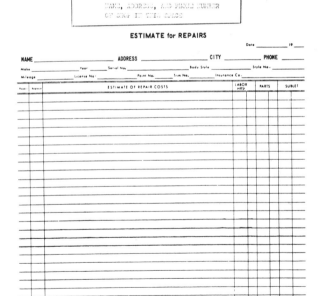

10-3 Combined estimate and repair order form.

equally important, particularly the degree of respect he earns in his day-to-day contacts with them. The latter is especially important to highly skilled people who know that their services are in demand.

He should be aware also that some ambitious people cannot be kept as long-term employees. Looking back on his own career, he probably knows that he disappointed a former employer when he decided to set up his own business. He should expect that other equally ambitious people will decide to do the same or accept other employment they see as more desirable. However, this does not change the fact that a well-run shop has a better chance of retaining good employees than one which is run in a slipshod manner.

THE PRODUCTION SCHEDULE

The production phase starts when the owner has signed the repair order or, if insurance is involved, the adjustor has issued his repair order. The immediate question is, when will the job be ready? This is of vital importance to the owner, because having his or her automobile out of service is at least an inconvenience and usually a hardship. The owner should be given a dependable answer based on the existing facts and good judgment.

In setting the promised delivery date, consideration should be given to the amount of work already in progress, the amount of work on the job in question, availability of needed parts, and a reasonable safety factor. Once a date is set, every reasonable effort should be made to meet it. When it is found that a delivery date cannot be met, it is always better business to notify the owner as soon as possible, rather than to wait until he or she comes for the automobile and finds it not ready.

There are many reasons why a job may be delayed beyond the promised delivery date, some excusable and some not. Such events as an unavoidable accident, equipment breakdown, or illness of a shop crew member are unavoidable. However, failure to find all of the

damage when making the estimate or checking parts availability is less excusable. The worst, however, is to name a delivery date, knowing when making the promise that it is impossible. When inexcusable delays occur too often, it is evidence of bad management.

Fouled-up deliveries due to production delays cannot be eliminated totally, but most of them can be avoided by entering each job on a schedule sheet as soon as it is started. A sample sheet is shown in Figure 10-4. This will serve as a reminder of all the work in progress if it is kept up to date and consulted before promising a job out. The schedule has its greatest value when the shop is working at or close to capacity and there is the possibility that other job-out promises will be forgotten. The sheet shown is intended only as a suggestion. Many shop managers use a sheet of this type but not necessarily the same as this one. A standard columnar pad, available from stationery or office supply stores, may be used, or a special form can be drawn up and printed by a job printing shop.

A feature of the suggested sheet is the side-by-side columns for estimated and actual times. This has a two-fold value: (1) it will provide a running check on the accuracy of estimating, and (2) eventually it will reveal which employees complete jobs in the estimated time and which ones consistently overrun. With such information, a good manager knows when he should change his estimating policy and which employees are deserving of extra reward in either wages or bonus.

A list of jobs promised to come in but not yet started should be kept in a separate appointment book or sheet. When making new appointments, the manager should check both the appointment book and the schedule sheet for conflicts. This is of particular importance when more than one person may be dealing with the customer.

Productive and Non-Productive Labor

Not all of the time expended in the day-to-day activities of the body shop is productive in the sense that it is used to perform actual repair operations. This extra time is non-productive. The amount of non-productive time required varies from job to job, but each job involves some. Before the first repair operation, some time will have been spent talking with the owner, making an estimate, probably contacting an insurance adjustor, and writing the repair order. Telephone calls or a trip away from the shop to obtain parts or materials may be required. After the repairs are finished, some more time will be spent in preparing the bill and delivering the automobile to the owner, who may have requested delivery to his or her home or place of business. Furthermore, time has to be spent with equipment and supply sales people, trips made to the bank, records kept, and housekeeping done on a regular schedule. If such duties are not performed, the operation may become a disaster.

Just as it is obvious that some time must be non-productive, it is equally obvious that the percentage of

10-4 Production schedule.

total time devoted to non-productive activities must be kept as low as possible.

REPAIR ORDER FILE

A wall file for repair orders, of the type shown in Figure 10-5, can be a convenience for the proprietor who spends much of his time at actual repair work. A separate pocket is used for the repair order and all other papers for each job in progress in the shop. Parts receipts, release forms, or any other papers should be put with the order when they come in. In this way, everything is available when the order is removed to make up the bill.

The Estimate File

The estimate file can be almost any suitable box or file holder, perhaps a drawer in a standard file cabinet. The shop's copy should be placed in it as soon as it is written, so that it will be available if and when the job is authorized.

The need for an estimate file stems from the fact that estimating is a form of competitive bidding, and not all of those written are sold. Many insurance companies ask for two or three estimates and authorize the job to the lowest bidder. A day or two, and sometimes weeks, may go by before an estimate is approved—and it may not be approved at all. When the job is authorized, the shop copy will be needed, so it should be kept in a safe place.

Most shops obtain estimate forms from the printer in bound pads; each sheet in the pad is perforated across the top for easy tear out. Some shops tear out the customer's copy and leave the shop copy in the pad. The result is that the first ones in the pad get quite a lot of handling before the pad is used up and often break loose or are torn out by mistake. This way there is great risk of losing an important estimate, which can be both embarrassing and inconvenient. It is far more desirable to remove and file every estimate when it is written.

The estimate file should be examined once a month, and those that are too old (usually a month) should be removed and either discarded or placed in a dead file. The value of a dead file may be questionable, but it will sometimes provide a copy of an original estimate when a job has been long delayed.

SUPERVISING REPAIR PROCEDURES

Under ideal circumstances, supervision of repair procedures is one of the manager's minor problems. That would mean that every repairman was competent and cooperative and assumed his responsibilities to the shop and the public. In the rare situation where the ideal conditions exist, most of the credit should be given to the manager, or proprietor-manager, and the rest to luck. The manager should get the credit for his ability to

choose and, perhaps, train competent people. Luck enters the picture, of course, because the right people are not always available.

One of the manager's most difficult tasks occurs when he finds a repairman in difficulty on a job and resentful of suggestions. This attitude is natural, because it is difficult for most people to admit error. Assuming the manager's competence to suggest or demonstrate better procedure, he still has to do so without offending the worker or exposing him to ridicule from other employees. This is a test of the manager's ability to handle personal relationships, rather than of his technical skill. One alternative is to allow the man to muddle along as best he can and hope that the result will be acceptable. Another is to be as discreet as possible in suggesting or demonstrating better procedure. Sometimes help is more readily accepted from another experienced man than from the "Boss." The last resort is to assign someone else to the job and either assign the replaced man to other work or discharge him. Any discharge should be handled carefully, particularly with a small group, to avoid creating new prolems with other employees.

A good test of the manager's ability shows up by how well he can plan the overall operation so that difficult situations do not arise. The probability of difficult employee relations, incompetence, undependability, or personality conflicts is much less in a smaller shop than in a large one, but it can happen in any group. The ability to handle employee relations can be a more important qualification for a body shop manager than knowledge of the trade. Sometimes the skilled tradesmen available to fill a managerial position in a large shop, particularly a dealership, are either unable or unwilling to develop the human relations and paper work skills necessary to be an effective supervisor. In such

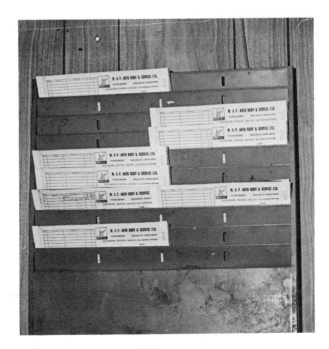

10-5 Repair order wall file.

cases, management has no alternative other than to appoint someone with these abilities even if he has little or no trade knowledge. It is a matter of choosing the lesser of two disadvantages. However, the skilled body repairman who has prepared himself for managerial responsibility would still have the advantage if all other things were equal.

DELIVERING THE FINISHED JOB

Delivering the finished job to the owner may seem a simple matter of having the necessary papers signed, taking the owner's money for whatever portion of the bill he or she is to pay, and handing over the keys. These must be done, but the *manner* in which they are done can affect the owner's satisfaction or dissatisfaction with the job. Owners often unconsciously express their resentment of what they consider ill treatment by being critical of the finished work, regardless of quality.

People in the body repair trade often either forget or never have recognized that their attitude towards automobiles may differ widely from that of most owners. To body repair people, automobiles represent the raw material with which they make their living and, certainly, a damaged one evokes no emotional response. The opposite attitude can be expected from most owners. Most owners have no reason to concern themselves with the technical details of construction and repair, although some may do so as a hobby. But many view their automobiles in much the same light as they regard their home and furnishings or good clothing. The sense of loss when their automobile is damaged is often far greater than the money value of the repair and the inconvenience involved.

It is natural for anyone to have some questions or mental reservations about the quality of a repair job involving the appearance and structural soundness of their automobile. The less familiar they are with the general subject of automobiles, the more they are apt to be concerned. Such persons' concern rightfully deserves understanding. It is not enough for the person delivering the job to know that the repair work has been done well, he should make sure that the owner knows, also. A courteous effort to answer any questions and ease the owner's fears may bring him or her back with more business. Failure to do so may generate complaint where none is justified and guarantee that that person will never come back.

PRICING THE WORK

Some beginning body shop managers find it difficult to set an exact price on their work, often preferring to quote their price after learning what a competitor has bid. This can be an easy way out of writing an estimate, but it is more nearly a guessing game than good business practice; the competitor may have been guessing, also. It is much better practice to set the price by making an itemized estimate of all parts, labor operations,

and materials, all of which represent money that must be paid out and should be recovered with a fair profit.

Any person qualified to operate a body shop should be able to examine a damaged automobile and list the parts, labor operations, and materials required, refer to a manual for parts and labor prices, and estimate time for the straightening or other variable operations. Labor times are usually set in hours and tenths of an hour for each labor operation. These are then added up and multiplied by the established hourly rate.

The Hourly Rate

As mentioned previously, the hourly rate is multiplied by the time estimated for the labor operations to determine the total labor price. In theory, its structure consists of separate allowances, usually expressed in percentages, for the repairman's hourly wage, operating expenses, and profit. The theory holds true reasonably well in practice, but local competition is usually the governing factor. As in any other business, competition sets the price level. Price level is actually a range, because different estimators looking at the same job do not always form the same conclusion as to time.

In many communities local associations agree on a common rate to be charged by all members. If everything else were equal, this would mean that all shops would charge the same price for a given job. In theory, the selection of the shop would be a matter of preference for reasons other than price. In practice, everything is not equal. Variable factors such as repair skills, quality of workmanship, special equipment, operating costs, and even the fact that one proprietor may be content to accept less than another will affect the situation. The result is price variation, even though the stated and agreed hourly rate is fixed.

A question of ethics can arise when the actual time required for a particular job is less than that estimated. This is a difficult question to resolve, because some variation is inevitable. If the average estimated and actual times are close, there should be no reason for criticism. When the average actual time is far less than the estimated, the suggestion of misrepresentation may arise. On the other hand, when actual time far overruns the estimated, the shop is in a losing situation.

Any question, ethical or otherwise, usually has two sides. For example, the automobile owner or insurance adjustor who would complain bitterly about what he or she felt was an overcharge would rarely be as forceful in insisting or paying the difference when the actual time overran the estimated.

LONG-RANGE PLANNING

Starting a body shop and getting it into self-supporting operation should be considered the first step of a long-range plan. The proprietor who has reached that point, often referred to as viability, should be pleased but not complacent; he must continue to plan for future steps, large or small, if his success is to continue. Problems such as cash for operating expenses, equipment wear, or availability of more desirable equipment have been discussed in the Budgeting section. Budgeting for the future is essential, but only a part of long-range planning. The successful proprietor should give considerable thought to several other areas where both opportunities and problems may arise, and be prepared to act when the time comes. Three important considerations are (1) public relations, (2) expansion, and (3) community change.

PUBLIC RELATIONS

One dictionary definition of public relations is: the state of the relationship between the general public and an institution of any kind. This includes body shops. In starting his business, the proprietor has as a prime concern earning enough public acceptance to survive. Having reached the state of viability, he has built an intangible asset in the relationship established with his community. The continued viability of the business is dependent on maintaining and expanding their relationship.

An important part of any business's public relations is that it is "there." The importance of a good location is that the people of the community see the shop as they go about their daily activities. The average person hopes to avoid being a customer of a body shop but, when involved in a traffic accident, will hurry to find one. The shop will get a percentage of the accident business simply because its services are available. The percentage will be affected by the appearance of the premises. The average person does not consider a collection of damaged automobiles attractive and considers an accumulation of junk parts repulsive. The proprietor who knows the value of good public relations will keep the appearance of his premises, inside and out, as attractive as possible.

Another part of public relations is the public reaction to dealing with the shop. Unfortunately, bad news spreads more rapidly than good. Most dissatisfied customers will be much more forceful in relating their experience to friends and acquaintances than the one who is perfectly satisfied. Furthermore, complaints will be accepted as fact more readily than recommendations, particularly if the listener is seeking advice about which shop to patronize.

The shop's relationship with the local insurance company representatives is a third and important element of public relations. The owner of a damaged automobile often leaves the choice of repair shop to the insurance adjustor or selects one from those recommended. In either case, the good will of the adjustor is valuable, sometimes to the point that some shop managers are tempted to overstep the bounds of ethical conduct in cultivating it. In the long run, this is a backward step that will lead to trouble. The best relationship with the local insurance company representatives is established by a reputation for quality work and a cooperative attitude. A good reputation can be earned, but not bought.

The proprietor is often much more aware of the value of good public relations than are his employees. It is unfortunate that some people who choose to work at a skilled trade have difficulty with ordinary human relations. The skilled repairman who takes pride in being "plain spoken" can offend customers who would otherwise be satisfied. That customer will remember his or her treatment and forget the quality of the repair work. One reason that many shop managers do not permit customers in the shop area is to avoid situations that can bring on "plain spokenness." The stated reason for the keep-out rule is insurance or safety regulations, but there is the unstated advantage of preventing undesirable contact with employees who fail to recognize that customer good will is as important to them as it is to management.

Participation in Community

Participation in community activities is an entirely different aspect of public relations from the actual conduct of the business. When starting out, most shop proprietors have been too busy surviving in business to give much thought or time to community affairs. When the business can be considered "established," the proprietor should recognize that the business has become a part of the community and that he has a community responsibility.

Community responsibility can be described only in general terms, but it has a direct bearing on activities such as schools, churches, local government, community planning, sports, clubs, and many others. Activities of this type depend on the services of local citizens, many of whom are successful business people. The extent to which a particular businessman should get involved is a personal matter. Although involvement should certainly not be for profit, communities do tend to support the business people who assume community responsibility unselfishly.

EXPANSION

Further expansion is a very normal process for the proprietor who has built a new business to the point of viability. Expansion that takes place as the result of a well-thought-out plan is usually healthy. However, too rapid expansion can be disastrous. The proprietor should consider at least three aspects of any planned expansion: (1) community need, (2) finances, and (3) the availability of skilled labor.

Determining community need is simply a continuation of the market survey discussed in a previous section. The difference at this point is that experience should enable the proprietor to evaluate the situation more accurately. However, there is always the risk that early success will lead to over-optimism. Good judgment is required to know the difference between a temporary and a growing demand. At this point it may be desirable to seek advice from other experienced business people who are not involved in the body shop business; their judgment will be more impartial.

Expansion requires capital. Any expansion that can be financed from accumulated funds is safer than one that requires borrowing. Regardless of how it is financed, there should be solid evidence that any planned expansion will pay for itself in reasonable time, or it may become a liability. Facts and figures accumulated by the proprietor are much more dependable than a glowing sales talk.

The availability of skilled labor will not be a problem if the planned expansion is simply to add new equipment that will improve the efficiency of the existing crew, but any major expansion will require additional skilled people. Traditionally, skilled body repairmen and those in related trades have been in short supply. One reason has been that not enough shops have made a serious effort to train new people; and one reason for this is that training new people is a skill that must be learned. The proprietor who has learned to train people in the necessary trade skills is risking much less in a major expansion than another who has not.

Training programs can be very informal. An exellent technique is to provide challenging work assignments from time to time. For example, an apprentice who spends full time sanding paint jobs learns little about either metal work or painting. However, if he is given an occasional opportunity to do some simple metal work or actually complete a paint job, his interest will be kept up, and he can develop into a more valuable employee. Many young men, including graduates of trade schools, accept such apprentice jobs but give up in disgust because they are never given a chance to develop into qualified tradesmen. Those who accept the challenge will often prove more valuable employees than another skilled man hired from another shop.

COMMUNITY CHANGE

Community changes will affect the continued success of the body shop in many ways, some perhaps beneficial and other definitely not. Neighborhoods rarely stand still over a long period; they usually develop or deteriorate. A trend in either direction will benefit some businesses and prove to be a hardship for others. For example, relocation of a major traffic route will increase the value of some real estate and decrease the value of others. The location of shopping centers, industrial plants, and real estate subdivisions can have similar effects. Not all such changes can be foreseen, but when they can, the proprietor affected should be alert to take advantage of any possible benefit and reduce the effect of any resultant hardships to the best of his ability.

The proprietor should be aware that he has made a change in the community by starting his business. Whether the effect was for better or worse depends on how the business is maintained. A body shop proprietor who permits the exterior appearance to deteriorate or fails to "keep house" properly may be contributing to the conditions that cause community decay.

ESTIMATING

The estimating procedures discussed in the following sections are intended to familiarize the beginner with the process of estimating the various panels and chassis parts requiring repair. Even though making estimates is ordinarily done by someone with wider experience, the beginner widens his experience by learning the business as well as the trade. His knowledge and ability to make a good estimate will be as important as his trade skills when he is being considered for advancement and even more so if he is considering starting his own business.

The nature of the goods and services sold by the body shop makes it impractical to set the price without first examining the individual job to evaluate it. The only fair and accurate way to do this is to prepare an itemized list of all repair operations and parts prices. Parts prices and the labor time allowances to install them can be determined from catalogs and flat rate labor annuals, but pricing the straightening operations is more complicated. Each straightening operation must be examined to estimate the time it will require. That time, multiplied by the shop's hourly labor rate, determines the labor charge. In the language of the body shop, setting the price is called *estimating*, even though only a part of it is actually estimated.

The importance of good estimating cannot be overemphasized. The price must be competitive; if it is too high the sale is lost, if too low the shop loses money. The success of the business depends on many factors, but none is more important than the performance of the estimator.

In the small independent shop, the proprietor usually does the estimating. In the large dealership shop, the body shop manager or an assistant will usually do it. In either case, the estimator should know enough about the body repair trades, metal work, frame straightening, painting, wheel alignment, and so on, to set fair time allowances and be methodical enough to be accurate. In addition, he should have enough sales ability to sell the job at the price he sets.

Some who feel that their interest is restricted to the mechanical part of their trade may question why they should be concerned with estimating, because it is a business matter rather than mechanical skill. This is really a short-sighted viewpoint. Those who find themselves in good jobs or owners of good businesses in the future will do so by learning the business as well as the trade.

This discussion of estimating is intended to give a general knowledge of estimating procedures. However, the pattern of estimate preparation used here is not presented as the only, or correct, way to prepare an estimate. The pattern, referring primarily to the sequence of entry on the estimate form, can vary widely and still accomplish the desired end result. The exact pattern is not as important as accuracy and clarity. Other people must be able to understand what the estimator has written, particularly in a large shop. The estimate serves an important purpose; it provides the list of parts to be ordered and the various repairmen take their directions from it. Common practice in large shops is to attach it to the hard copy of the repair order, so that it stays with the automobile during the process of repair.

OTHER ESTIMATING AGENCIES

Some of the automobiles that come to the shop to be repaired have already been estimated by the insurance company or an adjusting agency employed by the company. This practice was started in the early days of the automobile insurance business by some companies that were not satisfied with the original system of competitive bidding by which they were awarding repair jobs to the repair shops. They began training their adjustors in the various aspects of estimating, including such subjects as automobile construction and operation, how to inspect an automobile for damage, the principles of sheet metal repair, and a detailed plan of estimate writing. These companies require their adjustors to prepare their own estimate, even though the repair shop has an estimate already prepared.

Some other insurance companies have handled their losses by contracting with independent adjusting agencies that operate on a fee basis. Some of the agencies have adopted the practice of preparing their own estimates. A further refinement of the system, developed in recent years, has been the establishment of drive-in appraisal centers, some operated by insurance companies and others by appraisal agencies. In operation, the owner of a damaged automobile that is still drivable is requested to bring it to the drive-in when reporting a claim. After the claim has been approved and the estimate prepared, some companies award the job to a particular shop and others provide the owner with a copy of the estimate, on which the insurance company has agreed to pay the stated amount, and allows the owner to choose the shop.

In general, body shops welcome this method of estimating, because of convenience. In most cases the estimates are fair and reasonable and the shops are relieved of the task of preparing their own, which can require considerable non-productive time when the damage is extensive. However, they still have to prepare estimates on many damaged automobiles insured by companies that do not have their own esitmating systems or when the work is done at the owner's expense.

An inside view of a well-equipped drive-in appraisal center is shown in Figure 10-6. Many are not as well equipped as this one.

COMPUTERIZED ESTIMATING

The development of computerized estimate preparation promises to take much of the clerical work out of the estimator's job. The computer cannot relieve the esti-

mator of the responsibility of making the critical decisions, but it can relieve him of hours of tedious paperwork. The computer takes over after his decisions are made and pays for its use in time saved.

The computer system consists of two basic units: the central memory bank and the computer terminal in the body shop office. The computer company maintains the memory bank, which contains price and flat-rate labor allowances, plus any other pertinent information, for practically all automobiles. They lease the terminal to the body shop, so that the stored information is available to the body shop on demand. Instead of thumbing through a manual and laboriously writing information down, the estimator identifies the parts required on the terminal and gets an immediate print-out. The computer totals the estimate, delivers the required number of copies, and stores the information in memory for future recall if needed.

It is much more practical for the individual body shop to use the services of a computer firm on a lease or fee basis than to install its own computer, because of the tremendous volume of information required. Once assembled, this information can serve many shops as easily as one. Furthermore, the stored information must be updated as fast as changes occur; computer specialists can accomplish this faster and more economically than the individual user.

It must be emphasized that the value of the computer is in time saved and accuracy. It will not relieve the estimator of the responsibility of making critical decisions but, after the decisions are made, it will eliminate human error in processing the information fed into it. Obviously, the cost of computerized service must be weighed against the need. It is difficult to make any reasonably accurate prediction of the number of body shops that will adopt computerized estimating. The first use has been in the larger shops. As the systems are refined and improved, they may be adopted by a growing number of smaller shops; the final limit will be determined by the economics of the service.

10-6 The work area of a well-equipped appraisal center.

CHARGING FOR ESTIMATES

In the early days of the automobile insurance business, the standard practice was for the insurance company to instruct the owner to get two or three estimates from different shops and award the job to the lowest bidder. This practice is still followed to some extent, but body shops in general have tended to discourage it, for obvious reasons. The considerable time required to make an estimate on a large wreck is at best non-productive—and a dead loss if the job goes to another shop. This earlier system was further abused by some owners or insurance adjustors who "shopped around" before awarding the job.

Many shops in many communities have discouraged owner or insurance adjustor shopping by charging a substantial fee for making an estimate, with the understanding that the fee will be credited on the bill if the job is received. There are still many shops in many communities that do not charge for estimates. This is a matter to be decided by the management of the particular shop; what is good practice for one is not necessarily good for another.

THE ESTIMATOR'S QUALIFICATIONS

Certain personal traits are desirable for any person who wishes to become a good estimator. All of the time-honored maxims of honesty, good judgment, and a sense of fair play are important, just as they are for all other occupations. The true test of the estimator's ability is in how well he visualizes difficult repair procedures and determines fair time allowances. Listing parts and copying flat-rate labor allowances out of a manual are essentially clerical work. Guessing labor allowances for complicated straightening operations is a sure road to trouble. If the guess is too low, the shop loses money; if too high, the shop loses business. Even though estimating is a form of guessing, the guesswork can be reduced to tolerable limits by anyone with an understanding of the principles of metal repair work and the willingness to apply logical thought.

The skilled repairman has a definite advantage in estimating, if he possesses the other qualifications. However, there are many very successful estimators who have never done metal work. They are people who have had the opportunity to learn basic procedures by observing repairmen at work and who apply the knowledge in visualizing procedures to jobs they are estimating. When this is all summed up, the estimator's primary qualification is common sense.

ESTIMATING PROCEDURE

The operation of making an estimate of the damage on an automobile falls naturally into four steps: (1) inspecting the damage to determine its extent and the required repair procedures, (2) estimating time allowances for straightening operations, (3) filling in parts prices and flat-rate time allowances, (4) selling the estimate.

All of these steps are important, but the first two are the critical test of the estimator's ability. It is here that he must rely on his good judgment and knowledge of body repair to determine the time required to straighten or repair the various parts that are repairable and specify replacement for those that are not. He must be thorough enough in his inspection to find all of the damage and enter it on the estimate form. The third step has traditionally been a matter of taking the incomplete estimate to a desk where flat-rate labor books, parts price lists, and an adding machine were available to complete the pricing operation. There seems little doubt that the small independent shop will continue with the traditional system for a long time, but the availability of computerized estimating offers a means of shortcutting the clerical work for many high-volume shops. Once the estimator has compiled the basic information, the computer can print out the complete estimate in a fraction of the time required to do it manually.

The fourth step, selling the estimate, must be done, whether it has been prepared by the computer or laboriously hand written. In most businesses, selling is a matter of dealing with the buyer, who in the boy shop may be either the owner or an insurance adjustor. In shops where wage payments are geared to the individual's dollar volume production, the estimator may encounter additional sales resistance from the shop crew as well as from the public. The ability to meet such resistance will vary with the individual, but the greatest resistance will be directed at the estimator's judgment and thoroughness, not the method by which he put his judgment on the record.

The emphasis of this section is on the first two steps of the process. With those steps complete, finishing the estimate is a matter of routine and selling it is largely a matter of personality.

INSPECTION

The estimator's inspection of a damaged automobile should be considered as a two-phase operation. The first phse is a complete overall inspection to determine the extent of the damage. The second includes a part-by-part inspection, entering the information on the estimate form, and completing the estimate. The sequence of the first phase is determined by the conditions of the damage. The sequence of the second phase should be a predetermined routine.

In the first phase, the estimator's concern is to determine the extent of the damage. A minor dent may require no more than a single glance to see that straightening and refinishing an exterior panel is all that is involved. On more severe damage it should be obvious that some of the impact force has penetrated beyond the surface to affect structural parts of the body or frame. Almost always there will be some evidence of structural damage in the alignment of exterior sheet metal parts.

The estimator soon learns to recognize typical patterns of automobile damage. Although no two are exactly alike, many are quite similar. This is understandable, because automobiles operating in normal traffic conditions are subject to typical traffic accidents, with front-end, rear-end, or side collisions, and so on. Although the construction of automobiles varies, there is enough similarity to cause similar damage patterns.

ESTIMATING SEQUENCE

The primary purpose of following a definite sequence in preparing an estimate is to avoid missed items. In the preliminary inspection the estimator's attention may wander from one unit to another as he surveys the overall damage pattern. When starting to make the various entries on the estimate form, attention should be concentrated on one major unit at a time, complete the entry of all related items, then proceed to the next major item, complete all related items, and continue in this manner until all the damage has been itemized and the repair specified. Doing this in an exact, unvarying sequence will reduce the probability of missing items as much as possible. However, there is no one "best" sequence. The order of the sequence is not as important as the fact that one is adopted and followed.

Many independent repair shops follow the sequence

10-8 The damaged automobile on which the estimate in Fig. 10-7 was made.

found in the estimating manuals they use as a source of parts prices and flat-rate labor time information. This is simply to start at the front bumper assembly and work progressively to the rear, the first entry being the first damage found in the following list: front bumper assembly; head lamps, parking lights, and marker light; cooling system and any engine damage; air conditioning; hood, hinges, and lock; front fenders; front suspension; steering; frame; rocker panels; doors, front and rear; center pillar; roof; rear window; quarter panel; rear lid; trunk floor; fuel tank; rear lamps; and rear bumper assembly.

All parts related to each major assembly are listed with it before proceeding to the next one. The type of work to be done—repair or replace—is indicated either by a tick mark in the proper column on the left margin or a labor entry in the proper column. Estimated times are entered at this point; flat-rate prices are normally left to be filled in later at the desk or, if a computer is used, by the computer. Sample estimate forms are shown in Figures 10-2 and 10-3.

Many other sequences are practical and used with very satisfactoy results. One popular method is to place the parts and repair operations in separate groups. This is an advantage when filling in parts prices, because there is less chance of missing one when they are in a solid column.

The estimate in Figure 10-7 is a copy of one made by a dealership body shop in the author's hometown for the damage on the automobile shown in Figure 10-8. Names and parts prices have been deleted, as this is intended only to show a system in use.

Other systems are used by estimators in various shops. The test of any system is whether or not it works for the people using it.

Use of Abbreviations

Common practice is to abbreviate terms that must be

10-7 Copy of an estimate in which the parts and labor entries are made in separate blocks.

constantly repeated. Examples are right, left, front, rear, and so on. Used properly, abbreviations simplify by making the estimate easier to prepare and to read; when over-used, they are confusing, particularly to the owner who is not familiar with the language of the body shop. The safest policy is to limit the use of abbreviations to those that indicate position.

A list of some of the most commonly used body shop language and abbreviations is found at the end of this chapter.

THE ESTIMATOR'S QUICK CHECKS

Visual inspection is adequate for most body damage, but many of the operating units of the automobile should be checked thoroughly, if there is evidence to indicate the possibility of damage. The nature of the damage is usually an indication of what to expect. For example, a direct impact on the side of the front end would indicate the probability of suspension damage and suggest the possibility of steering linkage damage. If the impact has been hard enough to cause the automobile to skid sideways, there is a good possibility of wheel and suspension damage on the opposite side. Similar conditions often occur on the rear end.

Normally, it is not necessary to use precision gauges to determine if suspension or steering linkage parts are damaged so that repair or replacement is required. That type of equipment is essential to determine when the damaged unit has been straightened or rebuilt and readjusted to the manufacturer's specifications. When the unit is outside of specifications, the condition can usually be determined either visually or by simple measurements, often with a steel tape or a tram gauge. However, when the evidence of possible damage is strong but cannot be verified by quick checks, it may be best to resort to use of precision gauges. Whether the precision checking is done while the estimate is being prepared or the estimate is marked *open*, as explained in a following section, depends on the existing conditions.

Frame checking, both visual and by using gauges, is explained in Part 2 of Chapter 8 and not repeated here. Discussed in the next section are quick checks for front suspension, steering linkage, and wheels.

Front Suspension

The first and most practical check is to step back and look carefully at the position of the wheel in its opening in the fender. Even though the fender is damaged, the wheel position will usually provide some indication of misalignment. The wheel should be viewed also from the front, with the eye position close to the floor and any variation from the normal, nearly vertical position noted. A variation of more than one degree of camber should be noticeable.

The front end should be bounced up and down to check for binds in the shock absorbers. Excessively free

movement should be disregarded, because it is caused by normal wear, not collision damage.

Assuming that the frame is not collapsed in back of the front suspension and the opposite side is undamaged, a simple check for a bent control arm is to measure from its outer end to a reliable reference point on the frame or unitized body and compare to the same measurement on the opposite side. However, this measurement is meaningless if the frame is collapsed.

When the control arms are bent, the points of attachment to the frame and any shift of the position of the bushings should be checked. This applies particularly to the double-arm types that have two bushings each on both upper and lower. An impact that will drive the suspension back will tend to pull the front bushing outward and drive the rear one inward. Most single-arm suspensions have a strut rod from the outer end to an anchor point on the frame. This anchor position is often pulled out of place when the suspension is driven back. Any shifting of the attaching points should be noted and time alloted on the estimate form.

Steering Linkage

A visual check should locate any bends in the steering linkage, but careful attention should be given to the steering arms and pitman arm when severe damage is involved. On most modern automobiles, the steering arm is a part of the knuckle forging, but it may be a bolt-on part on some makes. However it is made, the distance between its outer end and the brake assembly should be the same on both sides. Pitman arms are usually relatively heavy forgings, but can bend and are apt to twist the pitman shaft of the steering gear to which they are attached by tapered splines.

Steering Gears

The pitman shaft of most steering gears can be checked for twist by looking at the inner end of the splines. There is usually enough of the splines left exposed, between the pitman arm and the steering gear housing, to be seen. If these are twisted, the pitman shaft and possible other parts or the complete gear assembly should be replaced.

Any steering gear that has been subjected to heavy force in a collision should be checked both ways through its full turning range with the wheels raised off the floor. If there is any roughness or binding, the gear should be disassembled for further inspection. Some rack and pinion gears, if forced hard against the end stops, can be damaged in making this check. Any gear of any type that operates smoothly and does not have excessive play in the steering wheel travel is usable as it is.

Toe-In or Toe-Out

Excessive toe-in or toe-out caused by a collision is

usually due to bent steering linkage or suspension parts. The estimator should look for the cause of any noticeable out-of-toe condition, rather than considering it as a condition to be corrected by itself. Re-adjustment of toe-in is a part of almost any front suspension parts replacement or adjustment operation.

A reasonably accurate estimate of toe-in or toe-out can be made visually if the front wheels are known to be straight and the tires are inflated properly. The procedure is to set the wheels in the streight-ahead postion and sight across the side of each front wheel to the corresponding rear one. The eye position should be in line with the fore and aft edges of the front tire and a mental estimate made of the amount of the rear tire tread visable. The estimate should then be compared to the opposite side. Excessive toe-in will reveal too much of the rear tire when viewed from the inside of each wheel; excessive toe-out will reveal too much of the rear when viewed from the outside of the wheels. Allowance must be made for differences in the front and rear tread width in making this check; there is a difference on many automobiles, but they do not vary the same amount.

Wheels

Any wheel that has been subjected to a strong side strain should be jecked up and rotated to check for lateral runout (wobble), even though it shows no evidence of damage. An appreciable in-and-out movement is easy to see by looking down as it rotates. If there is doubt, a pencil point or other slender object should be placed on a rigid support that will hold it in contact with the flat surface of the side of the tire rim. Ideally, the pencil should make contact all the way around the rim. If a half-turn shows a variation of ⅛ inch (3 mm), the wheel should be repaired. Simple runout of stamped steel wheels can be straightened in a press if not otherwise damaged. This does not apply to wire wheels and those made of various alloys; whether they can be repaired or must be replaced depends on too many variable conditions to answer here.

Open Entries

Sometimes a mechanical unit, transmission, water pump, axle housing, or other part cannot be checked to determine the extent of damage until it can be disassembled for inspection. Or extensive disassembly or straightening of other parts will be necessary to permit access to a particular unit. When this occurs, the usual practice is to list the unit on the estimate form as *open*, meaning that the extent of repair cannot be determined until further work is done.

Open items should be discussed with the buyer, usually the insurance adjustor, but the owner may be concerned also, and an agreement made. Whether the buyer will be willing to accept the report of conditions found after disassembly or will wish to be present depends entirely on the relations existing between him or her and the shop.

Right and Left Sides

It is standard practice throughout the automobile industry to consider right and left from the viewpoint of the driver, or other occupants, as they are seated within the car. Thus, the driver's position is on the left side of the automobile. The last digit of the part number of such parts as doors, fenders, moldings, and so on indicates whether it is right or left. On right-hand parts the last digit is even; on left-hand parts the last digit is odd.

Strict adherence to this rule is essential to avoid confusion, delay and expense. The greatest possibility for confusion arises when information is taken from conversation with the customer, who may not be aware of the convention. This is only natural, because it is customary to consider right and left from the viewer's position when looking at a scene or the printed page. Referring to right and left as the passenger or driver's side in conversations with the owner can eliminate errors.

WORDS OFTEN ABBREVIATED

It is common practice to abbreviate the following words when they are used on the estimate form or the repair order:

Air conditioning	AC.
Front	F.
Left	L.
Radiator	Rad.
Remove	Rem.
Replace	Rep.
Remove and replace	R & R
Refinish	Ref.
Sublet	Sub.
Spot refinish	Spt. Ref.

Excessive use of abbreviations should be avoided, because it can be confusing to persons not familiar with the body repair industry, particulary the owner of the automobile.

LANGUAGE OF THE BODY SHOP

Almost any industry of any size, including the body shop business, tends to develop a language of its own. Body shop language consists of parts names, terms used for various repair operations, and abbreviations used in writing repair orders and estimates. The safest practice in anything written is to use parts names as they appear in the manufacturer's parts catalog, but all parties should understand what is meant when other terms are used in conversation.

Some of the more commony used names and terms are listed below. This list is not intended to include all regional variations; to do so would probably add more confusion than it eliminated.

BELT	A line around the body at the base of the window openings, often covered with a belt molding.
CAMBER	Positive: outward tilt of the top of a wheel. Negative: inward tilt.
CANCER	Rusted body panels.
CORE	The finned section of the radiator assembly, but sometimes used in reference to the complete radiator assembly.
CORE SUPPORT	The frame that holds the radiator assembly and serves as the support for all of the front-end sheet metal on conventional construction.
COWL	The body passenger compartment forward of the front doors. May include the hinge pillars on some makes, but not on all.
DOG LEG	Four-door models only. The curved section of the quarter panel between the rear wheel opening and the edge of the rear door.
DOOR SKIN	The door outer panel, available as a replacement part for most doors.
DOOR PAD	The trim panel covering the inner surface of the door assembly. Past model door pads have been upholstered; many current door pads are made of molded plastic.
DOZER	A portable frame machine.
DRIVE LINE	The drive shaft and axles.
FACING	The front, rear, and lower surfaces of any door or the corresponding parts of the cowl, center pillar, and quarter panel.
FENDER	This term should be used only in reference to the front fenders. Quarter panels are often referred to as rear fenders. This is erroneous for almost all modern automobiles.
FRONT END	An indefinite term that usually refers to the front suspension system. Should be avoided when writing estimates and repair orders. Specify exact part names.
GARNISH	A molding around the inner edges of a window opening.
HARD TRIM	Body moldings. Should be avoided in writing estimates and repair orders.
HEADER	The upper reinforcement for the windshield and rear window openings. Sometimes used in reference to the upper door glass frame.
HINGE FACING	The door facing to which the hinges are attached.
HORSESHOE	Spring clip used to retain inside door handles on some makes of automobiles.
INDEPENDENT FRONT OR REAR SUSPENSION	See SUSPENSION
KICKUP	A raised section of the frame and body to provide clearance for the front and rear suspension system or axles.
LINKAGE	Any system of rods or links used to control an operating assembly (steering linkage, carburetor linkage, etc.). Specify exact part on repair orders or estimates.
LOCK	Any mechanism used to hold a hinged assembly closed. Some locks only latch, as no key is required.
LOCK FACING	The facing of a door to which the lock is attached.
LOCK PILLAR	The quarter panel facing to which the lock striker is attached. May be a part of the quarter panel stamping or a separate stamping welded to it.
MEMBER	A general term used in reference to the reinforced cross pieces of a frame. May be used in reference to reinforced body parts.
PAN	Body floors are usually referred to as *pans*. This term should be used on repair orders and estimates.
PITMAN ARM	The arm attached to the steering gear to operate the steering linkage.
QUARTER PANEL	The origin of this name goes back to the very early days of automobile body manufacturing when labor operations were performed by four-man teams, each taking a quarter, and has been retained in reference to the rear body side.
RECORE	The replacement of the core in a radiator assembly. The original tanks are removed from a damaged assembly and soldered to a new core.
REAR SUSPENSION	See SUSPENSION.
REGULATOR	Any mechanism used to control the movement of body glasses, manual or electric. Sometimes used in reference to the mechanism that provides fore-and-aft travel for the front seat.

ROCKER PANEL	The box-section panels forming the lower part of the door opening. Introduced in the early 1930s, the original rockers curved upward at the front end, suggesting the appearance of a chair rocker. The name has continued even though the appearance has changed.
ROOF RAIL	The reinforcement making up the upper part of a door opening. Should not be confused with the adjoining section of the roof.
RUN	A ridge formed in a wet coat of paint, caused by applying too much material. Sometimes referred to as "lace curtains."
SEAT TRACKS	The mechanism that provides fore-and-aft travel for the front seat.
SHELF	The shelf between the back of the rear seat and the rear window.
SPINDLE	The shaft that carries the bearings for the front wheel. Usually part of a larger forging that connects to the lower control arm and either the upper arm or MacPherson strut.
STEERING ARM	The lever, usually a forging, that connects the steering linkage to the steering knuckle.
STEERING LINKAGE	The system of rods that transfer steering effort from the steering gear pitman arm to the wheels.
STRIKER	The part that engages the lock assembly in closing.
SUSPENSION	The linkage and spring system that connects wheels to the chassis and absorbs road shock. Front or rear and right or left should be stated in estimate and repair order entries.
TANK	May refer to either the fuel tank or the upper and lower radiator tanks. The tank intended should be specified on repair orders and estimates.
TIE ROD	A part of the steering linkage.
TRIM	A general term usually used in reference to the fabrics, plastics, and metal parts used to upholster the interior of the passenger compartment. Trim parts are sometimes referred to as *hard* or *soft*, meaning metal and plastic or fabric. Exterior moldings should not be called trim on a repair order or estimate.
TUMBLE HOME	A rarely used term that refers to the inward slant of the upper edge of a door glass.
REVEAL	The edges of a body window opening.
REVEAL MOLDING	A molding that surrounds the reveal area of a body window.
VIXEN	The brand name used by one manufacturer of body files. Sometimes used erroneously in reference to all body files. This term is used much less than it was prior to introduction of plastic fillers.
UNSPRUNG WEIGHT	The weight of tires, wheels, hub assemblies, brake assemblies, etc., that work against the springs to transmit road shock into the chassis and body. Low unsprung weight is desirable for good riding qualities.

JOB OPPORTUNITIES

The fact that a young person has started learning the body repair trade is no indication that he or she should always work as a repairman. Many other related jobs can call for the unique qualifications given by a knowledge of the trade. Some of them may be within the present employer's firm, some with other firms' operating body shops, and still others in fields that service or otherwise relate to the automobile collision repair industry. Jobs and business opportunities in the total field are not limited to repairing automobiles. Body repair skills can be valuable qualifications for either promotion or employment in several related fields.

This is not a recommendation for the student to plan to change jobs because better opportunities are elsewhere. Body repair work is a job opportunity that enables many breadwinners and their families to enjoy above-average incomes as well as respect in their community. Many who possess the drive and ambition are able to set up their own shop and become completely independent. Others find repair work a satisfactory job and are happy to remain with it. However, a few people in all trades, including body repairmen, decide after a time that they should do something else. The advice to those is to make a change before it is too late and they become locked into a job that has become unsatisfactory. However, regardless of the skill level attained, experience in the body repair trade may be a marketable asset if the repairman makes *himself* marketable.

Personal marketability applies to more than just the person who finds himself in the wrong occupation. Many who have learned their trade well often wonder if their experience and ability could lead to different and more desirable jobs. Some in this group would be surprised if they could learn how often they have been silently appraised for promotion and rejected or if they knew that an employer in a related field has searched a large area, considered them, but looked farther. It is fortunate that these people do not know, because the answer would be hard to accept.

Personal marketability is difficult to define accurately, but it can be developed, or at least improved, by the person who is aware that it is a personal asset within his power to attain. However, it does come more easily to some than to others. It is some combination of reliability, common sense, and self-respect. It includes the ability to make self-appraisal and frank acknowledgment of error when an error is made. It is found in a range of personalities from the social, outgoing type to the extremely reserved, but it excludes the person who cannot get along with his co-workers. Also, it is a personal trait that leads to unexpected job offers.

It is to be hoped that the beginner at the body repair trade will be aware that his personal conduct and self-respect will shape his career as much as will his manual skill. Furthermore, these are factors within his control. There are probably openings in his area in the eight jobs discussed briefly in the following sections, and they will be filled from his own community. Sometimes the person employed deliberately sought the job; other times, the job sought the person. In either situation, the employer was probably influenced by personality factors as much as or more than by trade skills.

A job opportunity can be as simple as going from one employer to another to do the same work. Or it can mean leaving one type of work to take up another entirely different occupation. For example, a beginner is often forced to take whatever job is available, sometimes where the possibility of advancement is poor or non-existent. Under these circumstances, finding an opening in a progressive, well-managed shop would be a real opportunity.

Having made the move and proven competent, the beginner still has a future to consider. Competence implies quality work and efficient use of time; it also makes difficult work routine. This is a very satisfactory situation for some persons, but others find that it becomes boring because the sense of job satisfaction fades. An opening in another, related field can be as essential for the body man in this position as the first worthwhile job was for him when he was a beginner.

All jobs have advantages and disadvantages. Almost any job in a related field will require direct contact with the public and irregular hours, and will often necessitate traveling. Many require the ability to make decisions and defend them against strong opposition. Travel appeals to some people who feel tied to one location, but they soon find that it requires many days spent away from home and community activities.

ESTIMATOR

The attractiveness of the assignment as estimator can vary widely with the size of the shop and the policies of the shop's management. In a small operation, the estimating may be expected of the repairman as a part of his ordinary duties. In larger operations, particularly dealerships, it can become either a part of the shop foreman's responsibility or a separate assignment. Whatever the circumstances, the repairman hoping to improve his position with the company should look at the assignment as estimator as a logical first step.

There are many examples of repairmen who have accepted the added responsibility for estimating in a relatively small body shop and built it into a major operation under their supervision. In effect, they have built the job to which they have been promoted. Many successful independent proprietors have begun as estimators before opening their own repair shops. Others have continued their progress within a dealership past the level of shop manager. In most cases, their willingness to assume the responsibility for estimating has been a key factor in starting their progress.

Health is another reason for changing from repair work to estimating. Body repairmen develop health problems, just as other people do, sometimes temporary, sometimes lasting. Often the person is still active but unable to do the physical labor of body repair work. This can be simple hard luck, but many employers will do all they can to retain the services of a body man who

has proved worth retaining. An assignment as estimator is not always available, but if it is, it can solve the problem. The worker may develop a temporary assignment into further advancement by demonstrating the ability to perform under different circumstances.

The degree of responsibility assigned to, or sometimes assumed by, the estimator can vary widely. The determining factor is whether he must consult someone else or is personally able to determine the time allowances for estimated operations and decide whether particular parts should be repaired or replaced. A good estimator should know the job well enough to make decisions that will be respected by management, the shop crew, and the buyer, who is usually an insurance adjustor but may be anyone. If he does not know the job that well, the "estimator" is operating as an office clerk.

The competent estimator must assume part of the responsibility for the financial success of the shop. The position can be difficult for anyone who has trouble with personal relations.

The advantage of the estimator's job is that it is a first step toward advancement. It provides an opportunity to demonstrate the ability to assume responsibility.

BODY SHOP MANAGER AND FOREMAN

The titles body shop manager and foreman are usually associated with shops operated by automobile dealerships. The distinction between the two is not always clear, particularly in dealerships that could be classed as midsize. In some of the larger operations the body shop operates as a related but separate part of the service department. In a few, the body shop is set up as a separate division of the dealership corporation. In any large operation, both manager and foreman would be required for efficient operation. The manager's position would be an executive level.

At the other end of the scale, smaller dealerships may have only one or two repairmen in the body shop. In these instances the service manager may retain full responsibility for managing the body work, or one body man may be designated as foreman, but the degree of responsibility can vary widely.

The need for personal qualifications beyond trade skill increases with the size of the operation. However, that does not mean that a point is reached where the skills are unnecessary. Many large shops are managed by persons with no body repair experience. However, if the situation is examined closely, usually it will be found that the persons available for the job who had the trade skill lacked the other vital qualifications. With all the other qualifications equal, the man with trade skill would have an advantage, even though he reached a level of management where he only used that skill to understand the work he supervised.

The advantages and disadvantages of the body shop manager's and foreman's position vary from one shop to another, but in general, it is a step up. Success in either position requires self-confidence in dealing with the public and the people within the organization. The repairman considering either position should be aware that he will be judged by how well he can cope with difficult personal contacts where his sales ability rather than his mechanical skill will be on test. Either position can be a high-pressure, difficult job for the person who lacks the personal qualifications. The best mechanic does not always make the best shop manager or foreman, but that is no reason why he should not become one if he recognizes the situation and feels able to handle it.

Experience in body shop supervision at either level is excellent training for the person whose long-range intention is to set up his own shop. It will provide an on-the-job view of the business side of the operation that is difficult to obtain any other way.

SERVICE MANAGER

An automobile dealership service manager holds an executive position representing the firm in dealing with the service problems of the firm's clientele. He must keep the service department running smoothly and maintain good public relations. The non-technical aspects of the service manager's responsibilities are much greater than the technical—so much so, that many dealerships have selected service managers having little or no technical background. The reason is simply that it is easier for an intelligent person to learn what he needs to know than it is to alter the personality of another whose primary background is technical.

Many body repairmen have reached the service manager's position; some have acquired their own dealerships. Those who have done so have only used the same mental capacity that enabled them to become good mechanics to expand their ability into other fields. They have used their basic mechanical skills as a foundation on which to build a business career. It is quite probable that the same person, starting in a different business, would have reached a comparable level because of inherent ability.

INSURANCE ADJUSTORS AND APPRAISERS

The automobile insurance business employs many people as adjustors. Some companies require their adjustors to have legal training; others hire people with varied backgrounds. Some of the firms in the latter group consider body repair experience desirable if the applicant has the other necessary qualifications.

Physical damage appraisers are employed by specialty firms who contract with insurance companies for their services. The nature of their service varies to some degree, but the trend is to limit it to preparing estimates on automobiles assigned to them by the insurance company's adjustor. Not all appraisers are experienced body repairmen, but the body man is a prime candidate for the job if he meets the other requirements of the job.

The candidate for either the adjustor or the appraiser job must be able to meet and deal with the public. Both jobs carry considerable responsibility and require the ability to make and defend decisions, sometimes against considerable opposition. Some people thrive on that type of responsibility, and others find it burdensome. The man considering either job should make an accurate appraisal of his own personality and be sure that he will find it and the job compatible.

The repairman who succeeds in obtaining a position as an insurance adjustor or physical damage appraiser has taken a difficult step. Almost invariably he will start at a lower income level than he has had. The advantages are in the long-range prospects, because the possibilities of promotion are better. However, there is no guarantee of promotion. How far he goes will be determined by his job performance.

EQUIPMENT AND SUPPLY SALES

A sales position with a manufacturer or distributor of body shop equipment or supplies is sometimes available to a body repairman. Such positions often seem attractive, because they offer an opportunity to step into well-paying jobs that have good working conditions. Whether such an opportunity should be sought and accepted depends entirely on the personal likes and dislikes of the individual. Sales ability is a developed skill, but some persons develop it more easily than others. The primary question is how that particular person will adapt to sales work.

Many persons who are attracted to work requiring skilled hands are not comfortable in the situation that demands the type of face-to-face personal contact required in selling; these persons will find selling a hard and disagreeable job and are best advised to avoid it. Others, equally inclined toward skilled-trade-type work, find selling an agreeable task; those who do are sometimes able to attain good positions by combining their mechanical and selling abilities.

There are two general areas of the body shop equipment and supply sales field: (1) local jobber, selling directly to the repair trade, and (2) equipment or supply manufacturer, selling to the jobber trade or directly to the repair shop. Either can be rewarding to the repairman who is interested and is able to convince the firm's management that he is the man for the job. However, getting the job may be his biggest selling job.

The desire to enter the equipment or supply sales field is often the result of contact with sales people calling on the shop. The salesman may seem to have a more rewarding job. Others may seem to have inadequate knowledge of the body repair trade, leading the repairman to feel that he could do better. Whatever the reason, the repairman considering the change to sales must be prepared to be judged by a future employer on a set of standards entirely different from those that qualified him as a repairman. His trade knowledge will be considered as a part of his background that qualifies him for consideration, but only a part; many other factors will make up the total. The personal characteristics that make up sales ability are difficult to define accurately, but poise, intelligence, articulate speech, tact, and the personal drive to keep going under difficult circumstances are important factors. Also, the prospective salesman should have a general knowledge of business procedures or undertake a training program to develop it. Many employers will be as much impressed by the applicant's willingness to try to better himself as they are by what he learns.

SPECIALIST IN AN AUTOMOBILE MANUFACTURER'S SERVICE DEPARTMENT

Employment as a specialist in the service department of an automobile manufacturer is relatively difficult to obtain; there are many applicants for relatively few jobs. In general, this type of job requires an applicant who is much above average in trade skills and possesses the personal qualifications to operate at the professional level. He must be much more than just a well-qualified mechanic.

Many job opportunities in this field are for body men to conduct training programs in body-related service problems. These programs are well organized and are often conducted simultaneously in separate locations. A person willing and able to operate as a member of a well-organized team is needed for such a program.

The employer often goes to considerable effort to find persons of outstanding ability to fill a job of this type, rather than just choosing from a list of available applicants. The repairman wishing to qualify is advised to learn his trade well and improve his education as much as possible. In all probability, his trade skill will have been checked thoroughly *prior* to a job interview. In the job interview, he will be judged on his apparent ability to comprehend the responsibilities of the job and to act as a responsible representative of the company.

Any job of this type will almost always require some traveling, often quite a lot of it. Work schedules may vary widely, and sometimes special projects must be completed under pressure to meet a deadline.

SPECIALIST WITH AN EQUIPMENT OR SUPPLY MANUFACTURER

There are few specialist job openings with equipment or supply manufacturers. The number of manufacturers is small, and not all of them employ specialists. When an opening does occur, the selection will be made only after the qualifications of many candidates have been examined. Sometimes the candidate may not be aware that he is being considered. Often the job seeks the candidate, rather than the candidate seeking the job.

Job opportunities of this type usually are of two categories: instructor in a training program and field demonstrator. Job responsibilities with different companies would vary widely. In many, the person selected will be required to perform both duties as well as many others.

A few manufacturers of large straightening and front-end alignment equipment operate training programs as a service to purchasers of their equipment. An instructor in a program of this type must be above average in trade skills and know the product thoroughly. A very limited amount of applicable training is given by manufacturers of painting equipment.

Field demonstrations are usually done as part of the sales work. Operations of this type vary too widely to be described in detail, but often require the specialist to travel from city to city with a specially equipped truck. The job can vary from merely showing the equipment, with the truck as a portable showroom, to actually demonstrating it in use. This type of work is ordinarily done in sales meetings.

A part of the responsibility of this job may be preparing written material to be read by well-educated people, many of whom have little or no contact with a body shop other than as a customer. A lack of the ability to communicate in writing would be a difficult obstacle in obtaining the job and a source of embarrassment if the job was obtained.

Any tradesman interested in employment as a manufacturer's specialist should be aware that, first and foremost, he is a part of the company's sales activity, whether he actually engages in sales contacts or the work is strictly technical. His attitude toward his employer and the product cannot be hidden in his contacts with the public. A positive attitude toward both may make a worthwhile contribution, but a negative attitude will be a strong sales deterrent and cause for either a change of work assignment or dismissal.

AUTOBODY INSTRUCTOR

Relatively few body men enter the teaching profession as autobody instructors, because the requirements are high and only a limited number of openings are available. It can be a very rewarding or a very burdensome job, depending on the personality of the individual. The candidate for such a job should be aware that school administrators must consider many factors of his personality and educational background that have little relation to his skill level. They must also act within guidelines established by state, provincial, or other regulatory bodies.

A tradesman entering the teaching profession must adjust to an environment entirely different from that of the body shop. As a repairman, he has experienced directly the product of his efforts. He has made physical changes in the condition of the automobiles he has worked on, changes that can be seen and measured in terms of quality and dollars and cents. As a teacher, he develops an intangible product. Although he can see and grade the progress of his students, he cannot determine the long-range effect of his efforts, good or bad. As a man of good conscience, he knows that the example he sets has as much effect on his students as what he teaches them about his trade. If he lacks good conscience, he should not have been admitted to the classroom.

Educational requirements are the major problem for most tradesmen wishing to enter the teaching profession. State and provincial laws and regulations require teachers of all subjects to meet established educational standards. These vary in different jurisdictions to some degree, but all of them leave most tradesmen at a disadvantage as compared to the professional teacher; the teacher's early years have been spent in college or university learning the teaching profession, whereas the repairman has spent the corresponding years learning his trade. There are some exceptions, but most tradesmen will have to make up at least part of the deficiency by attending spare-time and special summer training sessions.

School administrators searching the field for suitable candidates for vocational teaching positions must consider the ability to speak and write. Ordinarily, this is associated closely with educational level, but there are many exceptions to the implied rule. Some persons are able to communicate, orally or in writing, better than their level of education would indicate. However, communication skills can be improved. Most school administrations would be favorably impressed by a tradesman who is making an effort to improve by attending classes in his spare time.

Anyone hoping to be considered for a position teaching his trade should evaluate his educational attainment carefully and attempt to fill in the gaps. This reevaluation usually occurs at the time of life when many persons begin to wish they had taken better advantage of their school years than they did.

ADDITIONAL JOB OPPORTUNITIES

The preceding job descriptions can provide only a glimpse of the total possible opportunities in the body repair field and related activities. The body shop industry furnishes employment for some persons in almost every community in the industrialized nations and in many that are less industrialized. In addition to the people in the primary repair activity, every community of appreciable size has people engaged in supporting activities, usually the distribution of supplies and material with a scattering of small manufacturers. When the large manufacturers of supplies and equipment and an important segment of the insurance industry are added to this, the total body shop industry appears as a large source of employment with tremendous opportunities for job improvement.

The student entering a body repair training program is coming in through one of the better gateways to this total field. Many successful people have begun in the same way. However, there is no way that success can be guaranteed to the student or any other beginner. Luck plays a part, but the primary effort determining success or failure is his responsibility. Good luck will help, and hard luck will hinder; but good luck rarely lasts long, and all but the worst hard luck can be overcome.

The message to the student is this: the opprotunity is there in many forms for you to take, but only *you* can take it. If you wish to look at other industries, you will find exactly the same reality.

INDEX